How Do We Know? The Social Dimension of Knowledge

ROYAL INSTITUTE OF PHILOSOPHY SUPPLEMENT: 89

EDITED BY

Julian Baggini

CAMBRIDGE
UNIVERSITY PRESS

PUBLISHED BY THE PRESS SYNDICATE OF THE UNIVERSITY OF CAMBRIDGE
The Pitt Building, Trumpington Street, Cambridge, CB2 1RP, United Kingdom

CAMBRIDGE UNIVERSITY PRESS
UPH, Shaftesbury Road, Cambridge CB2 8BS, United Kingdom
32 Avenue of the Americas, New York, NY 10013–2473, USA
477 Williamstown Road, Port Melbourne, VIC 3207, Australia
C/Orense, 4, planta 13, 28020 Madrid, Spain
Lower Ground Floor, Nautica Building, The Water Club, Beach Road, Granger Bay, 8005 Cape Town, South Africa

Printed in Great Britain by Bell & Bain Ltd, Glasgow.
Typeset by Techset Composition Ltd, Salisbury, UK

A catalogue record for this book is available from the British Library

ISBN 9781009077194
ISSN 1358-2461

Contents

Notes on the Contributors

Jennifer Lackey (j-lackey@northwestern.edu) *is the Wayne and Elizabeth Jones Professor of Philosophy at Northwestern University, the founder and Director of the Northwestern Prison Education Program, and Editor-in-Chief of* Philosophical Studies *and* Episteme. *Most of her research is in the area of social epistemology, with a focus on issues at the intersection of epistemology and the United States criminal legal system. She is the author of* The Epistemology of Groups *(Oxford University Press, 2021) and* Learning from Words: Testimony as a Source of Knowledge, *(Oxford: Oxford University Press, 2008).*

Katharine Jenkins (katharine.jenkins@glasgow.ac.uk) *is a Lecturer in Philosophy at the University of Glasgow. She is interested in questions to do with the relationship between social categories (especially gender and race) and social justice. Her published papers include 'Amelioration and Inclusion: Gender Identity and the Concept of Woman' (*Ethics, *2016), and 'Ontic Injustice' (*Journal of the American Philosophical Association, *2020).*

Linda Martín Alcoff (lmartina@hunter.cuny.edu) *is Professor of Philosophy at Hunter College and the Graduate Center, City University of New York. Recent publications include* Rape and Resistance *(Polity, 2018),* The Future of Whiteness *(Polity, 2015), and* Visible Identities: Race, Gender and the Self *(OUP, 2006), which won the Frantz Fanon Award.*

Ian James Kidd (ian.kidd@nottingham.ac.uk) *is Assistant Professor of Philosophy at the University of Nottingham. His interests include topics in epistemology and the philosophy of illness. Some recent publications include* Vice Epistemology, *co-edited with Heather Battaly and Quassim Cassam (Routledge, 2020) and* The Routledge Handbook to Epistemic Injustice, *co-edited with José Medina and Gaile Pohlhaus, Jr. (Routledge, 2016).*

Havi Carel (havi.carel@bristol.ac.uk) *is Professor of Philosophy at the University of Bristol. She works on philosophy of medicine, in particular*

doi:10.1017/S1358246121000163

on the experience of illness, as well as on phenomenology, epistemic injustice, and death. Her books include Phenomenology of Illness *(Oxford, 2016) and* Illness: The Cry of the Flesh *(3rd edition, Routledge, 2018).*

Alvin Goldman (goldman@philosophy.rutgers.edu) *earned his PhD degree at Princeton University. He taught primarily at the University of Michigan, University of Arizona (Tucson), and Rutgers, where he was Board of Governors and Distinguished Professor Emeritus of philosophy (and cognitive science). Currently he is Distinguished Research Associate at the University of California, Berkeley. He previously held visiting appointments at Yale University and Princeton University. A past President of the American Philosophical Association, Pacific Division, he is a Fellow of the American Academy of Arts and Sciences, and has also held a Guggenheim fellowship.*

Peter Adamson (peter.adamson@lrz.uni-muenchen.de) *is Professor of Late Ancient and Arabic Philosophy at the LMU in Munich. Recent publications include* Al-Razi *in the Oxford University Press series 'Great Medieval Thinkers'.*

Liam Kofi Bright (liamkbright@gmail.com) *is an Assistant Professor of Philosophy at the London School of Economics. His recent publications include 'Is Peer Review a Good Idea?' (*British Journal for the Philosophy of Science, *2020, co-authored with Remco Hessen) and 'Collective Responsibility and Fraud in Scientific Communities' (in the* Routledge Handbook of Collective Responsibility, *Routledge, 2020, co-authored with Bryce Huebner).*

Elizabeth Fricker (lizzie.fricker@magd.ox.ac.uk) *is an Emeritus Fellow of Magdalen College Oxford, and Emeritus Member of University of Oxford's Philosophy Faculty. Her main research interest is in the epistemology of testimony, and she has published many articles on this. She has also published in general epistemology and philosophy of mind. For research CV and recent publications, visit lizzie.fricker@academia.edu.*

Alessandra Tanesini (Tanesini@cardiff.ac.uk) *is Professor of Philosophy at Cardiff University. Her current work lies at the intersection of ethics, the philosophy of language, and epistemology with a focus* *on epistemic vice, silencing, prejudice and ignorance. Her new book* The Mismeasure of the Self: A Study in Vice Epistemology *is forthcoming with Oxford University Press.*

Sanford C. Goldberg (s-goldberg@northwestern.edu) *is Chester D. Tripp Professor in the Humanities and Professor of Philosophy at Northwestern University. His recent books include* Conversational Pressure *(OUP, 2020),* To the Best of Our Knowledge *(OUP, 2018),* Assertion *(OUP, 2015), and* Relying on Others *(OUP, 2010).*

Paul Giladi (p.giladi@mmu.ac.uk) *is Senior Lecturer in Philosophy at Manchester Metropolitan University. His recent publications include the edited collection* Hegel and the Frankfurt School *(Routledge, 2020) and the article 'A Foucauldian Critique of Scientific Naturalism: 'Docile Minds'' (*Critical Horizons, *21).*

Danielle Perherbridge (danielle.petherbridge@ucd.ie) *is in the School of Philosophy at University College Dublin. Her publications include:* Body/Self/Other: The Phenomenology of Social Encounters *(SUNY 2017); 'Habit, Attention and the Phenomenology of Recognition'* Convivium, *33 (2020); 'Beyond Empathy: Vulnerability, Relationality and Dementia',* International Journal of Philosophical Studies, *27 (2019).*

C. Thi Nguyen (c.thi.nguyen@utah.edu, @add_hawk) *is Associate Professor of Philosophy at University of Utah. He works on trust, art, games, echo chambers, and communities. Some recent works include 'Autonomy and Aesthetic Engagement' (*Mind, *2019), 'Echo Chambers and Epistemic Bubbles', (*Episteme, *2020), and* Games: Agency as Art *(OUP, 2020).*

Hugo Mercier (hugo.mercier@gmail.com) *is a researcher at the Jean Nicod Institute in Paris (CNRS). His recent publications include* Not Born Yesterday: The Science of Who we Trust *and* What we Believe *(PUP, 2020), and, with Dan Sperber,* The Enigma of Reason *(HUP, 2017).*

Notes on the Contributors

Lani Watson (lani.watson@philosophy.ox.ac.uk) *is a philosopher and Research Fellow with the Oxford Character Project, University of Oxford. Her work focuses on questions and political epistemology, including a forthcoming book,* The Right To Know: Epistemic Rights and Why We Need Them *(Routledge, 2021).*

Preface

When you think about thinking, what images come to mind? Perhaps Rodin's statue *The Thinker*, a genius like Einstein, or an old oil painting like that of the philosopher Kierkegaard, bent in concentration over his candlelit desk. In the popular imagination, thinking is almost always conceived of as a solitary pursuit, an act of deep engagement with one's own thoughts.

But if you think about, this is weird. Today, we might in fact say it is WEIRD: a strange quirk of Western, educated, industrialised, rich and democratic (WEIRD) societies (Henrich et al., 2010). In many other parts of the world and times in history, reasoning has widely been assumed to have been much more socially embedded. Confucius, for instance, described himself as 'a transmitter, not a maker, believing in and loving the ancients'.[1] He saw his task as preserving the accumulated wisdom of the past, not making a great, new original contribution. Even naming the school he figureheads 'Confucianism' is misleading since in China it has never been known by an individual's name but as *Rujia*, or the school of the *ru* (a scholar or learned man). 'Confucianism' was a 16th century Jesuit missionary coinage, the work of the proto-WEIRDS.

Indian philosophy is also characterised by adherence to schools rooted in deep traditions rather than in individuals. For example, the 8th-9th century thinker Śaṅkara (or Śaṅkarācārya) is indubitably a foundational figure in Advaita Vedanta, but its adherents trace its roots much further back than this and grant no individual the status of a founder. To them it would perhaps be like insisting on referring to transcendental idealism rather than Kantianism on the grounds that Kant's philosophy built on many before him and so should not bear his name alone.

In oral traditions, the role of the individual is even less important. Usually no one has any idea who, if anyone, came up with the core ideas that comprise their philosophies. In any case, what matters is that generations have found them to be true.

[1] Analects, Book 7 Ch 2, in Legge (1893, p. 195).

doi:10.1017/S135824612100014X

Yet in Western philosophy, reasoning has for many centuries been seen as a paradigmatically solitary activity. In Ancient Greece, Aristotle and Plato were already referring to certain ideas as those of named individuals, even though the culture also seemed to treat philosophy as something best done in a community. Plato had his Academy, Aristotle his Lyceum, and Epicurus his garden. In the centuries since, almost all the acknowledged great works of philosophy have been sole authored. You can count the exceptions on the fingers of one hand: Marx and Engels, Adorno and Horkheimer, Deleuze and Guattari. (We would now also add John Stuart Mill and Harriet Taylor Mill, but Taylor was not originally acknowledged as co-author, reflecting how until disturbingly recently the club of recognised solo thinkers has been male-only.)

And yet the social nature of thinking has been evident even in the individualistic West. In Europe and the Americas in the late 17th and 18th centuries people talked of 'The Republic of Letters' (*Respublica literaria*), a kind of long-distance intellectual community in which thinkers would discourse through letters. Descartes' *Meditations*, for example, reads like the work of someone alone in his study, but it was published along with a selection of objections from critics to whom Descartes sent his manuscript, along with his replies. This virtual symposium is longer than the book itself.

Both Edinburgh and Paris in the 18th centuries were centres of the Enlightenment where salons and literary societies were the focus of intellectual life. Universities have continued to uphold the communal nature of thinking, with their conventions of conferences, seminars and peer review.

Yet for many decades in philosophy, the theory of knowledge (epistemology) barely even acknowledged the role of the social in the formation of knowledge. For instance, for a long time many philosophers sought to define knowledge as some version of Plato's formulation *justified true belief*. That is to say, to know something is to have a belief that something is true, for that belief to be true, and for it to be properly justified. The key factors in this account are the knower (who has knowledge) and that thing in the world which the knowledge is of. There is no place in this account for the role played by the community of knowers.

The field of social epistemology opened up when a growing number of philosophers came to be dissatisfied with this. As one of the pioneers of social epistemology, Alvin Goldman, put it in an interview, 'Historically, epistemology focused on how you can get the truth about the world. The question for social epistemology is something like, how does the social affect people's attempts to get the truth?' (Baggini, 2008). This approach switches the focus in epistemology from definitions of what knowledge is to practical questions of what actually produces knowledge, and also the evaluative ('normative') questions of what we *should* count as knowledge.

If these issues ever appeared academic and remote, they certainly don't today. In the year in which the lecture series this book is based on were given, questions about who controls truth and knowledge were centre stage. The then President of the United States, Donald Trump, repeatedly dismissed well-evidenced claims as 'fake news' while peddling lies and myths on the basis of little more than personal conviction and here-say. The Black Lives Matter movement showed how whole sections of society are repeatedly denied a voice, their testimony disbelieved or ignored, even when pleading 'I can't breathe'. From when the last of our talks was postponed due to the global coronavirus pandemic, large parts of the population dismissed scientific accounts of what was happening, with a sizeable minority claiming that the virus was a hoax and that vaccines were dangerous.

The contributions to this volume help us to make better sense of these and many other issues that confuse us, in an age when people increasingly don't know who to believe, how to assess arguments or even if there is any such thing as truth.

Many of the contributors in this volume draw on JL Austin's concept of a speech act. Austin's central insight is that words do not only communicate information. In his terminology, words are only sometimes used in purely *locutionary* acts: ones that merely convey meaning. Words are also used in *illocutionary* acts, where the speaker intends to do or achieve something by speaking. For instance we might want to declare our love, make a request, give an instruction. Speech acts that actually result in a change in the world are *perlocutionary* acts, such as when you act on the basis of what I say.

I have to confess that although I've long found Austin's concept of speech acts invaluable, I often struggle to remember to which kinds *locutionary, illocutionary and perlocutionary* refer. It doesn't seem to matter, however, since the key insight is the simple one that we can do things with words. We can belittle and undermine people just as we can support and draw attention to them. We can discredit and we can give credibility. We can incite and we can calm down. You will come across numerous examples of such speech acts in several of the chapters to follow, demonstrating that how we speak really matters and that if free speech really means speech without any constraint, it can mean the freedom to do real harm.

Several chapters tackle a set of problems around what we might call epistemic authority. ('Epistemic' is an adjective meaning 'pertaining to knowledge'. So, for example, our 'epistemic goals' are what we want to achieve with regards to knowledge acquisition.) Why and how is it that some people's status as knowers is unjustly contested and their testimony is not believed? Several of our contributors refer back to the seminal work of Miranda Fricker on epistemic injustice: injustice that results from failures to communicate or attribute knowledge (Fricker, 2007). One such injustice she called 'testimonial injustice', which occurs when someone is unjustly ignored or not believed, because of an irrelevant factor such as their gender, race, or social class.

Another such injustice is hermeneutical injustice. Here, the injustice is a result of an inability to have the resources to properly understand what is happing and why it is unjust. For example, back in the 1960s women in the workplace were routinely the objects of unwanted sexual advances and even assaults. Many, perhaps most, women at the time thought they had to accept this as a fact of life: that is how men behaved. But in the 1970s the concept of 'sexual harassment' started to gain traction. Once familiar with this term, a woman could understand that what she had to endure was not natural or inevitable, it was an injustice.

These concepts play an important role in Jennifer Lackey's disturbing account of the role of confession in the criminal justice system. Confession is too often taken to be clinching evidence, but we know that confessions are often false, extracted by manipulative interrogation techniques. However, even when there is hard, forensic evidence that the confession must be false, judges and juries have often believed the confession, not the facts. This illustrates a peculiar form of testimonial injustice. Whereas usually the problem is that people are *not* believed, when people say negative things about themselves that fit negative stereotypes, they are believed too easily. Lackey's analysis of what is going here is a model of how philosophy can help us to understand important, real-life problems.

Katherine Jenkins also takes up Fricker's tools and puts them to important use. Jenkins argues that justice in cases of rape is hindered by three types of myth: that women routinely lie about rape, that in many rape cases the victim consented and only afterwards regretted it, and that women who are raped often bring it upon themselves. The problems here are not just that women are the victims of testimonial injustice. The structures of society also mean there are hermeneutical reasons why victims are not recognised. For instance, in England and Wales, marital rape was not even legally acknowledged until 1991. That meant that legally speaking, rape within marriage was conceptually impossible. Also, myths that women often say no to sex when they mean yes, perpetuated in many forms of pornography, means that their 'no' is perversely taken to be consent.

Related themes concern Linda Alcoff, who writes of the epistemic injustices faced by survivors of sexual violence. Their testimony, she argues, is not only vital for achieving justice, it 'can provide information and analysis about the patterns that reveal the nature of the problem. In speaking publicly, victims enact resistance by defying the stigma of shame and the likelihood of presumptive disbelief'. One vital point Alcoff argues is that it is a mistake to focus on the consistency of first-person accounts as a hallmark of their reliability. In traumatic situations, people often fail to remember details that are incidental, such as the exact time of day or what they assailants were wearing. Yet a failure to recall such things is too often assumed to be some kind of sign that their memories of what really matters are unreliable.

Havi Carel and Ian Kidd deal with questions of epistemic injustice in the context of healthcare. Medicine has traditionally been very hierarchical, with consultant doctors as gods and nurses as angels. Patients have had little power in this. And yet patients have an intimate knowledge of their own experience which makes them vital witnesses in any medical diagnosis and treatment. Some of Carel and Kidd's stories about how patients have nonetheless been ignored or disbelieved are shocking. Carel's many years of work with medical professionals is helping to change this, showing once again how social epistemology is a discipline with real-world impact.

Carel and Kidd's work shows the dangers of limiting epistemic authority to those with recognised expertise. But in recent years we have also seen problems when experts are not properly respected, resulting in unsubstantiated crank theories being given more credence than well-evidenced ones. Alvin Goldman tackles this problem head-on, asking how we can spot experts. Goldman provides no easy answers. Putative experts are not always genuine, and genuine experts do make mistakes. Expertise always presents a dilemma for the non-expert: you have to use your own intelligence to decide who to believe, but you don't know enough about the subject to make that judgement without relying on trust to some degree.

As Peter Adamson shows, this problem may be quite new in Western philosophy, but it would have been very familiar to the philosophers of the medieval Islamic world. He argues that like Goldman, al-Ghazālī believed reliance on experts is unavoidable. But this does not mean we are 'doomed to follow authority uncritically'. Uncritical acceptance of authority, *taqlīd*, is to be avoided whenever possible. One way to do this is to 'work at improving our ability to recognize the expertise of other people, so that we may responsibly give those people our credence.' If we follow this advice, we will have no choice but to be 'fairly modest in our pretensions of certainty'.

Just as excess reliance on expertise is irrational, outright distrust of expertise is not entirely irrational. Many experts have disgraced themselves and there have particular concerns in recent years over scientific fraud. But why do scientists lie when their entire discipline is the pursuit of truth? Liam Kofi Bright questions the standard theory that dishonesty is motivated by the desire for esteem. While accepting this is often true, the problem is that this desire is also a positive motivator. To imagine science can work without any pride is naive, but pride can also lead people astray. As with Goldman, we are offered no easy answers. Philosophy often brings greater clarity to an issue, helping us to understand it better, but certainty about what is the case does not always follow.

However much we depend on experts, the need to think for ourselves is inescapable. Yet as Elizabeth Fricker (Miranda's big sister) considers, new technologies are giving us various opportunities to opt-out of doing so. Algorithms can pick films and music for us, and fill our grocery baskets. Fricker focuses on the ability of satnav to save us the effort of navigating ourselves. On the face of it this might look like just another labour-saving piece of technology. But Fricker believes we lose something valuable when we wilfully de-skill ourselves in such a way. She is no luddite and appreciates the same could be said for using washing machines or dishwashers. She navigates this tricky terrain with care and skill, never on philosophical auto-pilot.

The web is not only responsible for bringing sat nav to every smart phone, it is also accused of coarsening public discourse. How we talk to each other is not just important for civic harmony, it also affects our ability to communicate effectively and to learn from each other. Questions and problems relating to this concerned several of our contributors.

Alessandra Tanesini cautions against taking calls for greater civility in public debate at face value. British readers may remember a recent male prime minister telling a female opposition member of parliament to 'calm down, dear', borrowing an advertisement catchphrase. For many this was an all-too common example of powerful people (usually men) using pleas for politeness as a means of dismissing grievances that are justly deeply-felt and emotionally expressed.

Anger, argues Tanesini, is sometimes exactly what is needed not only to 'assert one's moral authority' but to convey important knowledge about the seriousness of a complaint.

Still, as Tanesini accepts, much rudeness in public discourse in unwarranted. Is the very nature of online communication really to blame? Sandford Goldberg thinks it is. Like Fricker, he is no Luddite and believes the internet has brought huge benefits. But certain structural features of online exchanges makes it inevitable that they are often 'unproductive and unhappy affairs'. In short, effective communication requires sensitivity to the exact purpose and nature of each individual contribution, and online it is just difficult to judge these. The paper presents a challenge to developers to help devise tools that can work round these seemingly intrinsic limitations.

Paul Giladi and Danielle Petherbridge's contribution also concerns the problems of just public discourse. Their subject is Jürgen Habermas's influential notion of communicative action, which sees the goal of public discourse to establish consensus and mutual understanding, all of which is critical for a functioning democracy. Giladi and Petherbridge tease out the vulnerabilities that are inherent in this form of discourse, all of which make it fragile and difficult to make work in the idealised form Habermas envisages.

One way in which we are all vulnerable is that we are open to manipulation. C. Thi Nguyen dissects one powerful tool of manipulators: providing the illusion of clarity. Mental clarity is of course something we rightly seek, and Nguyen's paper itself provides a great deal. But there is also a kind of bogus clarity, in which solutions and ideas are provided that free us from the trouble of grappling with real complexities and instead make things more manageable. Nguyen's argument is not just a useful way to understand conspiracy theorists and other malevolent manipulators, it also provides a warning against the seductions of standardised, precise measurements of of performance in areas from healthcare to education.

You might worry that the manipulators are simply too powerful. Hasn't psychology demonstrated that human beings are stupid and gullible, led by their emotions and intuitions and not by their reason? Psychologist Hugo Mercier provides some reassurance for those who think human rationality has been debunked. He provides experimental evidence that human beings are actually very difficult to deceive. Nor are we as bad reasoners as received wisdom says. When we think collectively, with others, we actually get a lot right. We go wrong precisely when we head to our solitary garrets to think alone.

To have a psychologist in this collection should not be surprising. Philosophers are increasingly aware that many of the problems they address cannot be dealt with with the tools of philosophy alone. Social epistemologists in particular are aware that knowledge formation is a collective enterprise that should draw on relevant expertise wherever it is found and that work has to be done to get the facts right before we can start to reason. about them. Lani Watson has embraced this empirical and collaborative ethos in her work on the question of what counts as a question. The answer is both not as easy to arrive at as you might expect and at the same time almost obvious-sounding when it arrives. The paper is wonderful example of how philosophy can help us to question what we take for granted without always leading us into fantastical speculations.

The talks and this volume show how philosophy can be rigorous, accessible and of practical importance. I commend the essays that follow as demonstrations of as well as arguments about the social nature of knowledge formation.

Acknowledgements

It was a privilege to convene this series and I am very grateful to my predecessor, Anthony O'Hear, for selecting the theme and inviting several of the speakers. I am also indebted to Matt Hewson whose editorial work turned all the contributions into a coherent volume, and to colleagues at Cambridge University Press.

The lecture series on which this volume was based was made possible by the generous and professional hosting of Clive Judd and his teams at Foyles Bookshop. Videos of the talks are available on the Royal Institute of Philosophy's YouTube channel, thanks to videographer Kyle Cruise. At the RIP, an incredible amount of backroom work was done by James Garvey. Finally, my thanks to our new Chair, Lucy O'Brien, for stepping in and chairing talks I had to miss through illness.

Julian Baggini
Royal Institute Of Philosophy
jbaggini@royalinstitutephilosophy.org

References

Julian Baggini, 'The Real Thing?', *The Philosophers' Magazine*, 43, (2008), 88–93.

Miranda Fricker, *Epistemic Injustice: Power and the Ethics of Knowing*, (Oxford University Press, 2007).
Joseph Henrich, Steven J. Heine, Ara Norenzayan, 'The weirdest people in the world?', *Behavioral and Brain Sciences*, 33 (2010), 61–83.
James Legge, *The Chinese Classics* Vol. 1, (Oxford University Press, 1893).

False Confessions and Subverted Agency[1]

JENNIFER LACKEY

Abstract

In the criminal legal system, confessions have long been considered the 'gold standard' in evidence. An immediate problem arises for this gold standard, however, when the prevalence of false confessions is taken into account. In this paper, I take a close look at false confessions in connection with the phenomenon of testimonial injustice. I show that false confessions provide a unique and compelling challenge to the current conceptual tools used to understand this epistemic wrong. In particular, I argue that we cannot make sense of the unjust ways in which false confessions function in our criminal legal system by focusing exclusively on speakers getting less credibility than they deserve. I conclude that the way we conceive of testimonial injustice requires a significant expansion to include what I call agential testimonial injustice – where an unwarranted credibility excess is afforded to speakers when their epistemic agency has been denied or subverted in the obtaining of their testimony.

In the criminal legal system in the United States, confessions have long been considered the 'gold standard' in evidence. Indeed, according to Kassin et al. (2010), '[t]he U.S. Supreme Court has recognized that confession evidence is perhaps the most powerful evidence of guilt admissible in court (Miranda v. Arizona, 1966) – so powerful, in fact, that 'the introduction of a confession makes the other aspects of a trial in court superfluous, and the real trial, for all practical purposes, occurs when the confession is obtained' (2010, p. 9).

An immediate problem arises for this gold standard, however, when the prevalence of false confessions is taken into account. 'A false confession is an admission to a criminal act – usually accompanied by a narrative of how and why the crime occurred – that the confessor did not commit' (Kassin et al. 2010, p. 5). Since 1989, there have been 375 post-conviction DNA exonerations in the United States, and 29% of these involved false confessions.[2]

[1] The contents of this article were first presented in different form as Jennifer Lackey, 'False Confessions and Testimonial Injustice,' 110 *Journal of Criminal Law and Criminology*, 43–68 (2020).

[2] https://www.innocenceproject.org/dna-exonerations-in-the-united-states/, accessed 20 October 2020. As Kassin et al. (2010) note, however,

doi:10.1017/S1358246121000072

Moreover, false confessions involve everything from minor infractions to detailed accounts of violent crimes. In the largest sample ever studied, Drizin and Leo (2004) analyzed 125 cases of proven false confessions in the United States between 1971 and 2002 and found that 81% occurred in murder cases, followed by rape (8%) and arson (3%).

In this paper, I take a close look at false confessions in connection with the phenomenon of testimonial injustice. Roughly speaking, speakers are the victims of testimonial injustice when, due to prejudice or bias, their testimony is regarded as less credible than the evidence warrants.[3] I show that false confessions provide a unique and compelling challenge to the current conceptual tools used to understand this way of being wronged epistemically. In particular, I argue that we cannot make sense of the unjust ways in which false confessions function in our criminal legal system by focusing exclusively on speakers getting *less credibility* than they deserve. I conclude that the way we conceive of testimonial injustice requires a significant expansion to include what I call *agential testimonial injustice* – where an unwarranted credibility excess is afforded to speakers when their epistemic agency has been denied or subverted in the obtaining of their testimony. At the same time, I show that work by legal scholars and social scientists can benefit by viewing the practices that produce confessions through the lens of this expanded notion, and hence that epistemological tools can shed light on issues with enormous moral and practical consequences.

1. False Confessions

There are many factors that contribute to people falsely confessing to crimes that they didn't commit. First, there are *situational factors* that can significantly impact the likelihood of false confessions, including the length of the interrogation, sleep deprivation, the presentation of

---

'because this sample does not include those false confessions that are disproved before trial, many that result in guilty pleas, those in which DNA evidence is not available, those given to minor crimes that receive no post-conviction scrutiny, and those in juvenile proceedings that contain confidentiality provisions, the cases that are discovered most surely represent the tip of an iceberg' (2010, p. 3).

[3] I will discuss testimonial injustice in far greater detail later in this paper.

false evidence, and maximization and minimization tactics.[4] Let's examine these briefly in turn.

According to guidelines outlined by Inbau et al. (2001), it is advised that single interrogation sessions not exceed 4 hours. Yet Drizin and Leo (2004) found that in cases in which interrogation time was recorded, 34% lasted 6–12 hours, 39% lasted 12–24 hours, and the mean was 16.3 hours. Moreover, lengthy interrogations are often accompanied by other factors that can increase the likelihood of false confessions, such as isolation from significant others, which 'constitutes a form of deprivation that can heighten a suspect's distress and incentive to remove himself or herself from the situation,'[5] and sleep deprivation, which 'strongly impairs human functioning.'[6]

Regarding false evidence, it is permissible in the United States for police to outright lie to suspects, and so when involvement in criminal activity is denied, purportedly decisive evidence of guilt can be offered in response. Consider, for instance, the case of Marty Tankleff who, in 1989, was accused at the age of 17 of murdering his parents 'despite the complete absence of evidence against him. Tankleff vehemently denied the charges for several hours – until his interrogator told him that his hair was found within his mother's grasp, that a 'humidity test' indicated he had showered (hence, the presence of only one spot of blood on his shoulder), and that his hospitalized father had emerged from his coma to say that Marty was his assailant – all of which were untrue (the father never regained consciousness and died shortly thereafter).' Following these lies, Tankleff became disoriented and confessed, but then immediately recanted. 'Solely on the basis of that confession, Tankleff was convicted, only to have his conviction vacated and the charges dismissed 19 years later' (Kassin 2010, pp. 17-18). That the presentation of false evidence contributes to such confessions is reinforced by self-report studies, where suspects say that the reason they confessed is that they took themselves to be trapped by the weight of the evidence against them.[7]

4 These factors are highlighted in Kassin et al. (2010) because of the 'consistency in which they appear in cases involving proven false confessions' (p. 16).

5 Kassin et al. (2010).

6 Pilcher and Huffcut (1996).

7 Gudjonsson and Sigurdsson (1999) and Moston, Stephenson, & Williamson (1992).

There are also maximization and minimization tactics, which research has shown can lead to false confessions.[8] *Maximization* is a 'hard-sell' approach that involves the interrogator trying to scare or intimidate the witness, offering false claims about the evidence, and exaggerating the seriousness of not cooperating. Minimization is a 'soft-sell' approach in which the interrogator 'tries to lull' the witness into a 'false sense of security by offering sympathy, tolerance, face saving excuses, and even moral justification' (Kassin and McNall 1991, p. 235). Such techniques come in three different forms: 'those that minimize the moral consequences of confessing, those that minimize the psychological consequences of confessing, and those that minimize the legal consequences of confessing' (Kassim et al., 2010, p. 12). For instance, the interrogator may offer sympathy and understanding to normalize the crime, saying, for instance, 'I would have done the same thing;' the interrogator might offer minimizing explanations of the crime, such as that the murder was spontaneous or accidental; and the interrogator might communicate promises through pragmatic implication that the suspect will be punished less severely if he or she confesses. All three forms can put pressure of varying degrees on a suspect to confess to a crime that he or she did not commit, especially when used in combination with some of the other techniques, such as the presentation of false evidence.[9]

In addition to situational features, there are *dispositional factors* that increase the likelihood of false confessions, and the two most commonly cited concerns are juvenile status and mental impairment, including developmental disabilities and mental illness. This is supported by the fact that these groups are wildly overrepresented in the population of proven false confessions. For example, of the DNA exonerations in the U.S. involving false confessions, 31% of the false confessors were 18 years or younger and 9% had mental health or mental capacity issues known at trial.[10] In their sample of wrongful convictions, Gross, Jacoby, Matheson, Montgomery, and Patel (2005) found that 44% of the exonerated juveniles and 69% of exonerated persons with mental disabilities were wrongly convicted because of false confessions. There are a number of factors at work here. In both groups, for instance, there can be impairments in adjudicative competence, such as the ability

8 Klaver, Lee, and Rose (2008).

9 False confessions are an example of what McKinney (2016) calls 'extracted speech.'

10 https://innocenceproject.org/dna-exonerations-in-the-united-states/?gclid=Cj0KCQiArvX_BRCyARIsAKsnTxPQZoPRyGJCQpIXo4k_rgXKg6UAs0zWDwHnDJG4f--m2nSMyfDgvcwaAuDZEALw_wcB.

to assist in one's own defense. There can also be a diminished capacity to grasp legal terms, such as *Miranda* rights.

Finally, false confessions are often facilitated by the very innocence of the suspect. Awareness of one's own innocence leads people not only to waive their *Miranda* rights to silence and to counsel,[11] but also to be more open and forthcoming in their interactions with police.[12] If you have nothing to hide, you might wonder why you should remain silent and get an attorney. Yet it is not uncommon for the testimony of those who are innocent to be used against them, such as by calling into question their reliability or sincerity on the basis of minor inaccuracies. In addition, when a suspect confesses, this often leads the police to regard the case as solved, thereby closing the investigation and increasing the likelihood of overlooking exculpatory evidence.[13]

2. Testimonial Injustice

With these points in mind, let's now take a closer look at the phenomenon of testimonial injustice. The standard view is that a speaker is a victim of testimonial injustice when she is afforded a *credibility deficit* in virtue of a *prejudice* on the part of a hearer that targets her *social identity*.[14]

A speaker suffers a credibility deficit when the credibility that she is afforded by a hearer is less than the evidence that she is offering the truth, and a hearer has the relevant kind of identity prejudice when she has a prejudice against the speaker in virtue of the latter's membership in a social group. Prejudice here is being understood in terms of not being properly responsive to evidence. A prejudicial stereotype, for instance, is a generalization about a social group that fails to be sufficiently sensitive to relevant evidence. Where this prejudice 'tracks' the subject through different dimensions of social activity – economic, educational, professional, and so on – it is systematic, and the type that tracks people in this way is related to social identity, such as racial and gender identity. For instance, if a police officer

11 See Kassin and Norwick (2004).

12 Kassin (2005).

13 Leo and Ofshe (1998).

14 According to Miranda Fricker, for example, '[a] speaker sustains … testimonial injustice if and only if she receives a credibility deficit owing to identity prejudice in the hearer; so the central case of testimonial injustice is identity-prejudicial credibility deficit' (Fricker, 2007, p. 28).

rejects a woman's report of sexual assault merely because his sexism leads to him discrediting her, and despite evidence that supports her credibility, this would be a paradigmatic instance of testimonial injustice. In particular, the police officer's sexist beliefs manifest as a prejudice that targets the victim's gender identity in a way that results in her testimony being regarded as less credible than the evidence supports.[15]

When a hearer gives a speaker a credibility deficit in virtue of her social identity, Miranda Fricker argues that the speaker is wronged 'in her capacity as a knower,' and is thereby the victim of testimonial injustice. For the purposes of this paper, I will focus entirely on the claim that only credibility deficits are relevant to this phenomenon. Here, Fricker explicitly considers the question of whether credibility excesses can result in testimonial injustice, and denies that they can be, at least in the paradigmatic sense that is of interest to her. She writes:

> On the face of it, one might think that both credibility deficit and credibility excess are cases of testimonial injustice. Certainly there is a sense of 'injustice' that might naturally and quite properly be applied to cases of credibility excess, as when one might complain at the injustice of someone receiving unduly high credibility in what he said just because he spoke with a certain accent. At a stretch, this could be cast as a case of injustice as distributive unfairness – someone has got more than his fair share of a good – but that would be straining the idiom, for credibility is not a good that belongs with the distributive model of justice...those goods best suited to the distributive model are so suited principally

[15] Drawing on work by Patricia Hill Collins, Kristie Dotson focuses on a phenomenon very similar to testimonial injustice that she calls 'testimonial quieting,' which 'occurs when an audience fails to identify a speaker as a knower. A speaker needs an audience to identify, or at least recognize, her as a knower in order to offer testimony. This kind of testimonial oppression has long been discussed in the work of women of color. Take as an example a popular analysis of black women's lack of credibility found in the work of Patricia Hill Collins. In her book, *Black Feminist Thought* (Collins, 2000), she claims that by virtue of her being a U.S. black woman she will systematically be undervalued as a knower. This undervaluing is a way in which Collins and other black women's dependencies as speakers are not being met. To undervalue a black woman speaker is to take her status as a knower to be less than plausible. One of Collins's claims is that black women are less likely to be considered competent due to an audience's inability to discern the possession of credibility beyond 'controlling images' that stigmatize black women as a group' (Dotson, 2011, p. 242).

> because they are finite and at least potentially in short supply.... Such goods are those for which there is, or may soon be, a certain competition, and that is what gives rise to the ethical puzzle about the justice of this or that particular distribution. By contrast, credibility is not generally finite in this way, and so there is no analogous competitive demand to invite the distributive treatment. (Fricker, 2007, pp. 19-20).

Fricker grounds her denial that credibility excesses can lead to testimonial injustice in her rejection of a distributive model of credibility.[16] In particular, she argues that credibility is not finite in a way that lends itself to a distributive treatment.[17] Consider, for instance, finite goods, such as wealth, land, or food. Not everyone can own 20 acres because there is only a limited amount of land to go around. For some to have a lot of it necessitates that others have a little, or none at all. But other goods don't limit one another in this way. To give moral praise to one person need not be to deny it to another. We can say equally of Abraham Lincoln, Ida B. Wells, and Martin Luther King Jr. that they are exceptional moral agents. In this way, there is an important sense in which moral praise is an infinite good: there is often enough of it to go around.

Credibility, according to Fricker, is like moral praise rather than like land: it is an infinite good. If two friends tell me about their vacations this summer, believing that one of them snorkeled in Thailand need not impact my trusting that the other went hiking in Peru. I can

[16] José Medina agrees: 'Credibility is indeed not a finite good that can be in danger of becoming scarce in the same way that food and water can...' (Medina, 2011, p. 19). Similarly, he writes, 'The credibility excess assigned to some can be correlated to the credibility deficits assigned to others not because credibility is a scarce good (as the distributive model wrongly assumes), but because credibility is a comparative and contrastive quality, and an excessive attribution of it involves the privileged epistemic treatment of some (the members of the comparison class, i.e. those like the recipient) and the underprivileged epistemic treatment of others (the members of the contrast class, i.e. those unlike the recipient). An excessive attribution of credibility indirectly affects others who are, implicitly, unfairly treated as enjoying comparatively less epistemic trust. In my view, this is due to a disproportion in credibility an authority assigned to members of different groups. Credibility is not a scarce good that should be distributed with equal shares, but excesses and deficits are to be assessed by comparison with what is deemed a normal epistemic subject' (Medina, 2011, p. 20).

[17] Fricker also argues that credibility is a concept that 'wears its proper distribution on its sleeve'. For an argument against this, see Lackey (2018).

give them both as much credibility as I like since not only is there plenty to go around, but giving some of it to one need not take any away from the other. Because of this, it seems it isn't unjust to give someone more credibility than is owed since this doesn't deprive someone else of a good that is deserved.

3. Credibility Excesses and Testimonial Injustice

I began this paper by highlighting that the U.S. Supreme Court regards confession evidence as possibly the most powerful evidence of guilt admissible in court. At the same time, confessions are often acquired through coercion, manipulation, and deception – such as by using maximization tactics and presenting false evidence – as well as by targeting vulnerable suspects – such as those who have been sleep deprived, juveniles, and the mentally impaired. What I now want to show is that when the testimony of a confessing self is privileged over a recanting self because of prejudice, whether racial or otherwise, this results in a unique kind of testimonial injustice that is due to a credibility excess.[18]

This can be seen most clearly by focusing on several features of false confessions. First, false confessions are *highly resistant to counterevidence*, which, it might be recalled, is a key feature of the prejudicial stereotypes often at work in instances of testimonial injustice. Despite awareness of the reality and prevalence of false confessions, as well as their causes and effects, false confessions are frequently taken to be sufficient for grounding convictions. This occurs even when there is powerful evidence on behalf of defendants' innocence in particular cases, and the stakes simply couldn't be higher. In a recent article showing how false confessions trump exculpatory DNA evidence, for instance, Appleby and Kassin discuss the case of Juan Rivera, who was convicted of the rape and murder of an 11-year-old girl in Waukegan, IL on the basis of his confession, even after DNA testing of semen at the scene excluded him. 'The state's theory of why DNA belonging to someone other than the defendant was found in the victim was that the young girl had prior consensual sex with an unknown male, after which time Rivera raped her, failed to ejaculate, and then killed her' (Appleby and Kassin, 2016, p. 127). The fact that Rivera was convicted of

[18] Medina (2011) and Davis (2016) both discuss the relationship between credibility excesses and testimonial injustice, but neither does so in relation to phenomena at all like false confessions.

the child's murder shows that the state's outrageous theory was regarded as more credible than the possibility that he confessed to a crime he didn't commit – in other words, a single confession trumped evidence that would otherwise be taken to be decisively exculpatory. The most plausible explanation for this is that the false confession received a massive, unwarranted excess of credibility.

This is even more vivid when it is noticed that the totality of the evidence against confessions is often substantial, while the evidence in their favor is remarkably thin. Returning to the case of Juan Rivera, the evidence in favor of his innocence wasn't only the DNA that excluded him, and the fact that the state needed to construct an incredible theory to explain this. He was also a 19-year-old former special education student, who had been questioned by detectives for four days, during which he steadfastly denied any knowledge of the crime. Around midnight on the fourth day, after the interrogators became accusatory:

> he broke down, and purportedly nodded when asked if he had raped and killed [the 11-year-old girl]. The interrogation continued until 3:00 a.m., when investigators left to type a confession for Rivera to sign. Minutes later, jail personnel saw him beating his head against the wall of his cell in what was later termed a psychotic episode. Nevertheless, within a few hours, Rivera signed the typed confession that the investigators had prepared. The document, a narrative account of what the investigators claimed Rivera told them, was so riddled with incorrect and implausible information, that Lake County State's Attorney Michael Waller instructed investigators to resume the interrogation in an effort to clear up the inconsistencies. On October 30, despite Rivera's obvious fragile mental condition, the interrogation resumed, resulting in a second signed confession, which contained a plausible account of the crime.[19]

Because of trial errors and post-conviction DNA testing, Rivera had three separate jury trials and was found guilty and sentenced to life in prison on all three occasions. It wasn't until the Center on Wrongful Convictions became involved that the Illinois Appellate Court ruled in 2012 that Rivera's conviction was 'unjustified and cannot stand,' and thus that the state would dismiss all charges. Rivera had served 20 years in prison.

[19] https://www.innocenceproject.org/cases/juan-rivera/, accessed 18 February 2018.

If we look at the case of Rivera, the extent to which his false confession needs to be given an excess of credibility is not only undeniable, it is shocking. To see this, notice that knowledge is taken to be incompatible with the presence of defeaters, with can be either *doxastic* or *normative*, and either *rebutting* or *undercutting*.[20] A doxastic defeater is a doubt or belief that you have that indicates that one of your beliefs is either false (i.e., rebutting) or unreliably formed or sustained (i.e., undercutting). A normative defeater is similar, except it concerns doubts or beliefs that you *should have*, given the evidence available to you. So, for example, if I believe that the animal in my backyard is a bobcat by seeing one there, I might get powerful evidence that such a belief is false by you telling me that bobcats have never lived in my state, or that my basis is a poor one by my optometrist reporting to me how much my vision has deteriorated. If I accept both instances of testimony, then I have doxastic defeaters, rebutting in the first case, undercutting in the second. But even if I reject the testimony in question, I am still on the hook for this counterevidence if I do so for no good reason at all. Why? Because it is evidence that I *should have*.[21] The justification that my bobcat-belief might have initially enjoyed, then, has been normatively defeated.

These tools can help us see the extent to which Rivera's false confession was given, over the course of decades and by people at every stage of the process – including police officers, prosecutors, and jurors – a massive excess of credibility that resulted in a distinct form of testimonial injustice. Given all of the research discussed above, Rivera was, first and foremost, a prime candidate for providing a false confession: he was a special education student, who had endured multiple lengthy interrogations, was sleep-deprived, and was shown to be in the middle of a psychotic episode. Moreover, Rivera's original confession was riddled with inaccuracies and implausible information. All of this, by itself, should challenge the reliability of Rivera as a source of information about his guilt. In other words, those accepting Rivera's confession had undercutting defeaters (whether doxastic or normative), since they had evidence

[20] For various views of defeaters, approached in a number of different ways, see BonJour (1980 and 1985), Nozick (1981), Goldman (1986), Pollock (1986), Fricker (1987 and 1994), Chisholm (1989), Burge (1993 and 1997), Plantinga (1993), McDowell (1994), Audi (1997 and 1998), Bergmann (1997), Williams (1999), BonJour and Sosa (2003), Hawthorne (2004), Reed (2006), and Lackey (2008).

[21] For a very nice development of the notion of 'should have known,' see Goldberg (2015).

that clearly showed that their beliefs that Rivera raped and murdered the 11-year-old child were unreliably formed or sustained. That is, they had evidence that the source of their beliefs about Rivera's guilt – namely, Rivera himself – was not reliable under the interrogation conditions in question. But they also had doxastic rebutting defeaters, since the DNA evidence excluded him as a source of the semen at the scene of the crime, thereby calling into question the truth of their beliefs that he was guilty of the crimes.

When one has a defeater of any kind, the only way in which the target belief can be rationally retained is if one has a *defeater-defeater* – that is, a further belief or evidence that defeats the original belief or evidence. So, for instance, the rebutting defeater for my bobcat belief might itself be defeated if I come to learn that a bobcat recently escaped from the local zoo. Or the undercutting defeater might be defeated if I discover that my optometrist consulted the wrong chart when concluding that my vision is unreliable. But notice: there is simply no way in which the state's incredible theory in which the 11-year-old was sexually active with some unknown male, and Rivera didn't ejaculate despite raping her, successfully works as a defeater-defeater here. In other words, there is no interpretation of the available evidence that makes this theory *more plausible* than the alternative one: namely, that Rivera falsely confessed under duress to a crime he didn't commit.

That false confessions are resistant to counterevidence is further supported by looking at the sheer number of instances of testimony that often need to be discounted in order to retain belief in the correctness of a corresponding conviction. Consider, for analogy, how the testimony of victims of sexual assault is often rejected or discounted because of bias or prejudice,[22] but how numbers can sometimes add up to tip the balance.[23] So, for instance, a handful of girls and women accusing Larry Nassar of sexual harassment or assault wasn't enough for many to believe them, but when over 300 women came forward, the public started to side with their word over his denials.[24]

22 See, for instance, Tuerkheimer (2017).

23 It is instructive to compare this point to Charles Mills's discussion of the testimony of blacks: 'At one point in German South-West Africa, white settlers demanded 'that in court only the testimony of seven African witnesses could outweigh evidence presented by a single white person' (Cocker 1998, 317)' (Mills, 2007, p. 32).

24 https://www.chicagotribune.com/sports/college/ct-spt-michigan-state-larry-nassar-settlement-20180516-story.html, accessed 27 February 2019.

We saw something similar in the case of Bill Cosby, where 60 women reported being victimized at the hands of the once respected comedian and actor.[25] Now while this involves the addition of new testifiers, we can see a structurally similar problem at work in false confessions. A confessing self often reports guilt only once – under conditions of coercion, manipulation, deception, sleep deprivation, stress, and so on – while a recanting self reports innocence hundreds, even thousands of times, often over a period of years. And yet despite this, the one report of guilt utterly swamps the thousands of reports of innocence, with no justification for this radical asymmetry in treatment of confession versus recantations. This provides another lens through which we can see that false confessions are highly resistant to counterevidence.

Second, false confessions reveal how *credibility can be finite, and thus how its proper distribution is crucial* for assessing whether a speaker is the victim of testimonial injustice. Typically, when we talk about distributing credibility, we have in mind doing so across different people. If a woman says she was assaulted and the accused assailant denies this, then the question is: which person do we believe? But in cases of false confessions, we are talking about distributing credibility across different times in the life of the same person. There is the earlier, confessing self and the later, recanting self. The question then becomes, which self do we believe: the earlier or the later one?

Of course, the mere fact that two people disagree, even about matters of fact, does not by itself require that credibility be finite between them. I may tell you that a local restaurant is open while someone else tells you it's not. That we offer competing reports here does not require that only one of us be deemed worthy of trust or belief: you can be credible, even if wrong on a particular occasion, and I can lack credibility, even if right in a one-off case. Many disagreements are the product of innocent mistakes or lack of information, and so there can still be enough credibility to go around.

But not all disagreements are like this. It's precisely when someone's credibility itself is on the line that its finitude rears its head. False confessions provide the clearest case here: when someone confesses to murder and then recants shortly thereafter, there are no errors or gaps in evidence to explain the disagreement away. To give credibility to the confessing self is *ipso facto* to deny it to the

[25] https://www.usatoday.com/story/life/people/2018/04/27/bill-cosby-full-list-accusers/555144002/, accessed 27 February 2019.

recanting self. Credibility becomes scarce.[26] What this shows is that false confessions uniquely pit one against oneself, and reveal how an excess in credibility can lead to an egregious kind of testimonial injustice.[27]

Third, by virtue of the state saying that the reality described by the confessor in cases of false confessions – one that is reported only through coercion, manipulation, deception, sleep deprivation, and so on – represents her truest states, *the confessor's status as a knower is reduced to what she reports only under conditions devoid of, or with diminished, epistemic agency*. This is especially problematic since the question of whether one is a murderer can literally be a matter of life and death. So, while it is true that the recanter – the later self who accurately, consistently, and steadfastly describes a different reality that is not extracted through coercion, manipulation, or deception – is wronged in being afforded a massive credibility deficit, there is a unique and powerful epistemic wrong done to the earlier self who receives a credibility excess. Indeed, the excess given in false confessions quite literally amounts to the state saying that confessors are knowers with respect to the testimony in question only insofar as they are *not* epistemic agents.[28]

There is an instructive parallel here: in ancient Athens, the testimony of enslaved persons, who were the property of their masters or the state, was typically inadmissible in judicial proceedings except under torture. As Michael Gagarin writes, 'One of the most criticized features of classical Athenian law is the bizarre institution of … 'interrogation under torture'. A well-known rule held that in most cases the testimony of slaves was only admissible in court if it had been taken under torture, and in the surviving forensic speeches the orators frequently…praise the practice as most effective' (Gagarin, 1996, p. 1). Just as Athenian courts regarded the testimony

[26] I develop this in greater detail in Lackey (2018). I also make this point in https://blog.apaonline.org/2016/04/21/pitted-against-yourself-credibility-and-false-confessions/.

[27] While I have here focused on earlier-self credibility excesses, it should be clear that similar considerations apply to later selves. Suppose, for instance, that a false 'memory' of abuse is coercively extracted by people in power to serve their purposes, and the testimony of this 'later self' is given an excess of credibility in virtue of bias against her social identity. This would be an example of a later-self credibility excess, with a corresponding form of testimonial injustice.

[28] For an interesting and compelling discussion of a distinctive kind of epistemic wrong that targets the epistemic agency of knowers, see Leydon-Hardy (forthcoming).

of enslaved persons as reliable only when obtained via torture – and thus offered under conditions devoid of epistemic agency – so, too, do our courts privilege the testimony of confessing selves, even when confessions are extracted through interrogation techniques that undermine or compromise our epistemic agency. This is especially problematic when the confessing selves are vulnerable members of society, such as juveniles and those with developmental impairments, and when the credibility excesses are fueled by prejudice, such as racism and sexism.

We might take a step back here, then, and identify an interestingly different sort of testimonial injustice. More precisely, what I call *agential testimonial injustice* occurs when testimony is *extracted* from a speaker in a way that bypasses or subverts the speaker's epistemic agency and is then given an unwarranted *excess* of credibility. Agential testimonial injustice is extraordinarily vivid in cases of false confessions that have been extracted in various ways, but testimony obtained in ways that deny epistemic agency is not limited to such cases. Many abusive relationships, for instance, involve coercion of various degrees, including in testimonial contexts, and when what is reported under such conditions is unjustifiably privileged, one is the victim of this kind of testimonial injustice. Imagine, for instance, a woman testifying that her partner has never been abusive while he is sitting next to her in an interrogation room, but she then retracts this once she is able to extricate herself from his control. If the former testimony is weighed far more heavily than the latter for no good reason, particularly when one is aware of the broader context of the abuse, this would be an instance of what I'm calling agential testimonial injustice.

It is worth developing in a bit more detail the precise nature of two different epistemic wrongs involved in this kind of testimonial injustice. The first kind of wrong is the one highlighted above, which specifically involves *the excess of credibility given to the extracted testimony*. Here, one is epistemically wronged by virtue of being regarded as a testifier – a giver of knowledge – only when one's testimony is extracted and is thus the product of a process that subverts one's epistemic agency. This can be seen both by the weight that the confession is given relative to other evidence and, specifically, the privileging of the confessing testimony over the recanting testimony.

The second kind of epistemic wrong involved in agential testimonial injustice results from *the very act of extracting testimony from a speaker in a way that subverts her epistemic agency*. This can happen in different ways. The clearest and most extreme case is where the extraction, such as the interrogation tactics in question, leads subjects to believe in the truth of their own reports, either wholly or partially. For instance, following Kassin and Wrightsman (1985), Kassin et al. (2010) characterize 'coerced-internalized' false confessions as those in which 'innocent but malleable suspects, told that there is incontrovertible evidence of their involvement, come not only to capitulate in their behavior but also to believe that they may have committed the crime in question, sometimes confabulating false memories in the process' (2010, p. 15). In cases of coerced-internalized false confessions, then, both one's testimony and one's doxastic states have come under the will of another. By virtue of employing techniques that are coercive, manipulative, and deceptive, interrogators here are able to alienate a suspect from her own epistemic resources and bring about beliefs that are disconnected from her epistemic agency.[29]

These cases of coerced-internalized false confessions quite straightforwardly involve this second epistemic wrong. To see this, notice that epistemic agency is commonly understood as requiring a subject's responsiveness to reasons or evidence.[30] On a strong reading of this, I exercise my epistemic agency with respect to my belief that *p* when my belief that *p* is responsive to reasons. When interrogators are able to manipulate not only the testimony of suspects, but their doxastic states as well, they are quite clearly interfering with the reasons-responsiveness of the suspects' beliefs. This results in a clear instance of the second epistemic wrong involved in agential testimonial injustice since a subject's epistemic agency is being subverted in the obtaining of her confession.

But even when subjects don't internalize their own guilt, and thus continue to believe in their innocence despite saying otherwise, there is an important sense in which their epistemic agency is compromised *in the extraction of their testimony*. To make this clear, let's look at a couple of cases where a speaker reports what she herself does not believe but in a way that does not at all interfere with her epistemic agency.

Consider, first, lying – where a speaker states that *p*, believes that *p* is false, and states that *p* with the intention to be deceptive with respect to whether *p*.[31] Even though a liar aims to be deceptive in

[29] Coerced-internalized false confessions are an example of what Leydon-Hardy (forthcoming) calls epistemic infringement.

[30] See, for instance, Hieronymi (2008), McHugh (2013), and Reed (2013).

[31] See Lackey (2013).

her reports, this does not at all interfere with her *ability* to be responsive to reasons in her beliefs or her testimony. Indeed, a liar might even be a *responsible* epistemic agent regarding her doxastic states, despite the fact that her statements aim away from the truth. Consider, next, cases of *selfless assertion*,[32] where there are three components to this phenomenon: first, a subject, for purely non-epistemic reasons, does not believe that *p*; second, despite this lack of belief, the subject is aware that *p* is very well supported by all of the available evidence; and, third, because of this, the subject asserts that *p* without believing that *p*. A classic cases of a selfless assertion is where a Creationist teacher correctly reports that *Homo Sapiens* evolved from *Homo erectus* to her students, even though she doesn't believe this herself. Here, the reported belief in question is resistant to counterevidence, and so the belief itself is at least not properly responsive to reasons. Nevertheless, the reporting of the selfless assertion does not in any way violate the speaker's epistemic agency and, in fact, is grounded in it. In particular, the speaker in such cases fails to report what she herself believes, but she does so for straightforwardly epistemic reasons. In this way, she is appropriately sensitive to reasons, not with respect to her own beliefs, but with respect to her testimony. On my view, then, selfless assertions straightforwardly reflect epistemic agency.

Let's now turn to the case of extracted testimony. For instance, Kassin et al. (2010) discuss 'compliant false confessions,' which are 'those in which suspects are induced through interrogation to confess to a crime they did not commit. In those cases, the suspect acquiesces to the demand for a confession to escape a stressful situation, avoid punishment, or gain a promised or implied reward' (2010, p. 14). Here, even if the beliefs of the suspects are responsive to reasons, this is utterly disconnected from the obtaining of their testimony. Unlike in the case of selfless assertions, for instance, where the offering of the reports is precisely what is grounded in the responsiveness to reasons, the tactics used to extract the confessions – coercion, manipulation, deception – subvert the epistemic agency of the suspects. In so doing, such speakers are the victim of this second kind of epistemic wrong involved in agential testimonial injustice.

Finally, recall that Fricker's conception of testimonial injustice focuses specifically on credibility deficits that result from prejudices targeting a speaker's social identity, such as race or gender. We might ask, then, what social identity is relevant in cases of false confessions, especially since it is not only members of underrepresented groups

[32] See Lackey (2007) and (2008).

that are victims of the sort of credibility excess at issue in agential testimonial injustice. By way of response here, notice that Fricker's conception of social identity is unnecessarily narrow. While race and gender are certainly highly relevant to the credibility that speakers are given across many different contexts, there are other aspects of social identity that are important here as well, such as socioeconomic status, occupation, and so on. For instance, many people in the workplace find themselves on a hierarchy where those at the top are given more credibility than those lower down, even in areas that are entirely disconnected from their areas of expertise. In a hospital, physicians might be believed over nurses about questions that do not pertain to medicine, and if this happens regularly, and simply in virtue of professional status, it seems correct to say that the nurses are victims of testimonial injustice. Similarly, members of groups associated with delinquency, deviance, or moral deficiency, such as 'criminals' and 'prisoners,' are frequently the targets of systematic prejudice. A criminal record, for instance, presents a major barrier to employment,[33] the label of 'prisoner' or 'ex-con' is highly stigmatized,[34] and 'offenders' tend to be demonized as dangerous, dishonest, and disreputable.[35] Some have even extended this prejudice to 'suspects,' as Edwin Meese III famously said in 1985, while he was Attorney General of the United States, 'you don't have many suspects who are innocent of a crime. That's contradictory. If a person is innocent of a crime, then he is not a suspect'. [36] Thus, a plausible explanation is that at least one of the social identities targeted in cases of false confessions is 'criminal' or 'suspect,' triggering in others the belief that the confessor is guilty. Of course, this can combine with other prejudices, such as those involving race, ethnicity, and socioeconomic status. But, as we have seen, confessions alone can lead to egregious acts of testimonial injustice.

Agential testimonial injustice thus involves a testifier suffering two epistemic wrongs, both through the process by which the testimony is extracted and by virtue of the credibility excess it receives. I now want to briefly turn to why confessing selves might be given a credibility excess in the first place. And notice just how crucial it is to address this question. *For convictions based largely on false confessions*

33 See Devah (2007).

34 See Harding (2003), LeBel (2008), and Hirschfield and Piquero (2010).

35 See Gaubatz (1995) and Young (1999).

36 (https://www.latimes.com/archives/la-xpm-1985-10-09-me-16865-story.html).

can't be explained simply by pointing to the fact that recanting selves receive a credibility deficit. In many cases, if you subtract the confession, you lose the conviction, too.[37] So, for instance, even if a defendant's testimony of innocence at a later time is rejected, what is often also needed to convince a jury of his guilt is the veracity of the original confession. Put bluntly, calling the recanter a liar isn't enough for a conviction – the confessor also needs to be regarded as a truthteller.

4. Why?

The first, and perhaps most obvious, reason why the testimony of confessors is privileged is that most of us find it very difficult to imagine ourselves confessing to something we didn't do, and so we conclude that the suspect must be guilty. This is especially compelling when a violent crime is at issue, such as murder. The problem with this is that there is ample psychological research showing otherwise. For instance, in a well-known experiment by Kassin and Kiechel (1996), 69% of college students who were falsely accused of causing a computer to crash by pressing a key that they were told to avoid signed a confession. When false evidence is presented of guilt, this percentage is even higher, and it is not uncommon for suspects to even come to believe in their own guilt, either fully or partially. A study by Nash and Wade (2009) used digital editing software to fabricate evidence of participants 'stealing' money from a 'bank' during a computerized gambling experiment. When presented with this evidence, *all* of the subjects signed the confession form, with 63% fully internalizing the act and 20% partially internalizing the act. The authors conclude, 'a combination of social demand, phoney evidence and false suggestion from a credible source can lead a substantial number of people to falsely confess and believe they committed an act they never did' (Nash and Wade, 2009, p. 629). This can be seen in the case of Michael Crowe, whose sister was stabbed to death in her bedroom. 'After a series of interrogation sessions, during which time police presented Crowe with compelling false physical evidence of his guilt, he concluded that he was a killer, saying: 'I'm not sure how I did it. All I know is I did it'. Eventually, he was convinced that he has a split personality – that

[37] Consider, again, the case of Tankleff discussed above: '*Solely on the basis of that confession, Tankleff was convicted*, only to have his conviction vacated and the charges dismissed 19 years later (Firstman & Salpeter, 2008; Lambert, 2008)' (Kassin et al. 2010, p. 18, emphasis added).

'bad Michael' acted out of a jealous rage while 'good Michael' blocked the incident from memory. The charges against Crowe were later dropped when a drifter in the neighborhood that night was found with [his sister's] blood on his clothing' (Kassin et al., 2010, p. 15).

Another reason we favor the confessor over the recanter is that false confessions affect the perceptions of others, including eyewitnesses, alibi witnesses, and forensic experts. In one study, 61% of those who had witnessed a staged theft changed their identifications after learning that certain lineup members had confessed.[38] In another study, only 45% of participants maintained their support of an alibi for a suspect after being told that she confessed to stealing money, a number that dropped to 20% when the experimenter suggested that their support might imply their complicity with the alibi.[39] What this data shows is that false confessions not only mislead in the first instance, *they also beget additional misleading evidence downstream*. When this is combined with how counterintuitive false confessions seem to many, including judges and jurors, conditions become optimal for wrongful convictions.

Of particular relevance for our purposes here is that there is reason to believe that racial prejudice or bias is at work in convictions based on false confessions. Andrew Taslitz explains what happens when the interrogation techniques we discussed earlier are used in conjunction with racial discrimination:

> Now when we add race to the mix, the picture becomes clearer. Officers start with a presumption of the guilt of a young black male based upon one-sided and limited circumstantial evidence. The kid reacts with hostility and defensiveness. These reactions, combined with his powerless speech patterns, lead police to believe he is lying. They close off alternative theories, heightening the pressure on the kid about whose guilt they are now convinced. They make real evidence sound more inculpatory than it is, they deceive him into believing there is still more inculpatory evidence against him, they appeal to his self-interest, and they hammer away at him for hours. Young, isolated, cut off from family and friends, fearful, and rightly seeing no way out, he confesses. Falsely.
>
> Should the youth take the stand at a suppression hearing, the judge, drawing on the same racially-stigmatizing images of black youth, won't believe him. The case goes to trial, and the

38 See Kasel and Kassin (2009).
39 See Marion, Kukucka, Collins, Kassin, and Burke (2016).

> jury likely sees a film just of his confession.... the same defensiveness and linguistic barriers that made the kid seem to be a liar to the police prod the jury toward a similar conclusion. And the same stereotypes of black criminality and duplicity again favor jurors accepting the truthfulness of the confession rather than of its retraction. (Taslitz, 2006, pp. 131-32)

Given that 85% of juvenile exonerees who falsely confessed are African American,[40] there is further reason to conclude that racism is a significant factor when looking at why confessing selves are given a credibility excess.

Finally, the *practical interests* of those most responsible for securing justice often lead them, intentionally or unintentionally, to weigh confessions far too heavily, to disregard exculpatory evidence, and to rely on incredible theories to support their conclusions. This is often seen in the case of prosecutors, who can be blindly driven by a desire to 'win'. For instance, in a widely ridiculed interview on an episode of *60 Minutes*, 'Chicago: The False Confessions Capital,' then-State's Attorney Anita Alvarez discussed the case of the 'Dixmoor Five' in which DNA evidence ruled out five defendants who had falsely confessed to the rape and murder of a 14-year-old girl. After serving a total of 95 years behind bars, all five were exonerated in 2011, and the Illinois State Police settled in 2013 a civil rights case brought on their behalf for a record $40 million. Moreover, the semen found inside the 14-year-old matched Willie Randolph, who was a convicted rapist with 39 arrests. Despite all of this, when asked about this case in a 2015 interview, Alvarez still said that it was possible that the five defendants raped and murdered the girl, and that Randolph wandered past the field where her body was and committed an act of necrophilia.[41] Since the total evidence overwhelmingly tells against this outrageous theory, the most plausible explanation is that Alvarez was motivated by her practical interests, which she thinks will be served by refusing to admit mistakes by her office. Of course, we see this same phenomenon outside the courtroom as well. Climate change deniers will massively privilege one scientist's testimony over that of thousands of others because it suits their purposes, as do voters with the testimony of their preferred candidates for office. When such credibility excesses are driven by prejudices, they clearly result in acts of testimonial injustice.

40 Taslitz (2006).

41 http://blogs.chicagotribune.com/news_columnists_ezorn/2012/12/cook-county-states-attorney-alvarez-humiliates-herself-on-national-tv.html, accessed on 1 March 2018.

5. Conclusion

In this paper, I have argued that false confessions provide a unique, compelling, and practically urgent case in which an excess in credibility results in a distinctive kind of testimonial injustice. This reveals not only that credibility can, in fact, be finite, and that its proper distribution is often of critical importance – indeed, it can literally be the difference between life and death – but also that in privileging earlier, confessing selves over later, recanting selves, the state often reduces the confessor to a knower only insofar as she is devoid of epistemic agency. In doing so, the state is quite straightforwardly saying to its citizens – you are worthy of being believed only when we undermine your epistemic agency and extract information from you through coercive or manipulative methods. That this is a particularly pernicious form of testimonial injustice, carried out by institutions in which we place our trust, cries out for a radical change in the epistemic lens through which we view confessions in the criminal legal system.[42]

Northwestern University
j-lackey@northwestern.edu

References

Sara C. Appleby and Saul M. Kassin, 'When Self-Report Trumps Science: Effects of Confessions, DNA, and Prosecutorial Theories on Perceptions of Guilt.' *Psychology, Public Policy, and Law* 22 (2016) 127–40.

Robert Audi, 'The Place of Testimony in the Fabric of Knowledge and Justification.' *American Philosophical Quarterly* 34 (1997), 405–22.

Robert Audi. *Epistemology: A Contemporary Introduction to the Theory of Knowledge*, (London: Routledge, 1998).

Michael Bergmann, 'Internalism, Externalism and the No-Defeater Condition.' *Synthese* 110 (1997), 399–417.

[42] For very helpful comments on earlier drafts of this paper, I'm grateful to Tyrone Daniels, Lauren Leydon-Hardy, Baron Reed, Deb Tuerkheimer, and participants in the 2018 Summer School in Philosophy at the University of Cologne, Northern Illinois University, the University of Rochester, and the *2019 Journal of Criminal Law and Criminology* Symposium.

Laurence BonJour, 'Externalist Theories of Epistemic Justification.' *Midwest Studies in Philosophy* 5 (1980), 53–73.
Laurence BonJour. 1985. *The Structure of Empirical Knowledge*, (Cambridge, MA: Harvard University Press).
Laurence BonJour and Ernest Sosa, *Epistemic Justification: Internalism vs. Externalism, Foundations vs. Virtues,* (Oxford: Blackwell Publishing, 2003).
Tyler Burge, 'Content Preservation', *The Philosophical Review*, 102 (1993), 457–488.
Tyler Burge. 'Interlocution, Perception, and Memory', *Philosophical Studies* 86 (1997), 21–47.
Roderick M Chisholm, *Theory of Knowledge*, 3rd edn. (Englewood Cliffs, N.J.: Prentice-Hall, 1989).
Emmalon Davis, 'Typecasts, Tokens, and Spokespersons: A Case for Credibility Excess as Testimonial Injustice', *Hypatia* 31 (2016), 485–501.
Kristie Dotson, 'Tracking Epistemic Violence, Tracking Practices of Silencing.' *Hypatia* 26 (2011), 236–57.
Elizabeth Fricker, 'The Epistemology of Testimony.' *Proceedings of the Aristotelian Society*, supp. vol. 61 (1987), 57–83.
Elizabeth Fricker. 'Against Gullibility,' in Bimal Krishna Matilal and Arindam Chakrabarti (eds.), *Knowing from Words*, (Dordrecht: Kluwer Academic Publishers, 1994) 125–61.
Miranda Fricker, *Epistemic Injustice: Power & the Ethics of Knowing*, (Oxford: Oxford University Press, 2007).
Michael Gagarin, 'The Torture of Slaves in Athenian Law', *Classical Philology* 91 (1996), 1–18.
Kathlyn Taylor Gaubatz, *Crime in the Public Mind,* (Dearborn: University of Michigan Press, 1995).
Sanford Goldberg, 'Should Have Known', *Synthese* 194 (2015) 2863–94.
Alvin. I Goldman, *Epistemology and Cognition,* (Cambridge, MA: Harvard University Press, 1986).
Samuel R. Gross, Kristen Jacoby, Daniel J. Matheson, and Nicholas Montgomery, 'Exonerations in the United States 1989 Through 2003.' *Journal of Criminal Law and Criminology* 95 (2005) 523–60.
Gisli H. Gudjonsson, and Jon F. Sigurdssonb, 'The Gudjonsson Questionnaire-Revised (GCQ-R) Factor Structure and its Relationship with Personality', *Personality and Individual Differences* 27 (1999) 953–68.

David J. Harding, 'Jean Valjean's Dilemma: The Management of Ex-Convict Identity in the Search for Employment', *Deviant Behavior* 24 (2003) 571–95.

John Hawthorne, *Knowledge and Lotteries,* (Oxford: Oxford University Press, 2004).

Pamela Hieronymi, 'Responsibility for Believing', *Synthese* 161 (2008), 357–73.

Paul J. Hirschfield and Alex R. Piquero, 'Normalization and Legitimation: Modeling Stigmatizing Attitudes Toward Ex-Offenders' *Criminology* 48 (2010), 27–55.

Fred E. Inbau, John E. Reid, Joseph P. Buckley, and Brian C. Jayne, *Criminal Interrogation and Confessions* (4th ed.) (Gaithersberg, MD: Aspen, 2001).

Lisa E. Kasel and Saul M. Kassin, 'On the Presumption of Evidentiary Independence: Can Confessions Corrupt Eyewitness Identifications?' *Psychological Science* 20 (2009), 122–26.

Saul M. Kassin, 'On the Psychology of Confessions: Does Innocence Put Innocents at Risk? *American Psychologist* 60 (2005), 215–28.

Saul M. Kassin, Steven A. Drizin, Thomas Grisso, Gisli H. Gudjonsson, Richard A. Leo, and Allison D. Redlich, 'Police-Induced Confessions: Risk Factors and Recommendations.' *Law and Human Behavior* 34 (2010), 3–38.

Saul M. Kassin, and Katherine L. Kiechel, 'The Social Psychology of False Confessions:Compliance, Internalization, and Confabulation.' *Psychological Science* 7 (1996), 125–8.

Saul M. Kassin, and Karlyn McNall, 'Police Interrogations and Confessions: Communicating Promises and Threats by Pragmatic Implication.' *Law and Human Behavior* 15 (1991), 233–51.

Saul M. Kassin, and Rebecca J. Norwick, 'Why People Waive Their *Miranda* Rights: The Power of Innocence.' *Law and Human Behavior* 28 (2004) 211–21.

Saul M. Kassin, and Lawrence S. Wrightsman, 'Confession Evidence,' in Saul M. Kassin and Lawrence S. Wrightsman (eds.) *The Psychology of Evidence and Trial Procedure.* (Beverly Hills, CA: Sage, 1985) 67–94.

Jessica R. Klaver, Zina Lee, and V. Gordon Rose, 'Effects of Personality, Interrogation Techniques and Plausibility in an Experimental False Confession Paradigm.' *Legal and Criminal Psychology* 13 (2008), 71–88.

Jennifer Lackey, 'Norms of Assertion.' *Noûs* 41 (2007) 594–626.

Jennifer Lackey. *Learning from Words: Testimony as a Source of Knowledge*, (Oxford: Oxford University Press, 2008).

Jennifer Lackey. 'Lies and Deception: An Unhappy Divorce.' *Analysis* 73 (2013) 236–48.

Jennifer Lackey. 'Credibility and the Distribution of Epistemic Goods,' in Kevin McCain (ed.), *Believing in Accordance with the Evidence: New Essays on Evidentialism*, (Springer Publishing, 2018) 145–68.

Jennifer Lackey. 'False Confessions and Testimonial Injustice', *Journal of Criminal Law and Criminology* 110 (2020) 43–68.

Thomas P. LeBel, 'Perceptions of and Responses to Stigma', *Sociology Compass* 2 (2008) 409–32.

Richard A. Leo and Richard J. Ofshe, 'Consequences of False Confessions: Deprivations of Liberty and Miscarriages of Justice in the Age of Psychological Interrogation.' *Journal of Criminal Law and Criminology* 88 (1998) 429–96.

Lauren Leydon-Hardy, 'Predatory Grooming and Epistemic Infringement,' in Jennifer Lackey (ed.), *Applied Epistemology*, (Oxford: Oxford University Press, Forthcoming).

John McDowell, 'Knowledge by Hearsay,' in Bimal Krishna Matilal and Arindam Chakrabarti (eds.), *Knowing from Words*, (Dordrecht: Kluwer Academic Publishers, 1994) 195–224.

Conor McHugh, 'Epistemic Responsibility and Doxastic Agency.' *Philosophical Issues* 23 (2013) 132–57.

Rachel Ann McKinney, 'Extracted Speech', *Social Theory and Practice*, 42 (2016) 258–84.

Stéphanie B. Marion and Jeff Kukucka, Carisa Collins, Saul M. Kassin, and Tara M. Burke, 'Lost Proof of Innocence: The Impact of Confessions on Alibi Witnesses.' *Law and Human Behavior* 40 (2016) 65–71.

José Medina, 'The Relevance of Credibility Excess in a Proportional View of Epistemic Injustice: Differential Epistemic Authority and the Social Imaginary. *Social Epistemology* 25 (2011) 15–35.

Charles Mills, 'White Ignorance,' in Shannon Sullivan and Nancy Tuana (eds.), *Race and Epistemologies of Ignorance*, (Albany, NY: SUNY Press, 2007) 13–38.

Stephen Moston, Geoffrey M. Stephenson, and Thomas M. Williamson, 'The Effects of Case Characteristics on Suspect Behaviour During Police Questioning.' *British Journal of Criminology* 32 (1992) 23–39.

Robert A. Nash and Kimberly A. Wade, 'Innocent But Proven Guilty: Eliciting Internalized False Confessions Using Doctored-Video Evidence' *Applied Cognitive Psychology* 23 (2009) 624–37.

Robert Nozick, *Philosophical Explanations,* (Cambridge, MA: The Belknap Press, 1981).

Devah Pager, *Marked: Race, Crime, and Finding Work in an Era of Mass Incarceration,* (Chicago: The University of Chicago Press, 2007).

June J. Pilcher and Allen I. Huffcutt, 'Effects of Sleep Deprivation on Performance: A Meta-Analysis' *Sleep* 19 (1996) 318–26.

Alvin Plantinga, *Warrant and Proper Function* (Oxford: Oxford University Press, 1993).

John Pollock, *Contemporary Theories of Knowledge,* (Totowa, N.J.: Rowman and Littlefield, 1986).

Baron Reed, 'Epistemic Circularity Squared? Skepticism about Common Sense', *Philosophy and Phenomenological Research*, 73 (2006) 186–97.

Baron Reed. 'Fallibilism, Epistemic Possibility, and Epistemic Agency.' *Philosophical Issues* 23 (2013) 40–69.

Andrew E Taslitz, 'Wrongly Accused: Is Race a Factor in Convicting the Innocent?' *Ohio State Journal of Criminal Law* 4 (2006), 121–33.

Deborah Tuerkheimer, 'Incredible Women: Sexual Violence and the Credibility Discount.' *University of Pennsylvania Law Review* 166 (2017) 1–58.

Michael Williams, *Groundless Belief: An Essay on the Possibility of Epistemology*, 2nd edn. (Princeton: Princeton University Press, 1999).

Jock Young, *The Exclusive Society: Social Exclusion, Crime and Difference in Late Modernity*. (Thousand Oaks, CA: Sage, 1999).

Rape Myths: What are They and What can We do About Them?

KATHARINE JENKINS

Abstract

In this paper, I aim to shed some light on what rape myths are and what we can do about them. I start by giving a brief overview of some common rape myths. I then use two philosophical tools to offer a perspective on rape myths. First, I show that we can usefully see rape myths as an example of what Miranda Fricker has termed 'epistemic injustice', which is a type of wrong that concerns our role as knowers. Then, I show that it is important to recognise that rape myths are instances of misogyny. This word is of course a more familiar one, but I'll be drawing on a specific philosophical account of what misogyny is, developed by Kate Manne, that I think is useful here. Finally, I briefly consider some upshots of these claims.

1. Introduction

In January 2020, a high court appeal found that a family court judge, Robin Tolson, had incorrectly applied the law on rape in a ruling over custody. A woman had contested her former partner's claim for access to their son on the basis that the former partner had been controlling and had raped her. Tolson's ruling went against the woman, finding that no rape occurred because the woman did not attempt to physically resist the penetration. This judgement was overturned by the high court on appeal, in a ruling expressing concern and describing Tolson's approach as 'manifestly at odds with current jurisprudence, concomitant sexual behaviour, and what is currently acceptable socio-sexual conduct' (The Guardian, 2020). Tolson's ruling was certainly at odds with the law on rape, and with what is morally acceptable in terms of sexual conduct. However, it is not, unfortunately, out of line with many widely held mistaken attitudes about rape, or 'rape myths'. In this sense, far from being an anomaly, Tolson's ruling is in fact a paradigm example of how common rape myths affect many people's thinking when it comes to sexual violence.

In this paper, I aim to shed some light on what rape myths are and what we can do about them. I'll start by giving a brief overview of some common rape myths. I'll then use two philosophical tools to

doi:10.1017/S1358246121000126

offer a perspective on rape myths. First, I'll show that we can usefully see rape myths as an example of what Miranda Fricker has termed 'epistemic injustice', which is a type of wrong that concerns our role as knowers. Then, I'll show that it is important to recognise that rape myths are instances of misogyny. This word is of course a more familiar one, but I'll be drawing on a specific philosophical account of what misogyny is, developed by Kate Manne, that I think is useful here. Finally, I'll briefly consider some upshots of these claims.

Before I get started, though, I want to be clear about what philosophy can and cannot do for us in connection with this topic. In general, for me, doing philosophy means looking at the world around me and focusing on the things that seem urgent in the social situation in which I find myself to see if I can offer any kind of conceptual clarification or insight that might help move matters in a more positive, less oppressive, direction. In this case in particular, I think it is important to be clear from the start that philosophy is only one very small piece of the picture when it comes to understanding rape myths; empirical and theoretical work in sociology, social psychology, critical legal studies, and so on is also is essential. What's more, the analysis I am offering is by no means a radical departure from how we might in any case think about rape myths, both in general and within these adjacent disciplines. For example, I think it's not exactly startling or novel to say that we can think of rape myths as a form of misogyny. So I take myself to be doing something quite modest: using some philosophical tools to cast some already familiar thoughts in a more precise form. In the process, I hope to illustrate those philosophical tools, which I think are interesting ones, by showing them in action.

2. What are rape myths?

Here are some examples of common rape myths:

> 'If someone dresses or acts in a sexually provocative way, they are to blame if they are raped.'
>
> 'Rape always involves overwhelming physical force and a rape victim will always try to fight off their attacker.'
>
> 'Women often lie about rape for revenge or because they regret having sex.'

These are the kinds of things I have in mind when I say 'rape myths'. I take it that rape myths are 'in the waters', as it were: they are circulating in lots of areas of discourse, often below the surface. Rape myths can also come up in some quite specific contexts in some very stark ways, as we saw in the example of the family court judge. This is obviously an incorrect application of the law on rape, which focuses on the absence of consent and does not require active resistance. It also tallies with several of the rape myths I just mentioned: rape as always involving physical force and attempted resistance, and women as frequently lying about rape.

In this paper, I'm focusing on rape myths as applied to people who are perceived as women – which is to say, who are perceived as women *by whoever it is that holds the rape myth in question*. This could be another person, or it could be that someone is applying a rape myth to their own experiences. It's important to be really clear that rape myths affect women, men, and non-binary people, and that there are some rape myths that apply specifically to people who are perceived as men, for example. However, I think that by and large, these need a different treatment, and one that I cannot offer in this paper. So here I am adopting a specific focus on rape myths as they affect people perceived as women.

As this choice suggests, I think that gender is very important to rape myths – but it's far from being the only social category that matters. The way in which rape myths are applied and mobilised, and the shape that they take in particular instances of application, is deeply intersectional, in the sense that it involves and reveals the intermeshed nature of social categories that are often though about separately, such as 'gender' and 'race'. Here I'm aiming to take a fairly broad-brush approach: the hope is that most of what I want to say about rape myths as applied to those perceived as women is general enough that it applies across differences of race, class, sexuality, disability, and so on. This is not to deny that there are also lots of more specific things to be said about rape myths as applied to those who occupy these various intersections. Moreover, I recognise that this kind of approach is inherently risky: setting out to talk about 'women in general' always carries the danger of ending up implicitly centring the most privileged women. Constant checking is required if this pitfall is to be avoided, which is why I'm being explicit about the approach that I'm taking in this regard.

With these caveats out of the way, I'd like to give a taxonomy of different rape myths. I think rape myths can usefully be see as falling into three main families.

1. Dishonesty myths: Rape myths centring on the idea that women frequently lie about rape.

Examples of dishonesty myths include, 'Women have consensual sex and then say it was rape to avoid seeming like sluts', and 'Women tend to lie about rape as a way of getting revenge on men'.

Of course, these ideas have no foundation in fact. False allegations of rape are no higher than for other crimes – around 3%, according to Home Office statistics (Kelly et al., 2005). What's more, far from being over-reported, rape is extremely *under*-reported and there is an enormous drop-off at each stage as allegations of rape progress through the criminal justice system. Accounting for drop-offs at each stage after a rape has occurred (reporting, decision to charge, progression to trial, guilty verdict), only about 1.5% of the rapes that actually occur result in a criminal conviction (Ministry of Justice et al., 2013).

2. Consent myths: Rape myths that obscure what counts as consensual sex and what counts as rape.

Examples of consent myths include the following: 'Consent cannot be withdrawn partway through a sexual act'; 'Consent is automatically present if the people have recently had sex'; 'Non-consensual sex always involves overwhelming physical force'; 'Consent to one kind of sexual activity implies consent to other kinds of sexual activity'.

Consent myths are closely related to dishonesty myths because if a woman says she has been raped and then describes something that her interlocutor does not consider to meet the criteria for being rape – for example, because it does not involve overwhelming physical force – then it may well seem to her interlocutor as though she is lying.

To see how this family of rape myths are unfounded, we can consider the legal definition of rape in the UK, according to which person A rapes person B iff A intentionally penetrates the vagina, anus or mouth of B with his penis, and if B does not consent to the penetration and A does not reasonably believe that B consents. (There is also a counterpart crime of 'sexual assault by penetration', where the penetration is by something other than a penis, carrying same maximum penalty as rape.) In terms of how the law defines 'consent' in this context, it is understood that B consents to the penetration if they agree by choice and have the freedom and capacity to make that choice. In addition, consent is understood as ongoing and something that can be withdrawn at any time. This definition contradicts all of the consent myths listed above.

This is a good point at which to flag that not all rape myths can be neatly categorised in the taxonomy I am offering. Consider, for example, the myth, 'Rape is almost always perpetrated by strangers'. This is certainly a myth, because rape and sexual assault by penetration are overwhelmingly (90% of cases) perpetrated by people known to the victim, and often (56% of cases) by the victim's current or former partner (Ministry of Justice et al., 2013). But is it a dishonesty myth, because it implies that women who claim they have been raped by an acquaintance are lying? Is it a consent myth, because it makes it seem as though sex between acquaintances can't be rape? Is it neither? Both? I'm content to say that this myth is doing a few different things and does not fit perfectly into either of these categories. Nor does it fit into the third category:

3. Blame myths: Rape myths that place the blame for rape on the person who is raped.

Examples of blame myths include the following: 'Women who wear revealing clothing are to blame if they are raped'; 'Women who drink alcohol/take drugs are to blame if they are raped'; 'Women who flirt with men are to blame if they are raped'; 'Women who take men home/go home with men are to blame if they are raped'.

Again, the lines between these different categories emerge as slightly fuzzy. I think blame myths are often somewhat ambiguous between *blame* and *consent*. They can slide between, for example, 'Women who wear revealing clothing are to blame if they are raped', and 'A woman who wears revealing clothing is showing that she wants sex, and so what happened to her can't have been rape because she actually consented'.

Rape myths have various effects. Some of these concern the general discourse – how people talk about rape, how they respond to hearing about instances of rape from people close to them, or within their friendship circle or broader community, and so on. Others concern the criminal justice system, where particular attention has been paid to the effects on trials of jury members accepting rape myths (Ellison and Munro, 2009; Burrowes, 2013). Studying this typically involves mock trials, so that different factors such as the details of the case and the instructions given to the jury can be systematically varied, and they indicate that rape myth acceptance on the part of jury members does decrease the likelihood of a guilty verdict being returned.

A third effect of rape myths concerns the impact on a survivor's own understanding of what happened to them. One study (Peterson and Muehlenhard, 2004) looked at the relationship between rape myths and the phenomenon of 'unacknowledged rape', which is where someone has had an experience that meets the legal definition of rape in the relevant context but nevertheless does not consider themselves to have been raped. The study found that for certain rape myths, participants who had been raped in a way that corresponded to the myth and who accepted the myth were significantly less likely than other participants to have acknowledged the rape. These myths were, 'A woman who "teases" men deserves anything that might happen', and 'If a woman does not physically fight back, you cannot really say it was rape'. The first of these is a blame myth, and the second is a consent myth.

This third effect of rape myths – on the self-understandings of those who have been raped – is particularly interesting because it seems like it would still be important even in a society with very different social systems in place for responding to rape. For example, we might have deep-seated criticisms of the criminal justice system in its current form and even of 'criminal justice' as a broader concept or framing, and we might hope to bring about a radical transformation of this area of society. If such a shift were to be effected, the details of how rape myths affect juries' decisions may well cease to matter. But I struggle to envision a social shift in this regard that would mean that the effect of rape myths on *survivors' self-conceptions* would cease to matter. For one thing, this seems to matter intrinsically, independent of its role as a necessary condition for setting in motion a process of justice. For another, whatever form a process of justice might take, its being put into motion would surely depend to at least some extent on people conceptualising their experiences as wrongful and being moved to take some action based on this. So the ways in which rape myths can prevent people from conceptualising their own experiences of rape *as* rape is particularly interesting for this reason: it seems like it will continue to matter across a range of very different societies, including societies that we might prefer to our own and want to work to bring about.

3. Rape myths as epistemic injustice

Epistemic injustice is a broad term, coined by Miranda Fricker, to refer to practices of knowledge in which some people are prejudicially disadvantaged, for example through the workings of racism or sexism. As Fricker puts it, people who suffer epistemic injustice are wronged in their capacity as knowers (Fricker, 2007). Epistemic injustice has a number of varieties, one of which is 'testimonial injustice', which occurs when someone is perceived as less credible than they really are due to identity-based prejudice (Fricker, 2007, ch. 1). For example, a woman whose well-founded suspicions are dismissed as 'feminine intuition' by someone who holds sexist attitudes has suffered testimonial injustice: she has been perceived as less credible than she really is due to her listener holding a prejudice that relates to her identity as a woman.

Testimonial injustice is highly relevant to dishonesty myths. These myths present *women as a group* as untrustworthy with regard to sexual violence, suggesting that their testimony ought to be treated with suspicion. This highlights the way in which epistemic injustice is wrongful. If a woman is not believed when she speaks out about rape, this might have all sorts of bad consequences: she may find this re-traumatizing, an opportunity may be missed to prevent her rapist from committing further rapes in the future, and so on. But Fricker tells us that the *very fact of not being believed* can be wrongful *in and of itself,* and independently of any bad consequences, if the withholding of belief stems from an identity-based prejudice – and dishonesty myths fit this criterion.

Another type of epistemic injustice that Fricker defines is 'hermeneutical injustice', which consists of 'having some significant area of one's social experience obscured from collective understanding owing to hermeneutical marginalization' (Fricker, 2007, p. 158). To be hermeneutically marginalized, in this context, is to be hindered from contributing fully to the kinds of conversations that shape our collective understandings of the world. For instance, if women are – by law or by social convention – prevented from occupying influential roles in areas such as journalism, broadcasting, politics, the arts, and academia, then women will be less able to affect the direction of public conversations about a range of important topics (and thus the conceptual resources that arise from these conversations) and this would count as hermeneutical marginalisation. An example of hermeneutical injustice that Fricker gives is women who suffered sexual harassment in the workplace before there was a concept of 'sexual harassment'. This lack of a concept was not random, but rather was a result of women not being able to contribute equally to setting the terms of the conversation, due to not having the opportunity to have their voices heard to the same extent as men – that's the *hermeneutical marginalisation* part. What's more, without a concept of 'sexual harassment', a woman who was being sexually harassed might struggle to fully explain her experiences. She might try saying, for example, that she is being 'bullied'. And yet she might find this hard to substantiate, since it implies surface-level hostility and aggression, which might not be present. Or she might say something like, 'he behaves in ways that make me feel uncomfortable'. But this risks locating the problem in *her* subjective 'uncomfortable feelings', rather than in the objective facts about *his* inappropriate behaviour. So the concept of 'sexual harassment' does important work for us that none of these other descriptions can do: it bring a certain area of experience into focus. This is to say that the lack of a concept of 'sexual harassment' meant that an area of women's social experience was 'obscured from collective understanding' (Fricker, 2007, p. 158). Finally, women were worse off as a result of this: being unable to bring one's experience of sexual harassment into focus either in one's own understanding or in that of others is not a good situation to be in. In other words, these experiences are 'significant', and not being able to make them apparent to oneself or to others is a harm. Although this example of sexual harassment involves a *missing* concept – a 'conceptual lacuna' – hermeneutical injustice can also involve *faulty* concepts, such as a concept of 'citizen' that is such that it can only be applied to white men.

Hermeneutical injustice is particularly relevant to consent myths. Here, I want to distinguish between two different ways in which hermeneutical injustice can occur: it can involve a faulty *explicit* understanding of the concept of rape or of consent, or it can involve a faulty *implicit* understanding of the concept of rape or of consent (Jenkins, 2017).

Consider, first, the many ways in which legal concepts of rape have been problematic. For example, in England and Wales, non-consensual sex between a husband and wife did not count as rape prior to 1991. The concept of rape in circulation prior to that time was faulty: it excluded marital rape from the category of rape, even though as a matter of fact, in terms of what's wrongful or unjust, marital rape should be categorised with other instances of rape. In other words, this concept of rape obscured experiences of marital rape from collective understanding. This is an example of a faulty explicit concept, because rape was *explicitly* defined and understood in a way that excluded marital rape.

However, this kind of hermeneutical injustice does not capture many instances in which rape myths appear to interfere with how people hold and apply concepts of rape and of consent. Often, it seems, people can be conversant with a perfectly fine definition of rape or consent in the abstract, but fail to apply it correctly to a specific case. This might even be what happened in the family court judge case with which this paper began: we can easily imagine a judge having a correct belief about the *wording* of the law on rape, but applying an incorrect criteria for establishing whether a rape was committed in a particular instance.

Perhaps such cases are simply not instances of hermeneutical injustice? This seems unsatisfying to me; such cases seem to involve something going wrong with social concepts in a similar way to the paradigm cases of hermeneutical injustice. What's more, I think there is a straightforward way to bring them into the reach of that concept, which is to say that not being able to apply a concept properly *is* a way of holding a faulty concept.

A helpful distinction here is Sally Haslanger's (2012) distinction between manifest and operative concepts. Roughly, a manifest concept relates to the way in which we would explicitly define a concept if we were asked to do so. The operative concept, on the other hand, is the concept that would be extrapolated from our actual practices. So for example, suppose a school has a rule that any pupil arriving after 9 a.m. is to be recorded as 'late', but that in practice, teachers will only mark pupils 'late' if they arrive after the registration period ends, at ten past nine. In this case, the manifest concept of 'late' is 'arrived after 9 a.m.', and the operative concept is 'arrived after the end of the registration period'. My suggestion is that often rape myths function by leading people to hold a faulty operative concept of rape, even if the manifest concept is correct, and that this is a form of hermeneutical injustice – 'implicit' hermeneutical injustice, we might say.

So we've seen here that epistemic injustice helps us to understand the workings of two of the three varieties of rape myths that I identified. Dishonesty myths can be understood as examples of testimonial injustice, and consent myths can be understood as examples of hermeneutical injustice, which may come in an explicit or an implicit guise. What remains is to say something about blame myths, and here I'll reach for a different philosophical tool, which is the concept of *misogyny*.

4. Rape myths as misogyny

Unlike the term 'epistemic injustice', the term 'misogyny' is not immediately identifiable as a philosophical term of art. In appealing to it here, though, I have in mind a particular account of misogyny developed by the philosopher Kate Manne (2017). According to Manne, we should understand misogyny as 'the "law enforcement" branch of a patriarchal order, which has the overall function of policing and enforcing its governing ideology' (Manne, 2017, p. 78) Misogyny is thus the backlash or corrective response that occurs when a patriarchal social order is challenged. It puts women back in their place when they try to step out of line. For Manne, a social environment is misogynistic when girls and women (or some specific group of girls or women) face hostile social forces that affect them *because* they are girls/women, *and* in which these hostile social forces serve to police and reinforce a patriarchal social order (Manne, 2017, p. 19). Manne recognises, rightly in my view, that a patriarchal social order is always intersectional in nature, meaning that society is never just structured around divisions of gender but also of race, of class, and so on.

Misogyny, then is about protecting and upholding patriarchal social norms. And I think it's plausible to posit the following norm in many patriarchal societies: 'Women are not entitled to control when and with whom they have sex'. However, this can be made more specific; I don't think it's plausible to think that patriarchal social norms hold that *any* man is entitled to have sex with *any* woman under *any* circumstances. This is because patriarchy has a lot to do with policing men's access to certain women and protecting that access *from other men*. So according to patriarchy, only certain men are 'entitled' to sex with certain women; for example, husbands are entitled to have sex with their wives. My suggestion is that blame myths are an instance of misogyny that targets women and girls for objecting to sex *to which men are entitled according to patriarchal norms*.

Looking at blame myths in this way helps to explain two of their notable features. The first feature is that rape by a stranger is the form of rape that is least subject to blame myths. Women who are raped by complete strangers are the least likely to be blamed, although of course there can still be attitudes of blame towards these cases, perhaps focusing on clothing or alcohol. This fits with the idea that the norm that is being protected by blame myths is not one that grants all men blanket sexual access to all women, but a more specific norm that grants certain men sexual access to certain women.

The second feature is the *intersectional* nature of blame myths, and other rape myths. We don't live in a society that is *just* patriarchal, but in one that is *also* white supremacist, heterosexist, disablist, and so on. Under a white supremacist patriarchy, we can expect to see a racial asymmetry built in to norms about men's sexual access to women, with white men's sexual access to women of colour being specifically upheld and protected in a way that is not mirrored for men of colour and white women. This is exactly what we *do* see, a fact that has been explored in detail in the work of women of colour feminists in particular (Davis, 1983; Crenshaw, 1991). As Angela Davis argues, anti-rape activism must acknowledge both the racist deployment of fabricated rape charges against Black men, and the additional hostility and disbelief shown towards Black women who suffer rape. These dynamics from a duo, the 'twin myths' of the Black man as a rapist of white women, and of the Black woman as chronically promiscuous, and therefore welcoming all attentions from white men (Davis, 1983). An upshot of this is that blame myths are applied less often and less harshly to white women who say that they have been raped by Black men, and apply particularly often and particularly harshly to Black women who say that they have been raped by white men. This analysis fits neatly with the analysis of blame myths as an instance of misogyny that targets women and girls for objecting to sex that men are entitled to according to patriarchal norms – norms that are at the same time imbued with a white supremacist logic.

5. Concluding remarks

I've analysed rape myths as falling into three broad types: dishonesty myths, consent myths, and blame myths. And I've suggested that dishonesty myths can be understood as instances of epistemic injustice, that consent myths can be understood as instances of hermeneutical injustice, and that blame myths can be understood as instances of misogyny. As I said at the start, there's nothing particularly revolutionary about this analysis; it does not call for a radical upheaval in how people are already trying to counter rape myths and resist rape culture. It does, however, underline a few points that many people working in this area are already committed to, highlighting and explaining their importance. This is because strategies for tackling rape myths will be most effective if they take into account the ways in which rape myths are instances of epistemic injustice and of misogyny.

With regard to first of these, educating people about rape myths should not just involve telling people what the definitions of rape and consent are, but should involve encouraging and supporting people to actually apply those concepts to particular cases. This is crucial because, as we have seen, if you know the formal definition of a concept but you can't appropriately apply it to cases, you can't be said to fully have the concept (to be precise, you may have a faulty operative concept). Education must involve practical, engaged thinking about rape and consent in order to properly reverse the damaging effects of rape myths. With regard to misogyny, education about rape myths is going to need to be embedded in broader education challenging norms of male entitlement – which of course are racialised, classed, and so on – because those norms are underpinning and motivating those rape myths. The myths are a corrective or 'policing' response to perceived norm violations, which means that if we are not targeting the norms that are motivating then we are not getting to the root of the problem.

The call for thorough, practical, engaged education about rape and consent that is embedded in a wider program of challenging sexism is, as I have said, hardly a radical innovation. Given the importance of this call, though, it bears repeating. In repeating it here, in a philosophical way, I hope to have contributing to removing any shred of justification for continued inaction on this point.

University of Glasgow
Katharine.Jenkins@glasgow.ac.uk

References

Nina Burrowers, *Responding to the challenge of rape myths in court* (NB Research: London, 2013).

Kimberlé Crenshaw, 'Mapping the Margins: Intersectionality, Identity Politics, and Violence against Women of Color', *Stanford Law Review*, 43 (1991), 1241–99.

Angela Davis, *Women, Race and Class* (New York: Knopf Doubleday, 1983).

Louise Ellison and Vanessa E. Munro, 'Of "Normal Sex" and "Real Rape": Exploring The Use of Socio-Sexual Scripts in (Mock) Jury Deliberation', *Social & Legal Studies*, 18:3 (2009), 291–312.

Miranda Fricker, *Epistemic Injustice: Power and the Ethics of Knowing* (Oxford University Press, 2007).

The Guardian, 'Family judges could get training after row over comments on rape' (23.01.2020).

Sally Haslanger, 'What are we talking about?: The semantics and politics of social kinds' in S. Haslanger (ed.) *Resisting Reality: Social Construction and Social Critique*, (Oxford: Oxford University Press, 2012), 365–80.

Katharine Jenkins, 'Rape Myths and Domestic Abuse Myths as Hermeneutical Injustices', *Journal of Applied Philosophy* 34:2 (2017), 191–206.

Liz Kelly, Jo Lovett, and Linda Regan, *A gap or a chasm? Attrition in reported rape cases* (London: Home Office Research, Development and Statistics Directorate, 2005).

Kate Manne, *Down Girl: The Logic of Misogyny* (New York: Oxford University Press, 2017).

Ministry of Justice, Home Office, and the Office for National Statistics, *An Overview of Sexual Offending in England and*

Wales: Statistics Bulletin (Ministry of Justice, Home Office, and the Office for National Statistics, 2013).
Zoë D. Peterson and Charlene L. Muehlenhard, 'Was It Rape? The Function of Women's Rape Myth Acceptance and Definitions of Sex in Labeling Their Own Experiences', *Sex Roles*, 52 (2004), 129–44.

'To Possess the Power to Speak'

LINDA MARTÍN ALCOFF

Abstract
I argue here that first person speech on sexual violence remains an important dimension of the movement for social change in regard to sexual violence, and that the public speech of survivors faces at least three groups of obstacles: 1) the problem of epistemic injustice, that is, injustice in the sphere of knowledge 2) the problem of language and power, and 3) the problem of dominant discourses. I explain and develop these points and end with a final argument concerning the critical importance of speaking publicly on these areas of human experience.

Classical liberal philosophers in the modern period came to see that the ability to speak openly and freely in the public sphere was critical to social justice. Figures such as Kant imagined a civil society in which individuals could pursue their needs and interests, attain security, and operate within some realm of freedom, but all this required a realm of protected speech. For Hegel, however, this approach skips over a critical set of questions: who are these individuals? How did they come to be? How did they come to formulate their needs and interests?

For Hegel, the public sphere is necessary not merely to express and negotiate over individual interests, but to contrive and conceive them. Hegel's political philosophy suggests that, within what he calls the Sphere of Right, individuals are recognized 'rights bearers' (2005). But there is another sphere, the Sphere of Morality, in which individuals are not merely the passive bearers of rights, but participatory subjects who engage in the collective work of interpreting, enacting, and transforming their rights. In this public realm of open, deliberative discussion, subjects develop, and transform, their ideas about their needs and interests in debate with others who enter as equal participants. Following Hegel, then, it is important to understand that our interests are *formulated* in the public domain of speech and deliberation, rather than simply discovered or expressed.

The social taboos that exist in many societies, including the West, against speaking publicly about rape, especially when doing so in the first person, has precluded this process, inhibiting the development of understanding for both individual survivors and the public in general. When the victims of rape, sexual assault and sexual harassment are inhibited from speaking about their experiences, either

doi:10.1017/S1358246121000084

because of social taboos or preemptive discrediting, civil society is underdeveloped. What is at stake is not only the ability of survivors to articulate their experience and their demands, but their capacity to analyze their experience, rendering nascent ideas into knowledge and understanding.

Today, survivors of sexual violence are speaking around the world, inspiring and strengthening local movements and creating global echoes with cross-fertilizing effects. Often, this begins with social media, but high-profile accusations are then taken up by the mainstream media. Once it moves from the decentralized and unregulated space of social media to corporate media, the speech of survivors enters institutions that have the power to edit, interpret, curate, and spin the story. As a result, in some cases the speech of survivors is made use of for purposes that are quite contrary to their intention: to sell sensationalized celebrity stories for the purpose of media competition, or to legitimate unilateral military action or increased funding for carceral institutions. Dominant sectors also have an interest in portraying poorer nations, minority religions, or non-white communities as the primary locus of the problem. In this way, new information and analyses from survivors gets lost in the repetition of existing shibboleths. And thus, too often the response of the mainstream to anti-rape activism, even when it lets stories be heard, has little to do with achieving a greater understanding of the epidemic of sexual violence.

In this context, I will argue here that first person speech on sexual violence remains an important dimension of the movement for social change in regard to sexual violence, despite the ways it can be reinterpreted, distorted, and used for extraneous and nefarious purposes. What does this particular form of speech contribute that no other can?

1.

The political anthropologist Pierre Clastres studied the relation of power and speech in varied cultural contexts, and developed the following account:

> 'To speak is above all to possess the power to speak. Or again, the exercise of power ensures the domination of speech: only the masters can speak. As for the subjects: they are bound to the silence of respect, reverence, or terror…The man of power is always not only the man who speaks, but the sole source of legitimate speech' (Clastres, 1987, p. 151).

On Clastres' view, the organization of speech in a given social context is a way to map the organization of social power. And further, speech is a weapon of power, enacting domination in itself. Such a dire view may seem inapplicable to liberal, open societies which legally protect contentious speech. Yet conventions of authority, credibility and legitimacy – sometimes implicit, sometimes institutionally enacted and protected – thwart social movements of all sorts that offer new ideas about knowledge, expertise, and truth. For Clastres as well as for Foucault, these conventions should be understood as the real stakes of social conflict.

The current #MeToo movement, in its various iterations around the world, has taken up the issue of public speech as its central motif, and in this, it is far from new. Collective efforts to point out the ubiquity of sexual violations in the lives of women, girls, children, prisoners, and other vulnerable groups have been mushrooming steadily around the world since the 1980s, from New Delhi to Cairo to New York. This social activism has involved as a central feature the practice of survivors speaking publicly in 'Speak-Outs' and 'Take Back the Night' marches and rallies. The performative spectacles of 'Slut Walks' as well as demonstrations initiated by the '*Ni Una Menos*' movements in Latin America are also forms of public speech: enacting collective displays of defiance and solidarity that name the police and judicial system as collaborators in systemic sexual violence. These movements challenge existing norms about how to define sexual coercion as well as culpability.

Criminal justice institutions are arenas in which accusers can ostensibly enact their right to speak with conventional legitimacy. Yet it is important to note that the ability to make charges through judicial procedures is not the central or primary focus of the new global movement. Some very high-profile judicial cases have had a galvanizing effect, but the efforts to use public demonstrations, social media, and the anonymous circulation of lists of perpetrators bypasses conventional avenues for institutional redress. The effort at reforming court and police procedures is critically important, but the central focus has aimed to transform the broad sphere of public discourse.[1]

The tactic of victims coming forward publicly is not usually about making a charge against, and seeking legal redress from, an individual perpetrator. Many survivors conceal the name of their assailant, and simply describe their experience. The point is that through the mass of such disclosures the public at large can gain an appreciation of the

[1] See, for example, https://live-survivorsagendaorg.pantheonsite.io/wp-content/uploads/2020/09/2020-09-19_SurvAgenda_English-1.pdf

dimensions of the epidemic and also come to understand from the nature of the events that these should not be taken as inevitable or unavoidable. The recent movement has been particularly adept at focusing on the many institutions, from Hollywood to the Catholic Church, that not only excuse and protect but instigate and even procure victims. The problem is not simple human depravity but corrupt institutions. In this way, we may overcome the widespread fatalism about this sort of crime.

Toward this goal, first person testimony can be compelling, but more importantly, victim testimony can provide information and analysis about the patterns that reveal the nature of the problem. In speaking publicly, victims enact resistance by defying the stigma of shame and the likelihood of presumptive disbelief. Some reactions acknowledge that a crime occurred but dispute how survivor's characterize its significance – just 'twenty minutes of action' as one father of an accused young man characterized it. Some of the public continue to reserve their sympathy for the accused, since he's a 'genius' or 'simply troubled' or 'so young with his whole life before him now about to be ruined'. So there is a gamut of common responses that have the effect of dismissing the gravity of the victim's experience, its likely long term effects on her life, and in this way rejecting the credibility of her first person reports either about the incident or its impact. Susan Brison reports being constantly told she was 'just too sensitive' for having difficulties with normal life after a brutal rape and assault in which her assailant left her for dead in a ditch. There is a logic that she identifies behind such dismissive responses: 'As a society we live with the unbearable by pressuring those who have been traumatized to forget, and by rejecting the testimony of those who are forced to remember' (Brison, 2002, p. 5).

And yet, victims[2] stream forward. In the United States, after Supreme Court nominee Bret Kavanaugh was accused in riveting televised testimony, his accuser, Christine Blasey Ford was the subject of coast to coast vilification and threats, so much so that she had to move her family into a safe house as if she had threatened a Mafia crime boss. Still, sexual assault hotlines experienced an increase of 150% after Blasey Ford's testimony, and more accusers came forward in Hollywood, bringing the number of Weinstein's accusers to over 100.

[2] In this paper I will follow a common practice to make use of both the term 'victim' and the term 'survivor.' Despite the reifying tendency of the term 'victim,' it continues to be an apt descriptor, and some report that they don't yet feel they have achieved the status of 'survivor.'

The cost to victims who come forward and identified publicly remains quite high (Traister, 2019). They have lost jobs, careers, personal safety, relationships, and endangered their health. A woman who worked at Ford Motor Company lost her job, then lost her housing, then lost custody of her son, and now has to drive eight hours to visit him. Others have been deported to countries in which they are not safe.

The tactic of speaking out not only has great personal costs, but it is regularly coopted and misused. Corporate media markets may choose stories that have value as a form of sensationalism, while other stories may garner attention because they lend legitimacy to the carceral state, to racism, or to military operations in foreign countries. My own country of origin – Panama – was invaded in 1989 by the U.S. military after a week of daily media coverage of an episode in which Panamanian troops harassed U.S. soldiers and their wives. The persistent repetition of this relatively small incident helped to create public support for the subsequent unilateral military action that killed thousands of mostly poor Panamanians. That is the closest I have come to experiencing war in any direct way, as I spent many hours trying to reach my family members who were crouching under their dining room table as MIG fighters strafed buildings in their neighborhood.

Building on this overview, in this paper I will argue that the public speech of survivors faces at least three groups of obstacles: 1) the problem of epistemic injustice, that is, injustice in the sphere of knowledge 2) the problem of language and power, and 3) the problem of dominant discourses. I will explain and develop these points and end with a final argument, returning to Hegel, concerning the critical importance of speaking publicly on these areas of human experience.

2.

1) The problem of epistemic injustice

In the West, women have long been placed in a defensive posture about their credibility before they have uttered a word. 'Accusations of rape,' an eighteenth century lawyer argued, 'regrettably… place the life of a citizen in the hands of a woman' (E. Freedman, 2013, p. 17). His client, a wealthy New Yorker, was acquitted of raping a seamstress in his employ after a jury deliberation that lasted only fifteen minutes.

Ideas that correlate social identity with likely credibility have been promulgated throughout European history by some the most influential philosophers (Beard, 2017; Shapin, 1995). Socrates believed women's attention to their dress was proof of their intention to dissemble. Aristotle declaimed the tenor and pitch of women's voices as a sign of insincerity and depravity. Rousseau advocated the educational segregation of the sexes so that boys could achieve their potential for independence of thought, while girls would remain properly deferential to the opinions of others. Kant considered darkness of skin tone a contraindication of intelligence.

These ideas remain, though perhaps only implicit, but they are too rarely challenged. Few educational curricula spend the time necessary to debunk them. As a result, they retain their influence over our mental landscapes. Still today, female news anchors, as well as candidates for political office (such as, famously, Margaret Thatcher), employ voice coaches to help them lower their tone and achieve a 'masculine' depth. The normal tenor of a female voice lacks authority.

Steven Shapin's history of ideas about who could participate in the emergence of science traces the putative justifications behind some of these ideas. In early modern Europe, the illiteracy of peasants and women and the required obsequiousness of slaves were all taken to be disqualifying. Jews also lacked credibility because of their 'cunning', while interestingly, nobles were suspect as well since they were likely to be engaged in some court intrigue. Both of these latter groups were thought to be schooled in the arts of persuasive dissimulation. The issue for women actually combined several concerns: our purported sentimentality but also our economic dependence and subsequent need to flatter and manipulate. These ideas about the correlating criteria of credibility remain powerful today: witness the wide acquiescence to the idea that wealth enables political candidates to freely speak their mind. The common charge that female accusers have economic motives also resonates with this old history.

Achieving more epistemic justice for accusers means uncovering and critiquing these widespread ideas. What is the basis of skepticism about a given accusation, and is it a legitimate basis? Does a person's economic condition, level of education, sexual history, profession, or social identity in any way justify skepticism or even preemptive dismissal?

As a way to avoid problematic credibility judgments, putatively objective criteria can be put forward, such as consistency. Attorneys, and jurors, rely heavily today on the consistency of accusers' testimony as a way to assess their epistemic reliability (Lievore,

2004). This is an illusory solution. While consistency is certainly a legitimate part of everyday forms of judgment, it is also subject to manipulation in a way that mobilizes the sort of negative prejudices I just listed. When defense lawyers focus on *irrelevant* consistencies, they can then cast aspersions on an accuser's memory, reliability, integrity, and by implication, their motivations. In the Bret Kavanaugh hearings, Blasey Ford was asked a series of questions about the distance between her home and the house where the assault took place, about the names of all of the people present in the house at the time, about her reported fear of flying and her history of airplane travel as well as the reasons for and destinations of the flights she took. None of these questions were germane to establishing the credibility of Blasey Ford's charges, but were designed to erode her testimony through finding inconsistencies or inadequacies in her ability to report details. And it was the answers Blasey Ford gave to these questions that were used to discredit her account of what Kavanaugh had done to her at that party.

The criteria of consistency is today applied not only to statements in court, but also to informal communications by the accuser with their friends, family and co-workers through email and social media. Yet, consistency about such specifics as the exact date of an event, or the names of persons attending a house party, are not always telltale signs of faulty memory about the encounter itself. One prosecutor explains that, in her experience, 'victims of relatively isolated offences maintain a vivid, albeit distressing, recollection of the crimes. A victim may not remember what colour shorts she was wearing when, at eight years of age some 20 years ago her uncle put his finger in her vagina, but the victim remembers that event with certainty' (Shead, 2014, p. 60). Research indicates that exactitude about peripheral features can waver, but not necessarily the principle features of the encounter itself.

The findings of such research are intuitively plausible. Sexual violations, whether of a violent nature or of the more manipulative sort, tax the victims' mental capacities. She, or he, is sometimes trying to assess the danger and calibrate effective options while maintaining a conversation and a neutral facial expression. It's like taking a math test while swimming in the open sea. One's faculties are engaged in high-stakes multi-tasking. This can explain why our peripheral perceptions remain fuzzy even as we retain with crystal clarity the memory of the physical violation and the identity of the perpetrator. Such memories are reinforced after the fact by the need for survival, since we need to remember who to avoid.

I was assaulted as a child, stayed silent for many years out of fear, and as an adult endeavored to establish the period of time in which my assaults occurred. I had to look at old pictures, recall related school events, and gather up the courage to direct some questions to my mother. Some details continue to elude me, but, unfortunately, I have never forgotten the central events themselves.

Diverse conversational contexts that take place afterward will inevitably affect the precision and detail called for. In fact, some contexts may call for intentional misdirection, if we fear that the person we are speaking to about the event may try to pursue revenge against our perpetrator, for example.

The social identity of accusers should be irrelevant to how their credibility is judged, but it continues to play a role. Emphasizing apparently objective criteria such as consistency may be taken to be a corrective measure, but even this sort of criteria is subject to manipulation and misuse. The manipulation takes intentional advantage, I'd suggest, of the legacy of gender prejudice, which can be easily animated all the while concealed behind an alibi of unbiased judgment.

2) The problem of language and power

Clastres spent many years studying the conventions of speaking that operated in different types of societies. He concluded that speech and power are constitutively related, but in different ways in different societies. In societies with strong state-based institutional organization, such as our own, power is 'the sole source of legitimate speech' and the power of speech is 'detached from society as a whole' rather than held universally (1987, pp. 151–52). An accuser or defender may be allowed to speak in court and yet the ultimate epistemic assessment of their words is held exclusively by a judge or jury whose task is circumscribed by legal rules.

Of course, modes of allowing speech and distributing credibility change over time. As Michel Foucault reminds us, hundreds of years ago in Europe the mad were considered more reliable than most because they did not hesitate to speak their minds. Hence, the value of their role as court jesters was the ability to give tactless but truthful testimony (1988). Unlike those engaged in court intrigue, the mad were free of strategic agendas and foolish enough to speak the truth to kings. Because of this, the mad were epistemically useful, and credible.

Foucault suggests that, in more modern societies, the operations of power are not so centralized. Judicial courts increasingly rely on expert testimony from conventionally accredited authorities drawn from the social sciences, the academy, medicine, psychiatry and the police. Relations of compatibility between these diverse structures of authorization help shore up their acceptance: they need not be organized in pyramid form. Thus Foucault argues that the norms of credibility and expertise operate within a decentralized structure of institutions that resonate with one another. This too can be very difficult to dislodge or transform.

The confessional practices of the Catholic Church produced a structure of speaking relationships that today resonate in secular domains, creating a certain familiarity. A penitent confesses to his confessor, not merely about his actions, but also, and perhaps more importantly, about his dreams, desires, and thoughts. The priest passes judgment and gives absolution by instructing the recitation of a certain number of rosaries or other practices. In this speaking relation, the penitent provides the raw data, without analysis or judgment: the latter are provided exclusively by the priest. The penitent has first person privilege: they and they alone can report their innermost thoughts and feelings, but they have no privilege over the analysis of the level of venality, motivation, or cure. Talk therapy generally operates with the same form: the client details their experiences and thoughts, while the therapist provides the analysis, diagnosis, and behavioral advice.

Some years back a colleague and I analyzed the way in which victims of sexual violence were represented on television, during the period when this topic became a commonplace focal point in daytime talk shows (Alcoff and Gray, 1993). Inevitably, the shows began with riveting, emotional, first person testimony of victims to garner viewer attention. Since this topic was relatively new, it did garner viewer attention. Victims were prompted by a series of questions posed by the show's host, generally sympathetic (at least initially) but also sometimes asking the skeptical questions they believed their viewers might want answered. In this way the host positioned themselves as the representative of the public, just as the priests were representatives of the Church or of God. After a period of such questioning, a third figure almost inevitably appeared: a psychiatrist or psychologist, portrayed as dispassionate and objective, who could interpret what the victims said for the audience and offer their expert analysis. This analytical capacity was not accorded the victims themselves. Here, the confessional structure of the Church was replicated in a secular, public space where authorization was given by educational credentials rather than religious ones. Once again, the person giving first person testimony had limited epistemic privilege: they were put on the stand to be interpreted, judged and analyzed by others.

Clastres and Foucault both suggest that the organization of speaking roles manifest in such scenarios gain their credence more from historical legacy and cultural convention than considered epistemic judgment. To understand such scenarios, we need an analysis of language and power. How are the two related in our society, in our common conventions? Why do we assume that certain configurations of power ensure truthfulness and reliability? Why do first person experiential reports from individuals with lower status (generally because of their group identity) have to be judged by credentialed experts and authorities? How does this method restrict speech? For a very long time such methods have preempted speech by victims who accuse husbands, fathers, mothers, the rich, the Church, and the psychiatric establishment. As Clastres pointed out, the power of speech is not distributed universally across the population, with predictable effects on the distributions of power as well as the recalcitrance of these distributions to change.

3) The problem of dominant discourses

This problem connects to concerns just discussed about the supportive relations between existing organizations of power and the current conventions of speech, yet it involves the *content* of speech more than the *structure* of speaking relations or roles. The idea of a discourse is that our speech enters into a swirl of already existing and familiar beliefs, ideas, concepts, and framing assumptions by which they are interpreted and in some cases reshaped. In this way even new and original ideas can be domesticated, sometimes without intention on anyone's part. Discourses cannot determine truth: they cannot make it true that the moon is made of green cheese. But discourses can determine whether a claim is understood as meaningful enough to be pursued (Hacking, 2004). At one time the question of whether human beings could travel to the moon would have engendered puzzled stares. This was beyond the realm of meaningful plausibility, but so was the claim, much more easily investigated, one might think, that a husband raped his wife. Because dominant discourses affect which claims are taken to be intelligible and plausible enough to generate the search for evidence, they can have a determinate effect on new claims and new concepts.

In this context, consider the widely used concept of consent. Rape, sexual assault and sexual coercion are legally defined in relation to consent, in the sense that consent has become the key criterion used to distinguish morally blameworthy versus morally blameless sex. Given that bondage has become a popular practice, bruises and even injuries cannot suffice. What we want to know is whether all parties consented. Consent has not always been the principle focal point, but in the age of decreased religiosity, and an acceptance of sexual pluralism, the question has shifted from what the participants of a sexual encounter are doing, and whether it conforms to the religious dictum, for example, to simply whether they are all consenting. This concept has become hegemonic in everyday thinking about sexual practises well beyond the legal arena.

Its history is instructive. A century ago, laws in the United States as well as other countries referenced 'seduction' rather than consent (Freedman, 2013). Seduction roughly equaled breach of promise, as when a woman was pregnant out of wedlock. If she had engaged in sex under the promise of lawful marriage, yet found herself alone and bereft, she could bring legal charges. Pregnancy was indeed a crisis for unmarried women, since they could be legally fired and turned out of their housing. Thus, her crisis was a social crisis which seduction laws were designed to solve: if a marriage could be forced, society was off the hook. Interestingly, seduction law put the onus on men to explain themselves: trials centered on establishing the man's words as well as his actions. Women's own desire, will, and consent were beside the point.

The movement to replace seduction with consent laws was supported by a lot of men, some of whom may have been motivated by less than feminist concerns. Seduction laws put all men in danger of an accusation that could land them in prison if they had sex out of wedlock. Needless to say, these laws were far from foolproof: a man could marry a woman to avoid prison and then, shortly thereafter, leave town. Perhaps more importantly, these laws ignored the physical, economic, or emotional coercion women experienced. They were designed simply to force men to marry and provide economic support for pregnant women.

Against this backdrop, consent seemed to be a better approach. Consent focused on what is most morally blameworthy, coercion, rather than whether there was a lawful marriage. And yet consent has shifted the focus of trials to the question of what women said and did, even the way they dressed, in order to establish whether or not they consented. Hence, throughout the twentieth century, trials focused on women's attire, sexual past, and demeanor as the basis upon which juries and judges could pass judgement.

If we consider the way in which the concept of consent entered into dominant, gender-laden discourses, we can more clearly discern why it has proven to have such limitations and generated so much feminist critique (Pateman, 1980; Gauthier, 1999; Cahill, 2001). The idea of consent resonates with the contract tradition in western market societies, in which we make promises to deliver goods and services, as Carole Pateman has argued. To consent is to make a sort of contract, legally binding, in which ones promises to deliver a service over a specified time frame. This may give the person who receives the consent the dangerous idea that they are 'owed sex', as Ann Cahill has pointed out, and have been cheated if it was not delivered.

The language of contracts is phenomenologically inadequate for sexual encounters. Desire and arousal are not the kind of things that one can guarantee will be sustained. When the focal point is the consent of the woman in the encounter, this replicates, and resonates with, still prevalent ideas that men ask and women answer, that males are sexual aggressors and females are receptive, and in this way the focus on consent serves to reinforce heterosexual norms in which femininity is associated with receptivity and caring, while masculinity is associated with sexual needs and dominance (Gavey, 2005).

Most importantly, we know there are structural conditions that can predetermine consent, from economic dependence at work or at home, to status and ranking differences that produce what Jeffrey Gauthier calls 'the choice situation of the oppressed class' (Gauthier, 1999, p. 16). Choose this low paying job or that one, this abusive situation or an end to your career. In research by Nicola Gavey, women report that they consent in order not to be raped, as a way to reduce physical harm and trauma.

From this we can see how the concept of consent becomes capable of maintaining existing relations of power. Dropped into societies in which transactional relations are normalized, contractual relations are familiar and intuitive, and gender involves dominance, consent becomes domesticated, familiar, unobjectionable. Women's desire, will, and sexual pleasure may continue to remain off the map of consideration when consent is subtly coerced or chosen as the best of bad alternatives. Foucault notes that discourses are not simply collections of statements, but also involve practices, forms of subjectivity, and ways in which institutions are organized.

Consent is not unimportant, and I am not arguing it has no utility. But its position in our discourse as the obvious unassailable determinant of what is morally blameless sex needs to be understood as limited by the discursive context into which it has entered. Consent has served as the readily available cornerstone of many defense strategies, including Harvey Weinstein's: his solicitors have claimed that his accusers were actually consenting, as indicated by their friendly emails and relations after the assault. In this way consent is wielded as a weapon by which to remove the structural power relations from the frame of analysis. This problem is not determined by the meaning of the concept on its own, but by its discursive relations to ideas and framing assumptions still in dominance about sex, about women, and about men.

3.

Liberal societies that protect the rights of free and open speech have for too long ignored the ways in which the speech of the disempowered is in reality policed, disciplined, and restricted. Certain sorts of speech from disempowered groups, carefully chosen and curated, may be taken up and given circulation, but it is too often co-opted by those higher up in the chain of institutional power in ways that limit and distort its meanings and effects.

The sequestering of topics concerning sexual violence, especially institutionalized sexual violence, has meant that many women and other victims have not been able to enact their subjectivity in civil society. When survivors speak, their speech must often pass through media or legal domains in which it is interpreted, judged, and edited by others who have other interests besides addressing the problem. Informal conventions of assessing credibility have a similar ability to preempt discussion about the epidemic of sexual violence. We must begin to think past these stumbling blocks, and reconsider what would really be required to free up the speech of the subordinate.

Hunter College
City University of New York
lmartina@hunter.cuny.edu

References

Linda Alcoff and Laura Gray, 'Survivor Discourse: Transgression or Recuperation?' *SIGNS* 18 (1993) 260–90.

Mary Beard, *Women and Power: A Manifesto* (London: W.W. Norton and Company, 2017).

Susan Brison, *Aftermath: Violence and the Remaking of the Self* (Princeton: Princeton University Press, 2002).

Ann Cahill, *Rethinking Rape* (Ithaca, N.Y.: Cornell University Press, 2001).

Pierre Clastres, *Society Against the State* translated by Robert Hurley (Brooklyn, New York: Zone Books, 1987).

Estelle Freedman, *Redefining Rape: Sexual Violence in the Era of Suffrage and Segregation* (Cambridge, M.A.: Harvard University Press, 2013).

Michel Foucault, *Madness and Civilization: A History of Insanity in an Age of Reason* translated by Richard Howard (New York: Random House, 1988).

Jeffrey Gauthier, 'Consent, Coercion, and Sexual Autonomy' in *A Most Detestable Crime: New Philosophical Essays on Rape* edited by Kenneth Burgess-Jackson (New York: Oxford University Press, 1999) 71–89.

Nicola Gavey, *Just Sex? The Cultural Scaffolding of Rape* (New York: Routledge, 2005).

Ian Hacking, *Historical Ontology* (Cambridge, M.A.: Harvard University Press, 2004).

G. W. F. Hegel, *Philosophy of Right* Translated by S. W. Dyde. (Garden City, N.Y.: Dover Publications, (1820) 2005).

Denise Lievore, 'Victim Credibility in Adult Sexual Assault Cases' *Trends and Issues in Crime and Criminal Justice* (Canberra: Australian Institute of Criminology, 2004).

Carole Pateman, 'Women and Consent', *Political Theory* 8 (1980), 149–68.

Steven Shapin, *A Social History of Truth: Civility and Science in Seventeenth Century England* (Chicago: University of Chicago Press, 1995).

Karen Shead, 'Responding to Historical Child Sexual Abuse: A Prosecution Perspective on Current Challenges and Future Directions', *Current Issues in Criminal Justice* 26 (2014) 55–72.

Rebecca Traister, 'Was it Worth It?' *New York Magazine* September 30-October 13, (2019) 32–48.

The Predicament of Patients

IAN JAMES KIDD AND HAVI CAREL

Abstract
In this paper we propose that our understanding of pathocentric epistemic injustices can be enriched if they are theorised in terms of predicaments. These are the wider socially scaffolded structures of epistemic challenges, dangers, needs, and threats experienced by ill persons due to their particular emplacement within material, social, and epistemic structures. In previous work we have described certain aspects of these predicaments, such as pathocentric epistemic injustices and pathophobia. A wider systematic perspective is needed to integrate these and other concepts. By thinking predicamentally, we can better understand the interrelated social, epistemic, and practical obstacles experienced by ill persons and connect the many concepts available for theorising them (microaggessions, epistemic injustices, and so on).

1. Being ill

Being ill is hard. It is a time of fear, confusion, and uncertainty. It is often a time of pain, suffering and diminishment of freedom. It involves radical disruption to the ways one experiences the body – which often appears, for the first time, as something alien and other, as *a* body, and no long as *my* body. Those with chronic illness who choose to write illness narratives warn the unsuspecting healthy that their ability to anticipate these disruptions is more limited than they realise. Kathlyn Conway described the gulf between the cool, detached awareness of the inevitability and difficulty of illness and the felt realities of what it is actually like to be 'propelled into the dreaded world of illness' (Conway, 2013, p. 134). Havi Carel describes her diagnosis as 'a physical blow' and tells of how 'the realisation that everything was about to change, that a new era was about to begin, seared like burning oil on skin' (Carel, 2018, p. 5). Sometimes, the only way to really grasp the realities of illness is to experience them, to transition from the confident appraisal of abstract possibilities to the hotly felt intensity of what it is like to move into, and live within, that 'dreaded world'.

The realities of illness can often be made vivid by considering the intricacies of what for some people become regular experiences that are part of that dreaded world. Consider being hospitalised. This can

doi:10.1017/S1358246121000059

bring with it the institutionalised diminution of one's agency – the loss of privacy, dignity, freedom and agency. You enter a ward, are given a bed in a shared bay of six patients – anxious strangers, just like you. Your meals and daily schedule are supplied by others. You lie on that bed, witness to the bodily failures and personal pain of others, only minimally veiled from the sight of their suffering behind a thin blue curtain. Your body put on display to the entourage of doctors – alert and outfitted with the medical gaze – watching you as you speak your lines in the crushingly unfunny pantomime of the ward round. An obedient curio, you answer questions and, if the conditions for open discussion seem good, exchange views with the consultant as a dozen eyes watch intently.

The experience of hospitalisation can be analysed using the languages and concepts of qualitative healthcare research or feminist studies, or other theoretical approaches. Some people, though, will prefer less theoretically involved, more everyday language. If medical language can be alienating for some, so, too, can academic language. Whatever language one wants to speak, the ineradicable reality is that being a patient is hard, and not always in ways one can anticipate. One pivotal hardship is *epistemic*: that is, related to the patient's agency and status as a *knower*. When you become a patient, the views, knowledge, opinions, and preferences that provide the substance and texture of your distinctive individuality are not always sought, taken into account, and acted upon. Even when you offer your views, they can be rejected, ignored, or tuned out by the medical objective, scientific, and practical stance, which can be oblivious to the impact of words, gestures and of course, decisions, on the individual sitting in that hospital bed, wearing that compromising hospital gown, waiting for a life-changing word from the consultant.

The general experience of hospitalisation is, of course, made up of a multitude of encounters. Much can depend on the quality of specific interactions, especially when these turn on decisions, choices and requests. Consider the example of a patient (personal communication) being assessed for an organ transplant, taking a medication that has slowed down the rate of her disease progression. Without that medication, she would die within a few months, although it could potentially interfere with the wound healing process after the transplant. Although the medication would be washed out of the patient's body within a day or two, the theoretical risk has been noted in medical literature. A handful of medical reports discussing this risk in relation to the patient's own disease have been published. The patient had asked the consultant to remain on the medication while she is on the transplant waiting list, to prevent further deterioration and acute risk to her life. The consultant said he will think about it and let her know. He refused to accept copies of those medical reports from her.

When delivering his decision, the consultant invited the patient into a small room cramped with the entire transplant assessment team, none of whom, bar him, spoke. He then told the patient that she would not be permitted to stay on the drug while on the waiting list. Instead, she will have to choose whether to gamble on the new organ becoming available before her disease relapses, due to her being off the medication, or whether to stay on the drug but not have the transplant option. 'You see,', he explained, 'we want our transplant centre results to stay the best in Europe.'

This episode is a particular, but by no means unique, event in the predicament of the patient. Important, intimate decisions involving you, your body and your life, are made without sufficient tools to handle the differing views, perspectives, and tangible gaps in understanding between the patient's point of view and that of health professionals. Amid the desire for certainty, care, and cure, there is also a powerful desire – a need, even – to be heard, to be able to communicate the reality of one's circumstances and help others to understand. This is not merely a psychological need to be heard, although this is certainly important. It is the critical need for patients to be able to put forth views and preferences in order for these to be an integral part of decision-making process. 'Nothing about me without me', as the slogan goes.

Such poignant and painful needs to be seen, heard, and understood are a pervasive theme of the pathographic literature devoted to describing the lived experience of illness, a theme often signalled in their subtitles. Abby Norman's *Ask Me About My Uterus* is subtitled *A Quest to Make Doctors believe Women's Pain* (Norman, 2018). She reflects on the experiences of women whose testimonies about diseased bodies were ignored, citing the example of the American comedian, Gilda Radner, who died of stage IV ovarian cancer after her appeals to her doctors were ignored:

> What resonated with me about her story [...] was the deep knowing of her own body as a woman that is seeming unworthy of anyone's consideration or respect. I find that deeply unnerving: that I might be dying, and no-one would believe me, but that feeling of inescapable truth wouldn't leave me no matter how much other people denied it (Norman, 2018, p. 56).

Such cases are appalling and complex and provoke all sorts of moral and critical reactions. In her book, *Doing Harm*, feminist writer and critic Maya Dusenbery argues that modern healthcare systems cause women to suffer needlessly by trapping them within a 'knowledge gap' and a 'trust gap' (Dusenbery, 2018, chs. 1 and 2). Escaping that situation has been a key goal of the women's health movement since its inception, often in alliance with the disability rights and civil rights movements and other progressive groups aimed at radical cultural and institutional change (Edwards, 2013, chs. 3–5).

What these critics emphasise are the many enormous practical and epistemic constraints built into contemporary healthcare systems: the knowledge and trust gaps, the charged power dynamics between the medically trained and the rest, and the complicated relationships between the many actors – health professionals, other staff, managers, service providers, patients, families and sometimes lawyers, social workers and others. There are financial and political forces beyond the control of those acting within the immediate scene. There are the intellectual and moral failings of individual people, which can ramify when they interact with so many others. There are deeply entrenched structures of misogynistic assumptions and practices deeply baked into our social systems and cultural imagination. There is the systematic disenfranchisement of people who are struggling to have their voices heard against an intangible but steely backdrop of stigma and prejudice. Finally, there is the simple yet all-consuming state of being ill, in pain, suffering. A recent Patients Association report states that the top three terms patients used to describe being ill are: 'frustrating', 'frightened', and 'vulnerable'.[1]

What this describes is what we shall call the *predicament of the patient*. We take the term 'predicament' from José Medina, who uses it throughout his superb book, *The Epistemology of Resistance*. The book offers a sophisticated study of how oppressed people experience, understand, and try to cope with the entrenched systems of interpersonal and structural epistemic injustice that constitute the social world. It offers epistemological analysis in the service of social activism. One of Medina's convictions is that 'our epistemic lives are inextricably interwoven with our ethical and socio-political lives' and the consequent conviction that epistemological analysis must lead to 'deep personal changes' and commitment to 'transformative activism capable of changing social structures and relations' (Medina, 2012, p. 314). We need epistemology to grasp the full complexity of the systems of oppression built into the social world. But epistemology is not enough by itself.

[1] https://www.patients-association.org.uk/Handlers/Download.ashx?IDMF=2898fa05-69fa-4e66-b856-c150080d432c.

We use Medina's work to theorise what we call the epistemic predicament of patients as a way of developing some of our earlier work on epistemic injustice and illness. In what follows we discuss Medina's notion of predicament (section 2) and link this notion to Fricker's account of epistemic injustice, whilst introducing our own application of Fricker's term to illness (section 3). Section 4 develops what we call *pathophobic epistemic injustice*. The closing section offers thoughts on how predicamental thinking can advance and correct some of the limitations of the earlier and more restricted concept of epistemic injustice.

2. Predicament

Medina's analyses of gendered and racialized epistemic injustices are deeply informed by generations of excellent research on the intersectional character of our social identities as they play out in the social world. *The Epistemology of Resistance* offers conceptual tools for thinking critically about how best to understand and react to structurally epistemically unjust societies. One of those tools is the concept of a *predicament*. It starts from the foundational claim that people are embodied social agents whose epistemic identity and agency are shaped by their emplacement within systems of roles, relationships, and power relations. *Who we are* deeply shapes the sorts of knowledge we need to get by, the sorts of epistemic skills most useful to us, the sorts of concepts and ideas we need to master, and so on. The abstract figures familiar to many philosophical theories – like 'the knower' or 'the moral agent' – lack the embodied and socialised particularity needed to think properly about effective ways to organise one's epistemic and practical life. Knowers have bodies, genders, racialized identities, and so on, all of which must be included in serious answers to questions about their epistemic prospects and performance.

Medina does not define the term 'predicament', although from his uses of the term we can see what he has in mind. We are told, for instance, that our predicaments include differing degrees of susceptibility to 'lack of access to information', or whether and to what extent we 'lack a credible voice and authority', or whether we are likely to consistently experience 'epistemic exclusions and injustices' (Medina, 2012, pp. 29, 129). In some kinds of predicament, a person will '*struggle to make sense to themselves* of what they cannot yet communicate to others, especially to those who do not share their predicament'. In another kind, a person might face the challenge of being entrapped by an 'internalised ignorance that one may not even be able to recognise' (Medina, 2012, p. 98, original emphasis, p. 206). In these and other instances, Medina is emphasising the many ways our particular material and social circumstances affect the complexity and the quality of our epistemic lives.

Pulling this together, we define an *epistemic predicament* as the complex, contingent, and changing structure of epistemically-toned concerns, challenges, dangers, needs, risks, and threats that a person will experience as a result of their particular emplacement within a particular social world. Our epistemic predicament therefore fundamentally determines the kind of epistemic life that we have and the sorts of epistemic functioning, if not flourishing, we could reasonably anticipate.

Once we start to think about how the social conditions the epistemic, we can generate other features of epistemic predicaments. An epistemic predicament might generate ongoing concern with having to balance attempts to pursue one's epistemic goals while also responding to the hostile reactions and impositions of others. It may raise the challenge of constantly attempting to ensure proper uptake of one's testimonies among people who lack the appropriate sensibilities and hermeneutical resources. Another feature is the danger inherent in trying to defy oppressive socially entrenched expectations about how one should perform epistemically. There are others, too. The need to develop effective strategies for protecting one's fragile testimonial credibility in the face of constant efforts by others to erode it. The risk of having one's social experiences consistently subjected to highly distorting and often deliberate misunderstandings that can be as painful to endure as they can be to try to correct. And the threat of being epistemically downgraded in the eyes of others as a result of one's defiance of oppressive normative expectations about how one should epistemically behave.

Although we could extend this list, hopefully this suffices to give a sense of what we mean by an epistemic predicament. Looking at the list, it seems clear that many ill persons, and in particular psychiatric patients, elderly patients and child patients, have distinctive and entrenched epistemic predicaments. Illness narratives provide many examples of the new epistemic challenges, demands, needs, risks, threats, and vulnerabilities that come with being chronically ill. Some are spread throughout the social world, while others are confined to specific locations, such as hospitals.

Becoming ill means coming to occupy a new and difficult epistemic predicament. Susan Sontag famously said that to become ill is 'to take up one's residence in the kingdom of the ill'. She added that this kingdom has its own 'landscape' – its own stereotypes, prejudices, obstacles, and dangers (Sontag, 1978, p. 3). We can use that metaphor to think about the newly imposed epistemic predicaments of those who have become ill. One suddenly arrives at a strange, hostile new territory complete with new and disturbing features – looming obstacles, thorny thickets, impassable terrain, circuitous paths. One cannot make sense of this new environment and one therefore has to work hard to navigate it. There are medical terms to learn, services to find and new people to reluctantly involve in one's intimacies. There are decisions to be made, treatment options to consider, and practicalities to sort out. There are profound and bewildering changes to all aspects of one's life, that require mental energy, attention, emotional resources, and a lot of talking, thinking, and communicating. There is hard epistemic labour in being – and especially in becoming – ill (Carel, 2018).

Some of our existing epistemic skills work well enough, but others do not, so one is often uncertain and confused. The landscape is unfamiliar and it takes real work to survey it. The epistemic terrain is filled with strange new dangers and risks – like having one's testimonies about one's bodily condition ignored by other people. One's prior navigational skills are not always useful in these strange new conditions. New epistemic challenges come into view. New epistemic dangers become salient. Some epistemic risks one formerly encountered but rarely increase in frequency and severity. Epistemic needs that were once easily met now become momentous challenges. One is suddenly forced to make difficult trade-offs – between, for instance, *truthfulness* about the complexities of one's bodily condition and *acceptability* in the company of healthy people limited in their ability and willingness to understand. In the kingdom of the ill, the terrain is harsh and forbidding and the customs peculiar and so many of the people often cold and cruel to vulnerable strangers, newly arrived to this land.

Sontag's metaphor of the 'kingdom of the ill' can help us get a sense of what it may be like to suddenly occupy a strange and disturbing new epistemic predicament. One is now stuck in a strange land where one's testimonies and self-understanding suddenly seem to count for little. The interpersonal currency of credibility and trust is devalued. Everyday epistemic tasks become arduous marathons. Confusion is the new norm. The powers and privileges one used to enjoy in the kingdom of the healthy are now lost and the consequence is a frightening new predicament.

Contemporary scholars have described in vivid detail many of the realities of what we call the predicament of the ill. Some of the relevant phenomena are constant subjection to microaggressions, gaslighting and implicit biases (FitzGerald and Hurst, 2017; Freeman and Stewart, 2018). We agree with those accounts, although we want to interpret them as particular components of the wider predicament we describe here. To be ill is to inhabit a changed world with new challenges, needs, and risks that are tied into a complicated interpersonal world. Coping with their epistemic predicament is a major preoccupation of people with chronic somatic (bodily) illnesses, and of course of disabled people (we acknowledge the considerable overlap between the two groups) in their daily attempts to articulate their needs, pursue their life-projects, and cope with the world. What the concept of a predicament calls into view is the systematic character of these epistemic problems as revealed in the everyday experiences of those in the kingdom of the ill. In doing so, we ensure that we keep an appropriately broad perspective on the many interlinked epistemic problems faced by ill people.

3. From epistemic predicament to epistemic injustice

Experiences of illness are inherently diverse. They are shaped by pathological, psychological, situational, developmental, and sociocultural factors, which is one of the constant lessons of pathographies and research in the sociology and anthropology of illness. Indeed, one aspect of the epistemic predicament of ill persons is getting others to grasp the complexity and the particularity of their experiences. The problem is the delicate one of using general concepts and familiar tropes while at the same honouring the particularity of a specific ill person's own experiences. Rita Charon's book, *Narrative Medicine*, suggests that when reading illness narratives we are 'looking closely at individual human beings grappling with the conditions of life, attempts to illuminate the universals of the human condition by revealing the particular' (Charon, 2006, p. 9). Therefore, when thinking about the predicament of patients, we need to ensure that we do justice to the complex layering of personal and general features, to what a group of people share as participants in a common predicament and to the fact that our predicament is, in the final analysis, our *own*.

Before moving on, we offer three comments on epistemic predicaments. First, they are radically *plural*. Our predicaments are shaped by our subjective identity and the complex particularities of our embodied social circumstances. Granted, there will be commonalities among our predicaments, thanks to shared group identities and the common social and material structure of the world, as well as shared human features, such as our inherently social nature – what Heidegger calls *Mitsein*, our being-with-others (Heidegger, 1962). Second, predicaments are deeply *ambivalent*; it will always be too crude to characterise them as good or bad. Predicaments are complex structures of challenges and opportunities, deficiencies and resources, encouraging possibilities and forbidding inevitabilities. Third, predicaments are both changing and *changeable*, rather than immutable, permanent features of one's world. Predicaments change in response to changes in our personal character and orientation to the world, as well as changes in the social and material conditions of the world. Crucially, our predicaments can be changed through concerted effort, whether as individuals or as fellow participants in collective projects. Conversely, some people try to worsen the predicament of others deliberately as part of concerted projects of social and epistemic violence (Dotson, 2011).[2] Note that these three features pull together: the plurality and ambivalence of our predicaments ensures their changeability and means one has to reckon with the possibility of changes for better or for worse.

We want to explore the predicament of patients in relation to the well-studied vulnerability of ill persons to what, in earlier work, we have named *pathocentric epistemic injustices* (Kidd and Carel, 2018). These are wrongs done to an ill person specifically in their capacity as a *knower*, originally modelled on the analysis of epistemic injustice given by Miranda Fricker (2007). A flourishing literature has developed over the last decade devoted to pathocentric epistemic injustice in relation to a range of somatic and psychiatric illnesses.[3] Most of that work proceeds within Fricker's terms, specifically those of *testimonial* and *hermeneutical* injustices, although more recent work, this present piece included, explores some of the wider forms and conceptions of epistemic injustice (see the introduction to this volume and also Kidd, Medina, and Pohlhaus Jr. 2017, chs. 1-5).

The phenomenon of pathocentric epistemic injustice is a depressing dimension of the lived experience of ill persons within our societies. Unfortunately, it is but one dimension of their wider predicament. There are wider systems of epistemic violence, for one thing, and also a much broader range of problematic and harmful attitudes, practices, and structures whose collective effect

2 The term 'epistemic violence' was introduced by Gayatri Spivak (1998).

3 For a bibliography listing these publications see: https://ianjameskidd.weebly.com/epistemic-injustice-healthcare-and-illness-a-bibliography.html.

is to extend and intensify the suffering of those with illnesses. And of course, they are also ill and may be distressed, in pain, fatigued, or fearful, in addition to the epistemic dimension we focus on here. Interestingly, until recently there was no term for the variety of objectionable attitudes and behaviours directed at persons with chronic somatic illnesses. Sanism and ableism describe discriminatory attitudes that pertain to mental disorder and disabilities, while established terms like stigma refer to specific sources of that attitude, rather than the attitude itself.

In an effort to fill that gap, Ian James Kidd offers the term *pathophobia*. It captures the range of morally objectionable attitudes and behaviours directed towards those with chronic somatic illnesses (Kidd, 2019). It can take individual and collective forms and often intersects with other forms of oppression, such as sexism and ableism. Indeed, the deeply intersectional character of pathophobic experiences is often described in the testimonies and narratives of ill people. It is clear, too, that pathophobic attitudes and behaviour are extremely diverse. Kidd groups the main forms into five broad types: aversion, banality, callousness, insensitivity, and untruthfulness. They involve failures of interpersonal interaction and understanding, empathic caring, and sensitivity and truthfulness about the complexities of experiences of illness (Kidd, 2019, §4). Within the pages of pathographies, one finds stark examples of pathophobic attitudes and behaviours, whether at the individual or collective level – aversive behaviour from people on the street, banal ways of talking about illness, the callousness of healthcare practitioners and friends, insensitive comments and questions, and complex failures to communicate honestly with those suffering from chronic illnesses.

Pathophobia has many sources and it plays out in different ways. Its forms, frequency and severity is determined by medical, personal, sociocultural, situational, and structural factors. Some people are ignorant of what it is like to be ill. Some are indifferent to the suffering of others. Some are well-meaning but lack proper sensitivity. Some people struggle to make sense of lives very different from their own. Some people are cruel and selfish. Some people lack attentiveness to others. Other people might want to be sensitive, warm, and compassionate, but lack proper guidance on how to translate that into the rights sorts of behaviour. Appreciating all of this once again refers us to the idea of predicaments. The predicaments experienced by many ill persons are embedded within the pathophobic norms, structures, and cultures of the social world. Think of silencing and bright-siding, harms and violence, deflations of credibility and absence of empathy, lack of resources and construction of obstacles, humiliation and powerlessness; these are built into institutionalised practices, and the coiled webs of stigmatisation and social isolation. This is perhaps what Audre Lorde had in mind in her *Cancer Journals* when she announced her 'fury at the outside world's viciousness, the stupid, brutal lack of consciousness or concern that passes for the way things are' (Lorde, 1997, p. 24).

We think Lorde's fury was in part sustained by her acute realisation that the forms of pathophobic discrimination against her ill body was continuous with a 'whole pattern' of racism and sexism (Lorde, 1997, pp. 24, 11). Central to those patterns were recognisable forms of gendered, racialised, and pathophobic epistemic injustices. The first chapter of the *Cancer Journals* is titled 'The Transformation of Silence into Language and Action'. It speaks of the harms of the distortions of credibility and intelligibility, of voices silenced or muted and of social experiences obscured. Lorde describes how 'imposed silence about any area of our lives is a tool for separation and powerlessness', hence the need to launch 'a war against the tyrannies of silence':

> I have come to believe over and over again that what is most important to me must be spoken, made verbal and shared, even at the risk of having it bruised or misunderstood. That the speaking profits me, beyond any other effect [...] My silence had not protected me. Your silence will not protect you (Lorde, 1997, pp. 51, 55).

4. Pathocentric epistemic injustice

Armed with this background and the concepts of predicament and pathophobia, let us now turn to an analysis of a specific kind of epistemic predicament afflicting patients – what we have elsewhere called *pathocentric epistemic injustice* (Kidd and Carel, 2018). This is our term for epistemic injustices that target and track those with chronic somatic illnesses. They involve experiences – at once unfair and harmful – where a person is wronged as a *knower*, as a giver of knowledge or an interpreter of experiences. Sometimes we are right not to take someone seriously; and sometimes we cannot make sense of someone's social experiences, no matter how hard we try – these would not be epistemic injustices. To be an injustice, there must be *harm* and *unfairness*. Think, for instance, of the ways that prejudice can drive us to refuse to recognise someone *as* rational; or cases where contempt for a certain group shows itself as unwillingness to take up the concepts that would render their distinctive experiences intelligible.

A vigorous body of recent scholarship has confirmed and developed our proposal that there are distinctively pathocentric epistemic injustices. Recent work has described the epistemic injustices that track persons with chronic somatic and psychiatric illnesses (see, for example, Blease, Carel and Geraghy, 2016; Byrne, forthcoming; Crichton, Kidd and Carel, 2016; for a full list, see footnote 2). In a sense, what is being confirmed is what was being said all along in so many illness narratives, including Lorde's criticisms of 'tyrannies of silence'. Many ill persons continue to report that their testimonies, interpretations and other epistemic offerings are rejected, downgraded, or doubted by hearers, who are affected by negative prejudices and stereotypes about ill persons. The precise forms of those injustices are diverse, and much remains to be done in exploring them. But it is clear that systematic experiences of pathocentric epistemic injustices are an integral part of the predicaments of many ill persons and that ill persons are especially vulnerable to epistemic injustice (Carel and Kidd, 2014; Kidd and Carel, 2016).

Granted, chronic illness can damage cognitive capacities in ways that reduce one's credibility or epistemic authority. But we are clear that those are not cases of epistemic injustice because they are not unfair. The unfairness occurs when, for instance, the default presumption is that to be chronically ill necessarily entails epistemic incapacity, or when a person's testimonies are ignored despite their lucidity and precision, or when a person's efforts at rendering their own experiences intelligible are thwarted by the determination of others to refuse them intelligibility. Some of the tougher cases will involve hard-to-decide situations of fluctuating cognitive capacity, illnesses in penal contexts, epistemic injustices experienced by children, and psychiatric illnesses that involve delusions and other disruptions to epistemic functioning (see Burroughs and Tollefson, 2016; Carver, Morley, and Taylor, 2016; Critchley, 2019; Carel and Gyorffy, 2014).

Here are a few examples of pathocentric epistemic injustice. These come from patient testimonies, but additional examples can be found in healthcare reports, media stories, and the work of charities such as the Patients Association. As one example, we take the Report of the Mid Staffordshire NHS Foundation Trust Public Inquiry (2013), known as the Francis Report, after its chair, Robert Francis QS. The report documented the mistreatment and neglect of patients in that Trust.[4] It explains the 'appalling suffering of many patients

[4] The Francis Report can be downloaded at https://www.gov.uk/government/publications/report-of-the-mid-staffordshire-nhs-foundation-trust-public-inquiry

[was] primarily caused by a serious failure on the part of a provider Trust Board. *It did not listen sufficiently to its patients and staff* (Francis, 2013, p. 3, emphasis added). Such serious and systematic failings go far deeper than a lack of etiquette or poor bedside manner. They point to problems of a more global and enduring sort which, when manifested in healthcare environments, lead to the suffering and death (or premature death) of ill persons.

Outside of government reports, other accounts of pathocentric epistemic injustices can be found in illness narratives, blogs and vlogs, in online patient fora, and in the many other places where people testify about their experiences of being ill in an unjust and pathophobic world. Consider the following:

> I had acute epigastric pain going through to the back during the night but got no relief. It was implied that it was anxiety, and diazepam was prescribed with no effect. It seemed to me that in view of the massive and rapid changes in my body, a physical cause was quite likely. I felt the interest in me had waned and there was less understanding. No one took the pain seriously (quoted in Mandell and Spiro, 2013, p. 376).

> I had an abnormal cervical smear, so was sent to the large city teaching hospital for a coloscopy. I changed into the usual ties up the back gown, with the usual vital ties missing, and then went through for the examination. Lots of big sighs from the consultant with his head between my legs. Then off he goes, leaving the room. I'm told to follow. So, I arrive, naked under a gown which doesn't do up, slightly damp between the legs and a bit stressed as I have to sit down and I'm worried about leaving a wet patch. He goes on to tell me I need an operation. I hear blah blah blah as I'm perching and panicky [...] And it's very difficult to think without your pants on. I said nothing.[5]

An alarming feature of many pathocentric epistemic injustices is that they can nullify a person's capacity to resist the injustice being done. When subjected to an injustice, a natural response is to protest it, for instance, by deploying epistemic tools like arguing, criticising, and offering counter-evidence. But when suffering an epistemic injustice, one may undergo a depletion of epistemic authority. The ill person's testimonies are denied credibility; when

[5] This testimony was provided by a patient on the LAM Action patient support email group.

they make arguments, these are deprived of their force, since they are perceived as coming from an incompetent source.

The costs of epistemic injustice can be severe. Some of our everyday epistemic activities are mundane, but others are critical to our survival. Depending on context, being denied information, for instance, can be irritating or catastrophic. Having a person refuse to believe one's words can be frustrating or fatal. For these sorts of reasons, any impingement on our epistemic capacities can be a very serious problem – so serious that sometimes the results can be suffering and death. At the most extreme end of the spectrum we find simply no attempt to solicit patient testimony at all. The shocking case of Victoria Climbié is the starkest illustration of this stance. She was an eight year old Francophone child who suffered the most horrific abuse at the hands of her carers. The enquiry into her death identified at least sixty opportunities for professionals to intervene in the months preceding her death, when she was taken to hospital, health and social care appointments. Not once was she asked to provide any information about herself or to explain how her injuries were caused. 'At no point during her stay in the hospital did any doctor speak to Victoria in a formal attempt to find out what had happened to her, either with or without the assistance of an interpreter' (The Laming Enquiry, 2003, p. 256).[6]

Such cases painfully show that some of the worst predicaments are fatal. When one is silenced or otherwise invisible, one becomes at ever-greater risk of harm. This is why pathocentric epistemic injustices should be considered in relation to the various forms of pathophobia. Clearly, many of the structural factors that generate the one also generate the other. Pathocentric hermeneutical injustices, for instance, usually involve the absence or marginalisation of the hermeneutical resources and opportunities needed by ill persons. Such hermeneutical gaps will also be implicated in a lot of pathophobic banality – the variety of facile and superficial ways of understanding the particularity and complexity of experiences of chronic illnesses. Kathlyn Conway gives many examples of the banal things people said to her during her cancer:

> Some people recount positive stories of survival. I hear about one woman who had breast cancer and bicycled twenty miles a day throughout chemotherapy; another who looked gorgeous the

[6] The Laming Enquiry can be downloaded at https://assets.publishing.service.gov.uk/government/uploads/system/uploads/attachment_data/file/273183/5730.pdf

> entire time; and a third who told no one of her diagnosis and acted as if her life were absolutely normal. Why are these stories not consoling me? (Conway, 2007, p. 58)

Such trite assurances and glib comparisons underplay the complexity and awfulness of Conway's experience of cancer. They register failures not simply of communication, but of understanding. For that reason, pathophobic banality lies close to hermeneutical injustice. When those failures of interpersonal understanding are continuous and intense, they form part of our predicament. The social norms and structures that function to deprive ill persons of the credibility and intelligibility they deserve also sets them up for aversive, banal, callous, and insensitive treatment. Within the worst predicaments, the constant threats are silence and violence.

Understanding the predicament of patients ultimately means attending to the wider social and epistemic structures that have come to characterise our cultures. There are complex systems of norms, practices, and ways of organising our social practices and resources that tend systematically to harm persons with illnesses. This wider predicament involves an extremely complex interaction of oppressive ideologies and cultures that include pathophobia, misogyny, heteronormativity, and racism, along with others. What is crucial is to appreciate the dynamic conceptual and structural linkages between these invidious phenomena. At that point, we finally achieve a properly cognisant appreciation of the true complexity of the predicament of ill persons, of which pathocentric epistemic injustices are only one, albeit central, manifestation.

It should be clear that thinking predicamentally hugely increases the scale and complexity of the work. Local fixes might help, but only up to a point. Without a properly 'big picture' understanding, we risk becoming trapped in a futile game of ameliorative whack-a-mole that tries to deal with specific pathocentric epistemic injustices and localised instances of pathophobia without altering substantially the wider structures that generate and perpetuate them. We need to change the underlying structures, as the women's health movement has taught us for many decades. The titles of histories of that movement offer aphoristic clues to the sorts of changes we need – *More than Medicine* (Nelson, 2015) and *Into Our Own Hands* (Morgen, 2002). What ultimately needs to change is not just those individual pathophobic people who silence, shame, and harm those with illnesses, but rather what Audre Lorde called the 'outside world's viciousness, the stupid, brutal lack of consciousness or concern that passes for the way things are'.

5. Conclusion: thinking predicamentally

In this paper we proposed that our understanding of pathocentric epistemic injustices can be enriched if they are theorised predicamentally, that is, in ways that refer to the wider socially scaffolded structures of epistemic challenges, dangers, needs, and threats arising from the emplacement of ill persons within material, social, and epistemic structures.

As discussed in sections 3 and 4, Pathocentric epistemic injustices have come to be analysed in Miranda Fricker's (2007) terms of testimonial credibility and hermeneutical intelligibility, although since her original account many new forms of epistemic injustice have been identified. Moreover, some of the features of that account were amended (see Medina, 2017; Polhhaus Jr., 2017). Our earlier publications proceeded within Fricker's original framework (Carel and Kidd, 2014; Kidd and Carel, 2016). It's therefore salutary to consider ways that analyses of pathocentric epistemic injustices might be thickened to take advantage of new insights from within and beyond epistemic injustice studies.

Consider Fricker's discussion of cases where people with undiagnosed or poorly understood medical conditions suffer hermeneutical marginalisation. Other people cannot make proper sense of their social behaviours, seeing them as strange or erratic, which causes all sorts of interpersonal problems. Fricker suggests this is a case, not of hermeneutical injustice, but of 'circumstantial epistemic bad luck' (Fricker, 2007, p. 152). Against that judgment, Shelley Tremain suggests that this *is* an injustice: the social and hermeneutical disadvantages are sustained by stable background conditions that prevent others from making sense of those social behaviours – in which case, they amount to a hermeneutical injustice (Tremain, 2016, pp. 177–78). Interpreting those disadvantages situationally and individually as bad luck, rather than as systematic and structurally generated failings, is one way of concealing the full realities of the predicament of those with the relevant sorts of conditions and disabilities. As Nora Berenstain eloquently puts it, the problem is 'portraying medical gaslighting itself as a result of mere 'epistemic bad luck' rather than as the predictable and enduring consequence of the medicalization of disability within a materially harmful and ableist system of medical meaning-making' (Berenstain, forthcoming).

We need to appreciate that the predicaments of ill persons often include different sorts of obliviousness on the part of other people. Such obliviousness has at least three dimensions, each pertinent to properly understanding pathocentric epistemic injustices. First, one can fail to grasp the *enormity* of predicaments, maybe by supposing that cases of being ignored or silenced are occasional and irritating episodes, rather than constant problems. It can also include failures to appreciate how individually irksome limitations can, within the context of a predicament, become something far more significant. In her memoir of cancer, doctor Kate Granger reflects on the unfolding loss of putatively minor comforts and habits, like being able 'to sleep on my side, to have a bath, to share a bed with my husband' (Granger, 2014, p. 93). This restriction would not matter for a night or two, but becomes significant when enduring, and combined with the other miseries of illness.

Second, one might fail to grasp the *complexity* of predicaments, maybe by thinking that coping with illness is mainly a matter of seeking treatment and managing pain, rather than fighting to be believed when one talks about one's experiences. Coping with breast cancer is not just a matter of radiotherapy, scans, and tumours. It also involves coping with changes to one's relationship to a body that might now feel 'traitorous' and rethinking one's sexuality, as well as working out how one wants to relate to the public cultures of breast cancer. Barbara Ehrenreich speaks of the relentless 'bright-siding' built into the pink ribbon cancer cultures in the United States (Ehrenreich, 2009); Ann Boyer talks of the oppressive gendered pressures intrinsic to what she calls 'the cancer pavilion' (Boyer, 2019). Coping with cancer means coping with scans, treatment, and pain, but also with sexual identity, self-confidence, altered sense of embodiment, and so much more – all requiring epistemic, moral, and emotional labour, which largely goes unacknowledged.

A final sort of obliviousness to the predicaments of ill persons concerns the many ways that being an ill person intersects with one's social identities. An ill person is never just an ill person: they will have a gendered identity, a racialised identity, a sexual identity, a professional identity, and so on. Moreover, these many social identities are intersecting and not isolated from one another. Working class black women, for instance, suffer not just the individual costs of classism, racism, and sexism, but the compounded effects of those forms of discrimination. In a classic essay on intersectionality, Kimberlé Crenshaw emphasises that 'the failure to embrace the complexities of compoundedness is not simply a matter of political will, but is also due to the influence of a way of thinking about discrimination which structures politics so that struggles are categorized as singular issues' (Crenshaw, 1989, pp. 166–67).

By thinking predicamentally, we stand a much better chance of understanding pathocentric epistemic injustices in ways that honour their enormity, complexity, and intersectional detail. Our initial studies of pathocentric epistemic injustice did speak of *ill persons* as such, although more recently work has started to become more sensitive to the need for intersectional texture when studying the epistemic predicament of ill persons. Speaking of epistemic microaggressions, Freeman and Stuart emphasise much will depend on whether the patient is, for instance, an upper-middle class, white, heterosexual man or a working class, black, lesbian woman (Freeman and Stuart, 2018, p. 439). Our studies of pathocentric epistemic injustice should become more sensitive to the complexities and particularities of our intersectionally structured social identities. It is not just a matter of our diseased bodies, but of the ways they sit within wider structures of power, identity, and ideology.[7]

University of Nottingham
ian.kidd@nottingham.ac.uk

University of Bristol
havi.carel@bristol.ac.uk

References

Nora Berenstain, 'White Feminist Gaslighting' *Hypatia* (forthcoming).

Charlotte Blease, Havi Carel, and Keith Geraghty, 'Epistemic injustice in healthcare encounters: evidence from chronic fatigue syndrome', *Journal of Medical Ethics* 43 (2017), 549–57. doi:10.1136/medethics-2016-103691

Ann Boyer, *The Undying: A Meditation on Modern Illness* (London: Penguin, 2019).

Michael D. Burroughs and Deborah Tollefson, 'Learning to Listen: Epistemic Injustice and the Child', *Episteme* 13.3 (2016), 359–77.

Eleanor Alexandra Byrne, 'Striking the Balance with Epistemic Injustice in Healthcare: The Case of Chronic Fatigue Syndrome/Myalgic Encephalomyelitis', *Medicine, Health Care and Philosophy* (forthcoming).

Havi Carel, *Illness: The Cry of the Flesh,* (London: Routledge, 2018).

Havi Carel and Ian James Kidd, 'Epistemic Injustice in Healthcare: A Philosophical Analysis', *Medicine, Healthcare and Philosophy* 17(4) (2014), 529–40.

[7] We thank Julian Baggini for helpful comments and editorial suggestions.

Havi Carel and Gita Gyorffy, 'Seen but not heard: children and epistemic injustice', *The Lancet* 384 (2014), 1256–57.

L. Carver, S. Morley and P. Taylor, 'Voices of Deficit: Mental Health, Criminal Victimisation and Epistemic Injustice', *Illness, Crisis and Loss* 25 (2016), doi: 10.1177/1054137316675715

Rita Charon, *Narrative Medicine: Honoring the Stories of Illness* (Oxford: Oxford University Press, (2006).

Kathyln Conway, *Beyond Words: Illness and the Limits of Expression* (Albuquerque: University of New Mexico Press, 2013).

Paul Crichton, Havi Carel and Ian James Kidd, 'Epistemic Injustice in Psychiatry', *BJPsych Bulletin* 41(2016), 65–70.

Kimbelé Crenshaw, 'Demarginalizing the Intersection of Race and Sex: A Black Feminist Critique of Antidiscrimination Doctrine, Feminist Theory and Antiracist Politics', *University of Chicago Legal Forum* 1.8 (1989), 139–67.

Harry Critchley, 'Epistemic Injustice and Medical Neglect in Ontario Jails: The Case of Pregnant Women', Ben Sherman and Stacey Goguen (eds.) *Overcoming Epistemic Injustice: Social and Psychological Perspectives* (New York: Rowman and Littlefield, 2019), 237–51.

Ian James Kidd and Havi Carel, 'Epistemic Injustice and Illness', *Journal of Applied Philosophy* 3 (2016), 172–90.

Kristie Dotson, 'Tracking Epistemic Violence, Tracking Practices of Silencing,' *Hypatia* 26.2 (2011): 236–57.

Maya Dusenbery, *Doing Harm: The Truth About How Bad Medicine and Lazy Science Leave Women Dismissed, Misdiagnosed, and Sick* (New York: HarperCollins, 2018).

Laurie Edwards, *In the Kingdom of the Sick: A Social History of Chronic Illness in America* (London: Bloomsbury, 2013).

Barbara Ehrenreich, *Smile or Die: How Positive Thinking Fooled America and the World* (London: Granta, 2009).

Miranda Fricker, *Epistemic Injustice: Power and the Ethics of Knowing*, (Oxford: Oxford University Press, 2007).

C. FitzGerald, and S. Hurst, 'Implicit Bias in Healthcare Professionals: A Systematic Review', *BMC Med Ethics* 18, (2017).

The Francis Report (2013) ISBN 9780102981476, HC 947 2012-13.

Kate Granger, *The Other Side* (Kindle edition, 2014).

Lauren Freeman and Heather, Stewart, 'Microaggressions in Clinical Medicine', *Kennedy Institute Ethics Journal*, 28, (2018), 411–49.

Martin Heidegger, *Being and Time*, (London: Blackwell, (1962 [1927]).

Ian James Kidd, 'Pathophobia, Illness, and Vices', *International Journal of Philosophical Studies* 27.2 (2019), 286–306.

Ian James Kidd and Havi Carel, 'Epistemic Injustice and Illness', *Journal of Applied Philosophy* 3 (2018), 172–90.

Ian James Kidd and Havi Carel, 'Pathocentric Epistemic Injustice and Conceptions of Health', Benjamin R. Sherman and Stacey Goguen (eds.) *Overcoming Epistemic Injustice: Social and Psychological Perspectives* (New York: Rowman and Littlefield, 2018), 153–68.

Ian James Kidd, José Medina, Gaile Pohlhaus, Jr. (eds.), *The Routledge Handbook to Epistemic Injustice*, co-edited with (New York: Routledge, 2017).

Laming Report, *The Victoria Climbié Inquiry* (London: HMSO, 2003).

Audre Lorde, *The Cancer Journals* (San Francisco: Aunt Lute Books, 1997).

H.N. Mandell and H.M. Spiro (eds.), *When Doctors Get Sick* (Dordrecht: Springer, 2013).

José Medina, *The Epistemology of Resistance: Gender and Racial Oppression, Epistemic Injustice, and Resistant Imaginations* (Oxford: Oxford University Press, 2012).

Sandra Morgen, *Into Our Own Hands: The Women's Health Movement in the United States, 1969–1990* (New Brunswick: Rutgers University Press, 2002).

Jennifer Nelson, *More Than Medicine: A History of the Feminist Women's Health Movement* (New York: New York University Press, 2015).

Abby Norman, *Ask Me About My Uterus: A Quest to Make Doctor's Believe in Women's Pain*, (New York: Nation Books, 2018).

Susan Sontag, *Illness as Metaphor* (New York: Farrar, Straus and Giroux, 1978).

Gayatri Spivak, 'Can the Subaltern Speak?', in Cary Nelson and Lawrence Grossberg (eds.), *Marxism and the Interpretation of Culture* (Urbana: University of Illinois Press, 1998), 271–313.

Shelley Tremain, 'Knowing Disability, Differently', Ian James Kidd, José Medina, and Gaile Pohlhaus, Jr. (eds.) *The Routledge Handbook to Epistemic Injustice* (New York: Routledge, 2016), 175–83.

How Can You Spot the Experts? An Essay in Social Epistemology

ALVIN I. GOLDMAN

Abstract

In the history of western philosophy, people were often encouraged to seek knowledge by starting from their own minds and proceeding in a highly individualistic spirit. In recent contemporary philosophy, by contrast, there is a movement toward Social Epistemology, which urges people to seek knowledge from what others know. However, in selected fields some people are experts while others are laypersons. It is natural for self-acknowledged laypersons to seek help from the experts. But who, exactly, are the experts? Many people claiming to be experts are not the real thing. How can laypersons identify genuine experts? This essay explores the problems that arise, pointing out some of the mistakes that can be made and how to avoid them.

1. Introduction

Two of the most influential figures in Western philosophy were the French philosopher, Rene Descartes, and the English philosopher, John Locke. Each wrote very influentially in the field of epistemology, the field that studies how best to acquire genuine knowledge while avoiding serious mistakes. They shared the view that knowledge is best pursued in a highly individualistic way. Descartes held that we must start with knowledge of our own minds and extrapolate from there (Descartes, 1641). Locke also rejected intellectual reliance on others. As he put it, 'other men's opinions floating in one's brain do not constitute genuine knowledge' (Locke, 1690). In short, over hundreds of years, the Western study of epistemology has been a heavily individualistic affair. Each individual must determine what is true or false by his/her own devices. In the last few years, by contrast, there has been a movement toward *Social Epistemology*, a field that studies the prospects – and the risks – of trying to obtain knowledge from what other people know, or purport to know.[1] This is the theme of the present essay. In particular, we focus on two types of people: experts and laypersons. Experts have a great deal of knowledge and/or skill; laypersons lack that knowledge and skill.

[1] For a general overview of social epistemology, see Goldman and Whitcomb (2011) and Goldman and O'Connor (2019).

doi:10.1017/S1358246121000060

If a layperson seeks new knowledge, and hopes to acquire it from some purported expert or experts, what are the layperson's prospects for success, and what hazards should they be alert for?

2. Being an Expert and Distinguishing Experts from Frauds.

Around 2,500 years ago, the Greek philosopher Plato (in his dialogue, ***Charmides***) wrote as follows: 'If someone claims to be a doctor, how can I tell if he really is one?'.

That was a long time ago; but Plato's problem still confronts us. Given the complexity of the universe, the sophistication of our sciences, and the disputes that reign over difficult issues, people often feel – reasonably enough – that they are not as well informed as they need to be. Nor is it transparent who are the most knowledgeable and trustworthy people to consult with on this or that issue. People feel the need to consult experts who can answer their questions or execute various operations, such as repairing an automobile, performing surgery, or guiding one in making a financial investment. In each case one may ask oneself: Whom should I consult with, and whom can I trust the most? Suppose that one aims to launch a start-up company, but a tech specialist is required to run its digital arm. Who should be selected for that job? In each case, the layperson seeks someone with an appropriate kind of expertise. He or she is a novice, who candidly recognizes his own lack of the skills needed to meet with the challenge in question. However, the question then arises: how can such a layperson identify which of the available candidates would do the best job? Which should be chosen? (For present purposes, I ignore possible differences in the fees that potential experts might charge.) How can a layperson tell which of the numerous putative experts would really be good and which would turn out to be mere frauds or duffers?

Before proceeding, we should ask the following preliminary question: what does it take for someone to *be* an expert (in one or another field or domain)? We are not interested in enumerating all the different areas of expertise, which, of course, are legion. Rather, we are interested in the generic idea of what expertise consists in. What is required for a person to qualify as some kind of expert? Here are two different possible approaches:

(1) '*Reputational* approach'. An expert (in some specified field) is someone who has a reputation – at least in some circles – of being knowledgeable and/or skillful in the specified field.

(2) '*Realist* approach'. An expert (in some specified field) is someone who genuinely possesses appropriate knowledge and/or appropriate skills. In other words, he or she can correctly answer or resolve the kinds of questions or problems appropriate to that domain.

As between the two approaches to the nature of expertise – 'reputationalism' and 'realism' – I firmly side with realism. Being an expert does not require a reputation for possessing a high level of knowledge and skill. One can *be* an expert even if one keeps one's knowledge or skills quite private, rarely if ever displaying credentials or hanging out shingles to advertise one's skills or accomplishments. There can be genuine experts who have no clientele, following, or publicly established record.

We turn, then, to Realism. Realism is a bit tricky, however, because there are two elements, or two criteria, that need to be jointly satisfied for someone to qualify as an expert. The first criterion is a *comparative* criterion of expertise. This criterion requires of an expert that he/she *exceed most other people* in terms of knowing more correct answers to questions in the domain and knowing how to solve more problems in the domain than most people do. Meeting this comparative criterion, however, is not sufficient for being an expert. There is also an (admittedly vague) *absolute criterion* in addition to the initial, comparative criterion. If Terry holds false beliefs about *most* questions in the relevant domain, and false beliefs about how to solve problems in the domain, this is a very 'weak' performance that would disqualify him as an expert. And that disqualification will stand even if a large number of other people are even worse than Terry in terms of knowledge of the domain. In other words, one cannot qualify as an expert simply by there being *others* who have an even more inaccurate or misguided set of beliefs and problem-solving tendencies. The candidate must have a *substantial* amount of accurate knowledge and/or problem-solving ability to earn the status of expert.

This very broad characterization of expertise is intended to apply to a wide range of fields or domains, including natural sciences, medicine, law, automobile repair, finance, business management, music history, and so forth.

Although I highlight *knowledge* as a central component of being an expert, the types of knowledge in question here are not confined to narrowly 'intellectual' subjects that are devoted to what is or isn't a 'fact'. Being an expert can also involve having the ability to produce *actions* or *results*, such as curing physical ailments or identifying profitable investment plans.

3. What methods can laypersons deploy to select the best, or most useful, experts?

Now we focus on the question of how to identify the best experts.

(A) Appeals to training and credentials.

Putative experts are commonly people who have received specialized training, which – in the successful cases – may lead to expertise. They may study at universities, law schools, medical schools, technological institutes, and other specialized instructional entities. Such institutions will often confer degrees, licenses, and/or certificates to display in their offices. Seekers of expertise might consult and compare these degrees, licenses, and certificates as potential indicators of the relative quality of the competing experts.

But how much information can a layperson hope to extract by inspecting such licenses or certificates? A layperson may know very little about the relative strengths of the different schools or institutions that trained the putative experts. Moreover, if two competing experts have been trained at one and the same institution, it might still be unclear (to the layperson) who is the cleverest or most competently skilled trainee.

Patients' evaluations of doctors might be rather unhelpful for different reasons, especially when the patients lack medical knowledge. For example, patients may base their evaluation of a doctors' expertise more on the doctor's 'bed-side manner' than on the level of success relative to the severity of the symptoms. Good bedside manner will not, in general, be a reliable indicator of medical expertise.

(B) Appeal to the numbers.

Confronted with limited information and questionable reliability of a putative expert's knowledge and skills, a layperson might check to determine if the putative expert he initially encounters (expert #1) advocates a similar diagnosis or plan of action as other putative experts advocate. If *many* of them agree with the opinion of expert #1, whereas only a *few* concur with expert #2, shouldn't it be obvious that #1 should be selected rather than #2? This would be a case of 'trusting the numbers'. If most trained people agree that #1 is best, isn't #1 the better choice for the layperson? Unfortunately, matters are not so simple.

How so? Two groups of experts may be products of two different training schools. Suppose each group slavishly follows his/her own training school. It just so happens, however, that one school has more students, and therefore produces more trainees. This is what accounts for the numerical difference in response to the question at hand. However, a larger number does not prove that this group is more trustworthy than its competitor. Appealing to a larger number has merit only if and when the different consultants are *independent* of one another (as will be explained shortly). But independence does not hold in the present case in question.

The significance of *independence* can be illustrated by a different example. Suppose that Jones is a juror in a trial. He listens to witness #1 testify that he (#1) personally saw Schmitt commit the crime. This lends some initial support to Schmitt's being guilty. Next, Jones hears witness #2 also testify to Schmitt's guilt. But witness #2 did not personally witness the crime; he only heard about it from witness #1. Does the additional testimony from witness #2 strengthen Jones's evidence for Schmitt's guilt? No. Witness #2's evidence is not *independent* of witness #1's evidence; rather, it completely relies on witness #1. Therefore, witness #2's evidence adds no additional evidential weight (for juror Jones) with respect to Schmitt's guilt.[2]

(C) Comparing performances in a debate.

An entirely different method for trying to identify a superior expert is to attend, or listen, to a debate between competing experts. Preferably, the debate would be on the very subject matter on which the layperson seeks advice, for example, how best to treat a certain kind of cancer. Again, however, it is unlikely that an otherwise untrained layperson could profit much from hearing such a debate.

The problem is that such a debate is likely to be rife with technical terminology and lines of reasoning that might be familiar to experts but obscure to laypersons. The language in such a discussion would be highly esoteric, where 'esoteric' entails being beyond the ken of a typical layperson. It is therefore doubtful that a layperson could glean a great deal of usable, reliable information by watching or listening to such a debate.

(D) Track records

I suggest that the most helpful method – if it is available – is to check the past *track records* of the candidate experts' success rates. How

[2] For a more mathematical treatment of this matter, see Goldman (2001).

often did his or her advice generate an improved result, outcome, or state of affairs? How well did the putative experts prove themselves in the test cases? A track record consisting of a large percentage of successes and few if any failures would be a prime indicator of a candidate expert's quality.

Is it feasible, however, for laypersons to *verify the* past track records of multiple competing experts? This will depend, of course, on the kinds of tasks or problems that the experts in question have tried to tackle and the answers, or solutions, that they proposed. Are laypersons in a position to assess the accuracy or adequacy of the putative experts' solutions? Consider another medical example. Suppose a layperson learns that five years ago, Dr. Jones was confronted with the following problem: 'Patient Johnson suffers from symptoms X, Y, and Z. What would be the best way to treat his condition?' Suppose that the layperson intends to use this information to assess Dr. Jones's qualifications. Can he/she find out what treatment Jones delivered? That surely seems possible. But will our layperson be able to tell whether Dr. Jones' treatment was medically *sound*? That result is problematic, given the layperson's lack of medical training. Of course, the layperson may learn that patient Johnson eventually recuperated from his condition. Still, this would not provide sufficient guidance concerning the quality of Dr. Jones's diagnosis or the treatment of patient Johnson. (The patient may have recuperated all on his/her own.)

I do not mean to argue that appeals to past track-records are a totally fruitless method for addressing our problem. As indicated earlier, I think that tracking a putative expert's track record is a very good method to use, at least when used properly. Indeed, it may be the best method available. Here is an example (Goldman, 2001). Oscar is untutored in matters of astronomy. He hears Sidra claim that there will be a solar eclipse visible from London precisely one year hence. By itself this does not provide much (if any) evidence that Sidra has considerable expertise in astronomy; because as of yet Oscar has no clue as to whether Sidra's prediction will be right. However, suppose Oscar waits a year and then personally observes a solar eclipse in London, precisely as Sidra predicted. This would definitely supply evidence of Sidra's expertise (assuming she did not merely borrow this prediction from some astronomer friend of hers). The point is that this might be a legitimate example of how a novice can acquire genuine support for someone else's expertise, without having transformed himself into an expert.

To take simpler examples, laypersons can sometimes successfully identify cases in which their doctor, their mechanic, their investment advisor, etc. gives them just the sort of treatment, advice, etc. that palpably succeeds in generating sought-after results. To summarize, I do not claim that getting good evidence for various individuals' expertise is wholly beyond the grasp of laypersons. However, such evidence may be rather difficult to acquire – which is not to deny the value of utilizing such evidence whenever this is feasible.

4. Paying Attention to an Expert's Personal Interests.

An important additional factor to consider, of course, is the self-interest an expert might have in recommending one way of addressing a problem rather than another, for instance, by getting 'kickbacks' from choosing one investment outfit rather than another. In general, which expert to select for a given task will not depend exclusively on how knowledgeable or skillful the expert is, but also on how *trustworthy* the expert is in offering helpful advice to the layperson rather than advice that merely advances the expert's own self-interest. Other things being equal, it may be reasonable to avoid the guidance of an expert who clearly has a significant self-interest. Of course, it may sometimes be true that all potential experts stand to benefit from being employed for the same task. In such cases, the interest factor may not play a significant role. But where extremes of self-interest are significant, such information should not be ignored.

5. Mistakes to avoid in Assessing Levels of Expertise.

Psychologists and other scientists of cognition have identified a wide assortment of 'biases' or 'errors' in human thinking and reasoning. Some of these would apply to decisions concerning whom to trust as an expert.

(A) Overly confident expert.

Listeners are often blown away when they hear speakers assert things with considerable force and self-confidence. Listeners seem to assume that speakers' self-confidence is a reliable sign of authoritative knowledge. In fact, however, assertiveness and swagger are not very reliable indicators of truth possession (or expertise). The psychologist Philip Tetlock, for example, reported an experimental finding that experts who are most often accurate tend to be cautious, quiet, and somewhat more boring than their more self-confident and emphatic counterparts (Tetlock, 2006). Thus, if you want to identify a genuine expert, you may well be better off choosing a cautious character rather than a super-confident one.

(B) Confirmation bias.

Another belief-forming bias has been reported by the psychologists Lord, Ross, and Lepper (1979). They write: 'People tend to take at face value any evidence that confirms their prior beliefs, while subjecting evidence that disconfirms prior beliefs to intense critical evaluation'. Similarly, Ditto and Lopez (1992) report: 'Less information is required and less cognitive processing is devoted to reach conclusions we antecedently favor as opposed to conclusions we antecedently disfavor'.

(C) Conforming with the group.

Another common error people tend to make is trusting others when they have no reason to do so. Psychologist Solomon Asch (1951) devised an experiment in which groups of eight participants were shown a card with one line on the left and three lines of different lengths on the right. Their task was to identify which line on the right was of the same length as the line on the left. Meanwhile, seven members of the group were confederates of the researcher, instructed to choose the same *wrong line*. The subjects, answering last, could then either agree with the rest of the group – thereby picking the wrong line – or pick the right line. A significant number of subjects chose to go against the evidence of their own senses and instead conform with what the other group members said. This highlights the pitfalls of following, or *conforming* with, 'the crowd' (O'Connor and Weatherall, 2019, p. 81). As this example suggests, 'blind' *conformity* with others is a dubious basis for choosing an expert.

6. Choosing Between Bodies of Experts and a Skeptical Citizenry.

In the preceding discussion the focus has centered on the situation of a single person with a problem who needs the guidance of an expert but finds it difficult to decide which (putative) expert is the best or most reliable. In this section we consider a different kind of problem featuring experts. It is a case where there is a firm body of experts who agree that a certain type of action is desirable.

However, there is also a body of citizens who question or deny that this type of action is desirable. They do not necessarily claim a scientific basis for their opinion, but nonetheless deny that the relevant type of action is desirable. What course of action should be adopted by the largely untutored citizenry?

It might seem implausible to be concerned with this type of problem, except for the fact that there are actual bodies of contrasting opinions that exemplify such disputes, even in the most educationally advanced countries, such as the United States and England. Which group is being unreasonable, we might ask, and how or why have they gone wrong? What is the source (or sources) of the error? The discussion that follows is based heavily on the reporting of Jan Hoffman (2019.)

In August 2019 the United Kingdom lost its World Health Organization designation as a country that has eliminated measles, because of outbreaks that year. The same thing was expected to occur in 2020 for the United States. In both cases, this happened because of 'vaccine hesitancy', that is, the practice of declining to follow standard medical vaccination guidelines. The World Health Organization lists vaccine hesitancy as one of the top threats to global health. This is a reversal of the public's attitude toward vaccination, which had previously followed the dominant position of medical science. How or why was there such a change on the part of the public? Assuming that the change was a 'mistake' on their part, what were the sources of the mistake?

Hoffman (2019) offers several explanations. One major contributor to the emergence of anti-vaccine sentiment was the infamous publication by Andrew Wakefield, a British gastroenterologist, of an article in Lancet that associated the M.M.R. vaccine with autism (Wakefield, 1998). That study was later discredited and withdrawn by the publisher. The rest of the present discussion, however, focuses on events in the U.S.A.

According to Jan Hoffman (citing Paul A. Offit), scientists now report that science has 'lost its platform': 'Now, you simply declare your own truth'. She traces the constituents who make up the so-called 'vaccine resistant' come from disparate groups, including anti-government libertarians, apostles of the all-natural, and those who believe that doctors should not dictate medical decisions about children.

In a very different vein, Hoffman reports the sense among health experts that parents and even many doctors do not appreciate the severity of disease that immunizations have thwarted because they have not witnessed many actual cases of the disease. Thus, 'vaccines are a victim of their own success'. Another strong strain in Hoffman's explanation of the rise of vaccine resistance is 'groupthink parenting', facilitated by social media.

A different kind of explanation offered is failure to understand numerical risk. 'We pay more attention to numerators, such as "16 adverse events", than we do to denominators, such as "per million vaccine doses"'.

These points might reasonably be classified as 'mistakes' that (certain) parents are making. But there are other factors that certainly should not be counted as mistakes. One such factor is the lack of trust in 'Big Pharma'. Nobody can deny the humongous guilt of Big Pharma, especially with regard to Purdue's highly culpable role in the opioid catastrophe. Obviously, not every institution engaged in some sort of technical and profitable activity deserves uncritical obeisance. That is what makes our topic of expertise and responsiveness to expertise such a timely and significant topic for discussion and analysis in our time.

7. Selecting Educational Curricula and Governmental Policies

Most of the foregoing discussion focuses on a relatively narrow problem about expertise: namely, how laypersons can tell which of two self-styled experts is the better one to choose for guidance on the problem at hand? As already indicated, however, it would be a mistake to leave the impression that this is the only interesting and important question associated with expertise. Other issues have been raised by a variety of writers, primarily issues concerned with the role of expertise in public settings and venues. We shall illustrate these discussions in connection with two additional domains: (1) how should educational systems proceed in crafting curricula for public schools? and (2) what role should expertise play in guiding governmental policy- making?

> (A) Consider first educational systems, in which the contents of instruction are under the public's direction. Not infrequently (at least in the U.S.A), disputes arise about what scientists regard as established facts, giving rise to disputes about what should be included or excluded in the educational curriculum. Most prominently, there are disputes about creationism and human-caused climate change. (Creationism denies evolution and holds that God created all species in their present forms.)

Scientists are generally staunch endorsers of the truth of human-caused climate change and staunch critics of creationism. On the other hand, many families with children in school are supporters of creationism and skeptical of climate change. In such a scenario, one can readily imagine lively (if not heated) debates about which textbooks should or should not be adopted, as pertains to these contested issues. Assume that scientists – many of them, at least – are experts in their respective fields. They will likely argue for textbooks reflecting that (shared) expertise. Partisans of creationism and climate denial, on the other hand, will take issue with these curricular choices. Family members who disagree with the scientists might claim a different expertise of their own. Alternatively, they might simply challenge the alleged expertise of the scientists. They might grant certain expertise to the scientists but deny them any privileged role in guiding the educational curriculum.

This line of argument might readily lead to extremes. Shouldn't experts in mathematics, at least, get priority when it comes to hiring math teachers? Isn't education in general devoted to teaching *truths*, as far as it can achieve this? And haven't we characterized expertise, in the 'realist' sense, as the possession of knowledge, i.e., truth? Of course, which are the truths in any domain is open to debate.

(B) A second public arena in which expertise figures prominently is the (wider) political arena. A fundamental idea in democratic theory is that government must be guided, or determined, by 'the people', insofar as they elect representatives who in turn set policies. But governments – including democratic governments – also establish departments, each of which is dedicated to a specific domain, for example, agriculture, commerce, state, justice, defense, treasury, etc. In almost all of these departments it is common to appoint people with special knowledge and training in the appropriate areas, i.e., 'experts'. But if too much decision-making power is conferred on experts, won't this undercut the basic idea, or practice, of democracy? Exactly what role, then, should be assigned to experts in a democracy? This is a timely topic, currently receiving close attention. Drawing on the work of Michael Schudson (2006) and Alfred Moore (2017), consider these reflections on the prospects and pitfalls associated with expertise.

(C) Moore, writes as follows:

'A politician may pressure experts to reach a judgment that is favorable to the needs of the politician at that moment –

perhaps a declaration that a certain foodstuff is safe, or that there are known to be weapons of mass destruction in this or that place … [On the other hand] the expert would be constrained by her professional community from telling politicians what they want to hear – by concern for her reputation, by loyalty to her professional colleagues rather than her political clients. In this way, the independence and self-governance of professional communities is the source of their ability to tell truth to power…. The problem is how to ensure that democratic authority gives experts enough autonomy so that the voice of the expert represents the expert's expertise rather than the views of politicians or bureaucrats who pressure the expert into submission' (Moore: 2017: 47–48).

Or, as Schudson puts it: 'In other words, how can the leash be long enough to keep the expert from becoming a "toady?"' (Schudson 2006, 497). At the same time, is there a danger that experts might usurp the role of ordinary citizens in taking on their elected politicians?

8. Conclusion

How should individual novices and public organizations respond to the phenomenon of expertise? Much depends on a key concept, i.e., 'Knowledge'. Knowledge – by which I here mean 'true belief' – is an essential aspect of life. It plays a crucial role in achieving one's ends, and in avoiding mishaps and catastrophes.

Consider a simple example, not involving expertise. A pedestrian is crossing a street where there is a speeding car, or truck, bearing down on him. If the pedestrian forms a true belief that there is such a vehicle bearing down on him, he may be able to escape a disaster. But if he is ignorant of what is happening, disaster may befall him. So, knowledge is critical!

Or consider a second example. Charlie is visiting a new town. He loves Chinese food but doesn't know which of the many Chinese restaurants in town is the best. He therefore calls his friend, Sam, who purports to be an expert in Chinese cuisine. Sam recommends 'Szechwan Kitchen'. Now suppose that Sam really is an expert in Chinese cuisine. And he also has Charlie's culinary pleasure at heart. Thus, Sam's knowledge is very helpful. Charlie trusts Sam's expertise, and acts accordingly. The result is very satisfactory. Here reliance on expertise clearly 'works'.

Of course, I do not contend that trusting people who purport to be experts *always* has a happy ending. Trusting the work of Andrew Wakefield (1998) was clearly an unhappy event. Similarly, I would submit, ignoring the advice of the great consensus of climate scientists would certainly lead to disaster.

To sum up, putative experts are not *always* genuine experts (contrary to their frequent claims). And even the best of experts can be mistaken. Despite this, however, wisdom does not recommend systematic rejection of experts or expertise, as some thinkers have recommended. British Justice Secretary Michael Gove, for example, in explaining why he has not consulted experts on the wisdom of Brexit, said that 'people in this country have had enough of experts'.[3] I don't know if this is a common British attitude toward expertise. But I very much doubt that it is a wise stance to take in general.[4]

Rutgers University
goldman@philosophy.rutgers.edu

References

Solomon Asch, 'Effects of Group Pressure Upon the Modification and Distortion of Judgments' In *Groups, Leadership, and Men: Research in Human Relations*, edited by Harold Guetzkow, (Oxford: Carnegie Press, 1951) 222–36.

René Descartes, *Meditations on First Philosophy* (1641).

P.H. Ditto, and D.F. Lopez, 'Motivated skepticism: Use of differential decision criteria for preferred and nonpreferred conclusions'. *Journal of Personality and Social Psychology*, 63, (1992) 568–84.

Alvin I. Goldman, 'Experts: Which Ones Should You Trust?' *Philosophy and Phenomenological Research*, 63, (2001) 85–109.

Alvin I. Goldman and Dennis Whitcomb, *Social Epistemology, Essential Readings* (New York: Oxford University Press, 2011).

Alvin Goldman and Cailin O'Connor, 'Social Epistemology', *The Stanford Encyclopedia of Philosophy* (Fall 2019 Edition), Edward

[3] Mance (2016)

[4] I am greatly indebted to Holly M. Smith for her many contributions to this paper. I also wish to thank the audience at the Royal Institute of Philosophy who contributed a number of insights and challenging questions concerning this topic.

N. Zalta (ed.), URL=<https://plato.stanford.edu/archives/fall2019/entries/epistemology-social/>.

Jan Hoffman, 'How Anti-Vaccine Sentiment Took Hold in the United States', *The New York Times* (Sept. 23, 2019) https://www.nytimes.com/2019/09/23/health/anti-vaccination-movement-us.html?searchResultPosition=1

John Locke, An Essay Concerning Human Understanding (1690).

C. G. Lord, L. Ross, and M. R. Lepper, 'Biased assimilation and attitude polarization: The effects of prior theories on subsequently considered evidence', *Journal of Personality and Social Psychology*, 37 (1979) 2098–2109.

Henry Mance, 'Britain has had enough of experts, says Gove', *The Financial Times*. June 3, 2016. https://www.ft.com/content/3be49734-29cb-11e6-83e4-abc22d5d108c.

Alfred Moore, *Critical Elitism. Deliberation, Democracy, and the Problem of Expertise.* (Cambridge: Cambridge University Press, 2017).

Cailin O'Connor and James Owen Weatherall, *The Misinformation Age: How False Beliefs Spread* (New Haven and London: Yale University Press, 2019).

Michael Schudson, 'The Trouble with Experts – and Why Democracies Need Them', *Theory and Society* 35 (2006) 491-506.

Philip E. Tetlock, *Expert Political Judgment: How Good Is It? How Can We Know?* (Princeton, New Jersey: Princeton University Press, 2006).

Andrew Wakefield, et. al., 'Early Report RETRACTED: Ileal-lymphoid-nodular hyperplasia, non-specific colitis, and pervasive developmental disorder in children' *The Lancet* 351 (28 February 1998), 637–41.

Received Wisdom: The Use of Authority in Medieval Islamic Philosophy*

PETER ADAMSON

Abstract

In this paper I challenge the notion that medieval philosophy was characterized by strict adherence to authority. In particular, I argue that to the contrary, self-consciously critical reflection on authority was a widespread intellectual virtue in the Islamic world. The contrary vice, called 'taqlīd', was considered appropriate only for those outside the scholarly elite. I further suggest that this idea was originally developed in the context of Islamic law and was then passed on to authors who worked within the philosophical tradition.

In 1545, Girolamo Cardano (d.1576) published his *Great Art, or On the Rules of Algebra*. It begins: 'in this book, learned reader, you have rules of algebra. It is so replete with new discoveries and demonstrations by the author – more than seventy of them – that its forerunners are of little account' (trans. from Witmer, 1993, p. 1). It's ironic that a work that begins with boasts of its own originality should be notorious for having included an unoriginal result. One of the 'discoveries' Cardano revealed to his 'learned readers' was the method for solving cubic equations, that is, equations of the form $x^3 + ax = b$. It was not Cardano who discovered this method, nor indeed did he claim to have done so. As he openly explained in the *Great Art*, he had been shown it by his colleague Niccolò Tartaglia (d.1557), who wanted to publish it himself. But Cardano learned that Tartaglia's discovery was actually a *re*-discovery, since the method had already been established decades before by the now dead Scipione dal Ferro (d.1526). Cardano felt this gave him license to include the solution to the problem in his own book, much to the outrage of Tartaglia.

To our eyes this scholarly furore looks pretty familiar. In the modern world, scientists, mathematicians, and even philosophers

* This paper summarizes themes explored in greater detail in my forthcoming book *Don't Think for Yourself: Authority and Belief in Medieval Philosophy* (Notre Dame IN: University of Notre Dame Press, 2021). My thanks to Bethany Somma for helpful discussion.

doi:10.1017/S1358246121000011

are frequently anxious about publishing their results before they are 'scooped' by someone else. We know too that this phenomenon is not all that recent; just think of the famous dispute over who could take credit for inventing calculus. But in the sixteenth century, the phenomenon *was* recent. Very few medieval authors trumpeted their own originality the way Cardano does here, never mind bothering to give elaborate explanations about who should (and shouldn't) get credit for discovering what. In the midst of his explanation of the double discovery of the solution to cubic equations, Cardano comes out with a phrase that could appear in a twenty-first century footnote: methods presented in the book discovered by other scholars will receive explicit attribution, but 'those to which no name is attached are mine' (Witmer, 1993, p. 9).

Here we have a central paradox of the Italian Renaissance. This was an age where scholars were unearthing long ignored texts from antiquity, and extolling the unparalleled achievements of classical culture in such fields as of philosophy, history, literature, science, and mathematics (where the leading heroes were Pythagoras and Archimedes: see Rose, 1975; Joost-Gaugier, 2009). Yet it was also an age where originality was prized as a sign of genius, with that prize sometimes being bestowed by others (Vasari writing on Michelangelo) and sometimes awarded to oneself (Cardano). On both counts, the Renaissance seems to depart from the medieval mindset. Of course the whole point of speaking about 'renaissance' is that the study of antiquity was being 'reborn' after the long, moribund medieval age; and we standardly think of the medievals as being desperate to avoid giving the impression of originality. For the medievals, we are told, originality was not an asset to be claimed with pride but an accusation to be hurled at others. This was especially so in religious contexts, where novelty was at most only a step removed from heresy.

That, at least, is the received wisdom. In fact things were more complicated, and on both scores. The first point, about the recovery of texts unknown to the medievals, need not detain us here. But it is worth saying that while some ancient works were indeed rediscovered and had a major impact, a notable example being Lucretius *On the Nature of Things* (see Greenblatt, 2011), Renaissance philosophy also involved deep attention, and new approaches, to the Aristotelian corpus that had already been at the core of the medieval university curriculum (Schmitt, 1983). Furthermore, the Greek texts that inspired Renaissance philosophers and scientists were usually not so much rediscovered, as imported from Byzantium, where they had been preserved and known the whole time. For example Greek Byzantine commentaries on Aristotle's *Ethics* were an important influence on engagements with this text in Latin (Lines, 2012; Trizio, 2014). Finally, the fifteenth century was not the first time that ancient texts had been 'recovered' and given new attention. Scholars also speak of a 'twelfth century Renaissance' when discussing the contribution of philosophers like John of Salisbury (d.1180) and the Platonists associated with the city of Chartres, and even a 'Carolingian Renaissance' animated by scholars like Alcuin (d.804) and Eriugena (d. after 870).

But in what follows my focus will be on the second point. Were medieval thinkers really so authority-bound, so reluctant to think for themselves? Latin medieval culture offers many grounds for a negative answer. For starters, there were occasional thinkers who were happy to proclaim their own originality. The most flamboyantly unusual was Ramon Llull (d.1316), who developed a universal, combinatoric 'Art' for answering all possible questions in philosophy and theology. He unsuccessfully tried to get the scholastics in Paris to embrace this new method (Fidora, 2008), which he thought could even lead to world peace by establishing the truth of Christianity on rational grounds. Admittedly Llull is nobody's idea of a typical medieval philosopher. But about a generation earlier Roger Bacon was stressing the possibility, and urgency, of making new discoveries in philosophy and the sciences by taking recourse to empirical science (*scientia expermentalis*; see Hackett, 1995). Stubborn readers might say that Bacon too was more exception than rule. His empirical approach is often held up as an anticipation of trends in early modern European science, rather than being at home within medieval thought.

This assumption might be challenged, since it's not as if Bacon was the only medieval thinker with empirical leanings. But I instead want to consider a phenomenon that no one could deny to be typical of medieval thought, namely the scholastic 'disputed question'. This form of writing was based on actual teaching practices at the medieval universities. It is most likely to be familiar to you from Thomas Aquinas, but was used pervasively in scholastic philosophy from the thirteenth century onwards (extending, by the way, well into the 'Renaissance' and beyond thanks to the longevity of the scholastic tradition, but that's another story). In a disputed question, the term *auctoritas* refers not so much to a canonical *author* whose word is taken to be true without question, but to a given *passage* from a canonical author, whose word is worth at least taking seriously. (For example Aquinas regularly cites Averroes as an authoritative interpreter of Aristotle, but he also wrote a whole treatise critiquing Averroes' reading of the Aristotelian theory of mind.) Typically, in a disputed question such passages are arrayed to support alternative approaches to a problematic issue. The goal of the author is to show how the 'authorities' can be reconciled, interpreted, massaged, and occasionally set aside, in order to arrive at a position on the issue at hand that both makes intrinsic sense and fits the textual tradition.

In this context, an appeal to authority was not a discussion-ending move that precluded independent thought or creativity. To the contrary, it was an instrument for generating and exploring problems. A particular pure example of this tendency of authorities to create, rather than resolve, difficulties is the work *Sic et Non* (a title I like to translate *On the One Hand and On the Other Hand*) by the early scholastic Peter Abelard (d.1142). It simply sets out contradictory passages from the tradition without attempting to reconcile them. And we have other evidence that Abelard already considered the invocation of authority to be inadequate, by itself, for resolving intellectual problems. He tells a story in his own autobiography about a dispute with a colleague who accused him of having said something heretical (Radice and Clanchy 2003, pp. 21–22). When Abelard tried to explain himself, the colleague waved this away and demanded that he produce support in the form of an authoritative quotation. After Abelard did so, citing Augustine, the colleague insisted that Abelard was understanding the passage incorrectly. Abelard retorted that this was irrelevant, since the colleague was 'looking only for words, not interpretation'. Here we are not far from the refreshingly skeptical comment of Alan of Lille, that authorities are like a wax nose: they can be twisted in whichever direction you like (Stiefel, 1977, p. 359).

All this makes clear that the intellectuals of Latin Christendom did not learn to be wary of authority only in the Renaissance. But it is in medieval Islam that we see an even more thoroughgoing rejection of slavishness to authority. For in that culture, there was a specific word used to denigrate such slavishness: it was called *taqlīd*. Etymologically this term has to do with being 'bound' or 'gird', like a collar being hung around the neck of an animal. In English it is often translated as 'imitation' or, less pithily, 'uncritical acceptance of authority'. However it is translated, the important point is that it was a pejorative word. To accuse someone of *taqlīd* was to suggest that they were not thinking for themselves when they should be. That caveat ('when they should be') is important, because according to these same intellectuals, some people *should* engage in *taqlīd*. In fact, most people should. If one is not a trained scholar, one should not simply 'think for oneself' and make one's own determinations. Rather one should seek the advice of someone who *is* a trained scholar. But the scholars, called 'those who know (*ʿulamāʾ*)', were not supposed to be satisfied with merely quoting or imitating reputable authorities. In fact, it was arguably the avoidance of *taqlīd* that defined membership of the intellectual elite.

The original context of this idea was legal theory (El Shamsy, 2008; Ibrahim, 2016). In Islamic jurisprudence, the sources of legal injunctions are the Qurʾān itself and *ḥadīth*, meaning reports of things the Prophet Muḥammad said and did during his lifetime. Where an explicit injunction can be found in these sources, making a legal determination is relatively clear-cut. It says explicitly at Qurʾān 2:150, for instance, that one should face Mecca when praying, so no legal theory or independent reflection is required to determine that this is the correct direction to face in prayer. I say 'relatively' clear-cut because even here, of course, questions might arise. What should believers do if the time for prayer has come, and they are not sure which way Mecca lies? But the more acute problem is that many questions are not directly addressed in the Qurʾān and *ḥadīth* at all. One legal tradition, the *ẓāhirī* school, took the view that only the explicit injunctions are binding and everything else is permitted; the name of this school expresses their legal position, since they followed the *ẓāhir* or 'evident' meaning of the religious source texts. But the four main branches of Sunni jurisprudence allowed legal scholars to hand down rulings by extrapolating from what they could find in these source texts (Hallaq, 1997; Hallaq, 2005). To give the most famous example, wine is explicitly forbidden, so other alcoholic beverages are taken to be forbidden also, by 'analogy (*qiyās*)'.

This kind of reasoning was often called *ijtihād*, literally 'exerting oneself' to arrive at a considered judgment. In cases where a question is not straightforwardly settled by the religious source texts, the only alternative to *ijtihād* is *taqlīd*. Rather than working out such a judgment for oneself, one follows the reasoning offered by someone else. This might be, for example, one of the authoritative jurists who founded the aforementioned legal schools, or later jurisprudents working within one's school tradition. For this reason we can actually think about the use of *taqlīd* as being analogous to the legal concept of precedent (Jackson, 1996). A court may for instance hand down ten years punishment for a given crime simply because this is the amount that was given in the past, without giving much if any thought to the reasons why ten years are neither too few nor too many. But actually qualified jurists were not supposed to just follow these school founders by blindly repeating their judgments. That would be potentially dangerous, after all: if one does not understand the rationale for a previous ruling one might re-apply it in a situation where it is not relevant. Instead, jurists were encouraged to understand the 'rationale' or 'proof' (*ḥujja*) for the ruling.

There were degrees of independence here. The extremes would be pure *ijtihād*, which is figuring something out completely on your own, and pure *taqlīd*, which is taking the word of a legal authority without knowing why that authority decided as they did. A simple case might be someone consulting a judge about whether it is all right to snort cocaine, and simply accepting the answer 'no' without getting into the rationale for this answer, namely that it is intoxicating, and thus analogous to wine. This is *qubūl qawl bi-lā ḥujja*, 'accepting a position without any rationale'. Between the two extremes, one might make sure to understand the rationale by which a jurist made their decision. Or, one might make an effort to reach one's own decisions, but building on the precedent of one's chosen legal tradition. This was called '*ijtihād* within a school (*ijtihād fī l-madhhab*)' or 'affiliated *ijtihād* (*ijtihād muntasib*)'. It should also be noted that, while these points all come from the Sunni legal tradition, things were not that different in Shiite Islam, with the exception that the religious source texts are considerably expanded, with the Qurʾān and *ḥadīth* being supplemented by the teachings of the Shiite Imams.

There is some historical debate over the question of how much independence was allowed to jurists, and whether, as it is sometimes put, the 'gate of *ijtihād*' was ultimately closed, with legal theory giving way to strict following of precedent (Hallaq, 1984). But for our purposes it is sufficient to know that in the medieval period, legal scholars often reserved to themselves the right to engage in *ijtihād*. For the common run of people, those the Greeks called *hoi polloi*, the recommendation was to stick to *taqlīd* in order to avoid unwittingly violating God's law. As one legal theorist put it, 'it is incumbent on the ordinary person (*ʿāmmī*) to act by *taqlīd* if he is incapable of *ijtihād*' (Calder, 1989, p. 61).

Now, one thing that the medieval Christian and Islamic worlds had in common is that there was quite a bit of overlap between expertise in law and expertise in theology. As a result, the contrast between *ijtihād* and *taqlīd* also came to be applied to theological doctrines and religious belief in general. One might, for instance, believe in God simply because one was raised in a Muslim family; but one might also believe in Him because one was in a position to offer a proof (again, *ḥujja*) of His existence. In theology as in law, the scholarly elite prided themselves on avoiding *taqlīd*. As members of the *ʿulamāʾ*, the scholars could explain all their religious beliefs by offering their own rational argumentation and competent interpretation of the Scripture. Common folk were assumed to be incapable of this, whether because they lacked opportunity or lacked talent. A telling remark on this point comes from the theologian al-Isfarāʾīnī (d.1027), sorting such people into two categories:

> One [category] consists of people who are not wholly lacking in a kind of reasoning, even if it is imperfect in its expression and its grounding. Such people are truly believers and in the proper sense, know (*ʿārif*). The other [category] consists of people who are completely unenlightened in this respect and have no real knowledge, rather, since they believe through *taqlīd*, their belief lacks integrity and not one of them is free of uncertainty and doubt. (trans. Frank, 1989, p. 45)

Some theologians went even further, adopting not only a condescending tone towards people of pure *taqlīd*, but going so far as to say that for core religious beliefs every Muslim had a responsibility to gain at least a modest level of independent understanding. It is reported that in one West African community, for instance, ordinary Muslims were questioned philosophically by the scholars about the basis of their belief in the oneness of God (Van Dalen, 2016, p. 142). Usually though, *taqlīd* was felt to be appropriate for the simple believer, and inappropriate for the scholars.

Which raises the question, what is so bad about *taqlīd*? After all, if I am a Muslim wondering whether I can drink whiskey, it shouldn't matter whether I figure out that it is forbidden on my own, or am told it is forbidden by a legal scholar. The main thing is that I get the right answer, so that I may fulfill my religious obligations. Does *ijitihād* have anything to recommend it, apart from being the privilege of an elite class? One concern might be that figuring out one's religious obligations for oneself is itself a religious obligation, at least for those who are capable of it. Some Muslim theologians taught the following: 'whoever is capable of knowledge of God becomes an unbeliever if he does not apply knowledge to know God, regardless of whether he abandons knowledge to pursue *taqlīd*, doubt, conjecture, or ignorance' (trans. El Omari 2016, pp. 152–53). The thinking seems to be that if one has the capacity to reflect for oneself, then one would be failing to use this God-given gift by depending on the advice of others. To engage in *taqlīd* would be a kind of culpable laziness.

This view was echoed by figures working within the tradition of Aristotelian philosophy. Which is in a sense unsurprising, since Aristotle's depiction of the best or 'happy' life for humans revolves around the notion of making full use of one's inborn capacities. In particular, the power of reason is distinctive to human beings, and so being an excellent human demands making excellent use of reason. In the practical sphere this would consist in exercising reason to make virtuous choices. In the theoretical sphere, it would involve achieving full-blown scientific understanding. In neither case would it be sufficient to blindly follow the lead of other people. In the Islamic world, the Aristotelian philosopher who made this point most emphatically was Ibn Rushd, usually known under his Latinized name 'Averroes' (d.1198). He wrote that 'the name "human" is predicated equivocally of a human being who is perfected by a speculative science and of one who is not perfected by it or who does not have aptitude to be perfected by it' (Adamson, 2018, p. 93). A human who does not achieve scientific understanding is not a 'human' in the full and proper sense, just as an eye that cannot see is not an 'eye' in the full and proper sense, because it fails to carry out its natural function.

Averroes thought that this same message could be taken from the Qurʾān. His most widely-read work, *The Decisive Treatise* (*Faṣl al-maqāl*), begins with a series of scriptural quotations intended to establish that there is a religious *obligation* to engage in philosophical inquiry (trans. in Hourani, 1976). For example, 'reflect, you who have vision', and 'have they not reflected upon the kingdoms of heaven and earth, and whatever God has created?' (Qurʾān 59:2, 7:185). Now, even Averroes did not think that every Muslim has the responsibility to become versed in philosophy. But he did think that those who are *capable* of it are obligated to do so. As a faithful Aristotelian, he thought the guidelines to be followed here were laid out in Aristotle's logical writings, especially the *Posterior Analytics*, which offers an account of scientific, demonstrative understanding. Among the criteria such understanding must fulfill are the requirement to grasp the *reason* or *explanation* why things are true. (More technically: a demonstrative argument involves connecting two terms through an explanatory 'middle' term.) Having a demonstrative argument is the philosopher's analogue – or Averroes would have said, the philosopher's superior version – of the 'rationale' invoked in Islamic law and 'proof' offered in Islamic theology.

Just like the jurist and the theologian, then, the Averroist philosopher is a member of a self-appointed elite that is distinguished by the use of independent reasoning. And Averroes was certainly no less elitist than the jurists and theologians. He routinely contrasted 'the scholars (*al-ʿulamāʾ*)' to 'the many (*al-jumhūr*)' and in the *Decisive Treatise* explained that demonstrative arguments are for the former, since only they can understand such arguments. In a clear hint that he took this conception of elite reflection from the legal tradition, he even compared independent philosophical inquiry to the use of *ijtihād* in jurisprudence. 'The many', by contrast, should not even attempt to pursue such inquiry. It will only confuse them to be confronted with demonstrative discourse, which may even lead them into unbelief. An example might be that exposing common folk to proofs of God's incorporeality could convince them that God does not exist at all, if they cannot imagine a being with no body.

So when approaching these people – who will of course be the vast majority – one should instead use non-demonstrative discourse. This might be merely 'dialectical' argumentation, which draws on commonly accepted premises rather than establishing a chain of argument on the grounds of absolutely certain first principles, or 'rhetorical' discourse, which aims at mere persuasion. To believe that something is true because of dialectical or rhetorical discourse would be *taqlīd*, which from Averroes' point of view is entirely appropriate for the common believer. He was for the most part rather disdainful towards the theologians, whose vaunted proofs he thought were at best dialectical arguments, at worst just bogus sophistries. But he would have agreed with the Muʿtazilite theologian al-Kaʿbī (d. 931), who said that some people are 'obligated to apply *taqlīd* and conjecture: these are the laypeople (*al-ʿawāmm*), the slaves, and many women' (El Omari 2016, p. 159).

So this is one reason to avoid *taqlīd*: because if one has the talent and opportunity to do better by engaging in independent reasoning, then one also has the obligation to do so. But there is another reason. If I believe something merely on the basis of authority, then my belief will only be as reliable as the authority I have chosen. But how do I know that this authority is worth following? It could be that they are teaching me falsehoods. After all, I have not reflected for myself as to whether their claims are true, so how can I rule this out? In fact, even if what they have told me to believe is true, then it looks like I have wound up with a true belief only by luck. For a concrete example, we can consider a famous saying ascribed to the Prophet: 'every child is born in the innate condition (*fiṭra*) but his parents make him a Jew, Christian, or Magian'. From the Muslim point of view, Christian children are brought up believing falsehoods, such as that Christ was the incarnation of God or that God is a Trinity. If they had been more fortunate, they would have been born into Muslim families and thus would have had true instead of false beliefs. From the Christian point of view, of course, things are the other way around: Muslim children are unfortunate enough to be brought up thinking that Christ was not God and that Muḥammad was a genuine Prophet. But either way, the upshot is disconcerting.

In matters of such importance, it seems inadequate simply to hope that we've gotten lucky.

The problem is still with us, and discussed by philosophers of religion under the heading of 'religious pluralism'. Once you learn that there are believers in other religions (and people with no religious belief at all), how can you be satisfied with simply adopting the faith into which you happen to have been born? Actually, this worry about *taqlīd* would still arise even if there were no diversity of opinion. Even if every human on earth believes something, that doesn't prove it is true. What would prove it true would be, well, proof: and to have a proof is precisely not to believe by *taqlīd*. Still, we are more likely to worry about luck and unluck in belief where we are confronted by pluralism, that is, where there is observable difference of opinion. And the problem of specifically religious pluralism was certainly noticed by medieval philosophers. Here we might once again make mention of Ramón Llull, a Christian who grew up among Muslims on his native island of Majorca. He wrote a dialogue showing how his 'Art' could resolve disagreement between a Jew, a Muslim, and a Christian (trans. in Bonner, 1993). And Llull was, of course, only one of many medieval philosophers who believed that rational argument could show the viability of their favored Abrahamic religion and establish the incoherence of the rival faiths.

But I'd like to follow this line of thought in a work by someone who, famously, did not consider himself a 'philosopher (*faylasūf*)', at least in the sense this word carried in medieval Arabic. This was al-Ghazālī (d. 1111), who remains famous as a theologian and critic of Aristotelian 'philosophy (*falsafa*)' in the version put forward by Ibn Sīnā (Avicenna, d. 1037). He has this reputation on the basis of his *Incoherence of the Philosophers* (*Tahāfut al-falāsifa*, trans. Marmura, 1997), where he aimed many criticisms at Avicenna and other philosophers. Among those criticisms was the charge that they engaged in *taqlīd*, because they blindly followed authorities like Aristotle (Griffel, 2005). If you know anything about Avicenna you may find this accusation strange, or even risible. For in fact, Avicenna was distinguished by his innovative and occasionally even irreverent handling of Aristotelian philosophy, which he quite deliberately and explicitly reworked so as to produce a new and distinctive system (Gutas, 1988). But what we have seen so far in this paper may help explain why al-Ghazālī attacked Avicenna in these terms. The label of *taqlīd* was chosen to sting, since philosophers no less than jurists and theologians prided themselves on their independence of mind. It's what all members of the intellectual elite in the Islamic world had in common (so much for the notion that all medieval thinkers were happy to present themselves as being bound by authority and unoriginal).

For al-Ghazālī's own approach to authority and its use, we'll be better served by turning to another text, his intellectual autobiography the *Deliverer from Error* (*Munqidh min al-dalāl*, trans. in Watt 2000; I quote in my own translations from the edition in Jabre, 1969). In the opening section of this work, al-Ghazālī explains the background to a skeptical crisis he endured, when he came to think that none of his beliefs were absolutely certain. Beliefs grounded in sensation need sometimes to be corrected by reason. So how can we guarantee that reason itself stands in no need of correction, or validation, by a higher epistemic court of appeal (Jabre, 1969, p. 13)? The reason why this realization hit al-Ghazālī so hard is that he had made it his life's goal to achieve certainty, never contenting himself with beliefs formed through *taqlīd*:

> Thirst for grasping the true natures of things was a habit and practice of mine from early on in my life, an inborn and innate tendency (*gharīza wa-fiṭra*) given by God in my very nature, not chosen or contrived. So as I neared maturity the bonds of *taqlīd* weakened for me and I was emancipated from inherited beliefs. For I saw that young Christians always grew up to accept Christianity and young Jews to accept Judaism, while young Muslims always grew up to accept Islam. And I heard the *ḥadīth* related of the prophet, 'every child is born in the innate condition (*fiṭra*) but his parents make him a Jew, Christian, or Magian' (Jabre, 1969, pp. 10–11).

'Inherited beliefs' were not enough for the young al-Ghazālī, because he realized that religious communities who disagree strongly with one another are all following such inherited beliefs. In forming one's religious convictions, it is surely not enough to hope that one was lucky enough to be born into the right family. Thus he quotes exactly the aforementioned *ḥadīth*, drawing from it the lesson that *taqlīd* exposes one to the vagaries of epistemic luck.

Al-Ghazālī's struggle to overcome skepticism comes in several stages, which we do not need to discuss in detail here. In part his escape is thanks to a 'light cast into his breast' by God, which gives him a powerful subjective sense of certainty as concerns certain self-evident principles, like basic truths of logic and mathematics. But he does not try to ground his belief in Islam in such a feeling of certainty, perhaps because a 'Jew, Christian, or Magian' could do the same, again leaving al-Ghazālī on an epistemic par with those whose beliefs he considers false. Actually, it seems that al-Ghazālī could have made that move, simply saying that he feels certain he is right in his religious belief, and actually *is* right. Members of other religions might feel equally certain, but there would be a crucial difference: their beliefs happen to be wrong. This would satisfy some philosophers. For example Alvin Plantinga's 'reformed epistemology' allows the Christian to take belief in God as 'properly basic', which means the Christian can rationally commit to it without further argument or justification, even while recognizing that the belief is not basic for atheists. But such expedients do not seem to attract al-Ghazālī. He wants his beliefs to attain a standard of certainty such that *all* reasonable people would adopt them, if they were to perform due epistemic dilgence.

What al-Ghazālī needs, then, is a means of establishing with *certainty* that Muḥammad's prophecy was genuine, since the truth of Islam turns on this claim. A common way to do this would have been to appeal to miraculous feats performed by the prophet. In Islam, emphasis is placed on the Qurʾān itself, which is said to be 'inimitable' by normal human means (for the origins of this idea in Islamic theology see Martin, 1980). Indeed this is traditionally recognized as Muḥammad's *only* miracle. But again, this is a game that can be played by representatives of other Abhramic faiths. For instance Judah Hallevi's dialogue *Kuzari* shows a king being converted to Judaism on the strength of the well-attested miracles in Jewish history (for comparison between Hallevi and al-Ghazālī see Baneth, 1981; Kogan, 2002). Perhaps in part for this reason, al-Ghazālī rejects apparent miracles as insufficient grounds for accepting the veracity of a prophet. What seems to be a God-given miracle could be a trick worked by human means.

Instead, he proposes the following:

> If you are in doubt about whether a certain person is a prophet or not, certainty can be had only through knowledge of what he is like, either by personal observation or reports and testimony. If you have an understanding of medicine and jurisprudence, you can recognize jurists and doctors by observing what they are like, and listening to what they had to say, even if you haven't observed them. So you have no difficulty recognizing that al-Shāfiʿī was a jurist or Galen a doctor, this being knowledge of what is in fact the case and not a matter of *taqlīd* shown to another person. Rather, since you know something of jurisprudence and medicine, and you have perused their books and treatises, you have arrived at necessary knowledge about what they are like.

> Likewise, once you grasp the meaning of prophecy and then investigate the Quran and [*ḥadīth*] reports extensively, you arrive at necessary knowledge that [Muḥammad] is at the highest degree of prophecy. (Jabre, 1969, p. 43)

This passage offers a middle path between the blind obedience of *taqlīd* and the do-it-yourself ambitions of *ijtihād* and philosophical proof. Al-Ghazālī recommends obedience that is *not* blind, the acceptance of authority on good grounds. Just as one could verify that someone is a doctor by considering 'what he is like (*aḥwāluhu*)', so too we should convince ourselves that someone is a prophet by seeing the way he conducts himself, or reading about him. What we're looking for is not miracles, but wisdom, virtue, and holiness. This then would be al-Ghazālī's answer to the problem of religious pluralism: any fair-minded person who reads deeply about the life of Muḥammad will come away from this with the conviction that this man, surely, was a genuine Prophet, and therefore that Islam is the true faith.

While al-Ghazālī does not say quite as much about this process as we might wish, it is clear that the process is a fairly demanding one. As he says here regarding jurisprudence and medicine, you need to have 'perused the books and treatises' of these specialists. His idea is not, though, that you need to have transformed yourself into one of the specialists. Rather, the goal is to be in a position to verify the expertise of the genuine specialist without having such expertise oneself. We will only be in such a position once we have 'necessary knowledge' concerning the reliability of the specialist, or prophet. This is a term of art in Islamic theology: knowledge is 'necessary (*ḍarūrī*)' or 'immediate (*badīhī*)' if it leaves no room for doubt, as happens with first principles of reasoning and the immediate deliverances of sense-perception (Abrahamov, 1993). Some theologians say that necessary knowledge comes in part through the 'innate condition (*fiṭra*)', mentioned in that same Prophetic report about people born into different faiths.

Whatever its source, 'necessary knowledge' can provide the basis for further, 'acquired (*muktasab*)' knowledge, which stands in need of proof and is always less certain than necessary knowledge. For example speculative argumentation, in theology or any other field of science, would yield conclusions that have the status of acquired, not necessary, knowledge. Here we might return to the case of mathematics. When al-Ghazālī says that he had subjective certainty concerning mathematical truths, he means basic ones that are immediately obvious and thus constitute 'necessary knowledge', like 'ten is greater than three'. The conclusion of a complex mathematical proof would, by contrast, qualify as 'acquired' knowledge even if it takes its starting point from premises that are known necessarily. Al-Ghazālī's account of the verification of prophecy and expert knowledge has precisely this structure. We begin by familiarizing ourselves enough with the field of expertise that we are sure (that is, have 'necessary knowledge') who is an expert and who is not. Now we find an expert, and take their advice. This is not *taqlīd*, since that would be following an authority uncritically. But neither is it full-blown *ijtihād*, the pure use of independent judgment. Here, we do follow an authority figure, but do so after adopting a critical frame of mind and testing the credentials of that authority.

In the legal context that spawned the concept of *taqlīd*, and serves as one of al-Ghazālī's main examples, this approach might be contrasted to the aforementioned practice of 'affiliated *ijtihād*'. As we saw, that involved accepting the principles of a given legal school and then working out one's own legal judgments within those parameters. What al-Ghazālī describes has the reverse structure. Instead of taking one's starting points from an authority and working independently from there, he recommends using independent thought at the stage of choosing one's authorities, but thereafter depending on those authorities. In a juridical context this could mean, for instance, working out which of the founding legal scholars to follow, then following him. (It is no coincidence that in our key passage, al-Ghazālī mentions verifying al-Shāfiʿī's (d.820) expertise in law, since al-Ghazālī was himself a jurist of the Shāfiʿite school.)

This, I think, is an attractive answer to the question of how we should use authority. We can recognize the basic policy as one we use all the time, as when – to take al-Ghazālī's other example – we find a doctor we trust and then follow their advice. But remember that al-Ghazālī sets a fairly high bar when it comes to bestowing one's trust upon an expert. It's not good enough to choose a lawyer because they are wearing a sharp suit and carrying a briefcase, or a doctor because of their reassuring aura. Rather, you need to know something of law and medicine yourself in order to make an informed choice. In a modern context, al-Ghazālī might have in mind the extent of expertise you would build up over the course of taking an undergraduate degree. Your BA in literature doesn't qualify you to write books about Shakespeare, but it will help you verify that a certain Shakespeare scholar you meet at a party really knows their stuff. Of course, we will all still need to engage in *taqlīd* in many spheres of knowledge. You might be pretty good on Shakespeare, but when it comes to particle physics you have to surrender to epistemic luck, because you aren't even in a position to tell expert physicists apart from charlatans, never mind do physics yourself.

Even though al-Ghazālī's proposal comes from the rather special, and for us perhaps unfamiliar, context of a discussion of prophetic veracity, it applies with striking relevance to the problems we face in modern society. We are beset not just by religious pluralism but also disagreement over highly complex problems like climate change, the benefits of international trade agreements, and of course the best way to deal with a global pandemic. The first lesson we should take from al-Ghazālī is to be fairly modest in our pretensions of certainty. If you haven't devoted years of specialized study to climatology, economics, and epidemiology, then with respect to the issues just mentioned you are better off following the authoritative pronouncements of others than coming to your own, necessarily ill-informed, view. After all, none of us have time to become experts in all these fields. But this does not mean we are doomed to follow authority *uncritically*. Our goal should be to 'weaken the bonds of *taqlīd*', as al-Ghazālī put it. In other words, we should work at improving our ability to recognize the expertise of other people, so that we may responsibly give those people our credence. This policy, with its combination of humility and demandingness, might be medieval in inspiration, but it remains fit for purpose in today's world of widespread uncertainty.

LMU Munich
Peter.Adamson@lrz.uni-muenchen.de

References

Binyamin Abrahamov, 'Necessary Knowledge in Islamic Theology', *British Journal of Middle Eastern Studies* 20 (1993), 20–32.

Peter Adamson, 'Human and Animal Nature in the Philosophy of the Islamic World', in Peter Adamson and G. Fay Edwards (eds), *Animals: a History* (New York: Oxford University Press, 2018), 90–113.

David H. Baneth 'Judah Hallevi and al-Ghazali', in A. Jospe (ed.), *Studies in Jewish Thought* (Detroit: 1981), 181–99

Anthony Bonner (trans.), *Doctor Illuminatus: a Ramon Llull Reader* (Princeton: Princeton University Press, 1993).

Norman Calder, 'Doubt and Prerogative: the Emergence of an Imāmī Shīʿī Theory of *Ijtihād*', *Studia Islamica* 70 (1989), 57–78.

Racha El Omari, *The Theology of Abū l-Qāsim al-Balkhī/al-Kaʿbī (d.319/931)* (Leiden: Brill, 2016).

Ahmed El Shamsy, 'Rethinking *Taqlīd* in the Early Shāfiʿī School', *Journal of the American Oriental Society* 128 (2008), 1–23.

Alexander Fidora (ed.), *Raimundus Lullus: An Introduction to His Life, Works and Thought* (Turnhout: Brepols, 2008).

Richard M. Frank, 'Knowledge and *Taqlīd*: the Foundations of Religious Belief in Classical Ashʿarism', *Journal of the American Oriental Society* 109 (1989), 37–62.

Stephen Greenblatt, *The Swerve: How the World Became Modern* (New York: Norton, 2011).

Frank Griffel, '*Taqlīd* of the Philosophers: al-Ghazālī's Initial Accusation in the *Tahāfut*', in *Ideas, Images, and Methods of Portrayal: Insights Into Classical Arabic Literature and Islam*, ed. Sebastian Günther (Leiden: Brill, 2005), 273–96.

Dimitri Gutas, *Avicenna and the Aristotelian Tradition*: *Introduction to Reading Avicenna's Philosophical Works* (Leiden: Brill, 1988).

Jeremiah Hackett, '*Scientia experimentalis*: from Robert Grossteste to Roger Bacon', in James McEvoy (ed.), *Robert Grosseteste: New Perspectives on his Thought and Scholarship* (Dordrecht: Brepols, 1995), 89–120.

Wael B. Hallaq, 'Was the Gate of *Ijtihād* Closed?', *International Journal of Middle East Studies* 16 (1984), 3–41.

Wael B. Hallaq, *A History of Islamic Legal Theories* (Cambridge: Cambridge University Press, 1997).

Wael B. Hallaq, *The Origins and Evolution of Islamic Law* (Cambridge: Cambridge University Press, 2005).

George Hourani (trans.), *Averroes: On the Harmony of Religion and Philosophy* (London: Luzac, 1976).

Ahmed Fekry Ibrahim, 'Rethinking the *Taqlīd–ijtihād* Dichotomy: A Conceptual-Historical Approach', *Journal of the American Oriental Society*, 136 (2016), 285–303.

Farid Jabre (ed. and trans.), *Al-Ghazālī: al-Munqidh min al-dalāl* (*Erreur et Déliverance*) (Beirut: Commission Libanaise pour la Traduction des Chefs d'Oeuvre, 1969).

Sherman A. Jackson, '*Taqlīd,* Legal Scaffolding and the Scope of Legal Injunctions in Post-Formative Theory: *Muṭlaq* and *ʿāmm* in the Jurisprudence of Shihāb al-Dīn al-Qarāfī', *Islamic Law and Society*, 3 (1996), 165–92.

C.L. Joost-Gaugier, *Pythagoras and Renaissance Europe: Finding Heaven* (Cambridge: Cambridge University Press, 2009).

Barry Kogan, 'Al-Ghazali and Hallevi on Philosophy and the Philosophers', in *Medieval Philosophy and the Classic Tradition in Islam, Judaism and Christianity*, ed. J. Inglis (Richmond UK: 2002), 64–80.

David Lines, 'Aristotle's Ethics in the Renaissance', in Jon Miller (ed.), *The Reception of Aristotle's Ethics* (Cambridge: Cambridge University Press, 2012), 171–93.

Michael E. Marmura (trans.), *Al-Ghazālī: The Incoherence of the Philosophers* (Provo: Brigham Young University Press, 1997).

Richard C. Martin, 'The Role of the Basrah Muʿtazilah in Formulating the Doctrine of the Apologetic Miracle', *Journal of Near Eastern Studies* 39 (1980) 175–89.

Betty Radice and Michael T. Clanchy (trans.), *The Letters of Abelard and Heloise* (London: Penguin, 2003).

Paul Lawrence Rose, *The Italian Renaissance of Mathematics: Studies on Humanists and Mathematicians from Petrarch to Galileo* (Geneva: Droz, 1975).

Charles B. Schmitt, *Aristotle and the Renaissance* (Cambridge MA: Harvard University Press, 1983).

Tina Stiefel, 'The Heresy of Science: a Twelfth-Century Conceptual Revolution', *Isis* 68 (1977), 346–62.

Michele Trizio, 'From Anna Komnene to Dante: The Byzantine Roots of Western Debates on Aristotle's *Nicomachean Ethics*', in Jan M. Ziolkowski (ed.), *Dante and the Greeks* (Washington DC: Dumbarton Oaks, 2014), 105–140.

Dorrit van Dalen, *Doubt, Scholarship and Society in 17th-Century Central Sudanic Africa* (Leiden: Brill, 2016).

W. Montgomery Watt (trans.), *The Faith and Practice of al-Ghazālī* (London: Oneworld, 2000).

T. Richard Witmer (trans.), *Girolamo Cardano: Ars Magna or the Rules of Algebra* (New York: Dover, 1993).

Why Do Scientists Lie?

LIAM KOFI BRIGHT

Abstract
It's natural to think of scientists as truth seekers, people driven by an intense curiosity to understand the natural world. Yet this picture of scientists and scientific inquiry sits uncomfortably with the reality and prevalence of scientific fraud. If one wants to get at the truth about nature, why lie? Won't that just set inquiry back, as people pursue false leads? To understand why this occurs – and what can be done about it – we need to understand the social structures scientists work within, and how some of the institutions which enable science to be such a successful endeavour all things considered, also abet and encourage fraud.

Perhaps you have heard of Brian Wansink, or if not the man himself then certainly his results. Wansink was a nutritional scientist at Cornell, who specialised in the psychology of eating. He had authored 'studies suggesting people who grocery shop hungry buy more calories; that preordering lunch can help you choose healthier food; and that serving people out of large bowls encourage them to serve themselves larger portions', and on the basis of his expertise on these phenomena had been feted by the press and called to assist Google and the US Army run programmes designed to encourage healthy eating[1].The problem, however, was that he had not in fact produced evidence for these claims. On some occasions he had misreported his own data – that is to say, lied about what he had found. And on other occasions had more or less tortured his data with no regard to proper statistical method so as to give him something, anything, to publish. He knowingly entered falsehoods into the information stream of science, which is to say – he committed fraud (Bright, 2017 p. 291).

Brian Wansink misled scientific inquiry. An academic investigating Wansink's misconduct found that to the best of his knowledge (as of the 6th of April 2017) 'there are currently 42 publications from Wansink which are alleged to contain minor to very serious issues, which have been cited over 3,700 times, are published in over 25 different journals, and in eight books, spanning over 20

[1] https://www.vox.com/science-and-health/2018/9/19/17879102/brian-wansink-cornell-food-brand-lab-retractions-jama

doi:10.1017/S1358246121000102

years of research'.[2] When one considers that academic papers are typically reviewed by multiple scientists before publication, and many academics will reorient their research programmes to respond to well cited previously published literature, and the efforts of scientists to then uncover Wansink's misconduct – this is countless hours of time and effort from PhD researchers who could be doing more valuable things. And it is not just this opportunity cost to deplore – the practical interventions founded on Wansink's research were not free! For instance, the US government implemented a policy to redesign school cafeterias based on Wansink's 'findings' that cost nearly $20 million.[3] Scientific fraud can have serious consequences, and it's worth grappling with.

Philosophers have a bad habit of only concerning themselves with science done well, but when you think about it there is something puzzling about scientific fraud. Why bother to carry out scientific research if you are just going to lie about your results? Shouldn't scientists want to know what's true, and won't lying get in the way of that?

It can all seem more puzzling when one thinks about the sort of person who becomes an academic scientist. The average starting salary for a PhD physicist in the USA is $88,670[4], whereas someone with their skills has the option of going into the finance industry wherein 'entry-level quants with PhDs from top universities [may earn] base salaries as high as $125k and hedge funds offer up to $175k base salary'[5]. This is to say, to become an academic physicist it seems one must actively reject base pecuniary motives when making one's life choices. One might naturally think that therefore scientists are instead motivated by the sort of truth-seeking curiosity that makes fraud such a puzzle. Indeed, the scientific attitude has been defined as one of searching for truth and being willing to follow the evidence (Douglas, 2014; McIntyre, 2019). Yet the physics world has seen its share of fraud scandals all the same (for an engrossing deep dive into one such story see Reich, 2009). To state plainly the philosophical question that shall motivate us in the rest of this essay: what gives?

Well, sometimes the answer is clear enough. There are large industries quite uninterested in what is true except so far as it relates to their

[2] https://arstechnica.com/science/2017/04/the-peer-reviewed-saga-of-mindless-eating-mindless-research-is-bad-too/

[3] https://www.nytimes.com/2018/09/29/sunday-review/cornell-food-scientist-wansink-misconduct.html

[4] https://www.careerexplorer.com/careers/physicist/salary/

[5] https://www.efinancialcareers.com/news/2017/11/quant-trader-pay-phd-e-traders-automated-trading-salaries

ability to sell certain products. In some cases their interests might be harmed if the truth about those products were known. Prominent examples have been cigarette companies seeking to undermine public confidence in results showing that smoking caused cancer, or coal and oil companies seeking to discredit research demonstrating the reality and harms of human caused climate change (Oreskes & Conway, 2011). These industries sometimes pay scientists to lie which can evidently have pernicious effects (Holman & Bruner, 2015), and they have other more subtle and nefarious means of promoting untruth in science (Weatherall *et al,* 2020). The extent to which capitalist allocation of scientific resources is consistent with scientific honesty is dubious at best, and perhaps this whole way of arranging things needs to be rethought. But let us set aside these cases of fraud in profit-seeking-industry science. While the case of Wansink – academic at Cornell but also consultant at Google – shows that there is no strict division between academia and industry, on the whole commercial science comes with its own set of philosophical and ethical concerns (Pinto, 2015). Sufficient unto the day are the problems of academic science.

I said before that one might naturally think that if scientists are not in it for the money then they do what they do for curiosity's sake. When a philosopher says 'one might naturally think' something this is a prelude to telling you why it would be quite mistaken to do as much. And indeed the most common explanation for scientific fraud relies on a third option we haven't considered yet for what might motivate working scientists. Over the course of the twentieth century sociologists, historians, and economists collectively developed a theory of scientific motivation that they thought accounted for the prevalence of fraud. Coming into the twenty first century philosophers have started getting in on the act too, and we now have a fairly robust received view about why fraud occurs – and one which is suggestive of what may be done to stop it. Our first task shall thus be to spell out this theory, the theory of the credit economy of science, and credit motivated fraud.

Being a philosopher, I can't help but relate everything back to Plato. It will all be relevant in a moment, I promise! Plato famously divided the soul into three parts. There was the acquisitive element of the soul, epithumia, concerned with material comfort and the pleasures of the body. There was the spirited element of the soul, thumos, concerned with honour and esteem. And there was reason, nous, concerned with finding truth and the creation of harmony. Consequently, in his Republic, Plato suggested there were to be three castes of citizen in the ideal city corresponding to these elements of the soul. There was the many, primarily motivated by their acquisitive souls, carrying out the manual labour society needs to reproduce itself. The guardians, soldiers who are primarily governed by the sense of honour and esteem, and who are charged with protecting the city and its laws. And the philosophers, rulers, those elite few primarily moved by their sense of reason, naturally put in charge of the affairs of the city. One suspects that with this taxonomy in mind Plato would therefore have immediately seen the trick behind that 'one might naturally think' – in setting aside the idea that scientists are an acquisitive bunch, we moved straight to the hypothesis that they were truth seekers, something like the reason governed philosopher rulers. This then made fraud puzzling. But we missed a taxon! Between epithumia and nous there is a third option, thumos. Might the scientists be more akin to the guardians, governed by thumos above all?

So sociologists of science tell us! Starting with the pioneering work of Robert Merton in the 1960s (Merton, 1968; 1969) it has become increasingly common to talk of scientists as 'credit seekers'. That is to say, people who seek the honour, esteem, glory, of being well regarded in their field. To be a scientific credit seeker is to be someone who seeks status within a community, the community of peers in a scientific discipline. While there are still puzzles about how precisely to understand what counts as the relevant credit-conferring community (c.f. Lee, 2018), there is broad consensus that roughly put this is something that many scientists are in fact driven by. This can be at the level of individual motivation – science comes with a steep prestige and status hierarchy (Zuckerman, 1970; Cole & Cole, 1974) and scientists tend to want to climb that hierarchy. But even if they are not personally concerned with this, the way we have institutionally arranged science can essentially mandate acting as if one was such an honour, or credit, seeker.

We hand out resources through grants and prizes, we decide who gets a job and where, we decide which students will be placed with which academics – we do all of these tasks and many more in academia – primarily by deciding how 'impressive' we find candidates (Partha & David, 1994; Stephan, 1996). The informal judgements scientists routinely make about the quality of one another's work, and the potential or intellectual capacity of the scientists doing the work, are not just the stuff of idle gossip, but an essential element of how we in fact allocate the resources necessary to carry out scientific research. Hence even if you do not intrinsically care about your standing in the scientific community, if you want access to the resources necessary to play the game at all, you have to in fact gain scientific acclaim (Latour & Woolger, 1979, ch. 5). Hence everyone must to some extent act as if they are a credit-seeker.

Scientists win credit by establishing priority on new claims (Merton, 1957; Strevens, 2003). What this means is that scientists have to publish an adequate defence of some novel claim in some recognised venue (typically but not always a peer reviewed scientific journal) before anyone else has done so. What counts as 'an adequate defence' of a novel claim will vary from field to field – mathematicians may be required to produce a logically valid proof of a theorem, psychologists experimental support for a generalisation about human behaviour, philosophy professors an argumentative essay defending a key claim[6]. But the point is one needs to be the first to get such a thing out in one of the field-acknowledged venues for placing interesting work. If one does this, it counts to your credit – in the long run, the more interesting people in the field find the claim (or your defence of it) the more credit that accrues from having published it, and in the short run the more prestigious the venue you publish in the more credit is accrued to you (for more on the long-run/short-run credit distinction see Heesen & Bright, 2020, §3.5). Scientists are both intrinsically motivated, and de facto incentivised, to seek credit through establishing priority in this manner.

We are now in a position to state and understand the standard theory of scientific fraud. Scientists want and need credit for new results. To ensure their results are new, i,e, novel enough to have a plausible claim to establishing priority, scientists have to do their work sufficiently quickly that nobody else beats them to the punch (often referred to as being 'scooped' on a claim). And it is here problems arise. First, there are all sorts of points in the typical research process where scientists have relatively unconstrained choices to make about how to proceed, and an unscrupulous actor can mask questionable research practices by strategic choices (Simmons et al, 2011). In such a scenario the need for speed can produce temptations to cut corners and work to a lower standard (Heesen, 2018). This sort of perfidy seems to have been involved in Wansink's case, for instance. Second, even more brazen types of sheer data fabrication can be induced, in order to make results seem stronger and more interesting, sufficiently well supported to be worth publishing, or even just to wholesale invent phenomena (for a classic study of how credit seeking can incentivise this sort of brazen fraud see Broad & Wade,

[6] The inclusion of philosophers on this list is partly to signal that I am using 'scientist' is a very broad, rather old fashioned sense - much of what I say in this article would equally well go for philosophers, and other scholars of the humanities.

1982). Third and finally, the emphasis on novelty disincentives the sort of replication and checking work that would make catching fraudulent or unsupported claims more likely, removing or greatly reducing the threat of punishment that might otherwise deter fraud (Romero, 2016). Even when such checking work does occur, individual responsibility and thus punishment may be nigh impossible to assign (Huebner & Bright, 2020). And the mere fact that something has been shown false does not immediately prevent academics from accruing credit from having published it (LaCroix, et al forthcoming), so detection may not be sufficiently timely to actually discourage fraud if one can benefit from one's ill gotten credit gains in the mean time (Zollman, 2019; Heesen, 2020). The race for credit encourages fraud and generally low epistemic standards, and discourages the sort of work that might catch cheats out.

This analysis of what produces fraud is suggestive of a solution: replace thumos with nous! If the problem with scientists is that their desire for honour and esteem, credit, is tempting them to cut corners and commit fraud, we should try to discourage such glory-seeking behaviour. This can happen through motive modification (advocated in Du Bois, 1898; see Bright, 2018). In this sort of scheme one tries to both filter for scientists who are more concerned with the quest for truth than glory seeking when one looks for junior researchers. And one also engages in a kind of soul crafting (Appiah, 2005, ch.5), using the educational and cultural institutions of science to mould researchers' desires and sense of identity to be focussed much more on truth-seeking than worldly acclaim. This should also be paired with institutional redesign, so that people are not forced to become de facto credit seekers (Nosek et al, 2012), and replication and checking work is properly encouraged (Bruner, 2013; Romero, 2018). Credit-seeking caused fraud – removing credit-seeking is thus removing the cause of fraud. Not, of course, that soul-making and institutional design are trivial or simple matters! But we at least know roughly what we need to do, where we should be heading towards, do we not?

Well, maybe. (This is often the answer to philosophical questions, for what it is worth.) The problem is that I have not told you even half the story so far about thumos in science. We'll set aside the question of whether having scientists driven by nous rather than thumos would actually decrease fraud (on which see Bright, 2017[7]). Let us

[7] For more general concerns about the supposed superiority of nous to thumos see Zollman (2019).

admit that, yes, it is indeed plausible that credit seeking causes scientific fraud. Researchers from multiple different fields using multiple different methods have tended to arrive at that conclusion, it's about as well validated a causal claim as one is going to get in the social sciences. But the problem for this anti-fraud plan is that causing fraud is not all credit-seeking does!

In fact, much of the attention philosophers have given to the credit economy is precisely because at the close of the twentieth century it came to be appreciated that in many interesting ways credit seeking actually promotes surprisingly helpful behaviours for communities whose collective purpose is to seek the truth (Kitcher, 1990; Goldman, 1999, ch.8). I will give a couple of examples here. First, there is the phenomenon of scientific sharing. As has been long noted scientists see themselves as bound by what is called the 'communist norm' (cf Merton, 1942). According to this norm, it is required of scientists that they share their research with others, to make sure that whoever wants to have access to their research results and (in the ideal case) data may do so. Polling finds that scientists continue to support this norm (Anderson, 2010) and the recent growth of what is called the Open Science Movement[8] suggests the communist ideal still has the ability to inspire scientists to take action.

And communism is a good thing indeed! Sharing research speeds up the process of discovery by ensuring that people have access to the ideas and data they need to spur their own research forward. It fosters teamwork and checking of one's own research; by being able to easily compare what you and your lab are seeing with what is being found elsewhere one can correct mistakes and identify points of shared interest or possibilities for mutually advantageous collaboration. Finally, it makes fundamental research available to technologists and engineers, who can produce socially useful innovations by building off scientific work. How then does credit relate to this communist norm?

Well, it has been argued that it is exactly the quest for credit which can produce and sustain the communist norm (Heesen, 2017). Recall how it was that the quest for scientific credit encourages fraud – by encouraging people to rush their work, cut corners to get results before someone else could establish priority. Well, in the good case,

[8] http://www.unesco.org/new/en/communication-and-information/portals-and-platforms/goap/open-science-movement/#:~:text=Open%20Science%20is%20the%20movement,publish%20and%20communicate%20scientific%20knowledge.

the very same thumos which drives such things is also driving scientists to get their work out there and share it as soon as possible. To take a very famous example, Darwin apparently had evidence for his groundbreaking theories long before he published them. Historians debate precisely why he sat on the results so long (Van Wyhe, 2007), but it is evident that the risk of being scooped by the evolutionary theorising of Alfred Wallace played at least some role in prompting him to action. He didn't want to lose out on the possibility of gaining credit for his hard work, and this helped motivate him to get round to actually publishing his theory. Clearly we want such work to be shared for the good of science! And the nice thing about the credit motive given the priority rule is that it ensures that scientists have every reason to want other people to see what they have got as soon as it is presentable so as to gain the credit reward. What is more, they should want this work to be as widely accessible as possible so no one may be in any doubt as to who deserves priority, and have as wide an audience as possible may credit them with the discovery. If this is right then it is not just credit seeking in general, but the exact feature of credit seeking which brings about fraud which is at the same time responsible for this benefit!

For another example, consider the benefits of scientific pluralism. In general, we do not want every scientist to address the same problems via the same methods (Zollman, 2010). We do, of course, want some replication and double checking, and it is a problem that the credit incentive does not lead to enough such work. But we don't want everybody to be just doing the same thing as everyone else. For one thing, this would mean we simply fail to explore possibilities that might be fruitful if tapped for new discoveries. For another thing, this can mean errors go undetected – for the best way to expose some systematic flaw with a given scientific method is to show that approaching the same topic from a different angle consistently leads to divergent results. When we find that we tend to spend some examining our methods, and it is then that problems are uncovered and addressed. To take an example familiar from the lives of everyone on earth at the time I publish this, it is a very good thing indeed that multiple lines of inquiry were tried out simultaneously in developing vaccines for COVID-19. Because of this we have different vaccines which can act as an insurance against the possible failures of the others, and which may have different benefits for different populations. This is not unique to vaccines, but reflective of the aforementioned general features of science. So for science to function properly we need scientists to spread out in logical space, to explore various possible theories that might account for the data, and various possible methods for testing claims and generating and analysing data.

But this variety does not come easy! Indeed, from a certain angle, it can look rather puzzling for scientists to adopt different methods to address the same problems. If scientists all wanted to get at the truth, and were sharing their information about how effective various methods are, shouldn't they all use whatever is communally agreed to be the most effective truth-seeking method? Likewise and for similar reasons, should they not analyse data in light of what is communally agreed to be the most plausible theory? It is credit seeking that can help us avoid this rush to methodological conformism.

For credit can encourage scientists to adopt different methods or seek out novel problems (Kitcher, 1990; Zollman, 2018). For a junior scientist approaching a new problem, they may be well aware that the field validated methods and theories offer the most promising method of acquiring the truth on a given question. However, if they take the path more travelled they shall find themselves working in the wake of all the best minds of the previous generation, trying to say something novel where they have not. No easy task! Eventually it is better to take your chance on a perhaps less reliable or less well validated method – it may at least allow you to say something novel, and in this way gain priority on a claim, even if ultimately it is more likely to turn out to be mistaken in the long run. At the communal level, ensuring there is a regular supply of such people trying out new things (even if, individually, it often ends up in failure) is how science keeps itself fresh and avoids the stagnant conformity mooted above. It is the pursuit of credit in the scientific community that presently provides an avenue for such diversity to be incentivised.

We are now in a position to review. We were puzzled and concerned by the phenomenon of scientific fraud in academia. Puzzled because it did not seem like academic scientists should have the sort of base pecuniary motives that one might suspect lead to fraud. Concerned because, as in the case of Wansink, fraud can have serious intellectual and social consequences if not detected in time. So to explain why this fraud occurred we looked at the theory of the scientific credit economy. We saw that understanding scientists as governed by thumos, as engaged in the spirited pursuit of honour and esteem from their peers via claiming priority on new results, allowed us to explain how it is that scientific fraud occurred. What is even better, it is paired with a natural theory as to how to discourage fraud. But immediately upon realising that, we were forced to concede that thumos has its positive sides too, and can encourage behaviours which are useful for the scientific community's ability to carry out reliable inquiry, and which may be hard to motivate for truth seekers. So where does that leave us, and what should we do?

I don't know. Philosophy is hard.

That may seem somewhat despondent. This is, in part, just a reflection of a sad reality. We do not yet really know what to do, such is the state of our knowledge. Not that we have made no progress on the question. We have a good understanding of various of the effects of credit – we know how it can encourage fraud, and we also know how it encourages pluralism and sharing of one's work. So far so good. What we are sorely lacking, however, is any means of integrating our models or theories in this domain. That is to say, we do not have a sufficiently general and well confirmed theory of science as a social phenomenon that we can confidently predict and assess the overall effects of modifying our culture or institutional structure so as to decrease the significance of scientific thumos. Without that, it is very hard to say with any measure of confidence what we ought do.

Of course there is one bit of advice that would seem to fall out of this: study the problem more! And indeed my hope is that those who read this essay will see in it a call to arms. In the study of scientific fraud we have a puzzle that has it all. The scope and influence of science in contemporary society gives the problem an obvious and immediate practical importance – it's worth putting in the effort to do it right. By exploring the puzzle of scientific fraud we are led to a dilemma wherein it seems that the most natural method of reducing fraud would also reduce the incidence of positive phenomena. Are there other options we should seek, or if not how can we weigh the value of reducing fraud against the disvalue of reducing sharing and methodological diversity? These are deep questions about what is possible and what is desirable for us, touching upon matters in both ethics and epistemology. At all times we must be aware that science is a social enterprise, and to understand both how it operates and the likely effects of any intervention one proposes, one must understand how its cultures and institutions corral, inhibit, and generate possibilities for, the millions of scientists at work today. A keen social sensibility and understanding of social mechanisms is thus necessary here too.

The study of scientific fraud and how it may be reduced thus offers the student of philosophy a chance to practice that integrative skill for which our discipline aspires to be known. It is said that philosophers wish to know how things, in the broadest possible sense, hang together, in the broadest possible sense. I hope to have persuaded you that in considering those places where science is coming apart at the seams, one may gain valuable practice in just this sort of broad perspective taking, and do so in a way that addresses an urgent problem of our times.

It's easy to judge Wansink as a bad apple who cared too much for his career and not enough about the truth. But if the standard theory of fraud is even roughly correct, he was in some sense simply responding to the culture and institutions we have set up in academia. If you find people systematically breaking the rules the option is always available to you to shake your fists at them for their wicked ways and hope that sufficient moral condemnation will stem the tide of bad behaviour. But another option is to carefully study the social system giving rise to this behaviour, and with sleeves rolled up and an experimental attitude, get to work creating a better world.

LSE
liamkbright@gmail.com

References

Melissa S. Anderson, Emily A. Ronning, Raymond De Vries, and Brian C. Martinson, 'Extending the Mertonian norms: Scientists' subscription to norms of research'. *The Journal of Higher Education* 81 3 (2010), 366–93.

Kwame Anthony Appiah, *The ethics of identity* (Princeton University Press, 2005).

Liam Kofi Bright, 'On fraud' *Philosophical Studies* 174 (2017), 291–310.

Liam Kofi Bright, 'Du Bois' democratic defence of the value free ideal' *Synthese* 195 (2018), 2227–45.

William Broad and Nicholas Wade, *Betrayers of the Truth* (Simon & Schuster, 1982).

Justin P Bruner, 'Policing epistemic communities' *Episteme* 10 (2013), 403–416.

Jonathan R. Cole and Stephen Cole, *Social stratification in science* (University of Chicago Press, 1974).

Heather E Douglas, 'Scientific integrity in a politicized world', *Logic, methodology, and philosophy of science: proceedings of the fourteenth international congress.* (2014) 253–68.

WEB Du Bois, 'The study of the Negro problems', *The Annals of the American Academy of Political and Social Science* (1898), 1–23.

Alvin Goldman, *Knowledge in a Social World* (Oxford University Press, 1999).

Remco Heesen, 'Communism and the Incentive to Share in Science', *Philosophy of Science* 84 (2017), 698–716.

Remco Heesen, 'Why the reward structure of science makes reproducibility problems inevitable', *The journal of philosophy* 115 (2018), 661–74.

Remco Heesen, *Questionable Research Practices and Credit in Academic Careers* (2020) MS.

Remco Heesen and Liam Kofi Bright, 'Is peer review a good idea?', *The British Journal for the Philosophy of Science* (2020).

Bennett Holman and Justin P. Bruner, 'The problem of intransigently biased agents', *Philosophy of Science* 82.5 (2015), 956–68.

Bryce Huebner and Liam Kofi Bright, 'Collective responsibility and fraud in scientific communities', *The Routledge Handbook of Collective Responsibility* (2020), 358–72.

Philip Kitcher, 'The division of cognitive labor', *The Journal of Philosophy* 87 (1990), 5–22.

Travis LaCroix, Anders Geil, and Cailin O'Connor, 'The dynamics of retraction in epistemic networks', *Philosophy of Science* forthcoming.

Bruno Latour and Steve Woolgar, *Laboratory life: The construction of scientific facts*, (Princeton University Press, 1979).

Carole J. Lee, *The Reference Class Problem for Credit Valuation in Science*, (2018) MS.

Lee McIntyre, *The Scientific Attitude*, (MIT Press, 2019).

Robert K. Merton, 'A note on science and democracy', *Journal of the Legal & Political Sociology* (1942), 115–26.

Robert K. Merton, 'Priorities in scientific discovery: a chapter in the sociology of science.' *American sociological review* 22 (1957), 635–59.

Robert K. Merton, 'The Matthew effect in science: The reward and communication systems of science are considered', *Science* 159.3810 (1968), 56–63/

Robert K. Merton, 'Behavior patterns of scientists', *The American Scholar* (1969), 197–225.

Brian A. Nosek, Jeffrey R. Spies, and Matt Motyl, 'Scientific utopia: II. Restructuring incentives and practices to promote truth over publishability', *Perspectives on Psychological Science* 7.6 (2012), 615–31.

Naomi Oreskes and Erik M. Conway, *Merchants of doubt: How a handful of scientists obscured the truth on issues from tobacco smoke to global warming* (Bloomsbury Publishing USA, 2011).

Dasgupta Partha and Paul A. David, 'Toward a new economics of science', *Research policy* 23.5 (1994), 487–521.

Manuela Fernández Pinto, 'Commercialization and the limits of well-ordered science', *Perspectives on Science* 23.2 (2015), 173–191.

Eugenie Samuel Reich, *Plastic fantastic* Vol. 1 (Macmillan, 2009).

Felipe Romero, 'Can the behavioral sciences self-correct? A social epistemic study', *Studies in History and Philosophy of Science Part A* 60 (2016), 55–69.

Felipe Romero, 'Who should do replication labor?', *Advances in Methods and Practices in Psychological Science* 1.4 (2018), 516–537.

Joseph P. Simmons, Leif D. Nelson, and Uri Simonsohn, 'False-positive psychology: Undisclosed flexibility in data collection and analysis allows presenting anything as significant', *Psychological science* 22.11 (2011), 1359–66.

Paula E. Stephan, 'The economics of science.' *Journal of Economic literature*, 34.3 (1996), 1199–1235.

Michael Strevens, 'The role of the priority rule in science', *The Journal of Philosophy* 100.2 (2003), 55–79/

John Van Wyhe, 'Mind the gap: Did Darwin avoid publishing his theory for many years?', *Notes and records of the Royal Society* 61.2 (2007), 177–205.

James Owen Weatherall, Cailin O'Connor, and Justin P. Bruner. 'How to beat science and influence people: policymakers and propaganda in epistemic networks', *The British Journal for the Philosophy of Science* 71.4 (2020). 1157–86.

Harriet Zuckerman, 'Stratification in American science', *Sociological Inquiry* 40.2 (1970), 235–57.

Kevin JS Zollman, 'The Epistemic Benefit of Transient Diversity', *Erkenntnis* (2010), 17–35.

Kevin JS Zollman, 'The credit economy and the economic rationality of science', *The Journal of Philosophy* 115.1 (2018), 5–33.

Kevin JS Zollman, *The scientific ponzi scheme*, (2019) MS.

Should We Worry About Silicone Chip Technology De-Skilling Us?

ELIZABETH FRICKER

Abstract
It is argued that many means-end skills are mere drudgery, and there is no case from well-being to regret that the advance of technology has replaced them with machines. But a case is made that for humans possessing some skills is important for well-being, and that certain core skills are important for it. It is argued that these include navigational skills. While the march of technology has tended to promote human well-being, there is now some cause for concern that silicone chip technology is de-skilling us to an extent that impacts negatively on well-being.

1. Some important questions about human lives and the value of exercising skills

Consider two individuals, each of whom lives in London, and has booked a holiday cottage in Devon for a week. Each of them addresses the task of driving to their cottage. They employ very different means to navigate their way successfully to their destination. Iris has a good understanding of the geography of the UK. She knows that Devon is in the south west, with both a northern and southern coastline, to the east of Cornwall and west of Dorset, southwest of Somerset. She studies relevant road maps, and works out the best route to take: M4 motorway to Bristol, then on to the M5 until past Exeter, and so on. She utilises this knowledge as she makes her journey, referring occasionally to the map she has already studied to check. Bella, in contrast, has very little geographical knowledge. She knows that Devon has a coastline – her cottage is by the sea; and she vaguely understands that it is in the south of the UK; but beyond that she has little clue where it is relative to London and other parts of the country. She does not even know that she will be travelling west, not east, to get there from London. She does no research into maps of the area. Instead, on the day of travel, she simply inputs her desired destination into the GPS system in her phone, and then uncritically follows the instructions that its synthetic voice gives her at each decision point in her journey.[1]

[1] To serve the purpose of our present enquiry I have described two extremes. Most individual journey-makers will be somewhere between

doi:10.1017/S1358246121000138

Both Iris and Bella arrive safely at their destination. Each is happy with the method they use. Each method has been equally effective. My question in this discussion is: is there any reason to think one method preferable to the other? Iris has an understanding, a mental map, of the region of the UK she has travelled through, and of the relative positions in it of the origin and endpoint of her journey. She has deployed this knowledge, along with map-reading skills, in working out her route. Bella lacks these skills, and this geographical understanding and knowledge almost entirely; instead, she possesses the relatively limited skill of knowing how to input a destination into her GPS device, and then follow its instructions ('at the roundabout, take the second exit'; 'in a quarter of a mile, turn left onto Chapel Lane' – etc).

One reason for preferring to rely on one's own navigational skills, rather than a GPS device, is avoidance of risk. Whenever one relies entirely on a device to replace a skill for one, one incurs dependence on the device for the execution of the task in question, and so the risk of being let down if it fails. The GPS worked well on this occasion; but on another it might break down, or be unavailable. (If it is on one's phone, that might run out of battery, or there might be no satellite signal for it to detect one's current location.). But this argument cuts both ways: computational systems can fail, but so can humans, whose susceptibility to error for all kinds of reasons from tiredness to carelessness to drunkenness is constitutional.

In any case, I want here to do what we might, after J.S. Mill refer to as 'taking the higher ground' (Mill, 1998 (1863), Ch. 2)[2]. I will consider whether there is a case to be made that deploying one's own navigational skills and geographic understanding to make one's journey is somehow non-instrumentally better than delegating all understanding and responsibility to an electronic device, of which one knows only that it generally works, and how to follow its dictates.

Even the most skilful orienteering enthusiast might on occasion, for sheer lack of time, make a car journey to a destination without seeking to attain any understanding of its location or the route to it, instead resorting to a GPS device. So our question is a more

---

them. Using a GPS device critically, with some understanding of the task in hand, is very different from the uncritical use Bella is stipulated to make of it.

[2] In Mill's case, this consists in arguing the case for his proposed ethical theory, Utilitarianism, against the criticism that it is a 'doctrine for swine' by arguing that the 'higher' pleasures of intellect and sentiment are not just safer than bodily pleasures, but are intrinsically better qua pleasures.

general one comparing the methods employed by Iris and Bella respectively. Is it non-instrumentally better as a general practise to use the method of acquiring and deploying geographical knowledge and navigational skills, as one's way of getting about, as opposed to being content entirely to lack that knowledge and those skills, and to instead use the method of relying on a GPS or similar device that simulates this on one's behalf? By 'non-instrumentally better', I mean that a method is better, and is so not merely because it is more reliable, or efficient, or is in some other way likely to have better consequences.

More precisely, I will investigate whether we can find an argument for the conclusion that deploying navigational skills oneself is better, while invoking only uncontroversial evaluative theses in our arguments. Our argument must turn on the question of what things contribute value to a human life. There are philosophers who hold that exercising skills is part of what is distinctively valuable in a human life. (See for instance Aristotle, 2002). This premiss, if allowed, gives immediately the answer that a method of getting around that deploys one's own 'on-board' navigational skills is better, efficiency and reliability being equal, than one in which one lacks those skills, having instead only the very limited skill of knowing how to work and obey the instructions of a GPS device: if exercising skills is one of the goods of human life, then other things equal, achieving a task in a way that exercises one's skill is better than doing it in a way that does not – the first, and not the second, contributes non-instrumental value to one's life. (Of course other things may not be equal. For instance, even if there is something valuable in exercising arithmetical skills, spending many hours doing a complex calculation by hand would not be overall better, if inputting the data to a computer could get the result accurately in seconds – leaving one free to engage in other skilful activities.)

But such a case would not persuade Bella – who, remember, is content with her practise - that her life would be better if she were to learn some geography and navigational skills. An insistence that her preferred method of getting by car to her intended destinations – relying on her GPS – is objectively worse, according to an invoked conception of the good in human life that places value on skills, seems to be a mere exercise in elitist paternalism. If we are to provide an argument that can persuade Bella she is missing out on something she herself would consider of value, worth having in her life, then we must find one that invokes only an uncontroversial component of the good for human lives: well-being. The core idea of well-being is that it turns on how well an agent's life goes *for that agent*; it measures a life as better only if it is better for her, from her point of view. The main components of well-being, happiness and pleasure, are internally connected to desire and preference. (See Crisp, 2017). So if we can make a case to Bella that by relying on her GPS, and failing to acquire and exercise navigational skills, she is missing out on something that has the potential to contribute to how well her life goes for her, we will have pointed out something that she will surely recognise as giving her some reason to acquire and exercise navigational skills.

Happiness and pleasure are uncontroversial components of well-being. I will consider whether invoking only these, one can make an argument – not that one should never choose to make a journey by reliance on a GPS device; as remarked already, that would be absurdly strong – but make an argument that the kind of skills involved when one does one's navigation for oneself are basic ingredients of a good (viz. happy) human life[3]; so that having and sometimes exercising them tends to make one's life better (happier).

Our question comparing two methods of arriving at one's destination on a car journey instances a very broad general question:

> For every task whose performance involves the exercise of a (more or less complex) skill, is it in some way non-instrumentally better, other things being equal, to acquire and exercise the skill oneself to complete the task, rather than relying on another person who has that skill, or a device embodying the skill designed and built by other person(s), to do the task for one?

This question is to be understood so that it receives a positive answer just if for every skill one is capable of acquiring, exercising that skill would contribute some distinctive positive non-instrumental value to one's life. If this is so, then for every skill one is capable of acquiring, one has some reason – pro tanto reason – to acquire and exercise that skill.

A positive answer to the general question would yield our conclusion about the value of navigational skills as an instance. However, it could be that there is no general case for the non-instrumental betterness of deploying skills oneself rather than relying on others, but there is one in the special case of navigational skills. This is what I will make a case for in what follows.

[3] This statement should be understood as a generic. The claim I will here argue for is not that it is impossible for a human being to lead a happy life while lacking any navigational skills; but that this would be exceptional. Typical happy human lives involve some deployment of them.

Seeing our question as an instance of the broad general one suggests a case against it: it goes against a foundational feature of civilisation. The division of labour, and the development of specialist expertise, is a paradigmatic and essential feature of an economically and socially developed society. Some have a natural talent or bent for one thing, and go in for that; others' talents and inclinations point in a different direction. One person is good at growing crops, another at making pots, another at ironwork. So the blacksmith buys his corn, and sells his ploughshares to the corn-grower. No-one has both time and aptitude to acquire and deploy all the skills whose products contribute to a prosperous life, so each specialises in one department, and relies on the skills of others for other things.

But not so fast: this fact of the inevitable division of labour and specialisation of different people in different skills does not entail that our question receives a negative answer. It could be that, while I cannot both grow my own corn and make my own pottery, I have grounds to regret this fact. It could be that, for each skilful task, through failing to acquire and exercise its skill I am missing out on something worthwhile that I can't get in any other way. Sadly my limited capacities and circumstances mean I am restricted to acquiring only a few of the myriad of my potential skills. If this is so, then I have some reason – *pro tanto* reason – to learn to grow my own corn; although this reason is outweighed by circumstances that provide stronger counter-reasons in my case – I can't both grow my own corn and make my own pots, and I'm better at, and get more from, the latter. Generalising this point: if, for every skill I am capable of acquiring, exercising it would contribute some distinctive non-instrumental value to my life that I can't otherwise obtain, then for every such skill, I have some reason to acquire it; and some ground for regret if, given all the constraints of my situation, I cannot do so.

As remarked, no one human being can possibly acquire and exercise for herself all the skills whose outputs she will benefit from and rely on during her life. No-one can acquire all the skills of a car mechanic, an IT expert, a surgeon, a house builder...etc. So dependence on others in the form of reliance on them to exercise skills on one's behalf is part of the civilised human condition. But we still have choices to make, and questions to answer in this regard: should I seek over time to acquire and exercise as many skills as I can, thereby reducing my dependence on others? Which skills do I have some reason to acquire? Are there some core skills such that each one of us has some reason to acquire them?

So how we answer our question about the non-instrumental value of exercising skills has practical implications for how we should seek to lead our lives - what choices we should make about which skills to acquire, and which to continue to employ others (or devices created by others) to exercise on our behalf. Whether exercising skills contributes value to human life is an issue with normative practical implications for each one of us; it affects what we have reason to do, as we plan the course of our life over time.

And there is a broad concern that the advance of silicone-chip-based technology in the 21st century, of which GPS navigation is just one instance, should prompt us to raise: should we be worried that our human lives are at risk of becoming increasingly de-skilled, as ever more sophisticated electronic devices are developed, which take over skilled tasks that previously could only be done by suitably skilled humans?

2. Four Principles about Reason to Exercise Skills

Let us refine our issue. I next formulate four principles of differing strengths about reason to exercise skills. The rest of the paper will consider which, if any, has a plausible case for it based only on the uncontroversial components of well-being: happiness and pleasure or enjoyment. The domain of quantification here is humans.

Unrestricted RAS: For each one of us, for every skill that one lacks and is able to acquire, one has some reason to acquire and sometimes exercise that skill; and for every skill one has, one has some reason to maintain and sometimes exercise it; where this is not merely instrumental reason.

Certain RAS: For each one of us, there is a certain set of skills one has or is able to acquire such that one has some reason, for each skill in the set, if one lacks it, to acquire and sometimes exercise it; and if one has it, to maintain and sometimes exercise it; where this is not merely instrumental reason. (Note: which these are will differ from person to person)

Some-RAS: Each one of us has some reason to ensure that one has and sometimes exercises some skills – that one is not entirely skill-less; where this is not merely instrumental reason.

Core RAS: There is a certain set of broad skill-types such that each one of us has some reason to ensure, if she is able, for every skill-type in the set, that she has and sometimes exercises a skill of that type; where this is not merely instrumental reason.

The reasons mentioned in these principles are *pro tanto* reasons only, and the reason may be very weak. As regards Unrestricted-RAS and Certain-RAS, the reason to acquire a particular skill will inevitably in most cases be outweighed by other stronger reasons against since, as already remarked, no one has time to acquire all the skills they have the potential to master. However the reason is not destroyed, one still has some reason to acquire that skill though circumstance does not permit this; hence there is cause for regret about this fact. (Compare: suppose I want both to go to my friend's birthday party, and to attend the performance of the school play in which my daughter has a main role. Both are scheduled for the same time, so I cannot do both; I must lose out on one of these pleasures – there is cause for regret. While one reason is strongest and wins, the other is outweighed, not annulled.)

The reasons mentioned are not instrumental reasons: that is to say, the reason to acquire and exercise a skill obtains due to some value for one in that exercise itself, not due to beneficial further consequences of exercising it. (I have an instrumental reason to learn to play golf if taking part in my firm's golf days is an important means to further my career in the firm. This reason applies even if I hate playing golf, and get no enjoyment from doing so. In contrast, as will be argued below, the fact that I would enjoy playing golf provides some non-instrumental reason for me to learn to do so.)

There would be an instrumental reason to acquire skills if dependence on others was in itself bad, so that I have a reason to acquire skills to enable me to avoid this. We noted earlier that avoiding the risk of being let down by others provides one instrumental reason to avoid such dependence. This is not what I am interested in here. And in fact, dependence on others is in many cases itself part of a good. It is, for one thing, an essential part of caring personal relationships.

The reasons in our principles are normative reasons – reasons *for* acting in a certain way (See Raz 1999; Parfit 2011). There is for agent A a normative reason for her to perform an action of a certain kind φ-ing, when φ-ing would have some property that counts in favour of performing it, for agent A – there is something about φ-ing that makes it worth doing, for A. I am here concerned with properties of φ-ing that provide a prudential normative (PN) reason for A to φ; that is, something about φ-ing makes it good for A, from A's point of view. And I will assume that the property of φ-ing that confers such PN reason is that φ-ing would make a distinctive positive contribution not otherwise available to A's well-being - to how well A's life goes *for her*.

So: A has a PN reason to φ just if φ-ing will make a distinctive positive contribution to A's well-being. This principle tells us what needs to be shown, for each of our principles, to establish it: the possession and exercise of skills as specified in the principle must in itself directly contribute in a distinctive way to the agent's well-being. In my arguments regarding our principles I appeal only to uncontroversial ingredients of well-being that are undeniably motivating as features of prospective actions: pleasure and enjoyment, and happiness

I shall assume that, where an agent has the desire to acquire a skill, she has some PN reason to do so. (If someone desires to φ, then φ-ing has at least one evaluatively positive property for her that links to well-being: it fulfils her desire to φ. This involves some neglect of tricky issues: cases where someone is wrong about what she would enjoy, and desires for bad things). The more difficult task is to show that an agent has some PN reason to acquire and exercise a skill, even when she lacks any inclination so to do. To say she does is to maintain that she is missing out on some good of human life if she fails to acquire and exercise the skill – i.e. that exercising the skill would contribute directly to her wellbeing in a specific way not otherwise available.

In the rest of the paper I will argue that there is no case to be made invoking only well-being for our strongest principle, Unrestricted RAS, and it is likely false. We next see that there is a relatively straightforward case for Certain RAS: I have some reason to acquire and exercise any skill such that I would enjoy its exercise.[4] I then make an empirical case for Some-RAS; and I finish with a further empirically-backed argument for Core-RAS. But first I need to say a bit more about what skills are.

3. Task-achieving skills and skilful activities

Skills enable one to do things. One has the ability to φ just if one is sufficiently likely to succeed in φ-ing if one tries, and one is disposed to try over a sufficiently broad range of circumstances. (This second clause blocks abilities vacuously possessed by those who refuse ever to try to achieve anything; see Sosa, 2015, p. 95). Speaking of trying ensures that only things one does, that involve agency, count as abilities – falling over is not an ability, even if one does it frequently. (The clown who 'falls' intentionally and skilfully is

[4] This case turns on the account of pleasure that I adopt. Whether this account is necessarily true or is contingent and empirical is itself debatable.

another matter.) Skills are best seen as the mediators of abilities, hence more fine-grained than abilities. For instance, both Iris and Bella have the ability to reliably get by car to their intended destination; but they do so by means of different skills – skill at map-reading, versus at using a GPS device. (Clearly there are issues as to how finely skills are individuated: is someone who looks up a recipe online to bake a victoria sponge using a different skill from one who learned it from her mother and can remember it? These will not be pursued here.)

Skills can be sorted into epistemic or practical, however many involve elements of both. An epistemic skill is a knowledge base plus know-how or mastery of techniques that allows one to generate for oneself fresh knowledge in new circumstances, where one lacking that skill could not do so. Thus, for instance, a lab technician will be able to tell, from looking at a slide under a microscope, whether a certain virus is present in the sample, where a layman could not do so. And an expert on wild birds will be able to tell, from a variety of cues, what birds she is seeing or hearing while out on a hike. This skill is based in recognitional capacities for visual appearances and sounds of birds, mediated by relevant background knowledge, such as knowing that of two birds with similar appearance, one is common, the other very rare, in a certain region.

Being able to replace a worn-out clutch in a car is a practical skill: it has a practical result, a fixed car that can again be driven. Classifying skills thus by their outputs allows us to sort them as either epistemic or practical. A cabinet maker has the skill to make a fine chest of drawers and other items of polished wood furniture; a good baker has the skill to make a range of excellent breads and cakes. But this distinguishing criterion conceals the fact that most skills involve both epistemic and practical components: the mechanic both can diagnose what is amiss with my car, and knows how to fix it. Knowledge-base and skills to operate deftly are both involved, and are intermingled – a skilful worker 'knows what she is doing'.

Amongst practical skills, skills of doing something (other than generating new knowledge), there is an important distinction between skills that are, and are not, substantially teleological. The latter are skills that produce an end product, skilful means by which one achieves an end result that is distinct from the exercise of the skill, and (typically) remains after skilful activity stops. This is so of the cake-baker and cabinet maker. But other skills do not have an independent end-product, they are simply skilful activities. For instance swimming is a skill, but the only output it produces is itself, the activity of swimming. Of course one may swim to pursue further purposes such as winning a swimming race, but this is not an internal object of the skill itself. Cake-baking, in contrast, has producing a cake as its internal object; one who lacked it would not be engaging in the activity.

This distinction is significant when we consider our principles. Many substantially teleological skills are activities that humans only engage in because they are a necessary means to achieve their end-result. For most of us they are a tedious chore that must be done, and is only done, to get the desired end-product. Many domestic chores – washing clothes, house cleaning and so on – fit this model.

Skilled activities with no separate end-product do not fit the means-end model. There is no reason to engage in them unless either one finds them enjoyable, or they serve some further goal external to their identity – as with our reluctant golfer. Armed with this distinction, we will now consider the case for our principles.

4. No Case for Unrestricted RAS

For means-end skills whose exercise is not enjoyable for one, one has no PN-reason based in well-being to acquire and exercise the skill to attain its end-product, once a preferable alternative way of obtaining it is available – in the case of laundry, a washing machine. (A washing machine is a device invented and manufactured through the skills of others. In previous eras the wealthy would pay the less fortunate to engage in the drudgery of doing their laundry for them, without the aid of machines.) Many means-end skills such as doing housework and laundry are not enjoyable for most people, and so there is no cogent case from well-being to be made for Unrestricted-RAS. The falsity of Unrestricted-RAS is however contingent on the fact that many means-end skills are unpleasant drudgery: if, for every skill one is capable of acquiring, one would enjoy exercising it, then this principle would be contingently true for one. Invoking richer normative resources might also provide a case for its truth – for instance, if every piece of knowledge is of some value, and one can only know what it is like to exercise a skill by doing so. I find this implausible, and I conjecture that no convincing case can be made for Unrestricted-RAS, and that it is false.

Given that Unrestricted-RAS is false, contrary to this principle, there is nothing at all to regret about the invention of washing-machines, no distinctive aspect of human wellbeing is threatened or curtailed by their advent. On the contrary, it frees up people, mainly women, from the drudgery of scrubbing, rinsing and mangling, enabling them to spend their precious time on other more rewarding activities. What goes for washing machines goes for many other modern labour-saving devices: they are an unalloyed good, and their invention and widespread availability constitutes unambiguous human progress.

Equally, there is nothing to regret about the extensive social division of skills of labour. The division of labour and skills is a pervasive general good of civilisation and economic advance – so long as tastes and aptitudes are idiosyncratic, so some will gain satisfaction from exercising skills in activities that to others are just a boring chore. (Of course in our actual society who does what on behalf of whom is determined to a large extent by relative income and wealth, rather than differences in preferences. But the point about diverse preferences and aptitudes underwriting specialisation as welfare-promoting survives this fact.)

5. A Pleasure-Based Case for Certain-RAS

There are skills one possesses that one enjoys exercising; and there are other skills one currently lacks, but would enjoy exercising if one possessed them. It may seem a no-brainer that, for each such skill, one has some PN reason based in well-being to maintain and sometimes exercise that skill, if one already has it; and to acquire it and sometimes exercise it if one does not already. (Remember that these are only *pro tanto* reasons. Since, given my limitations of capacity and circumstance, I can only acquire a tiny proportion of the skills I am potentially capable of mastering, the reason to acquire a skill will be over-ridden by other competing factors in most cases. I have some PN reason derived from well-being to learn Russian, and Chinese, and Ancient Greek, and many other languages, since I would enjoy reading the literature written in them; but sadly it is way beyond my capability in my circumstances to learn them all.)

Not so fast. There is a fallacy in the inference here. One has some PN reason based in well-being to acquire a particular skill whose exercise one would enjoy, in virtue of that fact, only if the kind of enjoyment one would thereby get is distinctive, and cannot be obtained in another way; and its contribution to one's well-being consists in providing that distinctive kind. The pleasure of reading Russian poetry in the original must be something one can only obtain through doing just that, and that distinctive type of pleasure must contribute distinctively to one's well-being. If and only if this is so, then by not being able to read Russian, one is missing out on a good of human life that one cannot otherwise obtain; and so one has some reason to learn Russian.

So, if pleasure and enjoyment were a kind of uniform psychological stuff, a sensation caused by various activities and experiences but distinct from them, then the pleasure-based reason to engage in a pleasure-inducing activity would be only instrumental: in order to get the pleasure it causes; and, being one kind of stuff caused in different ways, any way of causing it would be equally good, as regards the pleasure. If this were so, then one would not need to learn to read Russian poetry in order to obtain the pleasure doing so induces; that same pleasure could equally be caused by many other pleasure-inducing activities, or indeed by suitable electrode-stimulation of the brain. There would be no hedonistic case for acquiring specific skills.

Pleasure and enjoyment are not like this. Pleasure is not one kind of sensation, but a variety of different pleasant experiences. And most of these experiences have complex representational content, and are inherently cognitive. Maybe there are some purely sensational pleasures: pleasant sensations such that their sensational quality is independent of any cognitive appreciation of their provenance and context. But the undeniable pleasures of our many pleasant skilled activities are not like this. And pure pleasant sensation independent of skill is rarer than one might think. Take tastes, for instance: surely these are simply pleasant (or unpleasant!) sensations, a sensory given that is independent of their cognitive setting? But try sipping a glass of milk thinking it is water – the result is very weird. Cognitive priming affects taste sensation; and in the same vein, relevant knowledge and discriminatory skill is involved in the background of taste experience. Think of the range of distinctive pleasant taste experiences enjoyed by an expert on fine wines. Her experiences are a product of her discriminatory skill and knowledge, and not available to one who lacks this. What she enjoys are the distinct specific tastes of particular wines. This not a generalised pleasantness with various different causes, nor is it a range of sensations whose availability and quality is independent of her background skills. (For an overview of accounts of pleasure, see Katz, 2016).

At the other extreme is Gilbert Ryle's view of pleasure as an aspect or manner of one's engagement in an activity (Ryle, 1949). If his view were correct, then one could only gain the pleasure when actually engaging in the activity. I will not adopt such an extreme view. Rather, I suggest that for our various skilled activities, the pleasure one gains from engaging in them is part of an inherently representational experience of one's engagement in the activity. This being so, one cannot enjoy the associated pleasure of a skill unless one has acquired the skill, with the discriminatory perceptual and action capacities that this involves. One cannot appreciate Chinese poetry if one cannot understand Chinese: accessing the pleasant experiences requires possession of the relevant skill. This is no less so in the case of various genres of music, which are also languages in the relevant sense. Appreciating a Mozart symphony, or a John Coltrane solo, involves hearing what is going on musically in its harmonic and rhythmic sequences, and this requires prior training of the ear. Enjoyment in this and many cases is a matter of appreciation, and this is a cognitive skill dependent on background knowledge and trained perceptual capacities. The same goes for many skilled activities: the enjoyable experiences of playing tennis, for example, are just that – experiences as of playing tennis; as such, they are available only to someone who has sufficient skill to play it. To have the enjoyable experiences of playing tennis one must know what it is like to play tennis; and this knowledge is only available to someone with some skill at it. (There are delicate issues about extent of skill required, of course. I cannot address these in this brief essay.)

Contrary to Ryle, I allow that one could on an occasion enjoy the pleasure of listening to a Mozart symphony through suitable stimulation of the brain to simulate the experience of actually hearing one (listening to a recording, after all, simulates the experience of hearing a live orchestra playing); and that one could enjoy the experience of playing tennis in, for instance, a vivid lifelike dream of doing so. But these pleasant experiences, with their complex representational content, are only available to one who in fact has the skill in question; and this requires having learned it, and exercised it on previous occasions.[5]

If this proposed account of the pleasure of skilled activities is correct, then Some-RAS is assured: one has some reason to acquire each skill such that one would enjoy exercising it since, on this account, there is no other way to obtain the distinctive pleasure in question. And that pleasure makes a distinctive contribution to one's well-being not otherwise obtainable. Which particular skills these are will, human nature admitting of variation, vary from one person to another. For the adventurous, the thrill of sky-diving and mountaineering are great; for others, the intellectual and homely pleasures of reading and knitting are preferable. As already remarked, this variation in human tastes and capacities makes specialisation in

[5] A more detailed treatment of these delicate issues is given in Fricker (2019).

skills beneficial to welfare. Some people like doing tax returns! The specialisation of skills allows them become tax accountants, while others become doctors, or performing artists, or farmers, or mechanics, or IT experts – and so on.

Our discussion above has shown how someone can have a PN reason based in well-being to acquire a skill, despite having no current desire to do so: she would gain a distinctive kind of enjoyment from exercising it, not obtainable in other ways. This reason applies to her, it is a reason for her to learn and deploy the skill, even if as things stand she does not appreciate this fact. Such normative reasons *for* acting are thus 'external' reasons for action: they apply to an individual in virtue of relevant facts about her and the world (Williams, 1979). The reason becomes 'internal', motivating, when she herself comes to appreciate the relevant facts. Our social interactions show sensitivity to such reasons – 'Come on, try it, I promise you you'll love it!' we say to someone, about a novel experience or skilled activity she at present has no desire to engage in. 'You don't know what you're missing!' – this is the basis of the case for trying the new skilled activity: the person would want to do it, if she knew what it would be like for her.

The advance of technology replaces human labour, mostly exhausting drudgery, with machines, freeing up humans' time so they can spend it on other less exhausting and more interesting activities. With the advent of these technologies human skills that they replace are lost, perhaps irretrievably; but from the standpoint of a view of the value of human life on which it consists entirely in well-being, we have so far found nothing to regret about this. The Luddite urge to resist the advance of technology is entirely understandable. The fear is primarily the loss of employment as machines replace skilled human workers; but a thought about the value of the skills being lost may also be a motivation. (Think of the resistance to the introduction of machine looms to textile mills in the UK in the 19th century.) I am told that, when writing was first introduced into the ancient world, there were those who lamented the loss of the skill of memorising long narratives by heart that this would herald.[6]

From what we have established so far, it seems there is no reason to acquire a skill, or to regret lacking it, unless one would gain a distinctive kind of enjoyment from exercising that skill. And so it seems that

6 Sadly I am no classical scholar, and I am indebted for this point to an audience member at a talk based on these ideas that I gave in the Philosophy Department at Edinburgh University.

lamentation of our loss of means-end skills in the face of advancing technology is misplaced. (Add to this the fact that, as one skill becomes obsolete, a new skill – of operating the technology in question – replaces it. Once long poems could be written down, there was no need to learn them by heart; but there was a new need – to become literate. And this new technology and its skill opened up new possibilities that were an essential part of the advance of civilisation.)

But our investigation is not over. What about our last two principles concerning skills? Even though, in itself, one has no reason to acquire a skill if one would not enjoy exercising it, it could be that Some-RAS holds: one has some PN reason based in well-being to ensure one is not entirely skill-less. If so, this would give one some reason to ensure one has some skills, even if one does not enjoy exercising any of them, so none is such that one has some reason to acquire and exercise it in particular. (Compare: it may be that I need, on a certain date, to be in the UK; even though there is no particular location in the UK such that I need, on that date, to be in it.) So, if Some-RAS holds, we may have cause to worry about the advance of technology rendering us skill-less, even if the particular skills we no longer need, because computers and robots do for us the skilled things we used to do for ourselves, are not distinctively enjoyable to exercise.

And the worry about the advance of technology robbing us of our skills might also be validated, if we found a case for Core-RAS. Core-RAS will be true if there are certain broad skill-types whose possession is a necessary condition for, or ingredient of, human well-being. If the current amazing advances in computing science and robotics are developing devices with the potential to replace one or more of these core skills, then there is cause for concern that aspects of what makes human life worth living may be undermined, threatened by them.

6. An empirical case for Some-RAS

An adult human with normal cognitive capacities cannot be happy without some degree of self-respect. Pleasures are fleeting and with a salient sensory component, and it may be one can experience some of these although one thinks oneself worthless; but one will not enjoy them fully if one feels bad about oneself. A sense of oneself as being of no value, useless and not worth anything, is like a background pain that prevents one from enjoying what would otherwise be enjoyable events. So enjoyment is hard for someone who lacks self-respect. This is yet more so for happiness. Happiness is a more stable and global feature of one's psychology, and one cannot be happy unless one is at ease with oneself; and this requires that one regard oneself as of some worth.[7] Thinking of oneself as of no value, as 'useless' is intimately linked to thinking of oneself as 'not good at anything'. So it is very hard to have self-respect, unless one believes oneself to be good at something, to have at least some skills.

Given these facts about human psychology, each one of us has a PN-reason based in wellbeing to ensure that she has self-respect. And, this being so, each one of us has some reason to ensure that she has some skills. Having some skills is a necessary precondition for enjoyment and happiness.[8] This psychological law admits of exceptions for very young children, and some adults who are cognitively limited and simpler, child-like. But it holds as a broad generalisation about human nature: it holds for all those who have the cognitive capacity to have an opinion or attitude (explicit or tacit) about their self-worth.

7. And One for Core-RAS

Ok, so we need to have some skills in order to be able to respect ourselves, and so to be able to enjoy life. But are there any particular skills we need to have to be able to enjoy life to the full? – Any particular skills that play an important role in enabling or enhancing one's level of well-being?

Our fourth principle, Core-RAS, will be a contingent nomological truth if there is a certain set of skills such that every human enjoys

[7] These empirical claims are validated in the empirical psychology literature. Du, King et al. (2017) states that '...studies have shown that self-esteem is an important predictor of subjective well-being.'

[8] Pedants may object that the case offered shows only that one must believe oneself to have some skills in order to have self-esteem, rather than that one must actually have them. Unlike beliefs on theoretical topics remote from everyday experience, it would be hard for a belief that one has a skill to survive long, if it were false; in any case, it is likely that the actual experience of exercising skills is what promotes self-esteem. It is true that someone may overestimate the extent of their skill; and the converse gap is a real issue: individuals who find it very hard to believe in their abilities, despite in fact having various skills. The case made for Some-RAS requires that having skills is a necessary condition for self-esteem, not that it is sufficient.

exercising them. But the issue I want to get at is whether the following thesis is true:

> (CS) There exist certain core skills (broad skill-types) whose possession is a generally necessary[9] facilitating condition for attaining and maintaining a happy human life.

One of the difficulties for determining whether (CS) is true, is that it is hard to place limits in advance on the diversity of possible types of happy human lives. Who knows how culture and social life will evolve, as technology produces new possibilities? Rather than seeking to anticipate all such possibilities and produce a thesis that holds necessarily, for all time, I will argue for a version of (CS) that holds as a lawlike truth regarding human life broadly as we know it now, in the early 21st century.

Human life has various broad features that recur across societies as we know them. The means of subsistence are scarce, so we need to be able to think and reason effectively about how to obtain them, as well as how to find a suitable mate. It is in our interests to understand the world we inhabit as fully as possible, in order to manipulate and control it, so a capacity for causal reasoning is a core skill. We are social creatures, and interpersonal communication and interactions including, in different circumstances, both cooperation and competition, are a fundamental aspect of our lives. So skills needed for social interaction are core. We need to have a capacity for mind-reading and empathetic understanding of others. We need to be able to communicate, so mastery of a common language is a core skill.

This much should be uncontroversial; but it is not my aim here to draw up a list of core skill-types. My aim is to sketch a case for the view that having a cognitive map of one's environment, and associated navigational skills for getting around in it, is among the core skills that each of us benefits greatly from having, since it greatly enhances one's possibilities for a happy life.

Why is knowing one's way around in one's environment conducive to well-being? Because it plays a fundamental role in enabling one to be in control of one's life, enabling one effectively to pursue one's goals. For most of one's projects and plans, being able to get to the right place at the right time is an essential ingredient in effectively pursuing them.

[9] By 'generally necessary' I mean that for the overwhelming majority of happy human lives it is a necessary enabling condition; but there can be exceptions. Cf footnote 11.

There are two components to being able get around independently in one's environment: one's cognitive map and associated navigational skills, and one's capacity and opportunity by some means actually to travel around in it. My current focus is on the first of these. (Of course her cognitive map is of little use in furthering her goals to someone who is trapped in one location – if, for example, she is imprisoned. And we all need some means of travel to be available. For the less able – for instance, someone confined to a wheelchair after an accident – this may require supporting means of transportation even for short journeys, and we all must resort to them for longer ones, too far to walk, which must made by bicycle, or car, or train, or bus, or ship, or plane.)

We are animals. And animals need to know how to get home, where the dangers are and where one can keep safe from them, where the food is, where one can find a mate, and so on – all represented in a cognitive map of one's environment with one's current location at its centre.[10] The ability to locate oneself in one's environment, in which one knows the locations of the features that are salient for one's needs, is basic to effective pursuit of one's goals. It is needed for, or at least highly conducive to, autonomy, being oneself in control of one's life; and this, because it enables one to fulfil one's goals, greatly enhances one's possibilities for happiness.

Consider again Iris and Bella. Iris is always interested in understanding the geographic layout of a place she visits, and placing this within a broader grasp of the layout of her environment; and she likes to navigate her way through it by deploying this understanding: she likes to 'know her way about'. Bella in contrast has no interest in understanding the layout of her environment. She is happy uncritically to follow the instructions of a GPS device when making a long journey by car; and when she is, say, visiting a city with friends, she lets them do all the navigation in getting from the hotel to the museum to the coffee shop to the park and back to the hotel, herself acquiring no understanding of their spatial relations, no mental representation of this.

So far so fine for Bella: this is a choice she has, explicitly or tacitly, made for herself and, you may object, there is no reduction in her capacities for well-being entailed by it. I concede this. My case for the core status of navigational skills is not that one cannot lead a

[10] 'Cognitive map' here should be understood broadly: I do not mean to commit as to the particular format of the mental representations, which could represent spatial information procedurally, rather than in the manner of a physical map.

happy life without employing them whenever possible, and extending them as much as one can. I only want to insist on a weaker, but still significant thesis: the skill that Bella fails to employ, when she gets to Devon using her GPS, without any grasp of the route, is an extension of a skill which, in its basic applications, is essential to being in control of one's life, and hence to well-being.

Knowing one's way about in one's environment is so basic that it is hard to imagine someone with a complete lack of it. Surely someone must at least know the way to her local supermarket, her children's school, her office; must have a mental map of their location relative to her home, and be able to deploy this to make her way there. And surely she must know how to get from the bedroom to the bathroom, from her home office in the attic to the kitchen in the basement! The capacity for mental representation of the layout of one's environment, together with navigational skills, which Iris but not Bella deploys in getting from London to Devon, is a cognitive resource that is fundamental to conducting one's everyday life. It is hard to see how one could get by, achieve one's most basic needs to survive, without deploying them to some extent. A complete inability to represent the spatial relations of significant objects and locations in one's environment, and correlated inability to navigate one's way to and from them, would render one reliant on specially devised compensating heuristics, or a suitable ever-present electronic device, or a faithful carer who leads one to where one next needs to be. There exist individuals who suffer from such topographical agnosia, or place-blindness, and one need only search the internet to find accounts from them of how disabling it is.

We have seen that some capacity to locate oneself and other objects of significance for one in a mental map of one's environment is a precondition, in the broad circumstances of human life as they currently are for most people, for effectively pursuing one's goals.[11] This makes it a key enabling condition for leading a happy life, and so a core skill. Is this a reason to value extending it beyond the level that is necessary for one's well-being? Should it motivate Bella, once we point this out to her, to stop using her GPS and instead apply herself to gain some understanding of geography and map-reading? There is no

[11] To re-emphasise: I am not claiming this as an exceptionless truth, even in current conditions. I do not intend to rule out that someone might lead a happy life of contemplation and abstract thought, while never leaving a small windowless room, food being delivered to them, and having no understanding of their environment. But this is radically a-typical for a human life.

entailment: the fact that one must use a certain skill in order to pursue one's goals in some circumstances (getting from the bedroom to the bathroom, say), does not in itself give one a reason to use it in other circumstances where an alternative – a GPS device – is available. Nonetheless, appreciating that in navigating for herself on her trip to Devon she would be cultivating a skill some exercises of which are necessary for being in control of her life, might make Bella think differently about whether it is worth investing the time to find out where Devon is, and learn to get there without using a GPS. Contemporary authors have written books emphasising the value and importance in human life of navigational skills (Huth, 2015; O'Connor, 2019). Moreover there is evidence of the importance for brain health of cultivating navigational skills. Recent neuroscience studies have identified the key role of the hippocampus in navigational tasks, during performance of which it is activated (O'Keefe and Nadel, 1978). It fails to be activated when a GPS is used, and is larger in those with good navigational skills (Javadi et al., 2017). And there are indications that brain function in general is protected against decline when navigational skills are developed and regularly employed, thus maintaining the size of the hippocampus (Konishi and Bohbot, 2013).

One could try another tack, and seek to persuade Bella that she would enjoy using a map to herself navigate her way to her Devon cottage. In fact the two strategies are not wholly distinct: a sense of being in control of what one is doing, the progress of one's current activity, is itself pleasant. So, showing that in navigating herself Bella would be exercising a core skill, one whose use is key to being in control of one's life, is ipso facto making a case that she would enjoy exercising that skill. Bella might or might not be persuaded to improve her map-reading skills. I have sought to show that she has some PN-reason based in well-being to do so: if she remains unmoved, this is because she does not know what she is missing.

Finally, what of the larger question of our title: should we be worried by the prospect that, with the advance of increasingly sophisticated silicone-chip-based technology, computers and robots are taking over ever more of what have always been exclusively human capabilities, and are progressively de-skilling us? We saw that there is no general case, from the standpoint of well-being, to regret the demise of means-end skills that were not enjoyable to exercise; and we concluded that the march of technology has had a largely positive impact on the quality of human life. As one skill is lost, other new ones arise and replace it, and we have not so far been de-skilled as a result of advancing technology. Self-driving cars, for instance, will allow to more of humanity what the rich already had in the form of a chauffeur, and not having to drive frees one up to work or read while travelling – as train and bus travel already permit.

But still – have we reached a new place now, in this march, where human skills that contribute value to our lives are threatened? This question is too big to answer decisively here. But if the case made here that navigational skills are core is sound, there is some reason for concern. We should at least step back from what is happening in silicone valley and in robotics labs elsewhere, and say: 'Hey, wait a minute, let's think about the implications of all these new robotic devices for what is valuable in our human lives'. That is the moral I hope you will take away from the discussion in this paper.[12]

Magdalen College
Lizzie.fricker@magd.ox.ac.uk

References

Aristotle trans. Rowe, C., ed. Broadie. S., *Nichomachean Ethics*. (Oxford: Oxford University Press, 2002).

Roger Crisp, 'Well-Being'. *Stanford Encyclopaedia of Philosophy*. ed. E. N. Zalta. (Stanford University: Stanford, 2017).

H. Du et al. 'Self-Esteem and Subjective Well-being Revisited.' *PLosONE*, 12(8) (2017), 1–17

Elizabeth Fricker, 'Epistemic and Practical Dependence and the Value of Skills Or: Satnavs, Good or Bad?' in *Trust in Epistemology*. ed. K. Dormandy, (Routledge: New York and London, 2019) 64–88.

[12] I have been mulling over the ideas in this paper for a long time, and they have developed in response to the numerous very valuable comments made by audiences on various occasions when I have presented them. Venues where I have done so include: Philosophy Dept, University of Edinburgh; Moral Sciences Club, University of Cambridge; Philosophy Department, University College Dublin; international epistemology conference in Bled, Slovenia; Philosophy Graduate Conference, University College London; and most recently, at a Royal Institute of Philosophy lecture in December 2019. My thanks to the many individuals in these audiences whose comments have improved and enriched the paper. A longer more detailed treatment including similar ideas is published in Fricker (2019).

John Edward Huth, *The Lost Art of Finding Our Way* (Belknap Press, 2015).

A. H. Javadi, et al. 'Hippocampal and prefontal processing of network topology to simulate the future.' *Nature Communications* 8, (2017), 1–11

Leonard D. Katz, 'Pleasure'. *Stanford Encyclopaedia of Philosophy*. ed. E. N. Zalta. (Stanford University: Stanford, 2016).

K. Konishi and V.D. Bohbot, 'Spatial navigational strategies correlate with gray matter in the hippocampus of healthy older adults tested in a virtual maze.' *Frontiers in Aging Neuroscience* 5(1) (2013), 1–8

John Stuart Mill, *Utilitarianism*. (Oxford: Oxford University Press, 1998 (1863)).

John O'Keefe and Lynn Nadel, *The Hippocampus as a Cognitive Map*. (Oxford: Clarendon Press, 1978).

M. R. O'Connor, *Wayfinding: The Science and Mystery of How Humans Navigate the World*. (New York: St. Martin's Press, 2019).

Derek Parfit, *On What Matters*. (Oxford: Oxford University Press, 2011).

Joseph Raz, *Engaging Reason*. (Oxford: Oxford University Press, 1999).

Gilbert Ryle, *The Concept of Mind*. (London: Penguin Books, 2000 (1949)).

Ernest Sosa, *Judgement and Agency* (Oxford: Oxford University Press, 2015).

Bernard Williams, 'Internal and External Reasons' in Harrison, R. ed *Rational Action: Studies in Philosophy and Social Science* (Cambridge University Press: Cambridge, 1979).

Passionate Speech: On the Uses and Abuses of Anger in Public Debate

ALESSANDRA TANESINI

Abstract
Anger dominates debates in the public sphere. In this article I argue that there are diverse forms of anger that merit different responses. My focus is especially on two types of anger that I label respectively *arrogant* and *resistant*. The first is the characteristic defensive response of those who unwarrantedly arrogate special privileges for themselves. The second is often a source of insight and a form of moral address. I detail some discursive manifestations of these two types of anger. I show that arrogant anger is responsible for attempts to intimidate and humiliate others with whom one disagrees. Whilst resistant anger can be intimidating, it is also essential in communicating moral demands.

Anger is, for better or worse, an important emotion in politics. Politicians often stoke it in the population when pursuing elections. But anger has also been described by leaders of social justice movements as an important tool in the fight against discrimination. Anger is often just below the surface in politics because it is a natural response to a perception that one (or those with whom one identifies) has been slighted. Hence, to the extent to which politics is concerned with justice, and the reduction of discrimination, it is concerned with phenomena that ordinarily elicit angry reactions. The focus of this paper is the use (and abuse) of anger in political debates and in politics more generally.

We begin to understand the functions of anger in political discourse, if we appreciate that anger is not a mere feeling, but that it is closely associated to moral judgment. In this paper I think of anger as the genus comprising a variety of emotional syndromes, that is clusters of thoughts, feelings, and dispositions to behave. These include anger as a reactive attitude of blaming someone for what they have done; but also rage which is a non-communicative form of anger. My interest here lies primarily in the communicative functions served by the expression of anger.

I argue that this focus on communicative functions gives us a principled way of distinguishing different kinds of anger and of making some progress toward understanding when angry words and actions are morally justified and when instead we should strive to avoid

doi:10.1017/S1358246121000047

them. In particular, I discuss two kinds of anger: arrogant and resistant. The first is a defensive form of status anger which is often intended to diminish or push down its targets. The second is a kind of anger that functions as a moral address in the shape of a demand. I treat these two species of anger as akin to speech acts that differ in what they are trying to achieve (perlocutionary aims) and in the kind of act they are (illocutionary force).

This paper consists of five sections. In the first I briefly argue that anger is inevitable in politics and that, furthermore, there are reasons against seeking to suppress its expression in every instance. Since there are also cases when the expression of anger seems bad in itself as well as leading to bad outcomes, we need to develop some criteria for when it is appropriate to use anger in politics. In the rest of the paper I make some progress toward this aim by distinguishing two kinds of anger on the basis of their different communicative functions. In the second section I offer an initial analysis of anger as a genus. I focus on three dimensions of this family of emotions: epistemic, communicative, and motivational. I analyse anger as a type of appraisal, a form of address, and a kind of energy that triggers and sustains action. In the third section I identify the distinctive characteristics of arrogant anger showing that it is a subordinating speech act that functions by humiliating or intimidating its targets. I argue that arrogantly angry speech acts are generally not apt but also not morally justified. In the fourth section I focus on resistant anger as the making of a demand for redress whose perlocutionary aim is the acknowledgment of a wrong and a commitment to do something about it. Resistant anger, provided that it is fitting because it is a response to a genuine wrong, is in many circumstances pro tanto justified since it is the vehicle for making moral claims that could not otherwise be made or at least heard. This leaves us with the problem that its expression, for which there might be some justification could nonetheless be counterproductive. I tackle this problem in the final section where I advocate acceptance of discomfort as a way of discerning arrogant from resistant angry reactions in other people.

1. Anger: A Political Emotion

Anger has often been a weapon in the toolbox of politicians and social leaders. For example, in the UK the successful Leave campaign leading to the referendum over exiting the EU relied on stoking in parts of the British population fear and anger directed at migrants as well as pride in the history of Empire. It is often said that

Remain failed because its campaign relied on facts, while Leave won because it managed to stir strong negative emotions. More recently, anger is the predominant sentiment animating the protests of social movements, like Black Lives Matter, against police brutality. Anger directed at entrenched injustice has been a dominant emotional colour of Afro-American lives for hundreds of years. James Baldwin conveys its all-consuming power when he writes in 'Notes of a Native Son' that '[t]here is not a Negro alive who does not have this rage in his blood–one has the choice, merely, of living with it consciously or surrendering to it. As for me, this fever has recurred in me, and does, and will until the day I die' (1998, p. 70).

These examples are not unique. It is sometimes argued that anger is essential to all politics that seeks to foment an us versus them mentality. Hence, anger would be pivotal to all two party systems but also to all oppositional radical social movements (Ost, 2004). Anger would thus be prevalent when the citizenry is divided or polarised, and when some sections of the population are systematically subjected to grave injustices.

Political disagreements that are marked by anger often exhibit distinctive characteristics. They are passionate and fiery. But they are also described as uncivil. Advocates of each side are not afraid to verbally insult, mock, humiliate and show contempt for one another. These behaviours were as prevalent during religious disputes in early modern Europe as they are today (Bejan, 2017). In order to avoid a descent into violence or even war, philosophers and political theorists in the seventeenth century and today advocate toleration and civility (Locke, 2003; Walzer, 1997).

In the same spirit, there is a long philosophical tradition recommending the regulation or even suppression of anger. Whilst Aristotle thought that anger – in the right measure and against the right target – was virtuous, the Stoics and Seneca wrote at length about the havoc caused by this emotion (Aristotle, 2007; Seneca, 2010). More recently, Nussbaum (2016a; 2016b) and Pettigrove (2012) have argued that we should not give in to anger but seek to cultivate meekness and forgiveness. Pettigrove and Tanaka (2014), for instance, cite empirical evidence showing that anger clouds moral judgment. It promotes a defensive attitude that leads one to perceive as slights or wrongs conduct that is morally acceptable. Anger is also responsible for loss of self-control and for morally unjustifiable aggressive behaviour. For these reasons they conclude that anger is everything considered harmful and therefore best avoided.

In addition, Nussbaum argues that anger is even irrational or self-stultifying because it motivates a desire for revenge that must fail to right the wrong that elicited it. For example, if I am angry with you because you killed my brother, what I really want is that my brother is still alive. However, if, because I am angry, I lash out and kill your brother in revenge, I fail to satisfy my want. My actions do not bring my brother back (Nussbaum, 2016a).

In direct contrast to this viewpoint, there is a long standing tradition of thought that is prevalent especially in the Afro-American tradition about the rightfulness of anger and its expression. Hence, Lorde (1996) praises trained anger for its ability to give one clarity of vision. Lugones (2003) describes some forms of anger as resistant. This kind of anger is in her opinion important to give one the courage to stand up against oppression, to build coalitions with other disempowered individuals, and to develop a sophisticated understanding of one's own condition. Anger reverberates in the speeches of Malcolm X but it also makes an appearance in addresses by Martin Luther King. Anger, so understood, is necessary if one is to retain dignity and self-respect in the face of systemic oppression (Cherry, 2019).[1]

While these two viewpoints on anger make diametrically opposed recommendations, they also both appear to be at least partially correct. Anger is on some occasions ill-fitting and morally unjustified. On other occasions it is instead a useful and necessary means in the pursuit of justice. In this paper I aim to make some progress toward formulating a principled distinction between these two types of case by way of isolating characteristics of two varieties of anger: arrogant anger and resistant anger.

2. What is Anger

Anger is an emotional syndrome that partly overlaps with rage, moral indignation, resentment and hard feelings. All of these have at times been called 'anger'. In what follows, I do not try to demarcate anger from these other emotions. Instead, I treat anger as a genus of which all of these emotions are species. Each is a syndrome; that is, it is a complex cluster of thoughts, feelings, desires, and behavioural dispositions which are usually but not necessarily associated. I restrict my attention here to so-called agential forms of anger. This is the kind of anger that is directed at other agents, rather than at things or creatures that do not have the capacities required to function as members of the moral community.

[1] Non-Western traditions also tend to be ambivalent about the value of anger. On Buddhism see McRae (2017).

Aristotle in his *Rhetoric* defines anger as a response to a perceived intentional slight inflicted on oneself or those close to one that is accompanied by a desire to get even (2007, 1378a, 30–33). Aristotle's definition is best suited to a special kind of anger that Nussbaum (2016a) has aptly labelled 'status anger'. It would be a response to a perception that another agent has slighted one by behaving in ways that do not befit one's social status. Hence, anger would be the response to being treated as occupying a lower social rank than one takes oneself to have. In addition, anger would trigger a revenge response that purports to re-establish social status by lowering the rank of the offender.

Aristotle's definition is too narrow in at least two dimensions. First, anger does not always concern social status. Second, it is not always associated with desires for revenge. For example, it is not uncommon for people to be angry with their friends when these have been inconsiderate. This anger often has nothing to do with social status. It might concern instead a breach of trust or the friend's unwillingness to sacrifice something for our benefit. It is also frequently associated with a demand of an apology, rather than a desire for revenge.

This initial characterisation of anger as a response to a perceived slight shows that anger, like some other emotions such as guilt, has both a focus and a target. The focus is the slight that triggers the angry response. The target is the person at whom the angry response is directed. In the case of anger this is the person responsible for the slight. In this regard anger differs from contempt, which is a related negative emotion. The latter is a global emotion since its focus is the agent that it targets, rather than, as is the case with anger, a specific feature or property of a person (Bell, 2013). This is why a person can be angry with another for something she did whilst also appreciating other aspects of the same person. When someone holds another in contempt, she cannot see anything admirable in the person she thinks is beyond the pale.

There are at least three dimensions to anger: epistemic, communicative and motivational. The first concerns anger as a kind of moral appraisal. The second pertains to anger as a form of moral address. The third applies to anger as a motivational force. I briefly explain each of these three aspect of anger in the remainder of this section.

Anger, like other emotions, is an evaluation. The person who is angry at the policeman who has stopped and handcuffed her without apparent cause evaluates the action of the enforcement agent to be wrongful. Hence, anger is a way of classifying behaviour as failing to meet moral standards and showing lack of good will (Shoemaker, 2015). Since it is an evaluation, anger is subject to the epistemic standard of propriety of correctness. Regardless of whether getting angry is the right thing to do in a given situation, anger can be accurate or not. It is accurate, apt or fitting when it presents as angersome actions that in actuality merit an angry response (D'Arms and Jacobsen, 2000). Thus, to be fitting or apt anger must focus on real slights. In addition, it must also be proportionate to the severity of the slight. Anger that is excessive or insufficient ill-fits the slight that it targets. These considerations support the view that anger can be an epistemically rational response. That is, one can supply evidence for the shape and size of one's anger that shows it to be an accurate presentation of how things are in the world.

Anger is no mere rating of an action as a slight. It is also a blame response and a way of holding the perpetrator accountable (Shoemaker, 2015). This idea is often expressed by noting that anger, like resentment and indignation, is a reactive attitude (Strawson, 2008). It is a response that is morally appropriate only when it is directed toward other moral agents. It is a responsibility response that consists in calling people to accounts by blaming them. There are various theories about the nature of blaming responses since these have been construed as akin to a punishment or a sanction (Smart, 1961), or a form of moral protest (Smith, 2013). Yet, another Strawsonian approach takes blame to serve a communicative function (Macnamara, 2015).[2] So understood, anger would be a form of moral address. One way of fleshing out this thought is that anger, but also other related emotional attitudes like resentment, are quasi speech acts because they are demands (Darwall, 2006, pp. 3, 120).[3] More specifically, these reactive attitudes are orders and as such they presuppose that the speakers have the authority to impose obligations onto the addressees. Darwall thinks of these prescriptions as second-personal because, if felicitous, they are instituted merely on the basis of the speakers' authority to impose new burdens on the addressees.[4]

[2] This is not to say that all anger is expressed. The point is that communication is what anger is for regardless as to whether in each particularly instance it succeeds in communicating (Macnamara, 2015).

[3] Macnamara (2013) argues that blame is a kind of moral address which does not take the form of a demand because we can blame people without taking ourselves to have the authority required to make a demand. I found her examples unconvincing but I lack the space to address the issue here.

[4] Obligations that are instituted by promises are also second personal. If I promise to you that I will come for dinner. I acquire a new responsibility toward you specifically and solely in virtue of my ability and willingness to acquire it.

This model of reactive attitudes as blaming responses that implicitly make demands on the targets of the attitudes provides a highly plausible account of the function of angry speech. Anger, unlike contempt, is an approach emotion since it moves the angry person to engage with the targets of anger rather than to avoid or shun them. Anger usually finds a verbal expression. Even when anger results in violence, it is rarely silent. Angry people usually shout or hurl abuses. These features of anger indicate that angry people want to make themselves heard. In short, anger is an attempt at communication of some sort.

It is also plausible to claim that the communication takes the form of a moral address. To see this consider what it takes for anger to be quelled. Sometimes anger stops, not because the angry person is exhausted or resigned, but because the reasons one had to be angry no longer hold. We can make sense of this idea if anger is not primarily an appraisal of a past wrong, but a form of address such as a request or a demand which stops once it has been satisfied. If anger is a mere appraisal of the existence of a past slight, if that evaluation is fitting, there is nothing after the event that can change its propriety. Thus, there would be no reason not to be angry forever (cf., Callard, 2017).[5] However, if anger is a form of moral address, once that address has received the response it sought, the addressee has a reason to stop being angry.[6]

In my view the address has the illocutionary force of an order, the issuing of a demand. That is, angry verbal or silent conduct is an exercitive quasi speech act that consists in an exercise of power to institute new obligations, prohibitions or permissions (Austin, 1976). The demand made in expressing anger is that the target of the angry response endorses the content presented in the angry expression, and thereby acknowledges a fault. This content is the moral evaluation of the situation as angersome. An example might help to clarify these points. Imagine a Black Lives Matter protester reacts angrily at being hit by a policeman with a baton. The protester's anger is a moral appraisal of the situation which is experienced as an assault by the policemen. The anger presents this assault as being wrong and responds to it by blaming the policeman. That is,

[5] In reality the matter is more complex as indicated by the ingenious solution proposed in Na'aman (2019).

[6] It should be noted that not all kinds of anger are a form of moral address. Rage, for instance, is often uncommunicative. It can for example be used to scare people away (Malatino, 2019). I return to this point in section 4 below.

the protester in being angry presents or makes manifest the following content: Your (the policeman's) hitting me with a baton has wronged me. This is the locutionary content of the angry response. Its illocutionary force is a demand that the addressee acknowledges his fault by coming to share the viewpoint of the speaker and that the addressee does so at least partly because the speaker demands it. That is, the protester orders that the policeman endorses the content: My hitting you with a baton has wronged you. This order is only fully successful when the policeman endorses that content in part as a recognition of the authority of the protester to issue this demand, which is to say, to subordinate the addressee's will to his own.[7]

I hasten to add that mere acknowledgement of the fault in the form of a sincere expression of guilt is usually insufficient to satisfy the person who is angry. The phenomenon of so-called white guilt is a case in point. Liberal white guilt does not cause anger to stop. Instead, it reenforces it. One of the reasons for this reaction is that the white person who reacts with guilt to white privilege is more concerned with her own moral standing than with social injustice. Her focus is on seeking forgiveness for herself rather than ending the oppression that provoked black people's anger. Hence, the white person has not come to share the angry person's moral appraisal of the situation because she perceive the damage done to her moral standing by the wrong she has committed to be more pressing than addressing the wrong itself. Thus, what the angry person seeks is a genuine acknowledgment of a fault. Feeling guilty is not sufficient and may not even be necessary. Instead, often an active engagement with a process of repair is required (Walker, 2006).[8]

I have explained above that fittingness is the norm of propriety of anger as a moral appraisal. Anger is apt or fitting only if the locutionary content of the angry expression is true.[9] Thus, its aptness is an epistemic reason to be angry. However, even when anger is fitting there might be reasons of another kind not to be angry. For example, being angry might be the morally wrong thing to do in

[7] In this regard anger is different from some other emotions like fear. Fear is also communicative in the sense that it usually elicits an uptake since witnessing another person's fear often causes one to become afraid. The communicative structure of anger is different since its uptake involves a recognition of the intentions of the angry person. This is why it is appropriate to think of anger as a quasi speech act.

[8] This is why as Cherry (2019) observes anger is compatible with love.

[9] As noted above, it also needs to be proportional to the seriousness of the slight or wrong.

the circumstances. It might be prudentially wrong or risky. Thus, there are also practical reasons to be or not be angry. Several critics of anger focus on this latter kind of reason to recommend that one refrains from anger. They note for example that anger is often met with anger. Hence, expressions of anger even when the anger is apt might prove politically counterproductive.[10]

This distinction between two kinds of reasons (epistemic and practical) to be angry is crucial to ascertain angry contributions to debate that are justified from those that constitute an abuse. I address these points in sections three and four below. For now, I restrict myself to two observations. First, anger that is not apt is never all things considered justified. Anger is not fitting when it presents as a slight something that is not a slight. It is also not apt if it is not proportional to the seriousness of the slight. This second requirement of aptness raises some delicate questions about the nature of the slighting conduct since this might have negligible consequences but have acquired a profound symbolic meaning. Thus, the person who reacts with extreme anger to a small aggression or insult might exhibit a fitting response because the size of the wrong inflicted is not determined by the gravity of the consequences of the conduct.

Second, one must tread carefully when reasoning that one should not be angry because one's anger is likely to be counterproductive. Considerations of political expediency are important and they might in some circumstances legitimately determine one's conduct. Nevertheless, it is important to remember that often apt anger backfires only because those who are responsible for, or complicit with, injustices are not prepared to acknowledge their role in wrongdoing. Unless this unwillingness to face injustice is tackled, it is hard to see how progress can be made in addressing systemic social injustice. Hence, even when one can predict that apt anger is going to be counterproductive in the short term, there might be a reason to express it nonetheless in order to shift the burden of emotional distress on those responsible for wrongdoing (Archer and Mills, 2019).

I have detailed the epistemic and communicative dimensions of anger. I now briefly turn to its motivating force. The fact that anger can help in the fight against injustice by making one fearless and perseverant is a recurring theme in the discussion of anger found in the writings of people of colour. Both Lorde (1996) and

[10] This conflict between different kinds of reasons is especially prevalent when one is subjected to systemic oppression. Srinivasan (2018) argues that having to manage it is a further unfair burden imposed on those who are subordinated.

Lugones (2003) remark that anger gives one courage to protest despite the risk of being subject to brutality, insults or in some cases incarceration. They also note that it gives one the strength to continue the fight for justice even when the prospects of success are limited. These motivational qualities of anger are, however, a double-edge sword. Continuous anger, expressed or suppressed, is damaging to mental and physical health. This is why Tessman (2005) has identified an angry disposition as a character trait that is helpful for those who engage in liberatory struggles, whilst also being a burden because of the toll it exacts on their mental and physical well-being.

In this section I have described expressions of anger as communicative acts that have the force of a demand that its targets share the moral outlook of the angry person and thus acknowledge the fault to which the anger would be an apt response. In the next section I turn to one species of anger that is often manifested in conduct designed to intimidate and humiliate people in order to diminish their social status. This anger is expressed in exercitives that seek to subordinate other people. I call it: arrogant anger.

3. Arrogant anger

There is a kind of anger that is characteristic of some social groups whose economic prospects and social standing are gradually diminishing. In the US and the UK this is the anger characteristic of white working class males whose working conditions have worsened and whose social standing as superior to people of colour and women of all races is being progressively eroded. There is no doubt that these people are being harmed and are genuinely suffering as a result. They struggle to make ends meet because of increasing levels of social inequality. However, these individuals have also incorporated a social identity that makes their sense of self-worth dependent on being superior to members of some other groups.[11]

This thought is perceptively captured by Baldwin when he writes that one of the reasons why black people are treated so cruelly in the United States is because social life is marked by a desire to ascend rung by rung in social and economic status. This conception of aspiration requires that some group functions as a marker of the lowest

11 Of course, this situation ultimately benefits those whose inherited wealth and status protects them from the risk of falling down the social ladder.

rank below which one may not fall without experiencing chaos and loss of self-esteem. In this context, 'the Negro tells us where the bottom is: *because he is there*, and *where* he is, beneath us, we know where the limits are and how far we must not fall. We must not fall beneath him' (Baldwin, 1998, pp. 218–19). It is this fear that is at the root of some white male anger that manifests itself as a form of aggrieved entitlement that is directed at women of all races and at people of colour. Particularly, those white men whose dignity is being harmed by extreme inequality struggle to preserve self-esteem by making sure that as they descend the rungs of society they keep themselves above some others whom in their eyes mark the places that must remain below them.[12]

I call this kind of anger 'arrogant' because it displays the characteristics of *superbia* understood as the tendency to 'do others down' in order to elevate oneself (Alighieri, 1994, Purg., XVII vv 115–117). Arrogance so conceived would be characteristic of those individuals whose sense of self-worth is at least partially dependent on thinking of themselves as superior to other social groups which one ranks as inferior. In describing this kind of anger as arrogant, I do not wish to imply that all those who occasionally exhibit this emotion are best thought of as being arrogant people. It is without doubt possible to behave in arrogant ways in some circumstances and toward some people even when the label arrogant is not an apt description of one's character. That said, people who are arrogant jerks often exhibit precisely this kind of arrogant entitled behaviour (James, 2014).

Given this initial characterisation, arrogant anger is best classified as a kind of status anger. This is anger that is a response to a perceived slight about one's social rank and is designed to reassert that status. Aristotle's original definition of anger cited above seems to have been formulated with precisely this kind of anger in mind. Status anger is a natural response to conduct that does not befit what one is entitled to given one's social standing. For instance, a woman

[12] For this reason I partly disagree with Kimmel's (2013) account of working class male rage as being misdirected toward minorities and women rather than corporations. White male blue collar anger is misdirected in the sense that corporations are the cause of the economic deprivation that is the main root of this rage. But it is also a kind of anger that is designed to assert one's social superiority. As such it is directed at the right targets, even though the anger itself is not fitting. I hasten to add that this anger is often stoked and manipulated by powerful groups whose interests are best served by fomenting discord among under privileged social groups.

who is asked by a participant to a meeting that she is about to chair that she make him a cup of coffee might feel both angry and resentful at the treatment. The anger is a reaction to the perception that one is treated as staff whose role is to service the meeting rather than to chair it. A characteristic feature of status anger is that it is often manifested in actions that are designed to re-establish one's social position by lowering the rank of the perceived offender. Thus, the chairwoman might decide to serve this participant coffee in front of other attendees before declaring the meeting open in order to embarrass the person who has simply presumed that she was the note taker. This behaviour is clearly designed to extract revenge by putting the prejudiced individual in his place.[13]

Examples such as this one illustrate two important features of status anger. Firstly, this form of anger can be fitting. It is often exhibited by subordinated individuals who assert their entitlements by putting down people who, through their conduct, have unfairly ranked them as inferior. Secondly, this kind of anger can be an effective response. To see why, one must first note that social ranking is often partly determined by the way in which people treat each other. In the absence of a formally sanctioned hierarchy, the group leader is simply the person that others treat as a leader and who behaves accordingly. In addition, even when a leader has been pre-selected this person's ability to occupy the role is severely curtailed when other members of the group do not recognise his or her authority. Status anger is a response to a perceived slight that ranks one as occupying a lower social position than one thinks one merits. As such the conduct that elicited the anger always at least threatens to actually reduce one's status. The angry response can effectively counteract the perceived slight because it can diminish the social rank of the person whose actions provoked the anger. In this manner, status anger has the power to correct for the perceived wrong that elicited it.

Arrogant anger is a kind of status anger that pertains to individuals who regularly exhibit anger directed toward members of some other social group partly because of their group membership and designed to rank them as inferior as a means of preserving the angry person's alleged social superiority.[14] The account of anger as a quasi-speech act elaborated above helps to supply a fuller characterisation of the structure of arrogant anger. The locutionary contents of these expression of anger are that the targets of the anger have slighted the angry

[13] The notion of status anger is discussed by Nussbaum (2016).

[14] I only have in mind social groups of people who share some identity such as gender, race, ethnicity, age or sexual orientation.

person. The target might be an individual, a collective or a whole social group. What is crucial is that the target's behaviour is interpreted as being a slight because of the angry person's perception of the targeted social group. For example, a plain clothed white policeman might experience a black woman's refusal to leave her car not as an expression of fear but as uppity or confrontational. He perceives her behaviour as a slight because he construes it as a challenge to his authority as a representative of law enforcement. The same policeman might instead generally interpret the same kind of refusal as expression of fear when it is expressed by an older clearly affluent white woman. Similarly, he might accept a refusal phrased as a demand that he makes himself known when it is issued by a self-assured white male driver wearing a sharp suit. The policeman's angry response is an example of arrogant anger if it is characteristic of his treatment of black women in general, and if he typically reacts in different ways in response to the same or similar behaviour when exhibited by white women or expensively dressed white men.

The illocutionary force of arrogantly angry responses is twofold. They are 'verdictives' similar to the verdict issued by juries because they are presented as being based on matters of fact. As such, angry responses implicitly rank members of the target's social group as inferior to the group of the arrogantly angry individual. This is because the angry response implicitly classifies the behaviour which elicits it as improper due to the social status of the target. The policeman of the example is not offended by the white man's request that he shows his police ID, because the policeman implicitly thinks of the other as an equal rather than as an inferior whose behaviour needs to be deferential. By responding angrily to the same demand if issued by a black woman, the policeman judges her to be ranked as inferior to him.

Arrogantly angry responses are also exercises of power (exercitives) since they subordinate others by being demands that their targets implicitly acknowledge their inferior status. In being angry, the angry person demands that the target shares his appraisal of the situation. Thus, the target is ordered both to acknowledge the angry person's authority to give him orders, and to acknowledge the angry person's ranking of her (as the target of the anger) as inferior to him in virtue of some of her social identities. In this manner arrogant anger is a way of legitimising subordination.[15] Finally, the perlocutionary goal of arrogant anger is to reduce the status of its targets,

[15] For the idea that some speech acts subordinate by being verdictives and exercitives see (Langton, 1993).

something it achieves in several ways including by subordinating them.

This characterisation of arrogant anger presupposes that it is a kind of status anger that is normally not apt. It is not fitting because it appraises as a slight conduct that is not in reality morally bad. The behaviour only seems insulting from the perspective of someone who wrongly thinks that people belonging to his social group are more worthy than members of some other social groups and thus deserving of special entitlement. Given the plausible assumption that all human beings possess dignity in equal measure, what is appraised as a slight in arrogant anger is often no such thing. Rather it might be conduct that treats one as an equal rather than one's superior or behaviour that resists illegitimate arrogation of entitlements on the part of the arrogantly angry individual. Arrogant anger, however, is not unfitting because it is a kind of status anger. Some of the examples above show that status anger can be apt. Individuals occupy different roles in society. Some have positions of legitimate authority over others. As such they are entitled to expect behaviour that befits their status. Arrogant anger is different. It presupposes inequalities of status among social groups such as races or genders. It is not fitting because there are no differences in worth or dignity among human beings.

Arrogant anger is at the root of several behaviours that are frequently observed when people debate with others with whom they disagree on both factual and normative matters (Tanesini, 2018). What I have in mind here are expressions of intolerance to criticism. There are reasons to believe that those who are prone to arrogant anger are especially unreceptive to taking criticism seriously. I have argued elsewhere (2016) that when speakers use assertions to tell something to an audience, they undertake commitments including, typically, a commitment to answer proper criticisms should these arise. It is a characteristic feature of people who behave in superior ways that they arrogate for themselves the authority not to be answerable to others for their claims.

I have compared this attitude to an arrogation of the special authoritativeness that is said by Catholics to pertain to ex-cathedra pronouncements by the Pope. These are meant to be akin to verdicts since they are said to be based on the facts but are not open to challenge by dissenting human beings. If this is right, individuals prone to arrogant anger take their assertions to have a special authority that those made by members of some other social groups are said to lack. It is because they implicitly take themselves not to be open to being challenged in debates by those whom they rank as inferior, that people who are prone to arrogant anger perceive these challenges as slights. These criticisms are interpreted as insults because they constitute failures to acknowledge the alleged entitlements arrogated by the speaker. This is why ordinary expressions of dissent elicit angry reactions in those who are prone to arrogant anger. These angry responses have usually one of two perlocutionary aims: humiliation and intimidation.

Manifestations of arrogant anger can humiliate their targets because as I indicated above this kind of anger is a subordinating speech act whose illocutionary force is to rank people as subordinate and to exercise authority to legitimise this ranking. In debates arrogantly angry interventions can lead to open mocking, eye rolling and expressions of incredulity at the stupidity of one's opponent in debate. They can also promote feigning a failure of understanding or adopting an attitude of condescension. Some of these behaviours are not themselves example of anger but they are among the aggressive consequences of an attitude of arrogantly angry intolerance of dissent.

Anger also often intimidates. This feature of anger is typically not a consequence of its communicative dimension. Anger as a syndrome frequently includes hot and aggressive feelings. These are especially dominant when anger is, like rage, uncommunicative. This kind of anger does not seek redress because instead it functions to push away its targets by threatening or scaring them. The intimidatory function of anger is not the sole preserve of arrogant anger, but it is often also present in the anger of members of subordinated groups, especially when they fear for their own physical integrity (Malatino, 2019). However, it is also an efficient weapon in the hands of those whose anger functions to push other people down so that they can emerge victorious. For example, intimidation, when successful, prompts other people to self-silence in order to avoid facing the wrath of the arrogant person. In this way, anger preempts the risk that one might be asked difficult questions when debating matters with opponents. In addition, intimidation also fosters in its targets a tendency to fake agreement to avoid the unpleasantness of aggression. As a result the claims made by those who exhibit a tendency to arrogant anger might seem to third parties to enjoy wider support than they in fact do. It is also possible that the appearance of agreement is taken as evidence of agreement by those who have a tendency to arrogant anger. In support of this hypothesis there is evidence that arrogant individuals tend to overestimate the extent to which others agree with their views (McGregor, Nail, Marigold and Kang, 2005).

The considerations raised in this section indicate that there are no good reasons to be arrogantly angry. Arrogant anger is a false appraisal of the situation. Therefore, it is a kind of epistemic mistake. In addition, it results in behaviours which, because they suppress criticism and disagreement, diminish access to information that would improve the epistemic quality of one's viewpoint. Arrogant anger is also manifested in morally reprehensible conduct such as acts of intimidation and humiliation. These are in most circumstances morally unacceptable. In short, there are both epistemic and moral reasons not to be angry, if one's anger is arrogant.

4. Resistant anger

There are also circumstances in which some people have plenty of reasons to be angry. When these reasons are present, it would seem that oftentimes anger is not merely permissible but desirable as an instrument in the fight for social justice and as a pre-requisite of self-respect. There is a well-established tradition, prevalent especially in Afro-American thought, that portrays anger along these lines both as a constant companion and as a tool in the struggle for liberation (Baldwin, 1998; Cherry, 2019; Lorde, 1996; Lugones, 2003). I borrow from Lugones (2003) the label 'resistant' to identify anger of this sort.

In what follows I detail some features of two kinds of resistant anger: communicative and non-communicative. It is, however, important to note first of all that anger does not come neatly packaged in distinct kinds. Some of the examples I provided above of arrogant anger included people who were also at the same time angry in other ways about different targets. The white collar worker who is angry at migrants because they take jobs that he thinks they should not be allowed to compete for is often also angry for different reasons with politicians who have little regard for his situation. Alternatively, a black person might direct some of her anger at another black person whom she sees as embodying the negative stereotypes attributed to racialised subjects. In short, people who suffer systematically from harm are angry often, and in different ways.[16] Sometimes their anger is arrogant and sometimes it is not.

Resistant anger is anger as a response to a perceived slight inflicted upon oneself or someone with whom one identifies because of

[16] On the risks of misdirected anger see also hooks (1995) as well as Lorde (1996).

membership in a stigmatised social group. Thus, resistant anger is anger in response to a perceived slight that is racist, misogynist, ageist, homophobic or so forth. So characterised, resistant anger is anger in response to a specific kind of slight that involves the ranking of some social group as inferior to others. There are thus different kinds of resistant anger. Some are examples of status anger. For instance, when a woman due to chair a meeting becomes angry when she is asked to serve the coffee, her anger is a response to a perceived slight that consists in the presumption that because she is a woman she cannot occupy the authoritative role of chair. But resistant anger need not concern diminutions of an individual's social status because of prejudice about that individual's social identity. The anger manifested by members of the Black Lives Matter movement is an example of resistant anger at racist injustice that is not particularly focused on matters of social status. Both these examples illustrate that resistant anger can be communicative.

Communicative anger, as explained in section two above, is a form of moral address. It is an exercitive speech act that demands of the targets of the anger that they share the angry person's moral appraisal of the circumstances and acknowledge that person's authority to issue this demand. Both arrogant and resistant anger are communicative as they constitute a form of engagement with the targets of the anger expecting them to acknowledge their fault and the other 'authoritativeness'. Because communicative anger is a form of moral address its presence is compatible with seeking to dialogue with those toward whom one's anger is addressed. This kind of anger when apt could, if appropriately received, be a stimulus to a process of addressing injustice and repairing damaged civic relationships.

Often, however, resistant anger is not communicative. Lugones (2003) identifies this kind of emotional response when she notes that sometimes those who are angry no longer care to be understood by, or communicate with, the targets of their anger. Rage is the best label for this emotion. It has found even fewer defenders than anger. Anger serves a purpose since it might succeed in moving those who are responsible for injustices to change their behaviours. Rage, since it fails to engage communicatively with them, would seem destined to be ineffective since it is usually completely unintelligible to those whose actions have caused it. Yet, as Lugones also points out, rage can be a source of information for those who witness it. Observing another's rage directed at a third party might alert one to the possibility that that person's emotion is a response to a grave harm. Hence, rage can indicate even when it does not communicate. As such, and especially when one can sympathise with the enraged person, even rage can be a tool of coalition building and a means to deepen one's understanding of injustice.

This characterisation of resistant anger and rage shows that these can be apt or fitting moral appraisals. Fitting moral emotions are sources of insight since they are correct presentations of the moral features of situations. As such resistant anger and rage can be a source of knowledge. These emotions are epistemically valuable since without them one might not have attended to the morally relevant aspects of the situation and thus would not have been able to understand that, for instance, some person's action is morally problematic (Lepoutre, 2018). In addition, when the conceptual resources required to understand the nature of some slight or wrong are not widely shared, resistant anger can alert one that something is not quite right. In so far as anger functions as a warning it can instigate reflection and inquiry aimed at making sense of one's experiences. Hence, provided anger is apt, there are epistemic reasons to be angry.

There are also practical reasons, based on the motivational force of anger, to be resistantly angry. When injustice is systemic, widespread and entrenched, as racism and misogyny undoubtedly are, it takes a lot of courage and perseverance to continue struggling against these injustices. Whilst in principle it might be possible for a human being to have these character strengths without the impetus that anger provides, in reality for ordinary humans it is likely to be the case that burning anger at the sight of repeated injustice supplies the necessary motivational stimulus not to give up because of exhaustion and despair (Tessman, 2005). Doreen Lawrence, for example, noted how it was her anger directed at the killers, but also at the police, that kept her going in the fight to get justice for her murdered son.[17]

In addition, at least when anger is communicative, this emotion constitutes a way of claiming moral authority for oneself. That is, it is a way of asserting one's entitlement to make moral demands upon others. In so far as the ability to issue such demands is an essential component of human agency, resistant anger in the face of systemic injustice can be a way of asserting one's self-worth and thus a manifestation of self-respect. As such, apt resistant anger, at least, is intrinsically morally valuable (Srinivasan, 2018). For this reason also, there are good moral reasons to be resistantly angry.

Resistant anger is an important tool to combat the destructive effects of arrogant anger on debates. Because resistant anger is an

[17] As reported by the Guardian https://www.theguardian.com/uk/1999/feb/14/race.world

instrument by which to assert one's moral authority, it is a means to communicate that one will not cower in the face of speech acts designed to mock or humiliate one. In addition, because anger makes one fearless, it gives one the ability to assert one's position when confronted with acts of intimidation. Hence, resistant anger is especially helpful as a way of counteracting those abuses of power that characterise the deployment of arrogant anger in debates.

To summarise, there are plenty of reasons to be resistantly angry and even raging. Resistant anger is a source of knowledge that can be communicated in debate, if interlocutors are willing to listen. It is a way of exercising moral agency by asserting one's authority and issuing moral demands that others acknowledge their faults. It is a way of building coalitions and fortifying one's character in the face of attempts to intimidate and humiliate one. Yet, these are reasons to be resistantly angry that should weighed up against all other considerations. One may grant these reasons and claim that they count for naught since anger is always strategically counterproductive. Anger would achieve nothing because those targeted by anger always react to anger with anger. Thus, although both sides wish to communicate to the other by means of anger, neither is listening and so no progress is ever made.

5. How to respond to anger

The last section raised the possibility that regardless of the existence of epistemic and practical reasons to be on occasion angry, ultimately anger is counterproductive since it does not make one's opponents want to listen to one's grievance. For this reason, one might conclude that even if anger is understandable, it is best avoided when one is trying to debate one's political adversaries. However, whilst there is no doubt that oftentimes it is strategically prudent to suppress one's anger when debating, it is important to note that people can control their anger. Hence, the burden of control should be fairly distributed. Especially in those cases where their anger is apt, people should not also have to shoulder the responsibility for regulating their emotions (Archer and Mills, 2019; Liebow and Glazer, 2019).

I conclude this section with a couple of recommendations on how to relate to others' anger if one is to behave in a manner that promotes justice rather than exacerbates injustice.[18] It is tempting to be quick

[18] These techniques are essentially designed to avoid immediately responding with anger to others' anger.

to judge other people's anger, to recommend that if they have a just cause, they should put their points across calmly and politely. It is easier, one may add, to hear a message when this is explained in an even tone. Yet, even though it is sometimes appropriate to criticise others for their anger, one must remain alert to the possibility that one's attitude is one of tone policing that silences some who might have been wronged (Berenstain, 2019; Jamieson, Volinsky, Weitz and Kenski, 2018). Thus, long before DiAngelo (2011) labelled the phenomenon 'white fragility', Lorde (1996) notes, in response to a white woman who asks her to mute her anger so that her addressee can hear the message, that she appears to think that her tone is a bigger problem than the injustice she highlights in her message (Bailey, 2018). Tone policing, and the calls for civility that accompany it, have little to recommend for themselves.

Since it is really hard when faced with others' anger directed at oneself to ascertain immediately whether their anger is apt, arrogant or resistant, it is essential that we train ourselves to dwell in our discomfort, rather than lash out in defence (Applebaum, 2017). If one avoids responding quickly and defensively to anger with anger, one can create the space to reflect and listen so that to have a better chance to understand whether the anger is fitting. Broadly speaking two strategies recommend themselves for dealing with the distress caused by being the recipient of others' anger. The first is a technique known as self-affirmation which consists in affirming the self by reflecting on the values that one cares most deeply about (McQueen and Klein, 2006). Self-affirmation has been shown to reduce defensiveness (Sherman and Cohen, 2006). It is also thought to mitigate arrogant behaviour (Haddock and Gebauer, 2011). The technique could be deployed when one is about to enter a situation where one expects to experience distress in response to others' anger. This technique is also useful to mitigate arrogant anger because this kind of anger is a defensive response to protect self-esteem.

The second technique is emotional self-regulation. It consists in the adoption of techniques designed to reduce emotional responses by consciously regulating one's cognitive processing. It could involve shifting attention away from one's own feelings to those of the other person whose actions have triggered the emotion. One might try to reappraise the situation by putting the stimulus of the emotion in a broader perspective so as to understand the causes of the behaviour. Finally one might simply try to suppress showing one's emotional response to the distress one is experiencing (Archer and Mills, 2019). In this manner one can put oneself in a mindset where one refrains from responding immediately to other people's anger in order to listen to what they are saying and to understand whether they have reasons to be angry.

To conclude, we should avoid adopting a blanket approach to anger. Some anger is best thought as arrogant. Anger of this kind is to be avoided because it is not fitting and is the likely cause of morally reprehensible debating behaviour. But anger can also be valuable when it is resistant. Anger of this second sort is an important source of knowledge and an important means to assert one's moral authority. Whilst it is true that even resistant anger is often met with anger and thus leads to a stalemate, the onus is on the targets of anger to be alert to the fact that the anger they face might be apt and justified. They can do this by regulating their emotions and by affirming the self through reflecting on the value of what they value.

Cardiff University
Tanesini@cardiff.ac.uk

References

Dante Alighieri, *La Commedia Secondo L'antica Vulgata,* (Firenze: Casa Editrice Le Lettere, 1994).

Barbara Applebaum, 'Comforting Discomfort As Complicity: White Fragility And The Pursuit Of Invulnerability', *Hypatia*, 32 (2017), 862–75.

Alfred Archer and Georgie Mills, 'Anger, Affective Injustice And Emotion Regulation', *Philosophical Topics*, 47 (2019), 75–94.

Aristotle, *On Rhetoric: A Theory Of Civic Discourse* (New York And Oxford: Oxford University Press, 2007).

John Langshaw Austin, *How To Do Things With Words* (Oxford; New York: Oxford University Press, 1976).

Alison Bailey, 'On Anger, Silence, And Epistemic Injustice', *Royal Institute Of Philosophy Supplement*, 84 (2018), 93–115.

James Baldwin, *Collected Essays* (New York: Library Of America, 1998).

Teresa M. Bejan, *Mere Civility: Disagreement And The Limits Of Toleration* (Cambridge, Massachusetts: Harvard University Press, 2017).

Macalester Bell, *Hard Feelings: The Moral Psychology Of Contempt* (New York: Oxford University Press, 2013).

Agnes Callard, 'The Reason To Be Angry Forever' In Myisha Cherry and Owen Flanagan, *The Moral Psychology Of*

Anger (London And New York: Rowman & Littlefield International, 2017), 123–37.

Myisha Cherry, 'Love, Anger And Racial Injustice' In Adrienne M. Martin, *The Routledge Handbook Of Love In Philosophy* (London And New York: Routledge, 2019), 157–68.

Justin D'Arms and Daniel Jacobsen, 'The Moralistic Fallacy: On The 'Appropriateness' Of Emotions', *Philosophy And Phenomenological Research*, 61 (2000), 65–90.

Stephen Darwall, *The Second-Person Standpoint: Morality, Respect, And Accountability* (Cambridge, Mass.: Harvard University Press, 2006).

Robin Diangelo, 'White Fragility', *International Journal Of Critical Pedagogy*, 3 (2011), 54–70.

Geoffrey Haddock And Jochen E. Gebauer, 'Defensive Self-Esteem Impacts Attention, Attitude Strength, And Self-Affirmation Processes', *Journal Of Experimental Social Psychology*, 47 (2011), 1276–84.

bell hooks, *Killing Rage: Ending Racism* (New York: Henry Holt, 1995).

Aaron James, *Assholes: A Theory* (New York: Anchor Books, 2014).

Michael Kimmel, *Angry White Men: American Masculinity At The End Of An Era* (New York: Nation Books, 2013).

Rae Langton, 'Speech Acts And Unspeakable Acts', *Philosophy And Public Affairs*, 22 (1993), 293–330.

Maxime Lepoutre, 'Rage Inside The Machine', *Politics, Philosophy & Economics*, 17 (2018), 398–426.

Nabina Liebow And Trip Glazer, 'White Tears: Emotion Regulation And White Fragility', *Inquiry*, (2019), 1–21.

John Locke, 'An Essay Concerning Toleration [1667; Published 1867]' *In Locke: Political Writings* (Indianapolis And Cambridge: Hackett Publishing, 2003), 186–210.

Audre Lorde, 'The Uses Of Anger: Women Responding To Racism' In Audre Lorde, *Sister Outsider In The Audre Lorde Compendium: Essays, Speeches, And Journals* (London: Pandora, 1996), 172–80.

María Lugones, *Pilgrimages/Peregrinajes: Theorizing Coalition Against Multiple Oppressions* (Lanham; Boulder; New York; Oxford: Rowman & Littlefield, 2003).

Coleen Macnamara, 'Reactive Attitudes As Communicative Entities', *Philosophy And Phenomenological Research*, 90 (2015), 546–69.

Coleen Macnamara, 'Taking Demands Out Of Blame' In D. Justin Coates and Neal A. Tognazzini, *Blame: Its Nature And Norms* (Oxford And New York: Oxford University Press, 2013), 141–61.

Hilary Malatino, 'Tough Breaks: Trans Rage And The Cultivation Of Resilience', *Hypatia*, 34 (2019), 121–40.

I. Mcgregor, P. R. Nail, D. C. Marigold and S. J. Kang, 'Defensive Pride And Consensus: Strength In Imaginary Numbers', *Journal Of Personality And Social Psychology*, 89 (2005), 978–96.

Amy Mcqueen And William M. P. Klein, 'Experimental Manipulations Of Self-Affirmation: A Systematic Review', *Self And Identity*, 5 (2006), 289–354.

Emily Mcrae, 'Anger And The Oppressed: Indo-Tibetan Buddhist Perspectives' In Myisha Cherry and Owen Flanagan, *The Moral Psychology Of Anger* (London And New York: Rowman & Littlefield International, 2017), 105–121.

Oded Na'aman, 'The Fitting Resolution Of Anger', *Philosophical Studies*, 177 (2019), 2417–30.

Martha C. Nussbaum, *Anger And Forgiveness: Resentment, Forgiveness, Justice* (New York: Oxford University Press, 2016).

David Ost, 'Politics As The Mobilization Of Anger', *European Journal Of Social Theory*, 7 (2004), 229–44.

Glen Pettigrove, 'Meekness And "Moral" Anger', *Ethics*, 122 (2012), 341–70.

Glen Pettigrove and Koji Tanaka, 'Anger And Moral Judgment', *Australasian Journal Of Philosophy*, 92 (2014), 269–86.

Lucius Annaeus Seneca, *Anger, Mercy, Revenge* (Chicago, Ill.: University Of Chicago Press, 2010).

David K. Sherman and Geoffrey L. Cohen, 'The Psychology Of Self-Defense: Self-Affirmation Theory' In Advances In Experimental Social Psychology Academic Press, 2006, 183–242.

David Shoemaker, *Responsibility From The Margins* (Oxford: Oxford University Press, 2015).

J. J. C. Smart, 'Free-Will, Praise And Blame', *Mind*, 70 (1961), 291–306.

Angela M. Smith, 'Moral Blame And Moral Protest' In D. Justin Coates and Neal A. Tognazzini, *Blame: Its Nature And Norms* (Oxford And New York: Oxford University Press, 2013), 27–48.

Amia Srinivasan, 'The Aptness Of Anger', *Journal Of Political Philosophy*, 26 (2018), 123–44.

P. F. Strawson, *Freedom And Resentment And Other Essays* (London: Routledge, 2008).

Alessandra Tanesini, 'Arrogance, Anger And Debate', *Symposion: Theoretical And Applied Inquiries In Philosophy And Social Sciences*, 5 (2018), 213–27.

Alessandra Tanesini, 'I – 'Calm Down, Dear': Intellectual Arrogance, Silencing And Ignorance', *Aristotelian Society Supplementary Volume*, 90 (2016), 71–92.
Lisa Tessman, *Burdened Virtues: Virtue Ethics For Liberatory Struggles* (New York And Oxford: Oxford University Press, 2005).
Margaret Urban Walker, *Moral Repair: Reconstructing Moral Relations After Wrongdoing* (Cambridge: Cambridge University Press, 2006).
Michael Walzer, *On Toleration* (New Haven, [Conn.] And London: Yale University Press, 1997).

The Promise and Pitfalls of Online 'Conversations'

SANFORD C. GOLDBERG

Abstract
Good conversations are one of the great joys of life. Online (social media) 'conversations' rarely seem to make the grade. In this paper I use some tools from philosophy in an attempt to illuminate what might be going wrong.

1. Introduction

Many of our conversations these days take place on social networks: Facebook, Twitter, ... In this respect, these networks are incredibly powerful tools: they provide a virtual 'place' for people to share things of interest to them with others all over the world in real time – whether the shared items are their own (verbally-expressed) thoughts, articles they found interesting, photographs, videos, or what have you. The social networks hold out the prospect of diminishing the significance of geographical constraints and democratizing the ability to get one's word out. And yet many people these days lament the poor quality of our exchanges in online networks.

In this paper I want to use a model of conversation from philosophy of language to diagnose some of the things that seem to be going wrong in our online 'conversations'. The model that I will introduce – what we might call the Stalnaker-Roberts' model of conversation[1] – is a rather simple model, and it employs some very idealized assumptions about the aim of conversations and the conditions under which they take place. As idealized and simple as it is, though, I think this model enables us to shed light on some of the challenges of online discourse, and it brings a fresh perspective on these. In fact, it might be *because* of the idealizations that the model sheds light on the challenges of our online conversations: many of the assumptions that the model needs to make either fail to hold in online conversations or it will be decidedly unclear to the conversational participants themselves whether these conditions hold. The fundamental claim I will

[1] See Stalnaker (1978; 2014) and Roberts (2012; 2018).

doi:10.1017/S1358246121000023

be making is that in this way we can shed light on at least *some* of the problems characteristic of our online discussions.

2. A conversational model

The Stalnaker-Roberts model of a conversation consists in (i) a model of the context of the conversation, (ii) the set of moves that can be made in a conversation, characterized in terms of their standard effects on context, and (iii) the participants in the conversation. We can get a sense of what this amounts to by oversimplifying a bit. Starting with (i), the context, this is understood to consist of (a) the set of propositions mutually accepted by all parties, (b) the question(s) under discussion, and (c) the plans in place, if any. Corresponding to this, the set of moves available to participants, (ii), is taken to involve three main types of acts: (a*) making an assertion, in which one proposes to add the propositional content of the act to the set of mutually accepted propositions; (b*) asking a question, in which one proposes to add a question to the set of questions under discussion, whether as a new question to be addressed, a subquestion of a previous question, or a clarification of an aspect of previous discourse; and (c*) issuing an instruction, in which one proposes to add to the list of plans (either immediate, or more long-term). In each case, those who observe one of these acts face the choice whether to allow the act to have its aimed-at effect on the context – that is, whether to accept the assertion (and so add its content to the set of mutually accepted propositions), and so on with questions and instructions as well.

This (highly oversimplified version of the) Stalnaker-Roberts model of assertion is helpful for thinking about the role of conversation in inquiry. Inquiry starts when there is a question to be addressed before a group of individuals, it involves giving and receiving instructions about how to plan the inquiry together, it proceeds as people add more information to the stock of information that is accepted, and it terminates when all but one of the answers to the main question under discussion is ruled out (leaving that answer as the response to the question).

Still, the model is rather simple, and it makes various simplifying assumptions. I what follows I will bring out some of these assumptions by trying to apply this model to the case of online 'conversations'; in some cases the inability to apply the model to these conversations will point to a shortcoming of the model itself, but in others it will illuminate features of online exchanges that make them less productive, and often less enjoyable, than we might like.

3. Three challenges

I want to highlight three challenges we face in applying this sort of model to online exchanges: (1) it is unclear how often the aim of online exchanges is correctly characterized as a conversation in the sense characterized by this model; (2) it is unclear how to characterize the scope of the participants; and (3) it is unclear how well the acts identified in the model correspond to the scope of acts performed online. In each of these ways, it is hard to see how to apply the model to online exchanges. After arguing that this may well point to sources of unproductiveness in online exchanges, I go on in the next section to argue that these sources of unproductiveness combine with certain aspects of the epistemological dimension of these exchanges, resulting in still further problematic features.

3.1 The Aim of Online Exchanges

Does the aim of online exchanges amount to or involve the sincere exchange of information? Though it might seem so at least for a good deal of our engagements online, a number of researchers have called into question how central an aim this is. Instead, researchers have pointed out how a good deal of online engagement has an expressive aim (Lynch, 2019), or alternatively aims at establishing one's group affiliation. If true, this (by now familiar) point has far-reaching implications: whereas standard conversations aim at or centrally involve the sincere exchange of information with the goal of arriving at the truth, online 'conversations' whose *raison d'etre* is establishing one's group affiliation need have no interesting connection to the truth. What is more, if the aim is to reinforce group cohesiveness, it would seem that participants will restrict themselves to what serves that aim, with the result that contributions that are seen to solidify one's identity will tend to get expressions of approval from others (likes and the like). This will loom large in the next section, when I consider the epistemic dimensions of online exchanges.

3.2 Scope of Participants

Consider ordinary face-to-face conversations. Typically, the participants know who is in the conversation and who is not. In part this is because there are conventions that enable us to discern the contours of the conversational participants. Thus, there are conventional ways to initiate a conversation with another (or others): for example, by addressing oneself to them in a way indicating one wishes to initiate a conversation with them. There are conventional ways to signal that one is or remains a participant in an ongoing conversation: for example, by shaking one's head to indicate uptake (or performing one or another action indicating that one is attending to the contributions). And there are conventional ways to conclude a conversation. What is more, in face-to-face settings, one can see all of those who are potentially participants in the conversation, enabling one to get a good deal of information regarding the participant status of each candidate.

The salient contrasts with online exchanges are many. For one thing, unless an individual contributes to the exchange (by posting, reposting, replying, liking the post, or what-have-you), there is no way to tell whether an individual in one's social network is a silent 'part' of the conversation. The contours of the participants, then, are hard to discern even if we assume that they are determinate. But there are grounds for doubting whether the contours are determinate: is one who glances at a post or a thread, registering a comment or two only to move on quickly, a part of the conversation or not? We might stipulate that only those are part of the online conversation who explicitly contribute to it in one way or another. But in that case our stipulation would eliminate the analogue in face-to-face encounters of the silent participant: the one who tracks what is going on, updates the context accordingly, but does not otherwise contribute.

Consider, too, the conventions available through which to signal an interest in initiating or concluding a conversation, as well as those for signaling one is still a participant. To be sure, posting might be considered a way to signal an interest in initiating a conversation: but with whom? With everyone in one's social network? With those on whose wall one's post is seen? We might also think of tagging as a way of calling one's attention to the conversation in the hope of including them; but not all tags are for that purpose, of course, so this signal is noisy. When it comes to indicating one's status as a participant in the conversation, of course, one can contribute to it (commenting, reposting, liking, etc.). Still, as signals of participation these acts (of commenting, reposting, liking, and the like) are also noisy, and it remains true that there would seem to be no way of doing so silently. Finally, there is no natural or conventional way to signal the end of the conversation, and it often happens that old posts (left for finished by those participating at the time) are revived when a new contributor makes a very belated contribution.

All of these differences are exacerbated by the temporal dimension of online exchanges: while technology would permit one to see who among the active participants is online at any given time, in a good many exchanges one interacts only with those who are actively participating at the time. Participants then can be remote from one another not only in space but also in time: I might reply tomorrow to a comment you made today, keeping alive the conversation even though the intervening 24 hours have been non-active.

There is an all-important corollary of not being able to discern the set of participants in an online discussion: we cannot discern the context set itself, that is, the set of propositions that are being mutually assumed for the sake of the exchange itself. The nature of the difficulty here can be characterized by contrasting two extreme views as to how to go about addressing this: what I will call a minimalist and a maximalist approach. On the *minimalist* approach, one assumes the minimal number of participants consistent with the nature of the exchange itself. These will include all and only those who have responded to another's post (whether by commenting or liking or reposting or what-have-you). Here, what is presupposed is only what we need to treat all of *these* individuals as mutually assuming in order to make sense of the exchange itself. On the *maximalist* approach, one regards the speaker's *entire social network* as in on the exchange, and what we as theorists regard as presupposed is what we need to make sense of the possibility of *anyone* of these individuals participating in this exchange. Obviously, how much this includes will depend on the diversity of views within one's social network, the salience of those views, and so forth.

I submit that neither the minimalist nor the maximalist approach to context-fixing is the right way to capture what is going on in the online "conversation," and that the reason for this will generalize to other (less extreme) attempts to capture the set of things that are mutually presupposed in the exchange. The trouble is that neither of these options appears to set the right constraints on what is to count as mutually presupposed in context, and so both will err in including either too much or not enough in the context set itself. Generalizing from this, I suspect that any attempt at some hard-and-fast technique for discerning the context set will make errors of one of these two sorts – either including too much in the context set, or not enough – even if the approach itself is not as extreme as either the minimalist or the maximalist approaches just described.

Let me give examples from the US and the UK to illustrate these worries about the minimalist and the maximalist approach to context-fixing.

Start with the minimalist approach. Suppose you reside in the US and you are among the majority of US voters who disapprove of

President Trump (56% as of July 2020[2]), where the majority of your network disapproves of him as well. Still, you might have a few pro-Trump people among your network, and they might be outspoken on those occasions when you make anti-Trump comments. If they do, does their participation in the thread you've initiated inviolate your attempt to presuppose (for the purpose of discussion) such things as that Trump is aiming to normalize political practices and behaviors that ought not to be normalized? Well, the cost of allowing this would be to allow all of the trolls to set the terms of our discussion. But if we insist that this should not be allowed, then it follows that the mere fact that a person is participating, or is trying to participate (e.g. by making comments on one's discussion thread), is not sufficient, by itself, to include their perspective as serving to fix the context set. To be sure, we might try to rectify this problem by de-friending trolls. But the problem is deeper than that: a troll who makes as if to participate properly throughout doesn't count as preventing one from presupposing what one wants to presuppose merely because the troll is quiet about matters. It seems that the mere fact that one is participating in an online discussion doesn't yet determine the role one plays in fixing the context set. Since minimalism assumes otherwise, it is not adequate.

Move to the maximalist approach. Suppose you reside in pre-Brexit UK and are a firm Remainer, where the vast majority of your online social network is in favor of Remain. (The point doesn't depend on the details of the politics; I use them for the purpose of illustration only.) Still, you might have the occasional Brexiteer among your network. (Suppose they are usually quiet and don't participate much, if at all, in your discussions.) Do their pro-Brexit views nevertheless help to fix what is mutually taken as presupposed for the purpose of your discussions? If so, you will not be able to have a discussion in which the Remain position is mutually taken for granted. But this seems weird: even if you don't always expect to be able to take that for granted, surely *sometimes* – in some online exchanges you initiate – you want to be able to do so, and you expect to be able to do so. So it can't be that the mere fact that you have a few Remainers among your social network prevents you from ever being able to do so. The maximalist approach can't be right.

What I think actually happens: we construct the context on the fly. Some posts make clear the sort of audience they have in mind: one's professional colleagues, or family members, or high school friends, or

2 This statistic is taken from the web site FiveThiryEight.com, cited 9 July, 2020.

the politically like-minded, or fellow cat-lovers, or fellow members of an interest group of some kind, etc. Other posts are sufficiently general that they might be aimed at a much wider audience, where the contours of that audience are themselves not clearly conceived in advance. Over the course of the evolution of the discussion, participants construct the context set as needed to make sense of the exchange. Insofar as some are regarded as calling into question the intended presuppositions of the conversation, they are ignored or disallowed to continue to 'hijack' the discussion. But if this is correct, it makes clear that there will be many cases in which the state of the context set at a given time will be far from clear to the participants, even to those centrally invested in a productive discussion.

3.3 Scope of acts performed online

To introduce the problems surrounding the scope of the speech acts performed online, I will need first to present some basic elements of speech act theory. To begin, note that the verbal use (or utterance) of a sentence is not just the production of sounds; it is rather a meaningful use of speech. Thus if I utter 'You will sit next to me' to you, intending thereby to be expressing what that English sentence says, I have performed a meaningful act. We can designate this act – the meaningful act one performs when one produces a sentence intending to be expressing what the sentence says – as a *locutionary* act. In knowing which locutionary act I have performed, you (my intended audience) thereby know what I have said. Still, as my intended audience you can know what locutionary act I have performed, and so know what I have said, without knowing how to *take* or *understand* what I've said: I might have said this as a *prediction* (I am predicting you won't know anyone else at the party), a *decision* (we are making seating arrangements for the upcoming wedding), or a *command* (I say it to you under my breath in a threatening tone). We can use 'illocutionary force' to designate that feature of a speech act that pertains to *how* what is said is to be taken or understood by the audience. Thus the illocutionary force of a prediction (= the way the speaker intends the audience to understand her locutionary act) differs from that of a decision, which in turn differs from that of a command. And we can use 'illocutionary act' to designate the resulting type of acts themselves: predictions are a different type of illocutionary act than are decisions or commands. The case above makes clear that one and the same (type of) locutionary act might be associated with various distinct types of illocutionary act.

For its part, the Stalnaker-Roberts model of conversation allows for three general types of illocutionary act: *assertions* (proposals to add information to the stock of propositions that re mutually presupposed), *questions* (proposals to add a query to the stock of questions under discussion, including subquestions of questions currently on the list as well as clarificatory questions about previous moves or other questions), and *directives* (proposals to add an action on the list of what is to be done). Using the notions introduced above, we can say that assertions constitute a type of illocutionary act with its own distinctive illocutionary force (= *assertoric* force), questions constitute a type of illocutionary act with its own distinctive illocutionary force (= *interrogative* force), and directives constitute a type of illocutionary act with its own distinctive illocutionary force (= *directive* force). The challenge is that there are actions performed in online settings whose illocutionary force is not obviously any one of these; and in addition even when it is clear (more or less) that an online act is of one of these three illocutionary types, it appears to be significantly different than standard acts of that type (in face-to-face settings). I will take these up in order.

There are many acts performed in the context of online discussions of which it is not obvious that their illocutionary force is one of the three just described. Here I mention four: posting, reposting/retweeting, liking, and (hash)tagging.

Of all of the 'speech acts' performed online, the post is the one that might seem the easiest to incorporate into the Stalnaker-Roberts model: isn't the act of posting simply the act of assertion itself – at least when one's post purports to say how things are? (By this I mean to exclude posts that are clearly intended as venting, or as merely expressive in some other way, as well as posts that extend invitations, etc.). There is much to recommend this analysis regarding posts in which one purports to say how things are. Still, there are two complications that are worth highlighting, as both of these render the construal of such posts as assertions less than fully happy.

Consider the question that one finds next to one's name when one signs on to one's Facebook account: *What's on your mind,* [*name*]*?* Interestingly, this question permits of at least two distinct readings: what I will call the *expressive* reading, and what I will call the *topical* reading. According to the expressive reading, the question asks one to *give expression to* one's own state of mind – whether that involves something one is thinking about, or an emotion one is feeling, or a reaction one is having, etc. According to the topical reading, the question asks one to *address oneself to a topic* and say something about that topic.

Suppose that a Facebook user interprets this question in terms of the expressive reading, and that her posts are informed by this aim. Then she might take it that what she is doing is simply giving expression to her states of mind. To be sure, we can still see her as making assertions in this case. Only if this is how she intended her post, its content will pertain in the first instance to her state of mind, rather than to the topic she is addressing. To illustrate, suppose she posts 'My friend Tom has misbehaved', intending thereby to be expressing 'what's on her mind' (as Facebook would put it). Then she will intend for her post to be understood as capturing e.g. the irritability she is presently feeling in response to something she takes Tom to have done. Even if it makes sense to regard her as having *asserted* as much (namely, that she is irritated etc.), such an assertion is very different from an assertion that is straightforwardly about Tom's behavior. To see this, notice that she might be taken aback by anyone who questions her: she regards herself as having done nothing more than having expressed her own state of mind, including her own take on the world, and any attempt to question this would, in her mind, be seen as challenging her authority to say what is on her mind. This is a very different sort of activity than the one we engage in when we make assertions about the world. To be sure, her 'take' on the world might be called into question (as in: Tom didn't do what she took him to have done); but if she is pressed with such an objection, she can always resort to the response, 'Well, this is how things struck me, and that's all I was saying in my post'.

I mention this not to defend this sort of maneuver, but rather to point to the possibility of some unclarity as to what, precisely, one is doing when one posts on Facebook. My claim is that this unclarity remains even if we restrict ourselves to posts in which one purports to say how things are. And so, even after we agree that posts are assertions in the Stalnaker-Roberts' sense, this possible unclarity makes it unclear what it is that is being asserted in any given case.

There is one other aspect of posting that makes it somewhat hard to accommodate it within the Stalnaker-Roberts model. Whereas that model aims to capture face-to-face exchanges between conversational participants, posts can have the feel of *public announcements* rather than *contributions to a conversation* itself. That is, one who posts is doing something more like *broadcasting to a wide (indeterminate) audience*, than *talking to a determinate set of individuals*. If this is right, of course, then the whole Stalnaker-Roberts model is not applicable in the first place – but then again, neither would it be correct to say that we engage in conversation online. I do not raise this to endorse the idea that we do not have conversations online.

On the contrary, I do think we engage in (something very much like) conversations online; my present point is only that they have very different features than those of face-to-face conversations. Seen in this light, posts can have the feel like public announcements more than they are claims made in the give-and-take of a speech exchange is one such feature.

But posts are not the only 'speech acts' online that are hard to fit into the Stalnaker-Roberts model. Consider next the *repost* or *retweet*, when another person's post, as such, is 'forwarded' in one's name. These are often (typically?) interpreted as a re-affirmation the content of the original post or tweet. And if things were this simple, reposts/retweets could be seen as a kind of assertion in which one re-asserts a content previously asserted by another – presumably with the point of extending the dissemination of that information to one's own social network. The difficulty is that not all retweets *are* endorsements. There are many motives for retweeting or reposting a previously-made post. At its most generic level, the rationale is that of bringing something to the attention of one's social network; but one can have all sorts of reasons for wanting to do this, not all of which include endorsement. (Perhaps it will be obvious to the most salient members of one's online social network that one regards the original post with contempt, or irony; perhaps the point is some sort of 'in'-joke among one's online social network; and so forth.) And even when one does endorse the content, sometimes the point of reposting/retweeting is not to re-assert what was asserted previously, but simply to register or signal *one's own endorsement* of it. (Such an act puts the focus on one's own attitude toward the content posted, rather than on the alleged truth of that post.) No doubt, the difficulty in interpreting a retweet or repost is related to the difficulty of discerning the contours of the conversation (who is included, and who is not), as well as the corresponding difficulty of discerning what is being presupposed in the context. But even if the difficulty of discerning the context is more fundamental, still, the challenge of assigning an illocutionary force to a retweet/repost, and even determining whether that force is one of the three main types postulated by the Stalnaker-Roberts model, remains.

Next, consider the act of 'liking' another's post. This act is even harder to interpret than is the act of retweeting or reposting. What we might call its 'pragmatic significance' – what it intends to convey regarding how it is to be taken by others in the conversation – can be any of the following: I endorse what you've posted; I like what you've posted; I support you in having posted this; I like you; I have read what you posted with interest; you are on my mind as you post this; I am following this thread with interest; and many others besides. To be sure, the set of possibilities here may be narrowed e.g. on Facebook, where one has other options: in addition to an emoji for 'like', there are emojis for 'love', 'care', 'ha ha', 'wow', 'sad', and 'angry' (the terms are from Facebook). And when the context makes things clear (but see below), interpretations may be narrowed further. Even so, there are a great many occasions on which it is hard to see how to interpret a mere 'like', and in any case it is far from clear how to fit this action into the tripartite list of actions postulated by the Stalnaker-Roberts model. These acts seem more expressive than any of the three acts postulated by that model: far from proposing to add information, or a question, or a task-to-be-done, they merely express one's attitude. No doubt, in this way they can be seen as adding the information that one expressed such an attitude to the common ground; but they are not thereby to be represented as an assertion. (As Stalnaker himself noted, all sorts of things add information to the common ground without counting as assertions: any salient public act one performs will do just this, as will salient events not involving any agent.)

Finally, consider the act of tagging. Here I have in mind tagging on both Facebook (an act involving the use of the person's Facebook name) or on Twitter (an act involving the use of the '@' sign followed by their Twitter handle). (Note that both of these are distinct from the use of the *hash*tag used on Twitter.) The act of tagging someone on a post can be performed with any of a variety of distinct intentions in doing so: to get the target's attention; to indicate to the target that s/he is being discussed; to indicate to the target that s/he is being thought about in connection with the post; to elicit from the target some response; and so forth. Assuming that the relevant intention is discerned by the audience (including but not limited to the target), once again, we might think that the statement that the speaker has the relevant intention is added to the common ground; but again this does not make the act one of assertion. The act would seem more like that of addressing oneself to someone than it would an assertion, though on occasion, when intended to elicit a response from the target, it might be construed as an instruction (to the target to respond). But since this will not cover all cases of tagging, the act of tagging itself is not of a type that should be identified with any of the three types of act postulated by the Stalnaker-Roberts model. (This is not particularly surprising; the point of the act of tagging is not to add any information or question or instruction to the common ground, so much as to capture another's attention for some purpose or other.)

While I will not have much to say about it, the act of hashtagging on Twitter is distinct from the act of tagging (whether on Facebook or Twitter). Though it can be directed at a single individual (whether explicitly, as in hashtagging them by name, or in some other way), the use of the hashtag is typically not so aimed. Instead, hashtagging is aimed at attracting the attention of the widest audience possible. Still, the intentions behind a hashtag can be varied. By their nature, hashtags allow followers of a topic to follow that topic, and might be seen as having that overarching aim. Still one might have various motives (with a greater or lesser degree of openness) for doing so: eliciting a response, capturing attention, adding to a conversation, and so forth. Once again, it is unsurprising that this act is not among the three postulated by the Stalnaker-Roberts model.

4. Disappointing conversations

I have been spending some time trying to highlight some of the features of online 'conversations' that appear difficult to understand in the terms provided by our best account of face-to-face conversations. My aim in doing so has been to prepare the way for an evaluative claim: these features of online exchanges – those highlighted in the previous section – are partially responsible for some of the disappointing outcomes our conversations online. To establish the latter claim, I need to supplement these features with some claims pertaining to the epistemological dimensions of our speech exchanges (whether face-to-face or online). It turns out that, once we understand some of these dimensions, we would predict some of the difficulties and problems that arise in online exchanges. Or so I will be arguing in this section.

A good proportion of the problems that arise in online exchanges reflect our uncertainty as to the context of the exchange itself, where 'context' is understood in terms of the Stalnaker-Roberts model. Such uncertainty, or more generally the failure to track the context as it evolves dynamically throughout the exchange, has at least some explanatory role in such phenomena as (i) the speed, extent, and ferocity of online shaming, (ii) groupthink, and (iii) belief polarization. I want to begin, then, by characterizing the source and nature of our uncertainty regarding the context, and the difficulties involved in tracking the dynamics of context as it evolves throughout an exchange.

I noted above that online exchanges on social media such as Facebook and Twitter make it practically impossible to know the contours of a conversation: while we can discern some of the participants in an exchange (namely, those who have actively contributed to it), we are unable to determine those who are silent participants to the exchange, those who are following the exchange albeit without weighing in. The implications of this ignorance are hard to overstate.

To see why this is, it will be helpful to identify the members of the class of inferences that are characteristically drawn from audience reactions to mutually observed contributions to a conversation. Here I highlight those inferences pertaining to the acceptability of a speaker's contribution. Suppose you are participating in a large face-to-face conversation in which a speaker is making claims about a topic on which you know little. The claims seem plausible, though you don't know enough even to be confident of your sense of their plausibility. Still, you see others nodding in agreement, and you take this to indicate their sense of the acceptability of what is being said, and you regard this as still further evidence of the likely truth of the claims. On this basis, you accept the speaker's say-so. Here, you are using the audience's apparent agreement as evidence (of a higher-order sort) indicating the acceptability of the speaker's say-so. Alternatively, if you observe that the audience is perplexed, or seems dubious, or is raising doubts, you might take this as some evidence that the speaker's say-so is *not* to be relied upon. In either case you are treating the audience's manifest reaction as offering evidence bearing on the acceptability of the assertion made in your mutual presence. Notice that you might do so even when the audience's reaction is one of silence itself. Reasoning that if they had harbored doubts they might have indicated this, you might think that their silence is attesting to their having accepted the say-so, in which case you are treating their silence as evidence of the acceptability of the say-so.

These are familiar features of face-to-face conversations involving multiple people. But now when these features are combined with our ignorance of who is following an online discussion, we can run into some serious problems. In particular, I suspect that this is partly responsible for such things as (i) the speed, extent, and ferocity of online shaming, (ii) groupthink, and (iii) belief polarization. Let me explain.

Suppose you observe a post on Facebook in which a Facebook friend writes of a situation that she finds worthy of contempt. You are aware that it will be regarded as such by your peer group as well, at least some of whom are Facebook friends with the one who posted. While you do not know what their ultimate views are, you worry about a scenario in which they too regard the situation as contemptible while simultaneously condemning those who don't so regard the situation. Once you see a friend join the speaker in expressing contempt for the situation, you decide that you too must quickly make clear that you find the situation worthy of contempt – lest others who are aware that you are Facebook friends with the writer might mistake your non-response for not caring. So you speak up in condemnation. Of course, many of your Facebook friends reason in the same way. The result is that many rush to join in the expression of contempt. Of course, once others see so many do so, they fear that not doing so might be taken (by those who think they are following this discussion) as a lack of contempt, and so they soon join in as well. What started out as a single person expressing contempt has become a pile-on.

Notice the role that ignorance of context plays in this scenario. There are various significant aspects of this ignorance. In general, you are ignorant of who is part of the conversation; and you are ignorant of the reactions of those who are part of the conversation but who are silent. The former ignorance might lead you to worry that there are far more participants than those who have been actively participating. The latter ignorance might leave you worrying about what those silent others (whoever they are) are thinking: what they think of the speaker's contribution, and also (perhaps more worryingly) what they think of *your* reaction to the speaker's contribution. All of this comes to a head in the form of the concern that others might take you to be following the conversation and might misconstrue your silence; this often leads you to respond as quickly and as vehemently as you did. And of course what goes for you goes for many others as well. What we have, in short, is a perfect storm in which everyone is ready to pounce on any shameful behavior mentioned online.[3]

I suspect that this sort of 'contextual ignorance' is explanatorily relevant not only to the speed, extent, and ferocity of online shaming, but also to groupthink and belief polarization.[4]

Groupthink is the phenomenon in which members who self-identify with a group shape their attitudes so as to bring them into line with those of the other group members, where this is driven by the desire to remain in the group's good standing. Groupthink itself can be seen in all settings, including face-to-face settings: Insofar as one wants to retain good standing in a group and one thinks that

[3] In highlighting the dimension of ignorance and its role in online shaming, I mean to be supplementing the account of online shaming in Ronson (2015).

[4] See e.g. Goldberg (2017b, 2020) for a detailed description.

this requires adopting a certain attitude, one is likely to adopt that attitude. But online settings can exacerbate the situation: insofar as one is ignorant of the contours of an online discussion and one worries about the inferences others might draw of one's silence, one is likely to signal one's attitude by contributing to that effect in the online discussion; and this only encourages other silent participants both to see the attitude as required by the group, and to manifest that they too possess it (by contributing to the discussion).

Belief polarization is the phenomenon whereby a group of likeminded individuals adopt increasingly radical views, or become more confident in their existing views, after discussion with fellow likeminded individuals, even though no new evidence has been introduced in the course of the discussion.[5] The phenomenon itself is seen in face-to-face discussions. But again online settings can exacerbate the problem. Given the dynamic just described, where an increasing number of people feel the pressure to signal that they, too, hold the view in question, this will give everyone more reason to think that the view is widely shared. And insofar as there is evidence to think that the view is widely shared, this gives those on the fence some reason to question their ambivalence, and it gives those who already have the attitude a reason for further confidence (on the assumption that so many people can't be wrong[6]).

I have just highlighted how the features of online discussions (as outlined in section 3) give rise to a kind of ignorance of the conversational context, with the result that discussions online are often sorry affairs in which (group-enhancing) ignorance proliferates. Stepping back from this, I would diagnose a more general challenge we face in our discussions online: not only is our route to information highly dependent on the say-so of others, but what is more the mechanisms in place to correct that say-so are themselves highly dependent on the say-so of our social network.[7] The result is that these correction mechanisms are only as good as the members of our social network are both knowledgeable and outspoken. If you

[5] That is: no new evidence *beyond the evidence pertaining to what others think on the matter*. For further discussion of the epistemological dimension of polarization, see Goldberg (2017b).

[6] It should go without saying but I will say it anyway: I am not endorsing this reasoning in such cases. My claims are rather that (1) such reasoning is common, and (2) such reasoning does capture something distinctively epistemic, in that evidence of what others think is a kind of evidence after all (even if it can be highly misleading as to what the truth of the matter actually is).

[7] See Rini (2017).

happen to reside in social networks where ignorance rather than knowledgeableness is pervasive, or where those who are knowledgeable do not speak up, you are out of luck. What is more, if you are in such a situation and you rely on the network itself to distinguish who among your network is knowledgeable, you are likely to compound the situation: not only do you fail to have knowledge, what is worse you will be *ignorant of your very ignorance*. If I am right to think that this is the state of many of us these days, it does not make for a happy world.

5. Conclusion

In this short essay, I have used a simplified version of the Stalnaker-Roberts' model of conversational dynamics to illuminate the features of online conversations that might explain why these are often such unproductive and unhappy affairs. I have identified two main sources of such unhappiness. The first source derives from the challenges we face in discerning the nature of contributions we make online in the first place. There is a question in each case whether our contributions are best thought of as contributions to a conversation, as opposed to reactions to a public announcement. And there is the challenge of discerning the (illocutionary force of the) the various acts we perform online (liking, tagging, hashtagging, and so forth). The second source the derives from the profundity of our ignorance of context and its evolution as the "conversation" progresses. I have tried to suggest how these sources combine to make online platforms ripe for the sort of ugly and unproductive exchanges that are all too common in our online exchanges.

Northwestern University
s-goldberg@northwestern.edu

References

Sanford Goldberg, 'Should Have Known', *Synthese*, 194 (2017a), 2863–94.

Sanford Goldberg, 'Can asserting that p improve the speaker's epistemic position (and is that a good thing)?' *Australasian Journal of Philosophy* 95 (2017b), 157–70.

Sanford Goldberg, *Conversational Pressure* (Oxford: Oxford University Press, 2020).
Michael Lynch, *Know-It-All Society: Truth and Arrogance in Political Culture* (New York: Liveright Publishing, 2019).
Regina Rini, 'Fake news and partisan epistemology', *Kennedy Institute of Ethics Journal* 27 (2017), 43–64.
Craige Roberts, 'Speech acts in discourse context'. In Fogal, D., Harris, D., Moss, M., eds. *New Work on Speech Acts*. (Oxford: Oxford University Press, 2018), 317–59.
Craige Roberts, 'Information structure: Towards an integrated formal theory of pragmatics', *Semantics and Pragmatics* 5 (2012), 1–69.
Jon Ronson, *So You've Been Publicly Shamed* (New York: Riverhead Books, 2015).
Robert Stalnaker, *Context* (Oxford: Oxford University Press, 2014).
Robert Stalnaker, 'Assertion' In Cole, P. ed., *Syntax and Semantics*: *Pragmatics* 9 (1978) 315–22.

The Vulnerable Dynamics of Discourse

PAUL GILADI AND DANIELLE PETHERBRIDGE

Abstract
In this paper, we offer some compelling reasons to think that issues relating to vulnerability play a significant – albeit thus far underacknowledged – role in Jürgen Habermas's notions of communicative action and discourse. We shall argue that the basic notions of discourse and communicative action presuppose a robust conception of vulnerability and that recognising vulnerability is essential for (i) making sense of the social character of knowledge, on the epistemic side of things, and for (ii) making sense of the possibility of deliberative democracy, on the political side of things. Our paper is divided into four principal sections. In Section 1, we provide a basic outline of Habermas on communicative action and discourse. In Section 2, we develop an account of vulnerability and communication in the context of speaker/hearer relations. We specifically focus on distorted communication, vulnerability and speech. In Section 3, we focus on elaborating epistemic pathologies in the context of epistemic oppression and testimonial injustice. In Section 4, we focus on explaining how Habermasian resources contribute to vulnerability theory, and how introducing vulnerability theory to Habermas broadens or deepens his theory of communication action and his discourse ethics theory.

I have spread my dreams under your feet; Tread softly because you tread on my dreams
W.B. Yeats

1. Communicative Action and Discourse

Jürgen Habermas places significant philosophical as well as socio-political emphasis on the intrinsically *social* character of language: meaning, normativity, and knowledge are mediated by practices that are rooted in *communicative action*.[1] For Habermas, communicative action is the type of action aimed at establishing *consensus* (i.e. mutual understanding) through the agonistic establishment of legitimate and valid norms for persons (i.e. language-using individuals). As Habermas frames it:

[1] By 'normativity', we mean the general idea of obligations, justifications, and values.

doi:10.1017/S1358246121000151

> The concept of communicative action presupposes language as the medium for a kind of reaching understanding, in the course of which the participants, through relating to a world, reciprocally raise validity claims that can be accepted or contested. (Habermas, 1984, p. 99)

Communicative action is not modelled on any kind of instrumentalised subject-object relationship and means-end framework. This is because communicative action is the variety of activity constituted by one of our knowledge-constitutive interests,[2] namely *communicative* interests: the function of communicative action is to *interpret* and to bring about the intelligibility of concepts such as justice and goodness under *public* reason. Communicative action, therefore, is directed at ends-in-themselves and to realising an intersubjective relationship between agents as much as possible. Specifically, the norms structuring communicative action simultaneously concern three different kinds of validity claims – a) claims to truth; b) claims to sincerity (truthfulness), and c) claims to normative rightness.[3] Tracing his intellectual lineage to Fichte's theory of recognition,[4] G.H. Mead's pragmatist social psychology, and J.L. Austin's speech act theory, Habermas's theory of communicative action draws on the following claims from Fichte, Mead, and Austin respectively.

On the Fichtean side of things, the 'I' must 'posit' (*Setzen*) itself as an individual for the 'I' to be an individual. In order to posit itself as an individual, the 'I' must recognise itself as 'summoned' by another individual. The summons (*Aufforderung*)[5] of another individual

[2] Viz. Habermas (1973, p. 196; p. 308).

[3] By 'normative rightness', we take Habermas to refer to intersubjectively and communicatively constituted forms of moral obligation and value orientations.

[4] Crucially, what we have written here is not meant to either ignore or downplay the significance of Hegel's theory of recognition for Habermas's position. In his iconic essay 'Labour and Interaction: Remarks on Hegel's Jena *Philosophy of Mind*', Habermas identifies and lays out what he sees as Hegel's *better* conception of intersubjectivity than Fichte's. From Habermas's perspective, given that Hegel – much like Fichte – articulates the communicative normative content of modern ethical life in *metaphysical* ways, neglecting the *pragmatic* dimensions of language-use and communication, Hegel, at best, multiplies beyond necessity his development of a proto-form of communicative rationality and action. Habermas construes his own postmetaphysical model as Hegelian without any 'metaphysical mortgages' (Habermas, 1987b, p. 316).

[5] *Aufforderung* ranges from 'begging' (*bitten*) to 'demanding' (*verlangen*).

limits the freedom of the 'I' out of respect for the freedom of the Other.[6] Such a practice of *mutual recognition* between individuals is a necessary condition for the possibility of personhood. On the Meadian side of things, the practice of navigating one's way in a team/group by understanding the various roles and behavioural habits/associations of 'the generalised other' enables a person to develop self-consciousness, which involves the internalisation of socialising practices.[7] Mead's well-known claim that individuation occurs through socialisation and his focus on both gestural and linguistic forms of interaction become central to Habermas's own theory. As Habermas writes:

> I see the more far-reaching contribution of Mead in his having taken up themes [such] that ... individuation is pictured not as the self-realisation of an independently acting subject carried out in isolation and freedom but as a linguistically mediated process of socialisation ... Individuality forms itself in relations of intersubjective acknowledgement and of intersubjectively mediated self-understanding ... Mead will shift all fundamental philosophical concepts from the basis of consciousness to that of language. (Habermas, 1992, pp. 152–53; p. 162)[8]

In other words, Habermas contends that Mead is credited with the foundational insight that language-use involves norms requiring *discursive exchange*, a variety of an *I-thou* relation, rather than the I-they and/or I-it relation, and that the most basic linguistic unit is 'the relationship between ego's speech-act and alter's taking a position' (Habermas, 1992, p. 163).

On the Austinian side of things, Habermas claims that 'a turn to the pragmatics of language ... concedes primacy to world-disclosing language – as the medium for the possibility of reaching understanding, for social cooperation ... – over world-generating subjectivity' (Habermas, 1992, p. 153).[9] Briefly put, Austin details three varieties of speech-acts,[10] where the latter two are especially relevant for our concerns and for making sense of Habermasian communication (and discourse):

– **Locutionary act**: uttering the literal meaning (*Bedeutung*) of a statement – i.e. stating the *pure semantic content* of a proposition.

[6] Viz. FNR (p. 31). Cf. Wood (2016, p. 83).
[7] Viz. MSS (p. 154).
[8] Cf. Taylor (1987, p. 13).
[9] See also Habermas (1984, pp. 288–95); Habermas (1998, pp. 66–88).
[10] See Austin (1975).

E.g. 'It's rather nippy in Boston during winter' = 'it's very cold in Boston during the winter months'

- **Illocutionary act**: the intended meaning (*Meinung*) of the speaker in the utterance of a sentence, namely the assertive/directive/commissive/expressive/declarative features of that sentence.

  E.g. 'Jim, it's rather nippy in Boston during winter' = 'Jim, please consider taking a down-coat with you when you travel to Boston in the winter'.
- **Perlocutionary act**: the consequential effects of an illocutionary act.

  E.g. After Sarah says 'It's rather nippy in Boston during winter' to Jim, Jim takes a down-coat with them when they travel to Boston in the winter.

Habermas himself identifies only illocutionary acts with communicative action, as, in his view, these acts are orientated to reaching mutual understanding and, in turn, such understanding is linked to reaching agreement and 'rationally motivated binding' or 'force' (Habermas, 1984, p. 278). For Habermas, then, 'communicative agreement has a rational basis [and] it cannot be imposed by either party, whether instrumentally through intervention in the situation directly or strategically through influencing the decisions of opponents' (Habermas, 1984, p. 287). In illocutionary acts a speaker partakes in communicative action *in* saying something such that she lets a hearer know she wants to be understood, in a perlocutionary act, the speaker aims to produce an effect *on* the hearer, and 'thereby brings about something in the world' (Habermas, 1984, pp. 288–89). Thus, according to Habermas's view, perlocutionary acts are associated with an intention and are considered a form of goal-directed action more generally. In Habermas's schema, perlocutionary acts then represent forms of strategic action given their intent is to bring about some particular end, rather than merely a form of communicative action directed toward mutual understanding.

Crucially, for Habermas, successful communication between agents involves the hearer being able to *transparently (and non-coercively)* grasp the reasons motivating the propositions put forward by the speaker:

> *We understand a speech act when we know what makes it acceptable.* From the standpoint of the speaker, the conditions of acceptability are identical to the conditions for his illocutionary success. Acceptability is not defined here in an objectivistic sense, from the perspective of an observer, but in the **performative attitude**

> **of a participant in communication**. (Habermas, 1984, pp. 297–98; emphasis added)

The pragmatics of language do not only reveal how individuality is mediated through a complex process of socialisation. Rather, illocutionary acts also point to *democratic potentialities*. This is because '[w]henever the speaker enters into an interpersonal relationship with a hearer, he also relates himself as an actor to a network of normative expectations' (Habermas, 1992, p. 190). Linguistic practice involves not just grasping the norms of assertion,[11] it also involves, to use Wilfrid Sellars's expression, knowing how to move in the *space of reasons*.[12] Successful navigation in the space of reasons requires grasping the plurality of communicative inferential commitments and entitlements one has in the *use* of words.

Importantly, as mentioned above, for Habermas, the norms structuring communicative action simultaneously concern three different kinds of validity claims – claims to truth; claims to sincerity (truthfulness); claims to normative rightness –, which directly correspond to three different kinds of formal 'world':

> [I]n communicative action a speaker selects a comprehensible linguistic expression only in order to come to an understanding *with* a hearer *about* something and thereby to make *himself* understandable. It belongs to the communicative intent of the speaker (a) that he perform a speech act that is right in respect to the given normative context, so that between him and the hearer an intersubjective relation will come about which is recognised as legitimate; (b) that he make a true statement ..., so that the hearer will accept and share the knowledge of the speaker; and (c) that he express truthfully his beliefs, intentions, feelings, desires, and the like, so that the hearer will give credence to what is said. (Habermas, 1992, pp. 307–308)

By engaging in illocutionary speech-acts – the 'bread and butter' linguistic practices of communicative action – (i) the intentional content of a speaker's propositions – i.e. to what the speaker is referring when they say things – is automatically directed to a *shared world* of agents. By virtue of, saying 'please consider', for example, the speaker is 'attempting to establish an interpersonal relation which the hearer will recognise as legitimate' (Niemi, 2005, p. 230); (ii) what the speaker is referring to in practices of communicative action is an *accessible,*

11 Viz. Grice (1975, pp. 26–30).
12 Viz. Sellars (1991, p. 169).

objective world; (iii) the speaker, just by virtue of performing an illocutionary speech-act ('Jim, you should seriously consider taking a down-coat with you when you travel to Boston in the winter') reveals a *subjective world* to the hearer. If Jim is to *genuinely* understand Sarah's advice, they must understand what it would mean to action her advice as well as understand that accepting Sarah's speech then commits them to take a down-coat with them when they travel to Boston in the winter.

Crucially, the emphasis on communication transforms the subject of experience from being voyeuristic to actively engaged. Habermas's position is, thus, allied with Kant's notion of *pragmatic anthropology*, which draws a distinction between *die Welt kennen* and *Welt haben*: 'the expressions "to know the world" and "to have the world" are rather far from each other in their meaning, since one only *understands* the play that one has watched, while the other has *participated* in it' (APPV, [120], p. 4). This empowers human beings by regarding their communicative practices as authoritative, since it is only through successful discursive exchanges that one can meaningfully develop notions of *autonomy* and *respect*. As such, for a practical relation-to-self to be healthy requires *progressive* intersubjective relations, ones which engender and sustain autonomy and respect.

On the corresponding socio-political front, Habermas contends that all social processes are assessed with respect to how well (or invariably not) they foster communicability and the development of 'discourse', namely *non-coercive* arenas for the agonistic, public use of reason. As he writes, '[an] ego-identity can only stabilise itself in the anticipation of symmetrical relations of unforced reciprocal recognition' (Habermas, 1992, p. 188). Democracy and communication are necessarily tied together and *mutually supporting*: the failure to develop communicative action is a barrier to democracy in the public sphere, and the failure to develop democratic values is a barrier to communicative action.

In Habermas's schema, when communicative practices fail or break down, participants can turn to discourse. Discourse, for Habermas, involves the public testing of claims to universal normative validity; as such, discourse is central to his modern critical social theory, to the extent that his discourse theory is effectively the rational reconstruction of Kant's moral theory implicitly embedded in the theory of communicative action. For Habermas, discourse comprises two key principles: the Discourse Principle (D) and the Universalisation Principle (U).

(D) concerns '[j]ust those action norms are valid to which all possibly affected persons could agree as participants in rational discourses' (Habermas, 1992, p. 107). In other words, valid norms are not extra-human dictates handed down to us. Rather, valid norms are, to use Robert Brandom's expression, (Brandom, 2002, p. 216) – *outcomes* of communicative action established and sustained by agents' intersubjective practices. These social achievements get their *normative* purchase by virtue of being assented to and acknowledged by a community of agents. Crucially, though, the practice of assenting to and acknowledging normative constraints and normative entitlements comprises determining 'the precise content of those implicit norms … through a 'process of *negotiation*' involving ourselves *and* those who attribute norms to us' (Houlgate, 2007, p. 139). By virtue of being a process of *negotiation*, norms are never *fixed* but always subject to 'further assessment, challenge, defence, and correction' (Brandom, 1994, p. 647).

(U) concerns the formal, pragmatic procedural justification of moral norms based on (D). In effect, Habermas construes (U) as the rational reconstruction of Kant's supreme principle of morality in the *Groundwork for the Metaphysics of Morals*. As he writes,

> [t]he Categorical Imperative is always already in the background here: the form of a general law legitimates the distribution of liberties, because it implies that a given law has passed the universalisation test and been found worthy in the court of reason. (Habermas, 1996, p. 120)[13]

Crucially, the Kantian universalisation test aims to establish which maxims and interests pass deliberative discursive articulation and challenge such that those maxims and interests are objectively valid (or universally and equally binding for any rational agent). By extension, democracy, for Habermas, is a constitutional state model structured in accordance with the principles of communicative action and discourse: the laws of a democratic constitutional state are legitimate insofar as we arrive at them through *discursive practices* that are wholly intersubjective and inclusive, since society can only be integrated peacefully in the long-run if social integration involves communicative action and discourse.[14]

In what immediately follows, we examine the vulnerability of speaking and communicating subjects in light of issues raised or neglected by Habermas's account of communicative action. We take vulnerability to be understood as a multifaceted concept, one that generally refers to our interdependence as human beings. Here

[13] See also Habermas (1996, p. 153).
[14] Viz. Habermas (2001).

vulnerability is understood to be a shared constitutive condition that evokes our needful openness to others and the open-ended nature of the human condition; it therefore points to power, injury and suffering, as much as it does to forms of care, social (inter)action and cooperation.[15] For our purposes, the notion of vulnerability becomes even more salient when we examine the forms of reciprocity, responsiveness and interdependence that we argue underpin Habermas's account of language-use, discourse and communicative action.

2.1 Vulnerability and Communication

A number of interpreters have questioned whether Habermas's critical theory is up to the task of accounting for various forms of power and subordination even within the normative account of communicative action. We argue that an alternative way of considering these issues and Habermas's theory more generally, is through a consideration of the potential vulnerabilities associated with speech and communicative action, specifically those related to power, injury and harm.

Thomas McCarthy, Amy Allen, and Nancy Fraser, to name a few, have drawn attention to the inadequacy of Habermas's critical theory in terms of accounting for forms of injury and harm associated with racial and gender subordination, for example. As Allen puts it, one major concern is that 'communicative action screens power out of the lifeworld', and as a consequence, adequate consideration is not given to the forms of subordination that are 'reproduced in the lifeworld domains of culture, society and personality' (Allen, 2007, p. 641), forms that are subsequently replicated in speech acts. McCarthy suggests that the resources for tackling these issues might be more readily found in Habermas's early work, where he more fully considers 'the relation between power, social practices and subjectivity' (McCarthy, 2001, p. 654 [cited in Allen (2007)]), or patterns of socialisation that impact on forms of communicative interaction. However, when Habermas moves to advance a formal pragmatic analysis of communication as well as his later theory of discourse ethics, it seems these insights drop away.

15 This way of phrasing the point is in Petherbridge (2016; 2018); that work provides a fuller account of the material on vulnerability. Sections of the material presented here in sections two and four have also been explored in Petherbridge (2021), but in the context of exploring the notions of recognition and trust.

Following McCarthy's insights, Allen suggests that one of the key problems for Habermas in the development of his formal pragmatics and later theory of communicative action, is the lack of an account of socialisation processes in the lifeworld that consequently adversely impact upon his critical theory of communication. For our purposes, this also points to one of the key sites of vulnerability in communicative practices more generally. As we will discuss below, this is also linked to a second but related form of vulnerability in speech practices, that is, the constitutive power of language in subject-formation, as well as the inherently vulnerable dynamic between speaker and hearer in speech acts.

Habermas's most developed attempt to address the problem of power and subordination in relation to forms of communication, can perhaps be found in his account of systematically distorted communication. He briefly discusses this phenomenon in *The Theory of Communicative Action Volume 1*, where he describes it as a form of concealed strategic action. As mentioned above, Habermas claims that perlocutionary acts represent forms of strategic action given their intent is to bring about some particular end, rather than merely a form of communicative action directed toward mutual understanding. Habermas argues the following:

> [systematically distorted] communication pathologies can be conceived of as the result of a confusion between actions orientated to reaching understanding and actions orientated to success. In situations of concealed strategic action, at least one of the parties behaves with an orientation to success, but leaves others to believe that all the presuppositions of communicative action are satisfied. This is the case of manipulation ... in connection with perlocutionary acts... [Furthermore,] [i]n such cases at least one of the parties is deceiving himself about the fact that he is acting with an attitude orientated to success and is only keeping up the appearance of communicative action. (Habermas, 1984, pp. 332–33)

In other texts, Habermas more directly links the problem of systematically distorted communication to the background context of the lifeworld and the problem of individual development. As Allen identifies, in his 'Reflections on Communicative Pathology' (1974), Habermas examines the phenomena of systematically distorted communication in regard to both the differentiation and connection between 'the external organisation of speech – roughly, its social context – and the internal organisation of speech – the universal and necessary presuppositions of communication' (Allen, 2007,

p. 645). As Allen has argued, this means we might also need to take account not only of systematically distorted communication but the forms of distorted subjectivity that arise in individual development that in turn impact on participants in communication.

For Habermas, though, the consequences of systematically distorted communication refer not only the disruptive effect they have on the social context in which speech acts take place, but also to the very 'validity basis of speech' itself. In this sense, Allen notes '[c]ommunication becomes systematically distorted when the external organisation of speech is overburdened, and this burden is shifted onto the internal organisation of speech' (Ibid.). This dynamic, however, occurs 'surreptitiously', in Habermas's view, without leading to a break in communication or to 'openly declared ... strategic action' (Habermas, 2001, p. 147 [cited in Allen (2007)]). The validity basis of speech is disrupted if at least one of the three universal validity claims – truth, normative rightness or sincerity – are violated even though communication nonetheless continues on the 'presumption' of it being communicative action orientated to reaching understanding, when in fact it conceals the speaker's strategic intent.

In this context, then, we suggest that Habermas's discussion and acknowledgement of the phenomena of systematically distorted communication discloses the kinds of vulnerability inherent not only in being a participant (speaker or hearer) in a speech act but also to the vulnerability contained in communicative action itself. This is the case both in relation to the vulnerabilities inherent to the identity development of subjects who enter into communicative acts such that the organisation of the social context impacts on the internal organisation of speech, but also to the vulnerability and unpredictability that might play out in speech acts themselves.

As the discussion of systematically distorted communication reveals, speech and communication are, then, subject to *at least* two kinds of vulnerability. Communicative practices are subject to a kind of vulnerability that is implicit to speech acts themselves, in the sense that not only the social context in which speech acts take place are vulnerable to relations of power relations, injury and harm, *but the very validity of speech becomes vulnerable*. As we will discuss further below, this is played out in the basic dynamics of speech acts themselves, where there is a vulnerability embedded in the basic relation between a speaker's performance and a hearer's response, such that certain conditions enable or constrain speech acts and are impacted upon by the 'situated identities of the persons' speaking and hearing.[16] In this sense, as Allen suggests, '[w]hen Habermas relates the concept of systematically distorted communication to the formation of identity' (Allen, 2007, p. 645), another tension is revealed. This is because for Habermas, as for other critical theorists such as Judith Butler and Axel Honneth, *identity is constituted through intersubjective recognition*.

However, as both Honneth and Butler reveal, the granting of recognition is inherently vulnerable; the intersubjective basis of subject-formation creates certain kinds of dependence on others but there is no guarantee that recognition will be forthcoming or when it might be withheld.[17] As Habermas himself identifies, this means that systematically distorted forms of identity indicate 'an asymmetrical distribution of power', and this dynamic is shifted onto the 'internal structure of speech' (Habermas, 2001, p. 147 [cited in Allen (2007)]). However, despite this acknowledgment, Habermas does not give due consideration to the way in which speech or language itself may also contribute to distorted forms of identity (for example, through 'interpellation', as Butler puts it).

In the preceding discussion, then, we have so far identified the following forms of vulnerability in relation to speech and communication:

1. The first manifestation of vulnerability is one associated with identity-formation, which, for Habermas, can be understood in terms of recognition. In this regard, we identified the way in which socialisation processes and forms of power reproduced in the lifeworld domains of culture, society and personality, render subjects vulnerable to distorted forms of identity which in turn impacts upon speech acts. This points not only to the vulnerability associated with recognition as intrinsic to subject-formation but to the constitutive power of language in subject-formation.
2. Such distorted forms of identity-formation may in turn impact upon the internal organisation of speech, leading to increased vulnerability. This is not only the case in terms of the social context in which particular speech acts take place but impacts on the very validity of speech itself.
3. This may play out directly in speech acts and the vulnerability associated with being a participant in communicative action, or in terms of the uncertainty about whether one's speech act is successful or not. This form of vulnerability is inherent to

16 Stawarska (2017, p. 185).
17 See Butler (2004).

> the relation between a speaker and listener, particularly in relation to the dynamic between a speaker's performance and a hearer's uptake.

We will now turn to a more detailed examination of the vulnerability entailed in the dynamics of speech acts and the potential for disruption or instability to the meaning and effect of such acts.

2.2 The Vulnerability of Speech Acts: Speaker Performance and Hearer Uptake

As discussed above, Habermas draws on Austin's analysis of speech acts in developing his account of communication and discourse, where the account of illocutionary acts is central to the theory of communication action (and the discourse theory of ethics). However, as we also saw, vulnerabilities were also identified in relation to inequality and power that distort the internal organisation of speech.

The interrelation between the performative nature of speech and inequality has been more fully addressed by philosophers such as Jennifer Hornsby and Rae Langton. Although these debates have seemingly not included a discussion of vulnerability as inherent to speech acts, we wish to draw attention here to this neglected aspect in the discourse here. Hornsby and Langton have highlighted the way in which, as speakers, certain people suffer what they term 'illocutionary silencing'. As they put it, 'people are silenced when they are prevented from doing certain illocutionary things with words. People who utter words but fail to perform the illocution they intend may be silenced' and this produces what they term 'illocutionary disablement'. In this scenario, a person's speech maybe said to 'misfire' and a person 'is deprived of illocutionary potential' (Hornsby and Langton, 1998, p. 21).

We would like to suggest that this kind of illocutionary silencing illustrates the kinds of vulnerability inherent to speech acts, and by extension, to communicative action. If there is uncertainty about whether a speaker's speech may misfire or be taken-up by a hearer, this causes certain vulnerabilities as a participant in communication. Here it is worth examining the dynamics of the vulnerabilities associated with illocutionary acts that Hornsby and Langton implicitly allude to in terms of their account of illocutionary silencing in more detail.

In many respects, Hornsby and Langton's reading and development of Austin's speech act theory accords with some of the basic interpretations also offered by Habermas. Hornsby and Langton point to the slightly unstable differentiation Austin marks out between illocutionary and perlocutionary acts, which in regard to the former, rest on 'the saying of certain words such that, *in* saying those words one performs an action', whilst in contrast the latter refers to 'the saying of words, such that *by* saying those words other things are done' (Hornsby and Langton, 1998, p. 24). As Hornsby and Langton remark (Ibid.), however, given that Austin ties illocutionary acts to a hearer's uptake, the outcome of the hearer's responsivity itself could be deemed a kind of consequence.

Nonetheless, like Habermas, Hornsby and Langton want to retain a distinction between illocutionary and perlocutionary acts. This is because, in their view, perlocutionary acts are not merely communicative but, 'introduce the idea of *extra-linguistic* or *incidental* consequences of speaking' (Ibid.), in other words, further actions follow from such acts that are not attached to the conventions of speech *per se*. Importantly, illocutionary speech acts are not only tied to, what Austin terms, 'felicity conditions' associated with certain formal conditions, conventions and institutions, such as an order, request or proposal, that ensure the force of a speech act. They are also related to certain conditions that involve 'the institution of language itself' (Hornsby and Langton, 1998, p. 25). In this regard, Hornsby and Langton point to the relation of recognition underlying a speaker and hearer in speech acts and argue that '[b]y involving the hearer as well as the speaker, illocutionary acts reveal language as communicative' (Ibid.).

In this sense, the success or otherwise of illocutionary acts relies upon the hearer's uptake but more generally also requires *mutual reciprocity and receptiveness of uptake*. As they explain,

> [u]ptake consists in the speaker being taken to be performing the very illocutionary act that, in being so taken, she (the speaker) is performing. Language use then relies in a mutual capacity for uptake, which involves a minimal receptiveness on the part of language users in the role of hearers. This minimal receptiveness does not mean the hearer will agree, or is even capable of agreeing, with what a speaker is saying; but it does mean that a hearer has a capacity to grasp what communicative act a speaker might intend to perform. (Ibid.)

Ultimately, then, mutual reciprocity is required for a speaker's utterance to do the work it means to do, and this brings Hornsby and Langton's view close to the spirit of Habermas's account.

However, in certain cases, this dynamic of illocutionary acts fails because as Hornsby and Langton point out, certain sayings are unspeakable for certain speakers. Some examples they give are, a man who tries to marry by saying 'I do', only to discover the celebrant was merely an unauthorised actor; or a woman living under Islamic law who wishes to divorce her husband who utters the word 'divorced'. These examples represent what Hornsby and Langton refer to as 'illocutionary disablement' (Hornsby and Langton, 1998, p. 26), in which the saying of something misfires as the speaker does not satisfy certain felicity conditions. Somewhat like Habermas, Hornsby and Langton refer to the centrality of a hearer's recognition of a speaker's intention in order for a speech act to be successful. Furthermore, they also point to the importance of reciprocity for such recognition conditions to be met. In their view, when reciprocity is at work, a hearer recognises the speaker's attempt to perform an illocution, and the speaker's attempt is performed. For example, in the situation of an unwanted sexual advance, a speaker says 'no' and the hearer recognises this as a refusal.[18] It is precisely when this kind of reciprocity fails and a speaker's illocution is not recognised for what it is, that a speaker is exposed to a particular form of vulnerability as she is unable to do things with words in the manner of successful illocution.

In a related manner, Quill Kukla (writing as Rebecca Kukla) has also drawn attention to the way in which a 'speaker's membership in an already disadvantaged social group makes it difficult or impossible for her to employ discursive conventions in the normal way, with the result that the performative force of her utterances is distorted in ways that enhance disadvantage' (Kukla, 2014, p. 441). However, Kukla questions how convincing it is to maintain a strict differentiation between illocutionary and perlocutionary acts. The argument is that sometimes the full force or consequences of an illocutionary act are not known or do not materialise in the act of speaking itself. Rather, as Kukla points out, recognition of the Other as a speaker as well as the form of responsiveness required for hearer uptake, in their view, do not seem solely intrinsic to illocution but are a perlocutionary effect.

The claim is that it is not really until people respond to a speech act that it can be deemed fully completed. It is only at this point that the effects of a speech act are really known, and in Kukla's view, this needs to be considered an 'integral part of the entire context of the utterance' (Kukla, 2014, p. 454). In other words, various norms and conventions contribute to determining not only whether a speaker is entitled to speak, but 'in placing that performance in social space after it is complete' (Kukla, 2014, p. 443). Moreover, certain sayings or words might be 'out of one's control' and vulnerable to

[18] Viz. Hornsby and Langton, 1998, pp. 27–28.

what Kukla helpfully terms a form of '*discursive injustice*' (Kukla, 2014, p. 445; 441). As Kukla explains, '[v]ictims of discursive injustice are, in virtue of their disadvantaged social identities, less able to skilfully negotiate and deploy discursive convention as tools for communication and action than others' (Kukla, 2014, p. 445). In this regard, Kukla draws attention not only to the recognition condition of a speech act that underpins Hornsby and Langton's view of the necessity of the recognition of a speaker's intention, but also to the impact such an act has in social space more generally.[19]

The types of illocutionary silencing that Hornsby and Langton name, and the notion of discursive injustice that Kukla highlights, not only demonstrate the vulnerability of speech and communication, but also have affinities with forms of epistemic injustice and discursive abuse, as we will discuss in Section 3.

However, before discussing these connections, it is important to consider the way in which a hearer might alternatively be vulnerable to injury and harm by way of a speaker's illocution, such that the vulnerability of the hearer is enhanced rather than that of the speaker. As Beata Stawarska suggests, a hearer's uptake not only enables a speech act to function but also 'plays an active role in shaping power relations' (Stawarska, 2017, p. 186), which points to the vulnerable dynamic involved in unjust speech. On one side, as Stawarska argues, some 'sayings have the potential to produce massive harm' (Stawarska, 2017, p. 185) that may or may not be intended, and on the other side, '[l]anguage users can re-shape the social world by being active listeners to those who have historically been disempowered' (Stawarska, 2017, p. 186), and whose illocutions often remain unrecognised. As Stawarska, suggests, 'we therefore need to expand the horizon' of communicative acts, 'to include the inherited social conditions of power and the received histories of the said words and the situated identities of the person's saying and hearing them' (Stawarska, 2017, p. 185).

Austin had already pointed to the way in which only those persons delegated with authority could successfully perform certain illocutionary acts, recognising that such authority whether celebrant or divorcee, is underwritten by an entire social order. However, Stawarska argues that historically disempowered or de-authorised groups can also come to 'make words speak somewhat differently than they did in the past' (Stawarska, 2017, p. 190). This requires recognising that linguistic meanings and language use are themselves vulnerable to change, in the sense that they have a certain 'socially contingent

[19] Viz. Kukla (2014, p. 444).

plasticity' (Ibid.) that has the potential to rupture inherited and sedimented meanings and usage.

There is, then, a two-pronged response to the phenomena of disempowered communicative participants: (1) there is what Stawarska, following Butler, refers to as the 'transgressive reclamation of socially harmful speech' by re-orientating the use and signification of certain words. In this manner, harmful or injurious speech can be turned around such that it becomes 'an empowering emancipatory practice' (Ibid.). In such cases, subordinated groups are themselves 'empowered to negotiate what words signify and what effects they may produce' (Ibid.). Thus, where once the saying of particular words might have been injurious, in the act of reclaiming them, disempowered groups are able to re-orientate the meaning and the affects that words produce in a self-affirming manner, and this also shifts the authority problem in linguistic encounters.[20] (2) Extending insights from Hornsby and Langton, this shift not only requires an alteration in terms of who has authority to speak, but also requires a form of 'active heeding' that enables forms of 're-authorisation' (Ibid.). Thus, akin to Hornsby and Langton, as Stawarska argues, the 'process of re-authorisation vitally depends on cultivating a stance of productive listening that empowers the utterance to become felicitous by virtue of the recognition it bestows upon the speaker' (Stawarska, 2017, p. 192).

Thus, the kind of vulnerability we wish to highlight is played out at what Stawarska terms the 'micro-level' of linguistic encounters, and this is particularly impacted by power relations between communicative partners to interaction.[21] The forms of vulnerability we refer to, then, include not only forms of injury and harm that can be inflicted through speech acts, but also the uncertainty and unpredictability of the receptive uptake of a hearer to the illocutionary acts of subordinated groups, as well as the vulnerability of the meaning of such speech acts themselves, which might be resisted, reclaimed, and negotiated.[22] Taking-up and extending the insights discussed above in relation to the notions of illocutionary silencing and discursive injustice, in what immediately follows, we focus on elaborating epistemic pathologies in the context of epistemic oppression and testimonial injustice.

[20] Viz. Stawarska (2017, p. 190).
[21] Viz. Stawarska (2017, p. 191).
[22] See Stawarska (2017, p. 191).

3. Epistemic Pathologies: Epistemic Oppression & Testimonial Injustice

Epistemic oppression refers to, as Kristie Dotson writes, 'a persistent and unwarranted infringement on the ability to utilise persuasively shared epistemic resources that hinders one's contributions to knowledge production' (Dotson, 2014, p. 115). According to Dotson, systemic practices of epistemic exclusion and oppression result in positions and communities that produce deficiencies in social knowledge, as evidenced by increasingly widespread, normalised virulent epistemic contempt for non-privileged groups. For example, distress at systemically reproduced institutional racism and police brutality is often dismissed, to the extent that the vocabulary of protest against racial oppression is viciously misrecognised to the point of erasure. As Robert Gooding-Williams writes, the reactionary view is 'a failure to regard the speech or actions of black people as manifesting thoughtful judgements about issues that concern all members of the political community' (Gooding-Williams, 2006, p. 14).

Black Lives Matter demonstrations typically involve the chant 'Hands Up, Don't Shoot!', where marchers raise their hands above their heads while chanting, as part of the effort to explicitly challenge the reactionary socio-epistemic paradigms which construe antiracist protestors as public threats. To quote José Medina here, '[t]his slogan performatively challenges the misplaced presumption that demonstrators pose a threat to public order, interrogating the underlying narratives that depict them as such a threat, while invoking alternative images of peaceful expressions of group agency' (Medina, 2018, p. 12). Furthermore, the chants 'Whose streets? Our streets!' and 'No Justice, No Peace!' are *deliberately* misinterpreted and misrecognised by reactionary groups to imply that the basic progressive claim 'black lives matter' is equivalent to 'black lives matter more than white lives'. Crucially, this forms a significant part of the explanation for why #AllLivesMatter is in fact reactionary, since #AllLivesMatter reveals itself as ignorant of structural racism and systemic misrecognition.

Related to, but conceptually and politically distinct from the concept of epistemic oppression, which is principally concerned with endemic patterns of structural exploitation and domination of specific epistemic communities, is the concept of epistemic injustice. To quote Miranda Fricker, epistemic injustice arises when a person is 'wronged in their capacity as a knower' (Fricker, 2007, p. 20). Such wronging usually happens in *at least* two ways: (1) through testimonial injustice, which *typically* occurs when a speaker's assertions are given *less credibility* than they deserve because the hearer has prejudices about a social group of which the speaker is a member;[23] (2) through hermeneutical injustice, which occurs when there is a gap in the collective interpretive resources of a given society that leaves a marginalised and socially powerless group unable to properly make sense of their social powerlessness. Crucially, the epistemic pathologies of misrecognising or not recognising individual knowledge-claims and/or social group knowledge-claims are particularly vicious forms of humiliation, in that they are a 'deformation of the normal human capacity for the evaluative perception of others' (Zurn, 2015, p. 101).

With regard to the kind of epistemic pathology of recognition in the context of testimonial injustice, in particular (for our specific focus here), it would be helpful to refer to Patricia Williams's autobiographical account of her experience of testimonial justice:

> I was shopping in Soho [in Benetton's] and saw a sweater that I wanted to buy for my mother. I pressed my round brown face to the window and my finger to the buzzer, seeking admittance. A narrow-eyed, white teenager … glared out, evaluating me for signs that would pit me against the limits of his social understanding. After about five seconds, he mouthed 'We're closed', and blew pink rubber at me. It was two Saturdays before Christmas, at one o'clock in the afternoon; there were several white people in the store who appeared to be shopping for things for *their* mothers. I was enraged … In the flicker of his judgemental grey eyes, that sales-child had transformed my brightly sentimental, joy-to-the-world, pre-Christmas spree to a shambles … [H]is refusal to let me into the store … was an outward manifestation of his never having let someone like me into the realm of his reality … (Williams, 1991, pp. 44–56)
>
> A rumour got started that the Benetton's story wasn't true, that I had made it up, that it was a fantasy, a lie that was probably the product of a diseased mind trying to make all white people feel guilty. At this point I realised … that the greater issue I had to face was the overwhelming weight of a disbelief that goes beyond mere disinclination to believe and becomes active suppression of anything I might have to say. The greater problem is a powerfully oppressive mechanism for denial of self-knowledge and expression. And this denial cannot be separated from

[23] See Davis (2016) and Giladi (forthcoming) for how credibility *excess* is an act of epistemic injustice.

> the simultaneously pathological willingness to believe certain things about blacks – not believe them, but things *about* them. (Ibid., p. 242)

In addition to being harmed by the salesperson's racism – Williams was racially barred from entry and consequently could not participate in the activity of buying Christmas presents for one's mother – Williams suffered a distinct, further wrong by having her testimony dismissed and not accorded serious communicative status. Specifically, in the Habermasian sense of validity claims involved with those speech acts conveying truthfulness and, above all, revealing and baring the *subjective world* of individual anxieties, hopes (and the like) to one's listener(s), Williams, rather than automatically receive the default level of epistemic respect, trust, and communicative appreciation provided by the Acceptance Principle,[24] is not only treated with epistemic scorn, she is also stripped of *any* normative authority. She is deemed as someone who violates the communicative norms of assertion. As such Williams's capacity for *speech* is violated – where, crucially, speech involves the vulnerability that comes with revealing oneself in the transparent communicative act of sharing sincere propositional content for uptake by the listener. This is why racism – at the epistemic level – is structured around the pathological norm of believing untrue things about black people, rather than believing black people about true things.

Testimonial injustice deprives Williams, a rational agent, of her rightful place as someone moving in the communicative space of reasons, and thereby leaves individuals like her who are systemically prejudiced against in a state of self-alienation and double-consciousness: Williams is forcibly alienated from her own speech and rationality, where these enable her to be a member of a community of inquirers and reliable narrators. As part of her self-conscious identification with fellow African-Americans in an African-American community, Williams communicatively self-interprets and finds such communicative action empowering. However, African-Americans (and other people of colour), as part of a racist world, are met with external and hostile web of meanings that radically distort such uplifting local self-conceptions. The power structure of racial oppression is pervasive such that the experiential relation Williams has to herself becomes distorted by how she views her agency from the perspective of white prejudicial attitudes, which aim to rob her of her position as a communicative subject, and instead treat her as an object of derision

24 See Burge (1993, p. 467).

and contempt. This is what we take her to mean when she argues that 'the greater problem is a powerfully oppressive mechanism for denial of self-knowledge and expression'. Crucially, the asymmetrical nature of the cognitive environment causes Williams to think and feel that the space of reasons, where communicative practices derive their sense of meaning and purpose, is not a space for *her*.

Given that epistemic oppression and testimonial injustice cause one to be alienated from both their own communicative rationality and from the speech-based practices which necessarily constitute discourse between peers, exclusion from the space of reasons amounts to 'discursive abuse'. The experience of discursive abuse 'carries with it the danger of an injury that can bring the identity of the person as a whole to the point of collapse' (Honneth, 1995, pp. 132–33), where the identity under threat here is a person's self-interpretation as *agential*,[25] since speech involves vulnerability with respect to revealing oneself in the transparent, trusting communicative act of sharing propositional content for uptake by the listener. To use Andrea Lobb's expression, the kind of 'epistemic injury' (Lobb, 2018, p. 1) endured here can be made sense of in relation to what Richard Rorty calls 'mute despair' and 'intense mental pain'. For Rorty, this notion of *agential pain* – the type of pain unique to agents

> reminds us that human beings who have been socialised ... can all be given a special kind of pain: they can all be humiliated by the forcible tearing down of the particular structures of language and belief in which they were socialised (or which they pride themselves on having formed for themselves). (Rorty, 1989, p. 177)

The failure to properly recognise and accord somebody the epistemic acknowledgement they merit is an act of abuse in the sense of forcibly depriving individuals of a progressive *communicative* environment in which the epistemic recognition accorded to them plays a significant role in enabling and fostering their self-confidence as a *communicative* agent. This includes:

i. External and forcible control over one's own communicative integrity.
ii. Violation of communicative integrity prevents one from trusting others and one's own capacities to the distressing extent that victims internalise culpability.
iii. Discursive abuse represents a type of disrespect that does lasting damage to one's basic confidence that one can

25 Cf. Fricker (2007, p. 55).

autonomously coordinate one's own communicative claims and even identify as a communicative subject or be recognised as one.

Understood in this manner, there is compelling reason to see how all three points above relate to the vulnerability associated with a) identity-formation, b) distorted identity-formation and the internal organisation of speech, and c) being a participant in communicative action, where c) especially concerns the dynamic between a speaker's performance and a hearer's uptake. Regressive recognition orders deliberately exploit intersubjective vulnerability and pervert communicative dynamics by making those excluded from the space of reasons think and feel as though their rejection is entirely the result of their failings. Epistemic oppression and systemic testimonial injustice permeate, to the extent that individuals and/or social groups are made to blame themselves for not being deemed worthy enough to be afforded credibility.[26]

4. Spreading One's Dreams at the Feet of the Other: Habermas and the Fragility of Communicating Subjects

The preceding discussion of illocutionary acts and silencing, as well as discursive injustice and abuse, raises questions about the neglected element of vulnerability inherent in being a participant in speech acts and more fully in communicative action. In turn, the vulnerability of participants in communicative action, flows through to the vulnerability of persons as knowers and participants in the space of reasons. What, then, do we draw from the above discussion in regard to the interrelation between vulnerability, speech and communication as it pertains to Habermas's work? In what follows, we conclude by considering, on the one hand, the manner in which an account of vulnerability enriches Habermas's overly formal notions of communicative action and discourse; on the other, we examine the ways in which Habermas's own account of communicative action is already oriented towards the vulnerability of speaking agents. This is evinced not only through the rules of communication and discourse that he goes to such lengths to construct, but also in claims he makes in regard to moral intuitions and discourse ethics.

As we have seen, Habermas builds an account of normativity and recognition into his theory of communicative action and discourse.

[26] For previous articulations of these points in section three, see Giladi (2018, 2020).

Implicitly, the formal structure of Habermas's theory of discourse and notion of the 'ideal speech situation', already acknowledges the vulnerability of speaking agents by providing measures aimed to protect persons in the realm of communicative action. His account of language-use points to what he regards as our primordial *inter*-dependence as language-users and the basic uncertainty of this endeavour. The account of the ideal speech situation makes a claim for equality of speaking-agents by having the opportunity to speak and to express one's viewpoint *without coercion or interference*. Moreover, Habermas argues for the need for free and equal argumentation and the use of reason in practical discourse, with the view to reaching mutual understanding and fostering mutual cooperation. However, he does not assume this process is seamless. Rather, he points to the fragilities and uncertainties of communicative freedom that arise with modernity due to particular developmental logics or dynamics (the decoupling of 'Lifeworld' and 'System'[27]), which in turn impact upon the internal structure of communicative action and the potential for rationality.

Notably, Habermas explicitly ties his account of discourse to a notion of vulnerability in texts such as *Moral Consciousness and Communicative Action*. In this text, he restates that '[a]rgumentation insures that all concerned in principle take part, freely and equally, in a cooperative search for truth, where nothing coerces anyone except the force of the better argument' (Habermas, 1990, p. 198). However, what is significant in this account is that Habermas also makes clear the anthropological claim underlying his discursive approach as it pertains to moral intuitions. As he writes:

> Moral intuitions are intuitions that instruct us on how best to behave in situations where is it in our power to counteract the extreme vulnerability of others by being thoughtful and considerate. In anthropological terms, morality is a safety device compensating for a vulnerability built into the sociocultural form of life. (Habermas, 1990, p. 199)

Here, it might be suggested, that Habermas makes clear that his theory of communicative action is in fact underpinned by a constitutive notion of vulnerability that is inherent to every social and

[27] Habermas makes a distinction between what he terms the 'Lifeworld', which refers the normatively underpinned public sphere as well as the private sphere of family life, in contrast to what he terms 'System', which includes the State and the activities of market capitalism steered by purely formal or instrumental mechanisms. See Habermas (1987a).

intersubjective context. It also brings Habermas within the vicinity of other vulnerability theorists when he ties this notion of vulnerability to our constitutive interdependence as human beings and to forms of subject-formation dependent upon recognition from others. For, as he states: '[t]he more the subject becomes individuated, the more he becomes entangled in a densely woven fabric of mutual recognition, that is, of reciprocal exposedness and vulnerability' (Habermas, 1990, p. 199).

In Habermas's view, then, moralities address or respond to what he terms the 'fragility of human beings individuated through socialisation' (Habermas, 1990, p. 200). But the protection of these fragilities requires a two-pronged approach that safeguards not only the individual subject but also the community in which that subject is embedded in a web of 'intersubjective relations of recognition' (Ibid.). These two elements point to two related principles that Habermas terms 'justice' and 'solidarity', and as he sees it, both principles are rooted in 'the specific vulnerability of the human species, which individuates itself through sociation' (Ibid.). In this respect, we argue that Habermas's theory should be taken seriously as a contribution to the discourse on vulnerability, particularly as it pertains to the neglected elements of speech and communication. In the essay 'Morality and Ethical Life', he even goes so far to say that 'linguistically mediated interaction, *is both the reason for the vulnerability of socialised* individuals and *the key resource they possess to compensate for that vulnerability*' (Habermas, 1990, p. 201). It is clear, then, that Habermas acknowledges that forms of vulnerability are inherent to speech and linguistically mediated interaction as well as to individual subject-development.

However, despite this anthropological claim in regard to linguistic forms of vulnerability, the way in which Habermas addresses this issue is ironically conceptualised at a rather formal and abstract level. As a consequence, he does not take adequate account of the more embodied, pre-reflexive and affective forms of interaction that characterise much of the literature in vulnerability theory. Indeed, even in his early work, Habermas's theory is based on the assumption that certain procedural rules are always already presupposed by human discourse and that these rules can be drawn on to validate moral principles, and thus normatively justify social interaction. Under this schema, rational consensus presupposes an ideal speech situation as a kind of meta-norm, a situation that significantly assumes a kind of symmetry and reciprocity, requiring all participants to adopt the standpoint of the 'generalised other'. In assuming this standpoint, though, participants must abstract from their individuality and concrete identity, thereby leaving behind their private and particular affiliations, and the specific social context in which they are embedded.[28] Through such a principle, Habermas suggests a rational consensus can be achieved in the context of conflicting opinions and interests *regardless* of differing traditions, cultural perspectives, or individual life-histories.

In order to make this claim, though, Habermas's moral theory relies upon a distinction he makes between *issues of justice* (morality) and *questions of the good life* (ethics), based upon a postmetaphysical argument shared with John Rawls's liberal egalitarianism (1971; 1985) that ontological questions must be separated from practical matters if the universalist normative presuppositions of communicative rationality are to succeed. In this respect, in Habermas's view, moral judgements are concerned only with right or just action, not with substantive values of the good or characteristics that pertain to individual needs and identities; only claims about rightness and just action are considered to provide norms that are obligatory for all persons universally and equally.[29] As a consequence, Habermas concludes that moral-practical dilemmas can be resolved on the basis of a universal sense of communicative reason, whereas questions relating to ethical identities can only be considered in terms of the ethical values within a particular form of life.

However, as Honneth, for example, has argued, normative claims are experienced and articulated by people in *everyday life* as disturbances that may, or may not, make mutual recognition possible *prior* to them reaching the level of discourse. These disturbances may therefore disclose the *processes* through which recognition is, or is not, achieved prior to the articulation of moral norms. Consequently, these are processes and conditions that individuals must feel are safeguarded even before they can attain the competency considered necessary by a theory of discourse ethics. In this respect, then, the Habermasian form of moral reasoning, as the impartial application of general principles, describes a restricted field of moral life concerned with public institutional forms of morality, but which, ironically ignore everyday motivational contexts despite their explicitly pragmatic orientation.[30] The universalist principle of Habermas's discourse ethics demands from interaction partners

[28] See Benhabib (1986). For a full account of the argument outlined here, see Petherbridge (2013).

[29] See Rehg (1994).

[30] Viz. Honneth (1995). See also Petherbridge (2013) a full account of this argument.

a willingness and refined ability to enable consideration of normative questions from a generalised standpoint whilst leaving aside their concrete relations with others in everyday experience.[31] However, such claims address dilemmas in social life that are not located at the abstract level of universalisation, but at the concrete level at which everyday forms of conflict occur. The proceduralism of Habermas's discourse theory and his overly formal account of linguistic action, therefore, means it is difficult to theorise how the *initial feelings of injury that motivate moral claims are converted into propositional attitudes (articulated linguistic claims) in the first place.*

As the above discussion of Allen revealed, it is then not only a matter of identifying forms of systematically distorted communication but equally forms of systematically distorted identity-formation that impact upon forms of communication. Thus, as Honneth and Allen have noted, normative criteria must not only be concerned with the intersubjective presuppositions of language but also the intersubjective presuppositions of human identity development that impact upon speech, communication, and the social scaffolding of the knower. Moreover, as Honneth identifies, Habermas's theory is also susceptible to the 'cultural exclusion' of oppressed social classes from the articulation of claims of injustice in the public sphere. Honneth draws attention to the silencing of forms of moral conflict or social feelings of injustice, that as he expresses it in early work, 'lie behind the façade of late-capitalist integration' (Honneth, 1995, p. 207).

This critique is aimed at Habermas's particular model of society and the public sphere, which unwittingly results in *the exclusion of certain voices and forms of moral protest from the public field of speech and communicative action*; in other words, Habermas's model fails to make sufficient sense of this type of discursive abuse, where such forms of discursive abuse reinforce the structural (epistemic) obstacles facing certain voices and forms of moral protest. These structural (epistemic) obstacles prevent certain voices and forms of moral protest from being publicly articulable and from becoming fully elaborated moral claims (Honneth, 1995, p. 207; p. 209). In this manner, forms of exclusion are related to deprivation of 'linguistic and symbolic means' (Honneth, 1995, p. 213), and this creates not only misrecognition and silencing, but the invisibilisation of disadvantaged groups. Indeed, what particularly motivates the inquiries of intersectional feminist epistemologists is precisely the focus on (i) the power dynamics of gender, race, class, sexuality, and disability; (ii) the role these dynamics of power play in the social conditions of

[31] Viz. Benhabib (1986, pp. 320–21).

knowing; and (iii) the ways in which the structures of existing social institutions affect the actual practices of knowers. As indicated above, intersectional feminist epistemologists are particularly concerned with (i) how the normative space of reasons is organised; (ii) how one negotiates the normative space of reasons; and (iii) how one gets into normative space at all. To put this more simply, the overriding focus is critically uncovering the substantive link between various types of power relations and epistemic practices. Arguably, the central question is '*who gets to know things?*'.

One problem, then, with Habermas's 'linguistification' of moral conflict and his account of justice, is that it potentially contributes to the very forms of silencing it seeks to overcome. This is due not only to the formal nature of his pragmatics but also implicit assumptions about the skills and capacities required for individuals and groups to enter into moral debate and discourse in the first place. Moreover, Habermas's account of communicative action and discourse relies upon certain democratic and discursively structured institutions and forms of political life. Here Habermas points to an important issue: communication free from power and distortion requires the establishment of robust modern democratic institutions, ones that are constituted through reciprocal relations and patterns of interaction. Such institutions must be underpinned by forms of reciprocal freedom that are grounded in relations of recognition. For such institutions to ensure forms of communicative action without coercion they must be immanently constituted from within the structure of recognition relations, or to put it another way, they must develop out of normative patterns of social interaction between social actors themselves in any given social context.[32]

Unfortunately, many existing modern institutions fall well short of the standards of Habermasian discourse and forms of recognition: they tend to have exclusionary epistemic habits and reveal a normalised contempt for non-privileged agents. To put this point more polemically, many existing modern institutions fail to be relational institutions, since they fail to promote practices of symmetrical recognition in communication; many institutions have substantive internal structural weaknesses; they often fail to encourage the quest for self-realisation and thereby leave people who are epistemically oppressed and marginalised in a constant state of alienation; many existing modern institutions, therefore, require radical change, rather than liberal tweaks. The goal of social critique, therefore, is to identify and shift unequal power relations that are directly responsible for

[32] See Honneth (2014).

forms of suffering and alienation that are produced by marginalisation and thereby further entrench forms of oppression.

On this score, Habermas's theory offers insights into the ways in which such institutions might be structured democratically in a manner that enables equal participation in communicative interaction. For, as Simone Chambers points out, in principle, discourse ethics combats the 'marketplace of ideas between elites in which interests and understandings compete with each other for domination' (Chambers, 1995, p. 176). Habermas's discourse theory (in principle) offers a model for mutual cooperation precisely *through* the acknowledgement of difference. These discursive spaces, however, can be opened up further by extending 'opportunities to participate, by including excluded voices, by democratising media access, by setting up 'town meetings', by politicising the depoliticised, by empowering the powerless, by decentralising decision-making ... and so on' (Chambers, 1995, pp. 176–77). These are all measures that might reinvigorate practices of discourse that are at the heart of Habermas's democratic project and address the fragilities associated not only with being a participant in communicative action but also interdependent subjects who rely upon recognition from others.

For as we have argued, participants in communication lay themselves bare in front of one another, and as Habermas suggests, there is an implicit trust built into communication that aims at reaching understanding. By drawing attention to the structure of communication with respect to the subjective world, Habermas highlights the need for the recognition of the *intentions* of the speaker in acts of communication. In doing so, he acknowledges the forms of interdependence, reciprocity and responsiveness that are intrinsic to vulnerability in a manner that might evoke an account of the intentions of the horizontally 'inclined', rather than vertically 'autonomous' speaker, to use Adriana Cavarero's terms.[33]

The desire to transform the practices of many existing modern institutions by recognising and embracing vulnerability crucially reminds us of precisely what we owe to one another. As evoked by the passage from Yeats with which this paper began, as communicating subjects, we 'spread our dreams' before one another thereby placing our trust in the other's moral responsiveness. Acknowledging the vulnerable dynamics of discourse advances democratic forms of association by fostering the protection of the individual as well as 'the well-being of the community to which he [or she] belongs' (Habermas, 1990, p. 200). As Habermas writes in one of his more recognitive

33 See Cavarero (2016).

moments, as 'creatures' constituted by 'profound vulnerability' we require communicative forms of moral attentiveness by which we can defend both 'the integrity of the individual' and preserve 'the vital ties of mutual recognition through which individuals reciprocally stabilise their fragile identities' (Habermas, 1990, p. 199; 200). Embracing mutual vulnerability, then, has the potential to provide the indispensable symbolic and material space for bringing about a better world.

Manchester Metropolitan University
P.Giladi@mmu.ac.uk

University College Dublin
danielle.petherbridge@ucd.ie

References

Amy Allen, 'Systematically Distorted Subjectivity? Habermas and the Critique of Power', *Philosophy and Social Criticism* 33 (2007), 641–50.

J.L. Austin, *How to do Things with Words*, eds. J. O. Urmson and Marina Sbisà, 2nd Edition (Oxford: Oxford University Press, 1975).

Seyla Benhabib, 'The Generalised and the Concrete Other: The Kohlberg-Gilligan Controversy', *Praxis International* 5 (1986), 402–424.

Seyla Benhabib *Critique, Norm and Utopia: A Study of the Foundations of Critical Theory* (New York, Columbia University Press, 1986).

Robert B. Brandom, *Making It Explicit: Reasoning, Representing, and Discursive Commitment,* (Cambridge, MA: Harvard University Press, 1994).

Robert B. Brandom *Tales of the Mighty Dead: Historical Essays in the Metaphysics of Intentionality*, (Cambridge, MA: Harvard University Press, 2002).

Tyler Burge, 'Content Preservation', *The Philosophical Review* 102 (1993), 457–88.

Judith Butler, *Precarious Life: The Powers of Mourning and Violence* (New York: Verso, 2004).

Simone Chambers, 'Feminist Discourse/Practical Discourse' in *Feminists Read Habermas: Gendering the Subject of Discourse*, ed. Johanna Meehan (New York & London, Routledge, 1995).

Emmalon Davis, 'Typecasts, Tokens, and Spokespersons: A Case for Credibility Excess as Testimonial Injustice', *Hypatia* 31 (2016), 485–501.

Kristie Dotson, 'Conceptualising Epistemic Oppression', *Social Epistemology* 28 (2014), 115–38.

J. G. Fichte, *Foundations of Natural Right*, ed. Frederick Neuhouser, trans. Michael Baur, (Cambridge: Cambridge University Press, 2000).

Miranda F. Fricker, *Epistemic Injustice: Power and the Ethics of Knowing* (Oxford: Oxford University Press, 2007).

Paul Giladi, 'Epistemic Exploitation and Ideological Recognition', in *Epistemic Injustice and the Philosophy of Recognition*, eds. Paul Giladi and Nicola McMillan (New York: Routledge, forthcoming).

Paul Giladi, 'Epistemic Injustice: A Role for Recognition?', *Philosophy & Social Criticism* 44 (2018), 141–158.

Paul Giladi, 'The Agent in Pain: Alienation and Discursive Abuse', *International Journal of Philosophical Studies* 28 (2020), 692–712.

Robert Gooding-Williams, *Look, a Negro!: Philosophical Essays on Race, Culture and Politics* (New York: Routledge, 2006).

Paul H. Grice, 'Logic and Conversation', in *Syntax and Semantics 3: Speech Acts*, eds. Peter Cole and Jerry L. Morgan (New York: Academic Press, 1975).

Jürgen Habermas, *Knowledge and Human Interests*, trans. J. J. Shapiro (Boston: Beacon Press, 1971).

Jürgen Habermas *Theory and Practice*, trans. John Viertel (Cambridge: Polity Press, 1973).

Jürgen Habermas *The Theory of Communicative Action: Volume One. Reason and the Rationalisation of Society*, trans. Thomas McCarthy (Beacon Press, Boston, 1984).

Jürgen Habermas *The Theory of Communicative Action: Volume Two. Lifeworld and System: A Critique of Functionalist Reason* (Beacon Press, Boston, 1987a).

Jürgen Habermas *The Philosophical Discourse of Modernity: Twelve Lectures*, trans. Frederick Lawrence (Cambridge: Polity Press, 1987b).

Jürgen Habermas 'Morality and Ethical Life: Does Hegel's Critique of Kant Apply to Discourse Ethics?' in *Moral Consciousness and Communicative Action*, trans. C. Lenhardt and S. Weber Nicholsen (Cambridge, MA: MIT Press, 1990).

Jürgen Habermas *Postmetaphysical Thinking*, trans. W. M. Hohengarten (Cambridge, MA: MIT Press, 1992).

Jürgen Habermas *Between Facts and Norms: Contributions to a Discourse Theory of Law and Democracy*, trans. William Rehg (Cambridge, MA: MIT Press, 1996).

Jürgen Habermas *On the Pragmatics of Social Interaction*, trans. Barbara Fultner (Cambridge, MA: MIT Press, 2001).

Axel Honneth, 'Moral Consciousness and Class Domination: Some Problems in the Analysis of Hidden Morality,' in *The Fragmented World of the Social: Essays in Social and Political Philosophy*, ed. C.W. Wright (Albany: SUNY Press, 1995).

Axel Honneth *The Struggle for Recognition: The Moral Grammar of Social Conflicts*, trans. Joel Anderson (Cambridge, MA: MIT Press, 1995).

Axel Honneth *Freedom's Right: The Social Foundations of Democratic Life*, trans. Joseph Ganahl (Cambridge: Polity Press, 2014).

Jennifer Hornsby and Rae Langton, 'Free Speech and Illocution', *Legal Theory* 4 (1998), 21–37.

Stephen Houlgate, 'Hegel and Brandom on Norms, Concepts and Logical Categories', in *German Idealism: Contemporary Perspectives*, ed. Espen Hammer (London: Routledge, 2007).

Immanuel Kant, *Anthropology from a Pragmatic Point of View*, trans. and ed. R. B. Louden, (Cambridge: Cambridge University Press, 2006).

Rebecca Kukla, 'Performative Force, Convention, and Discursive Injustice', *Hypatia* 29 (2014), 440–457.

Andrea Lobb, ''Prediscursive Epistemic Injury': Recognising Another Form of Epistemic Injustice?' *Feminist Philosophy Quarterly* 4 (2018 Article 3), 1–23.

Thomas McCarthy, 'Die politische Philosophie und das Problem der Rasse', in *Die Öffentlichkeit der Vernunft und die Vernunft der Öffentlichkeit: Festschrift für Jürgen Habermas*, eds. Lutz Wingert and Klaus Günther (Frankfurt, Suhrkamp, 2001).

G.H. Mead, *Mind, Self, and Society: The Definitive Edition*, eds. C. W. Morris, D. R. Huebner and H. Joas (Chicago: University of Chicago Press, 2015).

José Medina, 'Misrecognition and Epistemic Injustice', *Feminist Philosophy Quarterly* 4 (2018 Article 1), 1–16.

Jari I. Niemi, 'Habermas and Validity Claims', *International Journal of Philosophical Studies* 13 (2005), 227–244.

Danielle Petherbridge, *The Critical Theory of Axel Honneth* (Lanham, MD: Lexington Books, 2013).

Danielle Petherbridge 'What's Critical about Vulnerability? Rethinking Interdependence, Recognition and Power', *Hypatia* 31 (2016), 589–604.

Danielle Petherbridge 'How Do We Respond? Embodied Vulnerability and Ethical Responsiveness', in *New Feminist Perspectives on Embodiment* eds. Clara Fischer and Luna Dolezal (Palgrave MacMillan, 2018).

Danielle Petherbridge 'Recognition, Vulnerability and Trust', *International Journal of Philosophical Studies*, 29 (2021).

William Rehg, *Insight and Solidarity: A Study in the Discourse Ethics of Jürgen Habermas*, Berkeley, Los Angeles (London, University of California Press, 1994).

Richard Rorty, *Contingency, Irony, and Solidarity,* (Cambridge: Cambridge University Press, 1989).

Wilfrid Sellars, *Science, Perception and Reality,* (London: Routledge, 1991).

Beata Stawarska, 'Linguistic Encounters: The Performativity of Active Listening', in *Body/Self/Other: The Phenomenology of Social Encounters*, eds. Luna Dolezal and Danielle Petherbridge (Albany: SUNY Press, 2017).

Patricia J. Williams. *The Alchemy of Race and Rights: Diary of a Law Professor* (Cambridge, MA: Harvard University Press, 1991).

Christopher F. Zurn. *Axel Honneth: A Critical Theory of the Social* (Cambridge: Polity Press, 2015).

The Seductions of Clarity

C. THI NGUYEN

Abstract
The feeling of clarity can be dangerously seductive. It is the feeling associated with understanding things. And we use that feeling, in the rough-and-tumble of daily life, as a signal that we have investigated a matter sufficiently. The sense of clarity functions as a *thought-terminating heuristic*. In that case, our use of clarity creates significant cognitive vulnerability, which hostile forces can try to exploit. If an epistemic manipulator can imbue a belief system with an exaggerated sense of clarity, then they can induce us to terminate our inquiries too early – before we spot the flaws in the system. How might the sense of clarity be faked? Let's first consider the object of imitation: genuine understanding. Genuine understanding grants cognitive facility. When we understand something, we categorize its aspects more easily; we see more connections between its disparate elements; we can generate new explanations; and we can communicate our understanding. In order to encourage us to accept a system of thought, then, an epistemic manipulator will want the system to provide its users with an exaggerated sensation of cognitive facility. The system should provide its users with the feeling that they can easily and powerfully create categorizations, generate explanations, and communicate their understanding. And manipulators have a significant advantage in imbuing their systems with a pleasurable sense of clarity, since they are freed from the burdens of accuracy and reliability. I offer two case studies of seductively clear systems: conspiracy theories; and the standardized, quantified value systems of bureaucracies.

1. Introduction

Here is a worrying possibility: there is a significant gap between our feeling that something is clear and our actually understanding it. The sense of clarity can be a marker of cognitive success, but it can also be seductive. Oversimplifications slip easily into our minds and connive themselves into our deliberative processes.

In that case, the sense of clarity might be intentionally exaggerated for exploitative ends. Outside forces, with an interest in manipulating our beliefs and actions, can make use of clarity's appeal. Seduction, after all, often involves a seducer. Romantic seduction, in its more malicious form, involves manipulating the appearances of intimacy and romance in order to subvert the aims of the seduced. There is an analogous form of cognitive seduction, where hostile forces play

doi:10.1017/S1358246121000035

with the signals and appearances of clarity in order to lead our thinking astray.

The sense of clarity is a potent focal point for manipulation because of its crucial role in managing our cognitive resources. After all, we only have so much mental energy to go around; we need to prioritize our inquiries. In particular, we need some way to estimate that we've probably thought enough on some matter for the moment – that it's probably safe to move on to more pressing matters, even if we haven't gotten to the absolute rock bottom of the matter. Our sense of clarity, and its absence, plays a key role in our cognitive self-regulation. A sense of confusion is a signal that we need to think more. But when things feel clear to us, we are satisfied. A sense of clarity is a signal that we have, for the moment, thought enough. It is an imperfect signal, but it is one we often actually use in the quick-and-dirty of everyday practical deliberation. This shows why, say, manipulative interests might be particularly interested in aping clarity. If the sense of clarity is a thought-terminator, then successful imitations of clarity will be quite powerful. If somebody else can stimulate our sense of clarity, then they can gain control of a particular cognitive blind spot. They can hide their machinations behind a veil of apparent clarity.

Here's another way to put it: the moment when we come to understand often has a particular feel to it – what some philosophers have called the 'a-ha!' moment. The moment when we come to understand, says Alison Gopnik, is something like an intellectual orgasm (Gopnik, 1998). And, as John Kvanvig suggests, it is our internal sense of understanding – our sense of 'a-ha!' and 'Eureka!' – that provides a sense of closure to an investigation (Kvanvig, 2011, p. 88). The 'a-ha' feeling is both pleasurable and indicates that a matter has been investigated enough. If, then, hostile forces can learn to simulate that 'a-ha' feeling, then they have a very powerful weapon for epistemic manipulation.

I offer two sustained case studies of cognitive subversion through the seductions of clarity. First, I will look at the sorts of belief systems often promulgated by moral and political echo chambers, which offer simplistic pictures of a world full of hostile forces and conspiracy theories. Such belief systems can create an exaggerated sense of clarity, in which every event can be easily explained and every action easily categorized. Second, I will look at the seductive clarity of quantification. I borrow my use of 'seduction' from Sally Engle Merry's *The Seductions of Quantification* (2016), a study into how global institutions deploy metrics and indicators in the service of political influence. Merry focuses on the generation of indicators and metrics on the global stage, such as the Human Development Index, which attempts to sum up the quality of life across each country's entire citizenship in a single, numerical score. The HDI then compiles these scores to offer a single apparently authoritative ranking of all countries by their quality of life. Such systems of quantification can offer an exaggerated sense of clarity without an accompanying amount of understanding or knowledge. Their cognitive appeal can outstrip their cognitive value.

It is striking how quantified presentations of value seem to have a profound cognitive stickiness. The motivational draw of quantified values has been well-documented across many terrains (Porter, 1996; Merry, 2016; Espeland and Sauder, 2016). This motivational power is why so many companies and governments have become interested in the technologies of gamification. Gamification attempts to incorporate the mechanics of games – points, experience points, and leveling up – into non-game activities, in order to transform apparently 'boring' activity as work and education into something more engaging, compelling, and addictive (McGonigal, 2011; Walz et al, 2015; Lupton, 2016). I am worried, however, that gamification might increase motivation, but only at the cost of changing our goals in problematic ways. After all, step counts are not the same as health, and citation rates are not the same as wisdom (Nguyen, 2020, pp. 189–215; forthcoming). The, seductions of clarity are, I believe, one important mechanism through which gamification works.

Let me be clear: the present inquiry is not a study in ideal rationality, nor is it a study of epistemic vice and carelessness. It is a study in the vulnerabilities of limited, constrained cognitive agents, and how environmental features might exploit those vulnerabilities. It is a foray into what we might call *hostile epistemology*. Hostile epistemology includes the intentional efforts of epistemic manipulators, working to exploit those vulnerabilities for their own ends. We might call the study of these intentional epistemic hostilities *combat epistemology*. Hostile epistemology also includes the study of environmental features which present a danger to those vulnerabilities, made without hostile epistemic intent. Hostile environments, after all, don't always arise from hostile intent. Hostile environments include intentionally placed minefields, but also crumbling ruins, the deep sea, and Mars. An epistemically hostile environment contains features which, whether by accident, evolution, or design, attack our vulnerabilities.

I will focus for the early parts of this paper on cases of combat epistemology. I think this is the easiest place to see how certain sorts of systems have a hostile epistemic function. The cases of intentionally manufactured hostile environments will then help us to recognize cases of the unintentional formation of hostile epistemic environments. Hostile epistemic environments can arise from entirely well-intentioned, and even successful, pursuits of other purposes. A culinarily extraordinary pastry shop also presents an environment hostile to my attempts at healthy eating. In many bureaucratic cases, as we will see, systems of quantification often arise for very good reason: to efficiently manage large and complex institutional data-sets, or to increase accountability (Scott, 1998; Perrow, 2014). But these very design features also make them into epistemically hostile environments. Because of the magnetic motivational pull of quantification, the very features which render them good for efficient administration also functions to imbue them with seductive clarity.[1]

Other recent inquiries into hostile epistemology include discussions of epistemic injustice, propaganda, echo chambers, fake news, and more (Fricker, 2007; Medina 2012; Dotson 2014; Stanley, 2016; Rini 2017; Nguyen 2018b). Importantly, the study of hostile epistemology is distinct from the study of epistemic vice. The study of the epistemic vices – such as closed-mindedness, gullibility, active ignorance, and cynicism – is a study of epistemically problematic character traits. It is the study of failings in the epistemic agents themselves (Sullivan and Tuana, 2007; Proctor and Schiebinger, 2008; Cassam, 2016; Battaly, 2018). Hostile epistemology, on the other hand, is the study of how external features might subvert the efforts of epistemic agents. Of course, vice and hostility are often entangled. Hostile environments press on our vices and make it easier for us to fall more deeply into them. But vice and hostility represent two different potential loci of responsibility for epistemic failure.

This all might just seem like common sense. Of course people are drawn to oversimplifications; what's new in that? But there are important questions here, about why we're drawn to oversimplification and how culpable we are for giving in to it. Importantly, many

[1] I am influenced here by A.W. Eaton's discussion of artifact function, which draws on and develops Ruth Millikan's notion of function (Millikan, 1984, Eaton, 2020). Eaton argues that the intent of an artifact's designer does not determine that artifact's function. She suggests a more evolutionary model: An artifact may be unintentionally imbued with trait, but insofar as that trait is selectively reproduced in future artifacts, then its effect is part of those artifacts' function. So, if a bureaucracy generates a quantified metric for accounting purposes, but that quantified metric survives and is reproduced in further bureaucratic systems because of its seductive effect, then the seductiveness is part of those systems' function.

theorists treat our interest in oversimplification as straightforwardly irrational. In the psychological and social sciences, the appeal of oversimplification is usually explained as a mistake which can be understood in terms of individual psychological tendencies, such as motivated reasoning or the undue influence of the emotions. We accept oversimplifications, it is thought, because they make us feel smug, they comfort us, or they reinforce our sense of tribal identity (Kahan and Braman, 2006; Sunstein, 2017). Similarly, many philosophical accounts treat our susceptibility to oversimplification as a problem arising wholly from an individual's own personal failures of character – from their epistemic vices. Quassim Cassam, for example, tells the story of Oliver the conspiracy theorist, who believes that 9/11 was an inside job. Says Cassam, there isn't a good rational explanation for Oliver's beliefs. The best explanation is a failure of intellectual character. Oliver, says Cassam, is gullible and cynical; he lacks discernment (pp. 162–63).

I will present a picture that is far more sympathetic to the seduced. It is a picture in which exaggerated clarity plays upon specific structural weaknesses in our cognition. As cognitively limited beings, we need to rely on various heuristics, signals, and short-cuts to manage the cognitive barrage. But these strategies also leave us vulnerable to exploitation. Seductive clarity takes advantage of our cognitive vulnerabilities, which arise, in turn, from our perfectly reasonable attempts to cope with the world using our severely limited cognitive resources. And, certainly, the pull of seductive clarity will be worse if we give in to various epistemic vices. And, certainly, once we realize all this, we will want to act more vigorously to secure the vulnerable backdoors to our cognition. The general point, however, is that giving into the seductions of clarity isn't just some brute error, or the result of sheer laziness and epistemic negligence. Rather, it is driven, in significant degree, by systems and environments which function to exploit the cognitive vulnerabilities generated by the coping strategies of cognitively finite beings.

2. Clarity as thought-terminator

I have been speaking loosely so far; let me now stipulate some terminology. On the one hand, there are epistemically positive states: knowledge, understanding, and the like. On the other hand, there are the phenomenal states that are connected to those epistemically positive states. These are the *experiences* of being in an epistemically positive state – like the sense of understanding, the feeling of clarity. Loosely:

understanding is our successful grasp of parts of the world and their relationships, and the sense of clarity is the phenomenal state associated with understanding. For brevity's sake, let me use the terms 'clarity' and 'the sense of clarity' interchangeably, to refer to the phenomenal experience associated with understanding. I do not mean to be using 'clarity' in the Cartesian sense, where it is a perfect guarantee of knowledge. Clarity, in my usage, is merely an impression of a certain kind of cognitive success – what J.D. Trout has called the *sense* of understanding (Trout, 2002). Clarity may often accompany genuine understanding, but it is by no means a perfect indicator that we do, in fact, genuinely understand. So external forces can exploit the gap between genuine understanding and the feeling of understanding – that sense of clarity.

There are two general strategies for epistemic manipulation. There is *epistemic intimidation*: the strategy of trying to get an epistemic agent to accept something by making them afraid or uncomfortable to think otherwise. There is also *epistemic seduction*: the strategy of manipulating positive cognitive signals to get an epistemic agent to accept something. The manipulation of clarity is a form of epistemic seduction. It is the attempt to use our own cognitive processes against us, whispering pleasantly all the while.

How might clarity seduce? There are many potential pathways. For one thing, clarity seduces because it is pleasurable. But for the remainder of this discussion, I'll focus another, even more dangerous feature: that the sense of clarity can bring us to end our inquiries into a topic too early. This possibility arises because of the profoundly quick-and-dirty nature of daily decision-making. We are finite beings with limited cognitive resources.[2] In daily life, we need to figure out what to do: where to spend our money, who to vote for, which candidate to back. We face a constant barrage of potentially relevant information, evidence, and argument – far more than we could assess in any conclusive manner. So we need to figure out the best way to allocate our cognitive resources while leaving most of our investigations unfinished, in some cosmic sense.

When practically reasoning about the messy complexities of the real world, we are unlikely to arrive at any conclusive ground-floor, where we can know with any certainty that we're done.[3] So, for

[2] Two particularly relevant discussions on cognitive limitation and epistemology are Wimsatt (2007); Dallman (2017).

[3] As Elijah Millgram puts it, practical reasoning doesn't result in settled arguments to finalized conclusions. Practical reasoning produces only tentative conclusions. Practical conclusions are always open to defeat from

everyday practical deliberation, we need some method for determining that we've thought enough.[4] And that basis often needs to be fast and loose, to cope with the fast and loose manner of everyday practical deliberation. We need some basis for estimating that our

---

unexpected angles, and new forms of defeat may always surprise us (Millgram, 1997). The closest we can get to conclusiveness is to think that a certain piece of practical reasoning seems good enough, so far as we can tell. And even if you reject Millgram's view and believe that there were firm practical conclusions that we might eventually reach – surely, finding such firm conclusions is well beyond the reach of most human-scale practical deliberation in everyday circumstances.

[4] Very little has been written on how we decide to end our inquiries in practical deliberation. And much of that work has focused, not on fast-and-loose daily heuristics for terminating inquiry, but on when we can conclusively terminate inquiry. See, for example, Alan Millar and Kvanvig's debate about whether we need merely need knowledge to conclusively terminate inquiry, or whether we need to reflectively know that we know in order to terminate inquiry (Millar, 2011; Kvanvig, 2011). Trout himself argues that the 'sense of understanding' – that 'a-ha' feeling – is not of particular use in the sciences because it is quite vulnerable to cognitive biases and other corrupting psychological influences. In Trout's terms, the mere sense of understanding doesn't grant us what we really want in science, which is good explanations. We have other ways of recognizing good explanations, far more accurate than mere internal feelings. We know we have a good scientific explanation when our scientific model makes good predictions. We should, says Trout, therefore largely ignore the various internal signals of understanding, which will simply lead us astray. We should, instead, remain firmly fixed on the evidence that our scientific model provides good explanations, which are measured in the usual scientific methods: prediction, testing, and the like (Trout, 2002; 2017). Notice, however, that this sort of approach imagines the relevant epistemic agents to be cognitively ideal beings with essentially unlimited resources. It then asks how such cognitive beings should go about getting things right once and for all. And that might be the right idealization for thinking about how we should pursue long-term epistemic projects as parts of intergenerational communities, as we do in philosophy and science. But things look very different for cognitively limited beings in the quick-and-dirty of day-to-day decision-making. Sometimes we might be able to adopt some methodology with a pre-established threshold for terminating thought. Consider, for example, the cognitive strategy of satisficing: taking the first solution which crosses some pre-established minimal threshold (Simon, 1956). But what do we do when we aren't satisficing? In many cases, our investigations are more open-ended, without any sort of pre-established minimal threshold. For those sorts of investigations, we need some heuristic basis for attentional management.

understanding is probably good enough, so that we can make a decision and move on. We need something like a heuristic for terminating thought.

Here, then, is the ruling supposition for my inquiry: the sense of clarity is one of the signals we typically use to allocate our cognitive resources. (I do not claim that it is the only signal, though I do claim it is a significant one.) We often use our sense of confusion as a signal that we need to keep investigating, and our sense of clarity as a signal that we've thought enough.[5] Our sense of clarity is a signal that we can terminate an investigation. When a system of thought seems clear to us, then we have a heuristic reason to stop inquiring into it.[6]

I'm not claiming that this heuristic is a necessary part of all practical reasoning – only that the heuristic is currently under common usage. After all, heuristics are usually contingent tendencies and not necessary parts of our cognitive architecture. In fact, some research suggests that we can slowly change the heuristics we use (Reber and Unkelbach, 2010).

Here's my plan. First, we'll start to think about how powerful it would be if this supposition were true, and there were such a pleasurable and thought-terminating heuristic. I'll look at some evidence from the empirical literature on cognitive heuristics that supports something in the vicinity of my supposition. I'll show how the supposition, which concerns how we use our feeling of understanding, emerges from a recent discussion in the philosophy of science about the nature of genuine understanding. Then, I'll use the

[5] My discussion here heavily borrows structural features from Elijah Millgram's discussion of the function of boredom and interest in practical reason and agency. Millgram argues that a sense of interest is our signal that our values are good ones for us to have, and a sense of boredom is our signal that our values are bad for us to have, so we should change them (Millgram, 2004).

[6] As far as I know, Justin Dallman offers the only contemporary account of how our cognitive limitations force us to manage our efforts of inquiry. The best procedure to cope with cognitive limitation, he says, is to set up a priority queue. We assign priority levels to our various outstanding investigations, and then we proceed in order from highest priority to lowest (Dallman, 2017). But what basis do we have for assigning priority levels? To put my suggestion into Dallman's terms, we need some heuristic for quickly estimating priorities, and our sense of clarity functions as a heuristic basis assigning a low priority to its investigation. A sense of clarity can thus terminate a line of inquiry – not conclusively, but by lowering its priority below the barrage of other, more pressing matters.

supposition to think about what sorts systems and environments might successfully exploit the sense of clarity. I'll dig into some historical and sociological literature on echo chambers and on the social effect of simplistic quantification. The supposition will turn out to provide a unifying explanation for many of the documented effects of echo chambers and quantification. My argument in favor of the supposition, then, will be that it provides a unifying explanation for various observations from cognitive science, sociology, and history, while integrating neatly with a standard account of the nature of understanding. But this mode of argumentation can only render the supposition a plausible hypothesis; more empirical investigation is certainly called for.

3. Clarity as vulnerability

Suppose, then, that the sense of clarity plays a crucial role in the regulation of our cognitive resources, functioning as a signal that we can safely terminate a particular line of inquiry. Obviously, the sense of clarity can come apart from actual full understanding.[7] It must, in order for it to play a heuristic role in quick-and-dirty daily deliberation.[8] In order to know that we fully understood something, we would need to conduct an exhaustive and thorough investigation. The sense of clarity is far more accessible to us, so we can use it to make rough estimates about whether we've inquired enough.

If a hostile force could ape such clarity, then they would have a potent tool for getting us to accept their preferred systems of thought. This is because false clarity would provide an excellent cover for intellectual malfeasance. A sense of clarity could bring us to terminate our inquiry into something before we could discover its flaws. It would be something like an invisibility cloak – one that works by manipulating our attention. Our attention, after all, is narrow. We barely notice what's outside the focused spotlight of

[7] For an in-depth discussion of this point, see Trout's discussion of the gap between the sense of understanding in science, and actually possessing a genuine understanding (Trout, 2002). There is a useful further discussion in Grimm (2012, pp. 106–109), which defends Trout's claims against Linda Zagzebksi's claim that we always know when we understand (Zagzebski, 2001, p. 247). See also Strevens (2013).

[8] I am drawing here from the cognitive science literature on heuristics. Key relevant moments in that literature include Gigerenzer and Goldstein (1996); Kahneman (2013).

our attention. We can make something effectively disappear simply by directing their attention elsewhere.[9] One way to make something cognitively invisible, then, is by making it signal unimportance. The spy novelist John Le Carre – who had actually worked in British intelligence – describes, in his novel *Tinker Tailor Soldier Spy*, what a genuinely effective spy looks like. They aren't dashing and handsome, like some James Bond figure. An effective spy presents as entirely normal, bland, and dull. They can disappear because they have learned to magnify the signals of boringness. Similarly, the techniques of stage magic involve attentional misdirection. Stage magicians learn to signal boringness with the active hand while directing signals of interestingness elsewhere, in order to control their audience's attention. The sense of clarity can work in an analogous strategy of attentional misdirection. An epistemic manipulator who wants us to accept some system of thought should imbue that system with a sense of clarity, so that cognitive resources will be less likely to be directed towards it. The strategy will be even more effective if they simultaneously imbue some other target with a sense of confusion. The confusing object seizes our attention by signaling that we need to investigate it, which makes it easier for the clear-seeming system to recede into the shadows. The manipulator can thus gain control of their target's attention by manipulating their targets' priority queue for investigation.

Thus, hostile forces can manipulate the cognitive architecture of resource-management in order to bypass the safeguards provided by the various processes of cognitive inquiry. In the movies, the crooks are always hacking the system which controls the security cameras. Epistemic criminals will want to hack the cognitive equivalent.

4. Ease and fluency

The experience of clarity is complex and its phenomenal markers many. Let's start with a case study in one small and simple aspect of clarity – one which has been relatively well-studied in the psychological sciences. Consider the experience of cognitive ease – the

[9] The locus of the modern discussion of this sort of attentional blindness is in Christopher Chabris and Daniel Simons's influential experiments, including, famously, an experiment where half of the study subjects failed to notice a person in a gorilla suit walking across a room, and pounding their chest, when the subjects were instructed to perform a relatively simple counting task (Chabris and Simons, 2011).

relative degree to which it is easy to think about something. In the literature on cognitive heuristics, cognitive ease is part of the study of 'cognitive fluency', which is the 'subjective experience of ease or difficulty with which we are able to process information' (Oppenheimer, 2008, p. 237). Research has demonstrated that we do, in fact, often use fluency as a cognitive heuristic. If we comprehend an idea easily, we will be more likely to accept it. Cognitive difficulty, on the other hand, makes it more likely that we will reject an idea. This heuristic is not entirely unreasonable: we often experience cognitive ease in a domain precisely because we have a lot of experience with it. Cognitive ease often correlates with experience, which correlates with skill and accuracy. But, obviously, ease is separable from accuracy. Studies have demonstrated that one's mere familiarity with an idea makes one more likely to accept it. Familiarity creates a sense of cognitive ease, but without the need for any relevant skill or expertise. Studies have also shown that we are more likely to believe something written in a more legible font. Legibility leads to easier processing, which leads to readier acceptance. In other words: we are using our cognitive ease with some proposition or domain as a heuristic for our accuracy with that proposition or domain. Rolf Reber and Christian Unkelbach have argued that fluency heuristics are, in fact, often quite useful. Through a Bayesian analysis, they conclude that fluency is a good heuristic when the user's environment contains more true propositions than false ones – and the better the ratio of true to false propositions in their environment, the better the fluency heuristic will work (Reber and Unkelbach, 2010). But that heuristic can be gamed.[10]

Suppose that the usual fluency heuristic is in place. How might it be exploited? To game the fluency heuristic, a manipulator would want to offer their targets ideas expressed in some familiar manner, by using well-worn patterns of thought and forms of expression. This exploitative methodology should be quite familiar: it explains the rhetorical power of cliched slogans and Internet memes.

Suppose that the world has many such epistemic manipulators in it, and has become chock full of misleading ideas that have been engineered to seem familiar. Our best strategy to avoid manipulation would be to update our heuristics to close off this cognitive backdoor. As Reber and Unkelbach showed, we are capable of changing and

[10] Trout makes a similar point about fluency and the sense of understanding (Trout, 2017), although his concern is largely with attacking other accounts of understanding, and not providing a full picture of exploitation. I take myself to be filling in the details of his suggestion.

updating our heuristics when we receive evidence that they have led us astray. The manipulators, then, would want to mask from us any evidence that our use of the fluency heuristic was leading us astray. This is, however, easier to do in some domains than others. Some epistemic domains have obvious litmus tests. It is easy to check for mistaken reasoning in them because successes and failures are obvious to any onlooker. For example, we can tell that our theory of bridge-building has gone wrong if our new bridges keep falling down. But other epistemic domains have no such easy litmus tests – like the moral and aesthetic domains. If one's reasoning has been systematically subverted in such a subtle domain, there is no obvious error result that could function as a check.[11] So if manipulators wanted to gain control via the fluency heuristic, one good strategy would be to perform their fluency-manipulations over, say, claims about morality and value. Alternatively, they may want to devote their fluency-manipulations to complex and diffuse social phenomena or more esoteric scientific phenomenon. Some empirical claims cannot be straightforwardly checked by the layperson, such as scientific arguments for climate change or sociological claims how oppression perpetuates. If the manipulators' targets have been given a seductively clear explanation which dismiss, say, sociologists and climate change scientists as corrupt, those explanations will be quite hard to dislodge. Most targets will be unable to see that they have been led astray, and so won't update their heuristics (Nguyen, 2018b; 2018c).

5. Aping understanding

Perhaps it seems implausible to you that somebody would terminate a really important inquiry just because of fluency. There is, however, another much more sophisticated form of epistemic seduction which will more plausibly trigger the thought-terminating function. Hostile epistemic manipulators can try to imitate, not just ease, but a full *feeling* of understanding. They can present the phenomena associated with a positive and rich experience of clarity.

In order to see how one might fake the feeling of understanding, let's start by thinking about the nature of genuine understanding. For that, let's turn to a recent discussion of the nature of understanding in the philosophy of science. According to a recent strand of thinking, knowledge isn't actually the primary goal of much of our epistemic efforts. Knowledge is usually conceived of as something

[11] For an extensive discussion of litmus tests and expert-vetting, see Nguyen (2018a).

like the possession of true facts. Having knowledge, by the usual accounts, doesn't require any particular integration of those facts. But many of our intellectual efforts are aimed at getting something more than just knowing some disparate facts. We aim at something more holistic: understanding. The precise nature of understanding is still under some debate, but we can extract some common and largely uncontroversial ideas.[12] First, when we understand something, we not only possess a lot of independent facts, but we see how those facts connect. Understanding is of a system; it involves grasping a structure and not just independent nodes. Second, when we understand something, we possess some internal model or account of it which we can use to make predictions, conduct further investigations, and categorize new phenomena.[13]

That is an account of what it means to actually *have* understanding. So what are the experiential phenomena *associated with* understanding? What does it *feel* like to understand something? There are several distinct phenomena to consider here. First, there are the experiences associated with *coming to understand*. As Catherine Elgin puts it, when we come to understand, our way of looking at things suddenly shifts to accommodate new information. Understanding, she says, 'comes not through passively absorbing new information, but through incorporating it into a system of thought that is not, as it stands, quite ready to receive it' (Elgin, 2002, p. 14). When we come to understand, our system of thought changes and pieces of

[12] Much of the debate in that literature has turned on what is constitutive of understanding, and what is merely typically associated with understanding. For example, according to Steven Grimm and Henk de Regt, the skill of practical application is partially constitutive of understanding (Grimm, 2006; de Regt, 2009; Wilkenfeld, 2013; 2017). Michael Strevens, on the other hand, denies this constitutive relationship; skill typically follows from understanding, but isn't constitutive of it (Strevens, 2013). Note that we don't need to resolve debates like this for the current inquiry. Since we're interested what signs are associated with understanding, we don't really need to distinguish carefully between what is constitutive of understanding, and what follows from it. Finally, Kareem Khalifa has argument that these accounts of understanding can be reduced to the idea of knowing an explanation (Khalifa, 2012). My account here should be compatible with Khalifa's view – though, in his language, I would be talking about faking the feel of knowing an explanation.

[13] This discussion constitutes a fast-growing literature. I am particularly influenced by Catherine Elgin's account, Stephen Grimm's useful survey, and Michael Strevens' and Michael Patrick Lynch's discussions (Elgin, 2002, 2017; Grimm, 2012, Strevens, 2013; Lynch, 2018).

information that we could not accommodate before suddenly find a place. Kvanvig offers a similar account: to understand, he says, is to grasp a coherence relationship. It is to be aware of how the information fits together (Kvanvig 2003, p. 202). The experience of coming to understand, then, involves an experience of grasping a new and improved coherence. Let us call this the phenomenon of *cognitive epiphany*. And, as Gopnick points out, cognitive epiphanies are incredibly pleasurable.

Next, there are phenomena associated with *having an understanding*. Understanding involves a certain facility with the terrain. As Kvanvig puts it,

> ...To have mastered such explanatory relationships is valuable not only because it involves the finding of new truths but also because finding such relationships organizes and systematizes our thinking on a subject matter in a way beyond the mere addition of more true beliefs or even justified true beliefs. Such organization is pragmatically useful because it allows us to reason from one bit of information to another related information that is useful as a basis for action, where unorganized thinking provides no such basis for inference. Moreover, such organized elements of thought provide intrinsically satisfying closure to the process of inquiry, yielding a sense or feeling of completeness to our grasp of a particular subject matter. (p. 202)

When we understand a cognitive terrain, we can move between its nodes more quickly and easily. We can use our understanding to easily and powerfully generate relevant explanations. And if our understanding is fecund, these new explanations will serve to create even more useful connections. And, as Michael Strevens says, having an understanding also involves having the capacity to communicate that understanding – to explain to how the connections work (Strevens, 2013). Let's call all these the phenomena of *cognitive facility*.[14] And, at least in my own experience, the pleasure of clarity lies not only in Gopnick's moment of coming to understand, but also in the continuing joys of apparent facility and intellectual power. It feels incredibly good to be able to swiftly explain complex phenomena. It is the pleasure of engaging our skills and capacities to powerful effect.[15]

[14] I owe my framing to Laura Callahan's (2018, p. 442) useful discussion of understanding.

[15] For more on the aesthetic pleasure of one's own skillful action, see Nguyen (2020, pp. 101–120).

Let's enter into the mindset of the hostile epistemic manipulator. Our goal is to seduce with apparent clarity – to game other people's cognitive processes and heuristics so that they will accept our preferred system of thought. We'll want to engineer that system, then, to create the feeling of cognitive epiphany. We'll want to maximize, for our system's adopters, the sense that unexplained information is sliding into place, the feeling of newfound coherency. So we'll want to give the system easy-to-apply categorizations which are readily connected into a coherent network. And, once that system has been adopted, we'll want it to create the feeling of cognitive facility. We'll want to engineer it so that, once somebody adopts the system, thinking in its terrain will seem distinctly easier and more effective than before. We'll want it to give adopters a heightened sensation of forming connections and moving easily between them. We'll want it to create the impression of explanatory power, quickly and easily explaining any new phenomena that come up. And we would want to do all that while simultaneously masking its epistemic faults.

This might seem like an overwhelmingly difficult task for the aspiring manipulator. We manipulators, however, have some very significant advantages. First, we don't need to successfully imitate understanding all the way down. We simply need for our system to trigger the clarity heuristic early enough, before its adopters stumble across any of the flaws. If you're building a Potemkin village, you don't need to actually build any actual houses. You just need to build the facades – so long as those facades convince people not to try and enter the buildings. We manipulators, then, can hide our system's weakness and inferior performance behind a veil of apparent clarity.[16]

But our most significant advantage is that we are unburdened by the constraints of truth in engineering our extra-tasty system of thought. Epistemically sincere systems – that is, systems of thought generated for the sake of real knowledge and genuine understanding – are heavily constrained by their allegiance to getting things right.[17] We manipulators are unbound by any such obligations. We are free to

[16] This strategy exploits a cognitive error of over-weighting early evidence. For a discussion of why this is a cognitive error, see Kelly (2008). For an application of that discussion to conspiracy theories and echo chambers, see Nguyen (2018b).

[17] Elgin (2017) defends the use of idealizations and non-truths as parts of the models that help us to understand. However, the choice of models is still driven by an orientation towards getting the world right, in a more holistic way.

tweak our system to maximize its appealing clarity. This is similar, in a way, to how unhealthy restaurants are free to appeal more directly to our sense of deliciousness, because they are freed from considerations of health. (Or, at least, that's how my mother saw it.) We manipulators, then, can optimize our system to offer the sense of easily made connection and explanations. We can build a cartoon of understanding. And that cartoon will have a competitive advantage in the cognitive marketplace. It can be engineered for the sake of pleasure, and it will carry with it a signal that inquiry is finished, and that we should look elsewhere.

6. Two systems of cognitive seduction

Let's look at two case studies of the seductions of clarity: echo chambers and institutional quantification. The first case study of echo chambers will strike many, I suspect, as a plausible and familiar case of the seductions of clarity. The discussion of quantification may prove more surprising. And I hope that the differences between these two case studies will help us to hone in on the phenomenon's more general qualities.

Let's start with echo chambers. Most social scientists and journalists use the terms 'echo chamber' and 'epistemic bubble' synonymously. But, as I've argued, if we look at the original sources of these terms, we find two very different phenomena. An epistemic bubble is a social phenomenon of simple omission. It's bad connections in your information network – like if all your friends on Facebook share your politics, and you simply never run across the arguments presented by the other side. An echo chamber, on the other hand, is a social structure which discredits all outsiders. When you are in a bubble, you don't *hear* the other side. When you're in an echo chamber, you don't *trust* the other side. Echo chambers don't cut off lines of communication from the outside world; rather, they isolate their members by manipulating their members' trust (Nguyen, 2018b).

What matters for the present study is the particular content of the systems of thought which echo chambers use to manipulate trust. I'm drawing here on Kathleen Jamieson and Joseph Cappella's empirical analysis of the echo chamber around Rush Limbaugh and the Fox News ecosystem (Jamieson and Cappella, 2010). According to Jamieson and Cappella, Rush Limbaugh offers a world-view with some very distinctive features. First, Limbaugh presents a world of sharply divided forces locked in a life-or-death struggle. There are no onlookers or reasonable moderates. Either you're a Limbaugh follower – and so on the side of right – or you are one of the malevolent forces out to undermine the side of right. Limbaugh then offers an explanatory system in which most moral and political action can be understood in terms of that all-consuming struggle. Disagreement with Limbaugh's world view can be readily explained as the product of some organized, malevolent action to block the side of right. Most importantly, for our present purposes, the undermining function and the explanatory function are often accomplished with the help of conspiracy theories, which provide a ready explanation for disagreement from outsiders. The liberal media is in the grip of a nefarious network of elites, as are universities, and the academic sciences. These conspiracy theories offer to explain complex features of the world in terms of a single coherent narrative.

This is an obvious deployment of the seductions of clarity. First, Limbaugh's world-view offers the sensations of epiphany. Once his world-view is accepted, difficult-to-categorize actions suddenly become easily categorized. Previously hard-to-explain facts – like the existence of substantive moral disagreement between apparently sincere people – suddenly become easily explicable in terms of a secret war between good and evil. Second, the world-view offers the sensations of cognitive facility. The conspiracy theory offers a ready and neatly unified explanation for all sorts of behavior. And those explanations are easy to create. The world suddenly becomes more intellectually manageable. This is particularly vivid in some of communities around the wilder conspiracy theories. CNN recently conducted some quite telling interviews with some members of the fast-growing community of Flat Earth conspiracy theorists. Many theorists describe the satisfactions of being a Flat Earth theorist in in terms of cognitive facility. As Flat Earth theorist and filmmaker Mark Sargent puts it, 'You feel like you've got a better handle on life and the universe. It's now more manageable'. And Flat Earth theorist David Weiss says, 'When you find out the Earth is flat… then you become empowered' (Picheta, 2019).

Furthermore, well-designed echo chambers typically have systems of belief which can reinterpret incoming evidence in order to avoid refutation. For example, many echo chambers include sweeping scientific claims, such as denying the existence of climate change. Echo chamber members may have adopted belief systems with the help of the clarity heuristic. But, one might think, heuristics are defeasible – and contrary scientific evidence should surely bring members to abandon their settled acceptance of their belief system. However, a clever echo chamber can preemptively defuse such contrary evidence. A well-designed echo chamber can include, in its belief system, a conspiracy theory about how the media and the institutions of science were entirely corrupt and in the grip of a vast malicious conspiracy. This explanation performs a kind of intellectual judo. As Endre Begby (2020) points out, such a belief system transforms apparently contrary evidence into confirmations of the belief system – a process which he calls 'evidential pre-emption'. If Limbaugh predicts that the liberal media will accuse him of falsifying information, then when his followers hear such accusations from the liberal media, they will have reason to increase their trust in Limbaugh – since his predictions have been fulfilled! But notice that there is a secondary effect, beyond the simple confirmation Begby describes – an effect that arises from the seductions of clarity. The belief system makes it easy to create an explanation for incoming contrary evidence and to provide explanations that unify and connect that event with many others. This provides an experience of cognitive facility – which should trigger the clarity heuristic. This is an extremely well-designed epistemic trap, in which contrary evidence triggers two different defense mechanisms. First, the conspiracy theory pre-emptively predicts the presence of contrary evidence, and so confirms itself in the process of dismissing that contrary evidence. Second, the ease with which the conspiracy theory performs that prediction and dismissal is an experience of cognitive facility – which creates the sense of clarity, which, in turn, triggers the thought-terminating heuristic.

Such defensive conspiracy theories are an obvious case of the seductive, manipulative use of clarity. Let's now turn to a less obvious case. Consider the appeal of quantified systems. Consider, especially, the way in which large-scale institutions try to reduce complex, value-laden qualities to simple metrics and measures. In *Trust in Numbers,* a history of the culture of quantification, Theodore Porter notes that quantified systems are powerfully attractive. This is why, he says, politicians and bureaucrats love to cite the authority of quantified systems of analysis. Numbers, he says, smell of science. They have the ring of objectivity, and so they will be used in inappropriate circumstances in attempts to gain political control (Porter, 1996, p. 8). I think Porter is entirely right about the credibility advantage of numbers and their scientific feel – but I don't think this is the whole story. The details of his study offer us the opportunity to build a second account of the appeal of numbers, alongside his credibility account, in terms of the seductions of clarity.

There are, says Porter, qualitative ways of knowing and quantitative ways of knowing. Porter is not here making the crude claim that quantitative ways of knowing are inherently bad. Rather, he is interested in the relative advantages and disadvantages of each way of knowing. Qualitative ways of knowing, he says, are typically nuanced, sensitive, and rich in contextual detail, but they are not portable or aggregable. When we transition from qualitative to quantitative ways of knowing, we strip out much of the nuance and many of the contextual details. In return for this loss of informational richness, we get to express our knowledge in neat packages: in the form of numbers, whose meanings are portable, and which can be easily aggregated with other numerical results. This can be very valuable. Obviously, quantification is vital for modern science. And there are many administrative functions which quantification makes far more efficient. But, says Porter, contemporary culture seems to have lost sight of the distinctive value of qualitative ways of knowing. We tend to reach for quantitative ways of knowing compulsively, even when they aren't most appropriate for the task at hand.

In *The Seductions of Quantification*, Merry applies Porter's analysis to the recent rise of quantified metrics in international governance. She is interested in *indicators* – simple, quantified representations of complex global phenomena. One indicator is the UN's Human Development Index, which gives countries a single score for their performance in supporting the quality of life of their citizens. Another indicator is the US State Department's *Trafficking in Persons Reports*, which gives countries a score on their performance in reducing sex trafficking. Indicators present themselves in the form of a single, easy-to-use, easy-to-understand numerical score. These indicators, she says, hide the complexity and subjectivity of their manufacture. And that concealment is much of the point. Their power, says Merry, comes in significant part from their appearance of unambiguity. And once these indicators have been manufactured, they invariably become central in various governments' and politicians' decision-making processes. The very qualities which make them so powerful also make them blunt instruments, missing in much subtlety and detail. But, says Merry, they are incredibly hard to dislodge from the minds of the public and of policy-makers (Merry, 2016, pp. 1–43, 112–60).

Why are quantifications so sticky? The seductions of clarity offer an explanation. Quantified systems are, by design, highly usable and easily manipulable. They provide a powerful experience of cognitive facility. It is much easier to *do things* with grades and rubrics than it is with qualitative descriptions. We can offer justifications ('I averaged it according to the syllabus' directives'; 'I applied the rubric'). We can generate graphs and quantified summaries. And the sense of facility is even stronger in large-scale institutions, where the use of numbers has been stringently regularized. Because of the portability of numbers and the constancy and enforced regularity of typical institutional deliberation procedures, inside such institutions, it is vastly easier to use numbers to produce powerful and effective communications. And they are communications in terms which we know will be *understood* and *acted upon* – because the meanings and uses of these institutional terms has been so aggressively regularized.

In a university for which I once worked, all departments had to produce yearly assessment data which was supposed to demonstrate, in quantitative form, the quality of education that our students had received. Our assessments results had to be coded according to certain institutionally specified Educational Learning Outcomes (ELOs). So, the fact that our students scored well this year in their critical thinking multiple choice tests gets coded and entered into the system. Those scores now support our claim that a particular class succeeds in supporting certain university-wide learning: the Critical Thinking ELO, the Writing Skills ELO, the Moral Reflection ELO and the Mathematical Reasoning ELO. And the data for each particular class, in turn, is used to support the claim that our department as a whole supports the university-wide learning outcomes. And that claim, in turn, is used as support the claim that the University is succeeding in its mission, and achieving its stated Core Values: like Communication, Community, and Engagement. And the way in which class, departmental, and university ELO's link up are coded explicitly into our databasing system, so that new data can travel automatically up the chain. When I enter the latest batch of scores for my students, it produces an immediate effect into the system: all the reported ELOs up the chain will change. And this is possible precisely because the data I've entered has been rendered portable and because our outcomes reporting system has been set up to automatically take advantage of that portability.

Notice that all this gives me the experience of an enormous amount of apparently effective cognitive and communicative activity. I have a sense of grasping connections. I can see exactly how my class's ELOs support my department's ELOs, which in turn support my college's ELOs, which in turn support the university's ELOs and, in turn, the University Core Values. And my grasp of this system can give me a certain sense of cognitive facility. I can easily generate explanations of course content and generate evidence of teaching success. And I can know that they will be understood, since they have been expressed in the pre-prepared, standardized, and explicitly interconnected language of the institution. I know that my justifications will be incorporated into larger institutional aggregates, because my justifications occur in those intentionally stabilized terms. And I know that when I give justifications in those designated terms, they will usually generate pre-specified sorts of actions – ones which I can usually predict with some success. A stabilized, explicit system of quantified and systemized institutional value is designed so that its users can make themselves easily understood and their pronouncements quickly integrated into institutional systems of information processing and decision-making. In short, by using the provided terms of institutional discourse inside the institution, my speech and thinking will seem clear, precisely because they fit so well into a pre-established network of communication and justification. That pre-engineered fit creates a sense of cognitive facility, with all its associated pleasures. And the ring of clarity can trigger the thought-terminating heuristic in others who have also bought into the provided system of institutional discourse – ending inquiry into the apparently clear claim.

Of course, I'll have genuine cognitive facility if my various mental efforts actually track real elements in the world and process them in some epistemically valuable way. And, as Charles Perrow and Paul Du Gay have argued, bureaucracies certainly need regular methods and quantified systems in order to function and to administrate fairly (Du Gay, 2000; Perrow, 2014). The worry, though, is that we might set up systems that are useful for certain very specific data-collection and managerial function – but that can also exert a magnetic pull on our thinking in nearby domains. For example: GPAs and citations rates might be useful for certain particular tasks of bureaucratic administration. But, because they are so seductive, students and scholars may start using them as the primary lens through which they evaluate their own education and output.[18] And surely GPAs are not perfect indicators of a good education, and citations rates are not perfect indicators of good scholarship. A particular quantification can get an excess grip on our reasoning, even in contexts when it is less appropriate, by presenting an appealing sense of clarity. And we will fail to investigate whether this quantified metric is the most appropriate form of evaluation to use, precisely because its clarity terminates our investigations into its appropriateness.

[18] I offer a fuller discussion of how simplified and quantified systems of value can give their adopters the game-like pleasures of value clarity in Nguyen (2020).

So far, we've been concentrating on systems of thought whose contents themselves are seductively clear. But the seductions of clarity can also affect our judgments of the expertise and authority of the sources of those contents. The seductions of clarity can get us to accept a system by making its users and authors seem more credible or expert, precisely because they seem more clear. Recall that one of the standard signals of expertise is communicative facility. Non-experts trust purported experts when those experts are able to communicate their understanding – when the purported experts can explain to their audiences the connections between nodes, generate justifications, and the like. But consider what happens to the appearance of communicative facility inside a bureaucratized system of educational assessment. Those users willing to express themselves in the designated terms of that system have a considerable advantage in displaying communicative facility. They can easily generate justifications. They can easily make their reasons and requests understood and acted upon in institutional settings. They will seem clear because their communication will be readily taken up and acted upon. Their apparent facility will seem especially impressive to outsiders, who are out of contact with the subtler values involved with education. This is, obviously, a form of epistemic injustice (Fricker, 2007). Here, it is a form of epistemic injustice which gives a significant credibility advantage to anybody willing to speak in the terms provided by bureaucracies and institutions, which provide regularized systems of justification and languages of evaluation. And since the ability to create and disseminate such systems is usually held by those already in power, the bureaucratization of language will typically serve to amplify power differentials by granting more credibility to those who accept those bureaucratic terms of discourse.

To put it in Kristie Dotson's terms, epistemic oppression occurs when agents are denied the opportunity to use shared epistemic resources to participate in knowledge production (Dotson, 2014). Bureaucratic and institutionalized language can enable a particular kind of epistemic oppression. Ideas that can be easily expressed in the institutional language are readily entered into the shared knowledge base. But the standardization of language puts a special oppressive power in the hands of whoever creates the standardization. Once the standardization is in place and widely accepted, anybody who uses it will *demonstrate cognitive facility* and *demonstrate communicative facility*. They will *seem clear* precisely because they are using language for which a system of reception has been pre-prepared.

The sense of clarity is a terminator for inquiry, and ideas expressed in that regularized institutional language will bear that sense of clarity. So ideas expressed in that language are more likely to be accepted without question. Information that isn't placed into institutional language, on the other hand, will tend to be disappear. Such recalcitrant expressions will be less likely to be accepted, transmitted and remembered within the system. At the very least, since they seem confusing rather than clear, those recalcitrant expressions will be subject to constant questioning and inquiry, rather than quickly accepted. In a standardized system, non-standardized information will be subject to incredible friction. This creates a further competitive disadvantage. By the very fact that such information transmits slowly and poorly, the information and its authors will seem to have less communicative facility and so seem less credible. Those whose ideas don't fit comfortably into the regularized institutional language are at a significant disadvantage in participating in the production and dissemination of knowledge.

7. Nuance and closure

The point here is not to claim that quantified systems and conspiracy theories are always bad. Science and bureaucracy need quantification, and we certainly should accept conspiracy theories when there are actually conspiracies.[19] The point is, rather, that these sorts of ideas and methodologies are among the choicest tools for epistemic subversion. A ruthless epistemic manipulator, freed from the constraints of genuine inquiry, can re-formulate these sorts of systems to maximize their potential for seductiveness.

And this also offers us insights into unintentional cognitive seduction. Bureaucracies and institutions have very good reason to develop internally consistent and quantified systems of evaluation. Such systems make the administration of complex organizations possible. But insofar as such systems share a significant number of the traits and effects as those systems made for intentional manipulation – and especially insofar as such systems perpetuate because of their seductive effects – then such systems also function as seductively clear.

This suggests another reason to resist the seductions of clarity. Sometimes, we need to dwell in unclear systems of thought because we have not yet earned the right to clarity. In her study of metaphors,

[19] There is a very useful discussion of the occasional usefulness of conspiracy theories in Coady (2012, pp. 110–37); Dentith (2018; 2019).

Elizabeth Camp (2006) suggests that metaphors are most appropriate when we are still in the process of coming to understand. Metaphors are unclear by design. They are, says Camp, a special way of pointing to the world. We define simple nouns through simpler forms of pointing. 'Red' we define as looking like *that*. Metaphors let us point with a rough, waving gesture.

The reason we might want to do so, says Camp, is that such pointing lets us access the richness of the world in our talk. When I say, 'I don't understand what's going on with Robert very much, but his neurosis seems a lot like Liza's,' I'm not using some well-defined abstract predicate to describe Robert. I am pointing to Liza and to all the rich features of reality that are bound up with her. I am saying that I don't know what it is about Liza that matters, exactly, but it's something over there, where 'there' is a gesture in the direction of all the richness of Liza's actual self. And this sort of vague gesture is especially useful, says Camp, when we are trying to grapple with things we do not yet adequately understand. With metaphors, she says, we are gesturing vaguely at part the worlds.

Intentionally and openly vague forms of communication are very important. They remind us that our thinking – our concepts, our inquiries, our understanding – is not yet finished. Clarity is compelling, but signals us to end our inquiries. Seductively clear systems mask the fact that we should, in fact, be confused, and should be pressing on with our inquiries. They present themselves as finalized. On the other hand, metaphors and their kin wear their unfinishedness plainly on their faces. They are hard to use, and that difficulty reminds us that there is more work to be done. They leave the basement door open, so we know there is more to explore down there. When clarity seduces, it can prevent us from pushing on, from finding and dwelling on our confusions. Seductive clarity presents us with a false floor for our investigations into the world.

How do we resist the seductions of clarity? One possible defensive strategy is to develop new counter-heuristics, designed to sniff out the seductive manipulation of our original heuristics. Here's a rough analogy: a certain kind of culinary yumminess was once a decent heuristic for nutritious eating. But our nutritive environment changed, especially when various corporate forces figured out our heuristics and tendencies and started to aggressively game them. In response, we have had to adapt our heuristics. We have needed to become suspicious of *too much yumminess*. Many of us have already trained ourselves to notice when things are just a little too delicious. The crunchy, sweet, salty stuff that hits us just so – we have learned to taste in them the engineer's manipulative touch. We have developed an intuitive feel for designed craveability. This is a counter-heuristic, designed to trigger in response to signals that outside forces are trying to manipulate our more primitive heuristics. Sweetness, crunchiness, saltiness – our counter-heuristic makes as immediately suspicious when we find these in plenty.

In fighting the seductions of clarity, we need to develop new counter-heuristics in a similar key. The sense of clarity is something like cognitive sugar. Once upon a time, using our sense of clarity as a signal to terminate our inquiries might have been a good and useful heuristic. But now we live in an environment where we are surrounded by seductive clarity, much of it designed to exploit our heuristics. We now need to train ourselves to become suspicious of ideas and systems that go down just a little too sweetly – that are pleasurable and effortless and explain everything so wonderfully. Systems of thought that feel too clear should make us step up our investigative efforts instead of ending them. We need to learn to recognize, by feel, the seductions of clarity.[20]

University of Utah
c.thi.nguyen@utah.edu

References

Heather Battaly, 'Closed-Mindedness and Dogmatism', *Episteme* 15 (2018), 261–82.

Endre Begby, 'Evidential Preemption', *Philosophy and Phenomenological Research* 2020 https://doi.org/10.1111/phpr.12654

Laura Frances Callahan, 'Moral Testimony: A Re-Conceived Understanding Explanation' *Philosophical Quarterly* 68 (2018), 437–59.

Elisabeth Camp, 'Metaphor and That Certain 'Je Ne Sais Quoi'' *Philosophical Studies* 129 (2006), 1–25.

Quassim Cassam, 'Vice Epistemology' *The Monist* 99 (2016), 159–80.

[20] I'd like to thank, for all their help with this paper, Andrew Buskell, Josh DiPaolo, A.W. Eaton, Caitlin Dolan, Jon Ellis, Melinda Fagan, Keren Gorodeisky, Arata Hamakawa, Rob Hopkins, Jenny Judge, Samantha Matherne, Jay Miller, Stephanie Patridge, Antonia Peacocke, Geoff Pynn, Nick Riggle, David Spurrett, Madelaine Ransom, Jonah Schupbach, Tim Sundell, and Matt Strohl.

Christopher Chabris and Daniel Simons, *The Invisible Gorilla: How Our Intuitions Deceive Us* (Reprint edition: Harmony, 2011).

David Coady, *What to Believe Now: Applying Epistemology to Contemporary Issues* (Hoboken: Wiley-Blackwell, 2012).

Justin Dallmann, 'When Obstinacy Is a Better Policy' *Philosophers' Imprint* 17 (2017).

Matthew R. X. Dentith, 'The Problem of Conspiracism' *Argumenta* 3 (2018), 327–43.

M.R. X. Dentith, 'Conspiracy theories on the basis of evidence' *Synthese* 196 (2019), 2243–61.

Kristie Dotson, 'Conceptualizing Epistemic Oppression' *Social Epistemology* 28 (2014), 115–38.

A. W. Eaton, 'Artifacts and Their Functions' In *Oxford Handbook of History and Material Culture*. Edited by Ivan Gaskell and Sarah Anne Carter (Oxford: Oxford University Press, 2020).

Catherine Elgin, *True Enough,* (Cambridge: MIT Press, 2017).

Catherine Z. Elgin, 'Creation as Reconfiguration: Art in the Advancement of Science', *International Studies in the Philosophy of Science* 16 (2002), 13–25.

Wendy Nelson Espeland and Michael Sauder, *Engines of Anxiety: Academic Rankings, Reputation, and Accountability* (New York: Russell Sage Foundation, 2016).

Miranda Fricker, *Epistemic Injustice: Power and the Ethics of Knowing* (Clarendon Press, 2007).

Dr Paul du Gay, *In Praise of Bureaucracy: Weber - Organization - Ethics* (London: SAGE Publications Ltd., 2000).

Gerd Gigerenzer and Daniel G. Goldstein, 'Reasoning the Fast and Frugal Way: Models of Bounded Rationality', *Psychological Review* 103 (1996), 650–69.

Alison Gopnik, 'Explanation as Orgasm' *Minds and Machines* 8 (1998), 101–118.

Stephen R. Grimm, 'Is Understanding a Species of Knowledge?', *British Journal for the Philosophy of Science* 57 (2006), 515–35.

Stephen R. Grimm 'The Value of Understanding', *Philosophy Compass* 7 (2012), 103–117.

Kathleen Hall Jamieson and Joseph Cappella, *Echo Chamber: Rush Limbaugh and the Conservative Media Establishment* (Oxford: Oxford University Press, 2010).

Dan M. Kahan and Donald Braman, 'Cultural Cognition and Public Policy', *Yale Law & Policy Review* 24 (2006), 147–70.

Daniel Kahneman, *Thinking, Fast and Slow.* (New York: Farrar, Straus and Giroux, 2013, 1st Edition).

Thomas Kelly, 'Disagreement, Dogmatism, and Belief Polarization.' *Journal of Philosophy* 105 (2008), 611–33.

Kareem Khalifa, 'Inaugurating Understanding or Repackaging Explanation?', *Philosophy of Science* 79 (2012), 15–37.

Jonathan L. Kvanvig, *The Value of Knowledge and the Pursuit of Understanding,* (Cambridge: Cambridge University Press, 2003).

Jonathan L. Kvanvig. 'II–Jonathan L. Kvanvig: Millar on the Value of Knowledge', *Aristotelian Society Supplementary Volume* 85 (2011), 83–99.

Deborah Lupton, *The Quantified Self* (Cambridge: Polity, 2016).

Michael Lynch, 'Understanding and Coming to Understand' In *Making Sense of the World: New Essays on the Philosophy of Understanding,* edited by Stephen Grimm, (Oxford: Oxford University Press, 2018) 194–208.

Jane McGonigal, *Reality Is Broken: Why Games Make Us Better and How They Can Change the World.* (New York: Penguin Books, 2011).

Jose Medina, *The Epistemology of Resistance: Gender and Racial Oppression, Epistemic Injustice, and Resistant Imaginations* (Oxford, New York: Oxford University Press, 2012).

Sally Engle Merry, *The Seductions of Quantification: Measuring Human Rights, Gender Violence, and Sex Trafficking* (Chicago: University of Chicago Press, 2016).

Alan Millar, 'Why Knowledge Matters', *Aristotelian Society Supplementary Volume* 85 (2011), 63–81.

Elijah Millgram, *Practical Induction,* (Cambridge, Mass.: Harvard University Press, 1997).

Elijah Millgram 'On Being Bored Out of Your Mind', *Proceedings of the Aristotelian Society* 104 (2004), 163–84.

Ruth Garrett Millikan, 'Language, Thought and Other Biological Categories: New Foundations for Realism', *Philosophy of Science* 52 (1984), 477–78.

C. Thi Nguyen, 'Cognitive Islands and Runaway Echo Chambers: Problems for Epistemic Dependence on Experts', *Synthese* (2018a), https://doi.org/10.1007/s11229-018-1692-0.

C. Thi Nguyen 'Echo Chambers and Epistemic Bubbles', *Episteme* (2018b), https://doi.org/10.1017/epi.2018.32

C. Thi Nguyen 'Expertise and the Fragmentation of Intellectual Autonomy', *Philosophical Inquiries* 6 (2018c), 107–124.

C. Thi Nguyen *Games: Agency as Art* (New York: Oxford University Press, 2020).

C. Thi Nguyen 'How Twitter gamifies communication', *Applied Epistemology*, ed. Jennifer Lackey (New York: Oxford University Press, Forthcoming).

Daniel M. Oppenheimer, 'The Secret Life of Fluency.' *Trends in Cognitive Sciences* 12 (2008), 237–41.

Charles Perrow, *Complex Organizations: A Critical Essay*, (Brattleboro, Vermont: Echo Point Books & Media, 2014, 3rd edition).

Theodore Porter, *Trust in Numbers,* (Princeton: Princeton University Press, 1996).

Rob Picheta, 'The flat-Earth conspiracy is spreading around the globe. Does it hide a darker core?', *CNN* (Nov 18, 2019. Accessed July 10, 2020) https://www.cnn.com/2019/11/16/us/flat-earth-conference-conspiracy-theories-scli-intl/index.html

Robert Proctor and Londa L. Schiebinger, *Agnotology: The Making and Unmaking of Ignorance*, (Stanford University Press, 2008).

Rolf Reber and Christian Unkelbach, 'The Epistemic Status of Processing Fluency as Source for Judgments of Truth', *Review of Philosophy and Psychology*, 1 (2010), 563–81.

Henk W. de. Regt, 'The Epistemic Value of Understanding', *Philosophy of Science* 76 (2009), 585–97.

Regina Rini, 'Fake News and Partisan Epistemology', *Kennedy Institute of Ethics Journal* 27 (2017), 43–64.

James C. Scott, *Seeing Like a State: How Certain Schemes to Improve the Human Condition Have Failed* (New Haven: Yale University Press, 1998).

Herbert Simon, 'Rational Choice and the Structure of the Environment', *Psychological Review* 63 (1956), 129–38.

Jason Stanley, *How Propaganda Works,* (Princeton: Princeton University Press, 2016).

Michael Strevens, 'No Understanding Without Explanation.' *Studies in History and Philosophy of Science Part A* 44 (2013), 510–15.

Shannon Sullivan and Nancy Tuana, *Race and Epistemologies of Ignorance*, (SUNY Press, 2007).

Cass Sunstein, *#Republic,* (Princeton: Princeton University Press, 2017).

J. D. Trout, 'Scientific Explanation and the Sense of Understanding', *Philosophy of Science* 69 (2002), 212–33.

J. D. Trout 'Understanding and Fluency', In *Making Sense of the World: New Essays on the Philosophy of Understanding*. Edited by Stephen Grimm, (Oxford: Oxford University Press, 2017).

Daniel A. Wilkenfeld, 'Understanding as Representation Manipulability', *Synthese* 190 (2013), 997–1016.

Daniel A. Wilkenfeld 'MUDdy Understanding', *Synthese* 194 (2017), 1273–93.

William C. Wimsatt, *Re-Engineering Philosophy for Limited Beings: Piecewise Approximations to Reality,* (Cambridge, Mass: Harvard University Press, 2007).

Linda Zagzebski, 'Recovering Understanding', In *Knowledge, Truth, and Duty: Essays on Epistemic Justification, Responsibility, and Virtue*, edited by M. Steup, (Oxford: Oxford University Press, 2001).

Eric Zimmerman, Ian Bogost, Conor Linehan, Ben Kirman, Bryan Roche, Mark Pesce, Scott Rigby, et al., *The Gameful World: Approaches, Issues, Applications*. Edited by Steffen P. Walz and Sebastian Deterding, (Cambridge, Mass.: The MIT Press, 2015).

How Good Are We At Evaluating Communicated Information?

HUGO MERCIER

Abstract

Are we gullible? Can we be easily influenced by what others tell us, even if they do not deserve our trust? Many strands of research, from social psychology to cultural evolution suggest that humans are by nature conformist and eager to follow prestigious leaders. By contrast, an evolutionary perspective suggests that humans should be vigilant towards communicated information, so as not to be misled too often. Work in experimental psychology shows that humans are equipped with sophisticated mechanisms that allow them to carefully evaluate communicated information. These open vigilance mechanisms lead us to reject messages that clash with our prior beliefs, unless the source of the message has earned our trust, or provides good arguments, in which case we can adaptively change our minds. These mechanisms make us largely immune to mass persuasion, explaining why propaganda, political campaigns, advertising, and other attempts at persuading large groups nearly always fall in deaf ears. However, some false beliefs manage to spread through communication. I argue that most popular false beliefs are held reflectively, which means that they have little effect on our thoughts and behaviors, and that many false beliefs can be socially beneficial. Accepting such beliefs thus reflects a much weaker failure in our evaluation of communicated information than might at first appear.

History abounds with poor decisions that have been chalked up to gullibility – when people accept whatever they're told, even if they have no good reason for doing so. Demagogues have been accused of manipulating crowds into making risky, costly, or evil decisions. Religious leaders are supposed to convert whole crowds, and to turn peaceful flocks into crusading armies. Conspiracy theories appear to drive people to the craziest actions, whether it is storming a pizzeria in search of a paedophile ring, or burning 5 G towers to stave off cancer risk. Social psychology, in particular the Asch conformity experiments (Asch, 1956) and the Milgram obedience experiments (Milgram, 1963), is also often used to suggest that people are 'shackled by social pressure [and] overly deferential to authority' (Brennan, 2012, p. 8).

Could it possibly make sense to let others influence us so much, and so easily? The best explanation for the apparent ease with which humans are influenced can be found in the gene-culture co-evolution theory (Henrich, 2015; Richerson & Boyd, 2005). This

doi:10.1017/S1358246121000096

theory stresses the importance of cultural learning for human survival, but also the difficulty of knowing whom to learn from. To solve this problem, gene-culture coevolution suggests that humans have evolved a set of heuristics such as 'copy what the majority does', or 'copy what prestigious people do'. These heuristics would so greatly facilitate learning that people would follow them even if they lead to absurd conclusions, such as accepting blatantly false beliefs or engaging in costly behaviours.

Here, I want to challenge the idea that humans are easy to influence. First, I suggest that the costs of being easy to influence would be much too high: evolutionary theory suggests on the contrary that we should be quite difficult to influence, and in particular very resistant to harmful messages. Second, I review work in experimental psychology exploring the psychological mechanisms we use to decide when we should listen to others and believe them. Third, I review work in political science, advertising, history, showing that most attempts at mass persuasion fail completely, or have very small effects. Fourth, I attempt to explain why, if we are so hard to influence, and so good at evaluating what others tell us, some false beliefs still manage to spread widely.

1. The evolution of open vigilance

Within evolutionary biology, the evolution of communication is a well-studied field. Its main result is that, for communication to be evolutionarily stable, it has to benefit, on average, senders (those who emit the communicative signals), and receivers (those who receive them) (Maynard Smith & Harper, 2003; Scott-Phillips, 2008). If this isn't the case, senders evolve to stop sending signals, or receivers evolve to stop receiving signals. However, except for individuals whose interests are perfectly aligned (e.g. cells in a body), conflicts of interests between senders and receivers mean that senders often have an incentive to send signals that benefit them, but that do not benefit receivers – typically, by sending unreliable signals. As a result, for communication to remain stable, there must exist some mechanism that stops senders from taking advantage of receivers. The presence of such mechanisms can make communication possible in the most unlikely places, and their absence can spell doom for communication even when we expect it to work best.

The relationship between preys and predators appears purely adversarial, with no overlapping interests. In fact they do have one interest in common: if the prey is going to escape the predator anyway, then they are both better off if the predator doesn't chase the prey, since they both just waste much energy for nothing. However, if preys could send a signal conveying to predators 'I'm so fast you'll never catch me', all preys, regardless of their actual speed and stamina, would send that signal, and the predators would ignore it. Amazingly, several mechanisms – known as predator-deterrent signals – have evolved to allow preys to convince predators to not chase them. These mechanisms ensure that only preys that would, in fact, be likely to escape the predators can send the signals. For example, when Thomson's gazelles spot a pack of wild dogs, they often don't just run away; instead, they stot, jumping as high as possible on the same spot. This stotting often discourages the dogs from chasing the gazelles. Why? Because only a very fit gazelle, one that would likely escape the dogs, can stot well enough to convince the dogs to give up (Caro, 1986).

By contrast with the predator-prey relationship, the relationship between a mother and the foetus she carries appears entirely mutualistic. And yet they are waging a war over resources. The foetus is hungry for resources, in particular the sugar it gets from the mothers' blood, and tries to grab as much as possible. The mother's body happily provides resources to the foetus, but also wants to keep some for other pursuits. A tug of war ensues, in which the foetus, through the placenta, floods the mothers' blood with hormones to raiser her blood sugar level, while the mother produces high quantities of insulin to bring that blood sugar level back down. Because there's no mechanism to ensure the foetus only requests an amount that would be optimal for the mother, both sides waste resources to send signals that have no or very little net effect (Haig, 1993).

Humans rely hugely on communication for most of their decisions – what food to eat, whom to befriend, where to go, and so forth. This has likely been true for hundreds of thousands of years, as our ancestors already hunted, waged war, and raised children in collaboration with one another, and thus must have relied on communication. Moreover, we often cooperate and communicate with people who aren't our kin, and who have very different interests from ours. In these conditions, how is it possible that human communication has remained stable for so long? There must be mechanisms that ensure receivers of information benefit, on the whole, from communication, in particular by warding off unreliable and costly signals. We cannot afford to be gullible, overly easy to influence. Instead, we must be equipped with cognitive mechanisms that carefully evaluate what we're told, so we can decide what to accept and what to reject. I've called these mechanisms *open vigilance*, but they have been originally called *epistemic vigilance* (Sperber et al., 2010).

2. Cognitive underpinnings of open vigilance

Before delving into the details of how these cognitive mechanisms of open vigilance function, it's worth looking at their overall organization, contrasting two ways in which they could be organized. In the arms race view, senders and receivers become increasingly sophisticated in their attempts to, respectively, convey, and ward off unreliable information. For the receivers, that means starting from a state of relative gullibility and, as they become more sophisticated, learning to reject more information. This view equates lack of sophistication and gullibility; historically, it has been applied to animals, children, women, slaves, workers, the masses, which were all seen as both unsophisticated and easy to influence (i.e. they copy everything, they are easily manipulated by demagogues, they are subject to silly fads, etc.). Nowadays, this view is mostly present in dual process models which see the mind as divided between more basic System 1 processes, our intuitions and emotions, which are supposed to make us gullible, and System 2 processes, our reason, which supposedly allows us to critically evaluate what we're told, and reject what we would otherwise have naively accepted (Gilbert, 1991; Kahneman, 2011).

Another organization, in many ways opposite to the one suggested by the arms race view, draws on a different analogy: the evolution of omnivorous diets. Receivers would start from a state in which they only consume very specific forms of communication and, as they evolve to better evaluate what they're told, they become more open to a much wider range of communication – much like omnivores must be able to finely discriminate between edible and toxic foods in order to have a diverse but safe diet. Both perspectives make opposite predictions about how open vigilance mechanisms function, in particular what happens when the more sophisticated of these mechanisms cannot function properly. The first view, which draws on the arms race analogy, suggests that in the absence of more sophisticated mechanisms, we revert to a state of gullibility. The second view, which draws on the omnivorous diet analogy, suggests the exact opposite: in the absence of more sophisticated mechanisms, we revert to a state of conservatism in which we are very difficult to influence.

Unfortunately, there has been repeated attempts at forced persuasion grounded in the idea that stopping people from thinking carefully makes them gullible. The most infamous were subliminal advertising, in which some stimuli are flashed so quickly that we are not aware of them, and brainwashing, in which the victims are typically deprived of sleep and food, and subjected to indoctrination sessions, again with the hope that their higher thinking abilities would be impaired, making them more open to persuasion. The evidence clearly shows that neither of these techniques are efficient *at all*. Subliminal messages have no significant effect on us (Trappey, 1996), and brainwashing never worked on anyone (Carruthers, 2009). These (and other) results suggest that our open vigilance mechanisms are organized in such a way that the most basic of these mechanisms, those that are always active, are the most conservative, rejecting much of the information they encounter, and that more sophisticated mechanisms, when they are triggered, can overcome this initial negative reaction and make us accept more information.

The conservative mechanism that is at the heart of open vigilance is plausibility checking. It consists in comparing what we're told (or what we read) to what we already believe. Plausibility checking then drives us to reject information that clashes with our prior beliefs. Taking our prior beliefs into account is eminently reasonable – if you're told someone you respect has done something awful, say, you shouldn't just that this new information for granted. Moreover, we cannot help but relying on our priors: to understand a statement, you must use your beliefs and knowledge, and any clash is automatically recognized. As a result, plausibility checking provides a sound protection against unreliable messages. The issue, however, is that it is too conservative, as it makes changing our minds very difficult.

Several cognitive mechanisms can overcome our intuitive rejection of information that clashes with our prior beliefs. Reasoning, like plausibility checking, deals with the content of information, more specifically, with the quality of the arguments provided in support of a conclusion. Numerous experiments have shown that people are not only able to reject poor arguments (at least when the arguments challenge their beliefs), but also to recognize good arguments and change their minds accordingly (Mercier & Sperber, 2017). This is best demonstrated by small discussion groups, in which the exchange of arguments allows group members to adopt the best answer available, the answer that is supported by the best arguments, even if that means abandoning a confidently held belief (Laughlin, 2011; Mercier, 2016).

Some arguments rely on beliefs the audience already has, showing how the audience's beliefs are more consistent with accepting rather than rejecting the arguments' conclusion. This is for instance the case with mathematical or logical problems. Most arguments, however, require some trust for their premises to be accepted. Consider the argument 'vaccines do not cause autism because many studies have shown no such link': for this argument to be effective, the audience has to (i) trust the speaker that such studies exist and, (ii) trust that the studies were well conducted. This brings us to the second family of open vigilance mechanism, which deals not with content, but with the source of the messages.

When it comes to evaluating the source of a message, we seek to answer two main questions: Is the source right? Does the source have our best interests at heart? In briefly reviewing work on how people evaluate sources, I will draw on the developmental psychology literature, to illustrate how early-emerging these open vigilance mechanisms are (Clément, 2010; Harris et al., 2018).

How can we know whether a source is more or less likely to be right than us? An important cue is informational access. From at least the age of three, children are more likely to believe someone who has had visual access to relevant information (e.g. the content of a box) over someone who hasn't (Robinson, Champion, & Mitchell, 1999). In that situation, the children could see who had had informational access. In most situations, we rely instead on what people tell us: 'I saw Helen this morning, she told me she was pregnant' is a good reason to believe the speaker is well informed about Helen's pregnancy (assuming they aren't lying, see below). Three-year-olds are also able to take such reported informational access into account (Mercier, Bernard, & Clément, 2014).

Besides informational access, the main cue we use to decide whether someone knows best is their competence, or expertise, which in turn can be assessed in different ways. The most reliable manner of assessing someone's competence is to look at their track record: have they been consistently right in the past, in the relevant domain? Again, three-year-olds already believe an informant who has been right in the past over one who has been wrong (Clément et al., 2004). Small children are also able to use less direct cues of competence, in particular those based on domain-specific expertise. For instance, preschoolers know that they should direct questions about toys to another child rather than an adult, and questions about food to an adult rather than a child (VanderBorght & Jaswal, 2009). They also know that they should ask questions about living things to a doctor rather than a mechanic, and questions about objects to the mechanic rather than the doctor (Keil, Stein, Webb, Billings, & Rozenblit, 2008; Lutz & Keil, 2002.)

Finally, the last type of cue we use to ascertain who is right is consensus: if more people – who are themselves at least somewhat likely to be right – share an opinion, then we are more likely to believe them. More specifically, people appear quite apt at adjusting the weight they grant majority opinion as a function of the relative and absolute size of the majority (Morgan et al., 2012), skills that start to develop in the preschool years (Morgan et al., 2015). However, our ability to accurately assess majority opinion is dependent on how the majority opinion is presented: if we have fine-grained information about specific individuals and their opinions, we can weight them appropriately; by contrast, if all we have is statistical information (e.g. '97% of climate scientists say climate change is real'), then we tend to underweight majority opinion – even if it can still have an impact (Mercier & Miton, 2019; Mercier & Morin, 2019).

Figuring out whether someone holds accurate beliefs, however, is only the first step: if they have no intention of communicating these beliefs to us, we shouldn't let ourselves be influenced by what they say. Much work has been dedicated to the question of lie detection: are people able to spot whether someone is lying to them using behavioural cues such as gaze aversion? Decades of research have shown that people, including experts, are no better (or barely better) than chance at spotting liars using such cues (DePaulo et al., 2003; Hartwig & Bond, 2011; Vrij, 2000). Don't these results clash with the current framework, which argues that people are well able to evaluate communicated information? In fact, there are no reasons why liars would behave in any recognizable manner, and thus why people should be able to spot them using behavioural cues. This doesn't mean that receivers are helpless; on the contrary, they can rely on a variety of cues to decide who they can trust. Some cues pertain to the sender's past behaviour: do they have a track record of being helpful? For instance, three-year-olds are more likely to believe an informant who has been nice to one who has been mean (Mascaro & Sperber, 2009). However, even people who've been good to us can't be trusted when our incentives diverge – you wouldn't trust your best friend if they tell you, playing poker, that they have a great hand and you should fold. Like adults, children spontaneously discount self-interested statements (Mills & Keil, 2005; 2008.).

3. Mass persuasion

I have argued on evolutionary grounds that humans should be endowed with cognitive mechanisms allowing them both to accept communicated information that is beneficial to them, and to reject that which is harmful. The experimental psychology literature confirms that humans, both adults and children, pay attention to a variety of sound cues pertaining to the content and source of messages to decide what to accept. Moreover, these mechanisms are organized in such a way that in the absence of cues suggesting we should accept a message – good arguments, a history of trust in the source – we revert to the rejection of messages that clash with our prior beliefs. This means that most attempts at mass persuasion should be largely ineffective: when you are harangued by a demagogue, see an ad, or listen to propaganda on the radio, you don't know the source personally, and you can't exchange arguments with them. You have, as a rule, not much ground for changing your mind. Yet it is commonly believed that humans are easily manipulated by mass persuasion, whether it comes from demagogues, preachers, advertising, or propaganda. What gives? These beliefs in mass persuasion's power of influence are simply false. A mountain of evidence shows that mass persuasion attempts fail to persuade.

Since ancient Greece, scholars have been concerned with the possibility that a demagogue could pervert democracy by suborning the masses to their will. There is no evidence that this is the case. Instead, demagogues gain in popularity if they are skilled at figuring out what people want to hear, at giving people a voice. For instance, historian Ian Kershaw shows Hitler was elected in 1933 because he 'embodied an already well-established, extensive, ideological consensus' (Kershaw, 1987, p. 46). For example, during his electoral campaign, Hitler had to strongly tune down his anti-Semitism, stressing instead his more popular anti-communism. Moreover, quantitative studies of his campaign speeches suggests they had little or no impact on the Nazi vote share (Selb & Munzert, 2018).

Maybe preachers have more success, converting whole crowds, imposing a strict ideology, convincing people to engage in a variety of costly behaviours, from fasting to the tithe? The rise of Christianity, going from one individual to most of the population of the Roman Empire, and then its domination over Western Europe for centuries, appears to illustrate the power of religious mass persuasion. In fact, like all religions, Christianity spread slowly – a growth rate below 5% a year –, and through personal networks, as people recruited family members or close associates (Stark, 1996; Stark, 1984). Even when it had become the dominant, official religion, Christianity – like all dogmatic religions – found it very difficult to end pagan practices, which it often ended up recycling instead (Abercrombie et al., 1980; Delumeau, 1977; Le Bras,

1955; Thomas, 1971). Finally, the population complained about any imposition by the Church, from paying the tithe to going to confession, and they used many Church mandated activity as excuses – going to church to barter or gossip, using religious holidays to drink and party, etc. (see, e.g., Murray, 1974).

What happens, though, when an authoritarian regime controls all the media and can drown the population in propaganda? Even then, mass persuasion doesn't seem to have much persuasive effect. The example of Nazi propaganda is the best studied. Using a variety of materials – from archival documents to surveys – researchers have found that Nazi propaganda often failed completely, and that when it did appear to have some effect, it was unrelated to the intensity of propaganda, being modulated instead by prior opinions (Kershaw, 1983; Adena, Enikolopov, Petrova, Santarosa, & Zhuravskaya, 2015; Voigtländer & Voth, 2015). For example, Nazi propaganda might have allowed people who were already anti-Semitic to act on their prejudices – by signalling that the government would back them up – but it had the opposite effect on areas with lower anti-Semitism (Adena *et al.*, 2015). The same patterns are found in other authoritarian regimes, from Stalinist Russia to Maoist China – two countries which now largely rely on propaganda techniques that do not require straightforward persuasion, but attempt instead to sow confusion and distrust, or simply to distract people from issues the regime finds problematic (Roberts, 2018).

Even if they are, in many ways, vastly more sophisticated than authoritarian propaganda, political campaigns in democracies also have surprisingly limited effects. As in other fields, the gold standard for evidence is the randomized control trial: for example, deploying a given campaign act – distributing fliers, robocalling, etc. – in only a random half of electoral districts, and measuring whether voting intention or voting behaviours changed. Studies using these methods suggest that the effects of campaign acts are often null, and at best small (Kalla & Broockman, 2018). This is particularly true in widely publicized elections – presidential elections, say – and the effects of political campaigns increase when voters cannot rely on simple heuristics such as voting for their preferred party to make a decision (e.g. for primaries or ballot measures). On the whole, the media (and, to some extent, political campaigns) do have an effect on voters, but 'by conveying candidates' positions on important issues' (Gelman & King, 1993, p. 409): during a campaign, most people will learn at least some basic facts about the candidates, such as what party they belong to, and this will inform their decisions – a phenomenon quite distinct from mass persuasion.

In terms of amounts invested, advertising dwarves political campaigns – yet it does not seem to have stronger persuasive power. A recent study of the effects of TV advertising, which was comprehensive and methodologically superior to its predecessors, revealed that the effects of the vast majority of TV ads were small at best, with 'a sizable percentage of statistically insignificant or negative estimates' (Shapiro et al., 2019). Another recent and large scale study – with billions of observations – of online display ad effectiveness also points to very small or null effects for the vast majority of ad campaigns, with a few positive outliers, and half of the (limited) effect of advertising being to merely make people buy earlier a product they would have bought anyway (Johnson et al., 2017).

There are different ways for mass persuasion attempts to succeed. Propaganda demonstrates the strength of the regime. Spending on political ads displays that a politician has a well-funded campaign. But mass persuasion fails to persuade the audience of its outward message. This makes sense, given that mass persuasion attempts, as a rule, do not provide us with any good reason to change our mind and accept the messages.

4. Explaining the cultural success of (some) false beliefs

Even if they do not spread though mass persuasion, it is undeniable that some false beliefs have proven culturally successful, from flat earth theory to rumours of paedophiles infiltrating the government, or a belief that bleeding someone will cure just about every ailment they might suffer from. Doesn't the success of these apparently absurd ideas belie the claimed effectiveness of our open vigilance mechanisms? How can people accept such hogwash and not be gullible?

The last six chapters of *Not Born Yesterday* are dedicated to answering these questions, leading up to the conclusion that not only is the success of some false beliefs consistent with the existence of efficient open vigilance mechanisms, but that in fact these mechanisms are crucial to make sense of why some false beliefs spread (while most don't). Not every one of these arguments can be summarized here, and I will focus on two points: 'belief' takes different forms, and holding false beliefs can be socially beneficial.

When we talk about 'beliefs,' we put in the same category very different things, such as 'Olivia thinks relativity theory is correct' and 'Olivia thinks her keys are in the drawer.' However, cognitively, beliefs come in two different varieties: intuitive and reflective beliefs (Sperber, 1997). Intuitive beliefs are the type of beliefs we share with other animals, that are formed (or could have been formed) through perception and basic inference, and that we use to draw further inferences and guide our behaviour. For instance, Olivia might have seen her keys in the drawer recently, and use that belief to guide her inferences and behaviour (e.g. where to look for her keys if she needs them). By contrast, reflective beliefs take a different form, they are metarepresentations: instead of simple believing '*p*' one can believe '*p* is true.' That humans can hold such metarepresentations is obvious in the case of views we do not actually entertain, such as '*p* is false.' In that case, there is a clear distinction between '*p*,' which we do not believe, and '*p* is false,' which we believe, and it is clear that we will not act on the basis of '*p*,' as it is insulated from other beliefs, inferences, and planning mechanisms. What is less obvious is that the same can be true for things we do believe. For example, there are contents that our minds are not well-equipped to process (reflective concepts, see, Sperber, 1997), and which are bound to remain within a metarepresentational embedding. If I tried to add 'relativity theory' to my intuitive beliefs, I would have no idea what to do: what inferences to draw from it, what behaviour should follow. The best I can do is hold the reflective belief 'relativity theory is correct.'

Within this framework it is thus perfectly possible for people to genuinely hold beliefs that have very little impact on their other beliefs or their behaviours, because they are only held reflectively. As is argued at length in the book, many popular false beliefs are held in this reflective manner – and we can tell because people do not behave as one would expect if they held the same beliefs intuitively. Consider the example of pizzagate, a widespread conspiracy theory according to which high ranking Democrats were abusing children in the basement of a Washington D.C. pizzeria. One man, Edgar Maddison Welch, stormed the pizzeria with his assault weapon, demanding that the children be freed. It is plausible that he had formed an intuitive belief that children were being abused, the police was too corrupt to act, etc. – in which case, his behaviour was, arguably, moral and rational. By contrast, the millions of Americans who, according to polls, endorsed pizzagate mostly failed to act on that belief. At best, they wrote one star reviews on the pizzeria's page, noting that their that they harbour paedophiles, *and that their pizza isn't great*. Such behaviour would be completely incongruous for someone who intuitively believed that children were being abused. We can thus safely conclude that the vast majority of people who believed in pizzagate only did so reflectively.

Holding a false belief reflectively, instead of intuitively, is much less of a failure of open vigilance, given that there are, as a rule, few practical consequences for doing so. Indeed, in quite a few cases there might actually be benefits for (reflectively) holding false beliefs, benefits that further explain why these beliefs might pass the filters of open vigilance. Some false beliefs are worth entertaining because they would be very relevant if they were true (Altay et al., 2020; Blaine & Boyer, 2018). In particular, information about threats – such as potential paedophiles – is worth considering, even if we're not sure it's true. Moreover, since people are keen on being aware of potential threats, they tend to reward, reputationally, those who share such beliefs, deeming them more competent (Boyer & Parren, 2015). As a result, false beliefs about threats can spread, even if they do not have much effect on people's behaviour.

Another way through which false beliefs can spread while having a limited direct causal impact is as justifications. People like to be able to justify their beliefs and behaviours. As a result, when there is disagreement over a belief or a behaviour in a community, this creates a market for beliefs that justify the belief or behaviour. People who suggest such justifications can be rewarded reputationally or professionally, and their audience is not particularly critical of the justifications, since these justifications have no effect on the audience's beliefs or behaviours. A striking example is provided by Galen's humoral theory of disease, which was prominent in the Western medical canon for centuries, and associated with the practice of bloodletting. At first, it might seem that this theory has done much damage, by prompting people to rely on a harmful therapy. In fact, bloodletting is one of the most common forms of medical therapies worldwide, being present in dozens of cultures that have never heard of Galen (Miton et al., 2015). It appears that bloodletting is an intuitive form of therapy, and that Galen's theories mostly justified the practice, rather than cause its success.

There are many other reasons why professing false beliefs might be beneficial: that they help us look nicer (Altay & Mercier, 2020) or more dominant (de Araujo et al., 2020), that they allow us to credibly signal our commitment to a group (Mercier, 2020), and many others (see, e.g., McKay & Dennett, 2009). Given that there is, as a rule, little personal cost to holding these beliefs – as they are held reflectively – and that there can be reputational benefits, it is not so surprising that they are allowed to pass through by our epistemic vigilance mechanisms.

The belief that large swathes of humanity are gullible, in spite of its historical pedigree and theoretical rationale, is simply false.

Convergent evidence from many fields – psychology, political science, marketing, anthropology, history, economics – shows that people are well able to evaluate communicated information. In particular, they are largely inured to mass persuasion attempts, in which no good reason for changing their minds is provided. Instead of focusing on why people sometimes accept false information, it appears much more productive to understand how we can help good information spread by tapping into our open vigilance mechanisms.[1]

Institut Jean Nicod
Ecole Normale Supérieure
hugo.mercier@gmail.com

References

Abercrombie, N., Hill, S., & Turner, B. S. (1980). *The dominant ideology thesis*. Allen & Unwin.

Altay, S., de Araujo, E., & Mercier, H. (2020). *'If this account is true, it is most enormously wonderful': Interestingness-if-true and the sharing of true and false news*.

S. Altay, & H. Mercier, *Happy Thoughts: The Role of Communion in Accepting and Sharing Epistemically Suspect Beliefs* (2020).

S. E. Asch, 'Studies of independence and conformity: A minority of one against a unanimous majority', *Psychological Monographs*, 70 (1956), 1–70.

T. Blaine & P. Boyer, 'Origins of sinister rumors: A preference for threat-related material in the supply and demand of information', *Evolution and Human Behavior*, 39 (2018), 67–75.

P. Boyer & N. Parren, 'Threat-related information suggests competence: A possible factor in the spread of rumors', *PloS One*, 10 (2015), e0128421.

J. Brennan, *The ethics of voting*, (Princeton University Press, 2012).

T. M. Caro, 'The functions of stotting: A review of the hypotheses', *Animal Behaviour*, 34 (1986), 649–62.

S. L. Carruthers, *Cold War Captives: Imprisonment, Escape, and Brainwashing*, (University of California Press, 2009).

F. Clément, 'To Trust or not to trust? Children's social epistemology', *Review of Philosophy and Psychology*, 1 (2010), 1–19.

[1] *Acknowledgements*. This work was funded by two ANR grants, ANR-17-EURE-0017 and ANR-10-IDEX-0001-02.

F. Clément, M.A. Koenig, & P. Harris, 'The ontogeny of trust', *Mind and Language*, 19 (2004), 360–79.

E. de Araujo, S. Altay, A. Bor, & H. Mercier, *Dominant Jerks: Sharing Offensive Statements can be Used to Demonstrate Dominance* (2020).

J. Delumeau, *Catholicism Between Luther and Voltaire* (Westminster Press, 1977).

B. M. DePaulo, J. J. Lindsay, B. E. Malone, L. Muhlenbruck, K. Charlton & H. Cooper 'Cues to deception', *Psychological Bulletin*, 129 (2003), 74–118.

A. Gelman & G. King, 'Why are American presidential election campaign polls so variable when votes are so predictable?', *British Journal of Political Science*, 23 (1993), 409–451.

D. T. Gilbert, 'How mental systems believe', *American Psychologist*, 46 (1991), 107–119.

D. Haig, 'Genetic conflicts in human pregnancy', *Quarterly Review of Biology*, (1993) 495–532.

P. L. Harris, M. A. Koenig, K. H. Corriveau, V.K. Jaswal, 'Cognitive foundations of learning from testimony', *Annual Review of Psychology*, 69 (2018).

M. Hartwig, & C.H. Bond, 'Why do lie-catchers fail? A lens model meta-analysis of human lie judgments'. *Psychological Bulletin*, 137 (2011), 643.

J. Henrich, *The secret of our success: How culture is driving human evolution, domesticating our species, and making us smarter*, (Princeton University Press, 2015).

G.A. Johnson, R.A. Lewis, E.I. Nubbemeyer, 'Ghost ads: Improving the economics of measuring online ad effectiveness', *Journal of Marketing Research*, 54 (2017), 867–84.

D. Kahneman, *Thinking, fast and slow*, (Farrar Straus & Giroux, 2011).

J. L. Kalla & D.E. Broockman, 'The minimal persuasive effects of campaign contact in general elections: Evidence from 49 field experiments', *American Political Science Review*, 112 (2018), 148–66.

F. C. Keil, C. Stein, L. Webb, V.D. Billings, & L. Rozenblit, 'Discerning the division of cognitive labor: An emerging understanding of how knowledge is clustered in other minds', *Cognitive Science*, 32 (2008), 259–300.

I. Kershaw, 'How effective was Nazi propaganda'. In D. Welch (Ed.), *Nazi propaganda: The power and the limitations* (Croom Helm, 1983) 180–205.

I. Kershaw, *The Hitler Myth: Image and Reality in the Third Reich*, (Oxford University Press, 1987).

M. A. Koenig, 'Beyond semantic accuracy: Preschoolers evaluate a speaker's reasons', *Child Development*, 83 (2012), 1051–1063.

P. R. Laughlin, *Group problem solving*, (Princeton University Press, 2011).

G. Le Bras, *Etudes de sociologie religieuse* (Presses Universitaires de France, 1955).

D. J. Lutz & F.C. Keil, 'Early understanding of the division of cognitive labor', *Child Development* (2002), 1073–1084.

O. Mascaro & D. Sperber, 'The moral, epistemic, and mindreading components of children's vigilance towards deception', *Cognition*, 112 (2009), 367–380.

J. Maynard Smith & D. Harper, *Animal signals*, (Oxford University Press, 2003).

R.T. McKay, & D.C. Dennett, 'The evolution of misbelief', *Behavioral and Brain Sciences*, 32 (2009), 493–510.

H. Mercier, 'The argumentative theory: Predictions and empirical evidence', *Trends in Cognitive Sciences*, 20 (2016), 689–700.

H. Mercier, *Not Born Yesterday: The Science of Who we Trust and What we Believe*, (Princeton University Press, 2020).

H. Mercier, S. Bernard, & F. Clément, 'Early sensitivity to arguments: How preschoolers weight circular arguments', *Journal of Experimental Child Psychology*, 125 (2014), 102–109.

H. Mercier & H. Miton, 'Utilizing simple cues to informational dependency', *Evolution and Human Behavior*, 40 (2019), 301–314.

H. Mercier & O. Morin, 'Majority rules: How good are we at aggregating convergent opinions?' *Evolutionary Human Sciences*, 1 (2019), e6.

H. Mercier & D. Sperber *The Enigma of Reason*, (Harvard University Press, 2017).

S. Milgram, 'Behavioral study of obedience', *Journal of Abnormal and Social Psychology*, 67 (1963), 371–78.

C. M. Mills, F.C. Keil, 'The Development of Cynicism', *Psychological Science*, 16 (2005), 385–90.

C.M. Mills, & F.C. Keil, 'Children's developing notions of (im)partiality', *Cognition*, 107 (2008), 528.

H. Miton, N. Claidière, & H. Mercier, 'Universal cognitive mechanisms explain the cultural success of bloodletting', *Evolution and Human Behavior*, 36 (2015), 303–312.

T. J. H. Morgan, K.N. Laland, & P.L. Harris, 'The development of adaptive conformity in young children: Effects of uncertainty and consensus', *Developmental Science*, 18 (2015), 511–24.

T. J. H. Morgan, L.E. Rendell, M. Ehn, W. Hoppitt, & K.N. Laland, 'The evolutionary basis of human social learning'. *Proceedings of the Royal Society of London B: Biological Sciences*, 279 (2012), 653–62.

A. Murray, 'Religion among the poor in thirteenth-century France: The testimony of Humbert de Romans'. *Traditio*, (1974) 285–324.

P.J. Richerson & R. Boyd, *Not by genes alone*, (University of Chicago Press, 2005).

M. E. Roberts, *Censored: Distraction and Diversion Inside Chinas Great Firewall*, (Princeton University Press, 2018).

E.J. Robinson, H. Champion, & P. Mitchell, 'Children's ability to infer uterrance veracity from speaker informedness', *Developmental Psychology*, 35 (1999), 535–46.

T.C. Scott-Phillips, 'Defining biological communication', *Journal of Evolutionary Biology*, 21 (2008), 387–95.

P. Selb & S. Munzert, 'Examining a Most Likely Case for Strong Campaign Effects: Hitler's Speeches and the Rise of the Nazi Party, 1927–1933', *American Political Science Review*, 112 (2018), 1050–1066.

B. Shapiro, G.J. Hitsch, & A. Tuchman, 'Generalizable and robust TV advertising effects' (2019), *Available at SSRN 3273476.*

D. Sperber, 'Intuitive and reflective beliefs', *Mind and Language*, 12 (1997), 67–83.

R. Stark, 'The rise of a new world faith', *Review of Religious Research*, (1984) 18–27.

R. Stark, *The Rise of Christianity: A Sociologist Reconsiders History*, (Princeton University Press, 1996).

K. Thomas, *Religion and the Decline of Magic*, (Weidenfeld and Nicolson, 1971).

C. Trappey, 'A meta-analysis of consumer choice and subliminal advertising', *Psychology & Marketing*, 13 (1996), 517–30.

M. VanderBorght & V.K. Jaswal, 'Who knows best? Preschoolers sometimes prefer child informants over adult informants', *Infant and Child Development: An International Journal of Research and Practice*, 18 (2009), 61–71.

N. Voigtländer & H.J. Voth, 'Nazi indoctrination and anti-Semitic beliefs in Germany', *Proceedings of the National Academy of Sciences*, 112 (2015), 7931–36.

A. Vrij, *Detecting lies and deceit: The psychology of lying and the implications for professional practice*, (Wiley, 2000).

What is a Question

LANI WATSON

Abstract
Questions are, in many respects, the hallmarks of the philosopher's trade. They are passed down from one generation to the next and yet, throughout history, philosophers have had relatively little to say about questions. In particular, few have asked or tried to answer the question 'what is a question'. I call this the 'Question Question' and I offer an answer to it in this paper, furnishing philosophical analysis with the results of a large online survey, which has been running for more than a decade.

Philosophers are well known for dealing in questions. They are, in many respects, the hallmark of the trade. It is surprising, then, to find that philosophers have had relatively little to say *about* questions throughout intellectual history. Socrates, for instance, the provocative street philosopher of ancient Athens and great-grandfather of Western philosophy, was, among other things, renowned for his distinctive questioning style. Yet, as far as we know, Socrates never asked what a question is. The same can be said of many other philosophical greats, at least according to their surviving works. In fact, there exists no sustained examination of questions in the philosophical canon at all (or, as far as I have found, in any 'non-canonical' philosophical works). There is plenty to be said about this surprising lack of philosophical attention and I will not distract us with a discussion of that here. It is nonetheless worth noting, at the outset, that throughout history philosophers have simply not asked or tried to answer the question 'what is a question'.

I call this the 'Question Question' and I offer an answer in this paper. As a philosopher, I have been thinking and writing about questions for about ten years and I believe that the answer I offer here is a good one. That being said, I am more interested in prompting philosophical thinking about questions – their value and significance in our lives – than I am in providing a final or definitive account of what they are. Readers should, therefore, view the following as a provocation for further thought and discussion about questions and an invitation to engage critically with the analysis on offer. There are many ways to cut the conceptual cake when constructing a definition of questions and I am presenting just one; perhaps it will inspire others to do the same. At the least, it seems there is room for a more sustained,

doi:10.1017/S1358246121000114

philosophically-informed public discussion of the Question Question. I hope that by offering an answer, I can play a worthwhile role in stimulating, advancing, or opening up that discussion.

1. Answering the Question Question

The Question Question first presented itself to me when I started thinking and writing about questions. At that time, I was primarily occupied by work on questions in logic and the philosophy of language. For, while it is true that philosophers throughout history have not attempted to answer the Question Question, there is, nonetheless, a specialised field dedicated to the study of questions in logic and linguistics, which emerged in the twentieth century.[1] In general terms, a question is defined by theorists working in this field, in terms of the propositions that answer it (also known as the question's 'answer-set'). As one theorist observed in the late 1990s:

> 'The most influential proposals...have, in fact, proposed a very specific characterisation of what a question is: namely, that a question is a property of propositions, that property which specifies what it is to be an exhaustive answer' (Ginzburg, 1997, p. 386).

We will not be grappling with the details of this analysis in what follows. However, two things are worth noting about the quotation, for present purposes. Firstly, it is one of a relatively small number of instances, in any philosophical literature, where an answer to the Question Question is articulated. Secondly, in order to understand it, one must have a relatively advanced grasp of various technical notions in logic and linguistics. In other words, it is far from intuitive. This is not something that logicians or linguists need to worry about in order to do valuable work on questions. However, when it comes to answering the Question Question, I think it is problematic.

That is because I believe a satisfying answer to the Question Question should reflect an everyday conception of questions. It should reveal the idea of a question that we learn to use as infants

[1] For a range of seminal work in this field, see Whately (1826; 1828), Cohen (1929), Prior and Prior (1955), Harrah (1961), Åqvist (1965), Belnap (1966), Bromberger (1966), Hamblin (1973), Belnap and Steel (1977), Karttunen (1977), Groenendijk and Stokhof (1984), Hintikka (1985; 1989), Kiefer (1988), Groenendijk (1999), Wisniewski (2003), Aloni (2005), Jaworski (2009), Ciardelli (2010), Roelofsen (2013).

and carry around with us in daily life: the concept that is embedded in our cognitive architecture, so to speak. The 'logician's answer' quoted above, is not this (and arguably it is not intended as an answer the Question Question, in the sense I intend). At any rate, my aim here is to present an answer that anyone familiar with questions can understand and recognise. Questions are, after all, part of the stock of the world and a ubiquitous feature of human life. Any answer to the Question Question that seeks to capture the value and significance of questions in our lives should respond to and reflect the everyday conception we have of them. It is undeniable, I think, that there is a gap between this conception and work on questions in logic and linguistics.

In response to this gap, I began constructing a definition of questions. It was also at that time that I began collecting questions and initiated what is now an extensive and unruly question collection. As it turns out, this has also played a role in answering the Question Question. I started the collection by asking one hundred people to write down the first ten questions that came into their head. With the exception of 'how are you', none of the resulting one thousand questions were the same ('how are you' was repeated four times). The questions ranged from 'do you want cashback' to 'do you love me', and include gems such as 'am I getting uglier', 'is a giraffe bigger than an elephant', and 'how long does a pack of cheese last'. To these, I added the first one hundred questions that came into my own head, the first one hundred questions that I found in the philosophy books on my bookshelves, the top one hundred questions typed into Google that year, and one hundred quiz show questions. Since then, I have added questions that I have been asked, have heard asked, and have read or witnessed in a whole variety of settings, from supermarket queues to newspaper headlines.[2]

As you might expect, the question collection contains a dizzying variety of questions. This is one of the most intriguing things about it. Moreover, it constitutes a valuable data-set when answering the Question Question. Indeed, curating the collection is itself an exercise in conceptual analysis. In order to determine what should and shouldn't be included in the collection, one must determine what, if anything, serves to unify such a seemingly diverse array. In other words, one must decide what counts as a question. Even with an answer in mind, the question collection continues to serve as a valuable resource in refining the contours of the analysis. Importantly,

[2] You can visit the question collection at: www.philosophyofquestions.com/questioncollection/.

the collection contains many questions from everyday life; the questions that people ask and answer on a daily basis. This is what makes the collection particularly valuable to me in arriving at a satisfying answer to the Question Question.

A second loosely empirical method that has shaped my answer to the Question Question is an online survey. The survey, which has been running via my website, again for about ten years, aims to provoke reflection on the nature of questions and expose some basic intuitions (aka 'folk intuitions') about what they are. It focuses on understanding what questions look and feel like from the perspective of everyday questioners (aka 'the folk'). The survey describes ten short scenarios, revolving around a day in the life of an imagined school teacher called Sarah. In each case, survey participants are asked to make a judgment about whether or not the scenario contains a question. They are also invited (but not obligated) to explain their response. The results offer a valuable insight into the way that people identify and conceptualise questions, again providing an important data-set when it comes to answering the Question Question.[3]

Like the question collection, the survey, which has received over 6,000 responses to date (as of 23 Oct 2020), has played a role in constructing a definition of questions. Both of these methods have encouraged analysis via a process of elimination: examining what a question isn't, rather than what a question is. Consequently, I will follow this process in the remainder of the paper, beginning by ruling out some plausible answers and then constructing the answer at which I have arrived. I will discuss the results of the survey along the way. Readers who have not taken part in the survey may wish to complete it before continuing. The survey takes an average of twelve minutes to complete and can be accessed at: www.philosophyofquestions.com/questionnaire/.

2. What a question is not

The process of elimination just described has to start somewhere and there are many places one could start: a question is not a cup of tea, or

[3] A large proportion of the current survey responses were collected when the survey was included as an optional introductory task as part of the University of Edinburgh's free 'Introduction to Philosophy' Massive Open Online Course (MOOC). Since then, the survey has been open and free for visitors to my website. Survey participants are 49% female, 51% male, 62% are under 40, and 51% have never studied philosophy.

a waterfall, or a night sky. Of course, it makes sense to start with an answer that has some initial plausibility. An examination of definitions offered in reference sources, such as dictionaries and reference websites, provides a useful starting point. The Oxford English Dictionary (3rd edition, 2010), for example, defines a question as 'a sentence worded or expressed so as to elicit information' (p.1455). The same definition is found when typing the phrase 'what is a question' into Google (as of 23 Oct 2020). Wikipedia defines a question as 'an utterance which typically functions as a request for information, which is expected to be provided in the form of an answer' (as of 23 Oct 2020). Dictionary.com defines a question as 'A sentence in an interrogative form, addressed to someone in order to get information in reply' (as of 23 Oct 2020). Likewise, the Merriam-Webster Online Dictionary defines a question as 'a sentence, phrase, or word that asks for information or is used to test someone's knowledge' (as of 23 Oct 2020). Finally, the Collins Concise English Dictionary (8th edition, 2012) defines a question as 'a form of words addressed to a person in order to elicit information or evoke a response; interrogative sentence' (p. 1359, emphasis added).

Notably, in all of these, a question is defined in terms of its manifestation as some form of linguistic expression: a word, sentence, phrase or utterance. I will start, then, with the idea that a question is a specific type of sentence: an interrogative sentence. An interrogative sentence is precisely a sentence that asks or expresses a question. Interrogatives are one of the basic sentence types. As such, defining a question as an interrogative sentence is a neat way to categorise questions as a fundamental feature of language (which they are). Despite this, I argue that questions are not always interrogative sentences. As such, we must look beyond interrogatives for a definition of questions. Moreover, I argue that questions are not always expressed in language. As such, we must ultimately look beyond language entirely, in order to answer the Question Question.

2.1 Questions are not always interrogative sentences.

Interrogatives are distinguished from other basic sentence types, such as declaratives, in virtue of their grammatical form. Consequently, defining a question as an interrogative sentence is akin to defining a question in terms of its grammatical form. This can be classed as a *formal* approach to the Question Question: one that prioritises question form as a means of identifying and analysing questions. I will return to the formal approach later. Before doing so, it will be instructive to take a first look at two key results from the survey. These will help to establish the conclusion that questions are not always interrogative sentences.

The first result comes in response to a scenario I call GOOGLE. In this scenario, our protagonist, Sarah, is attempting to find out where the nearest butchers to her house is, on behalf of a friend. As she is a vegetarian, Sarah herself has no interest in this information but, nevertheless, she types 'local Edinburgh butchers' into Google and notes down the location. In response to this scenario, 72% of the survey participants (to date) judge there to be a question (3,515 participants), 20% judge there to be no question (996 participants), and 8% are unsure (365 participants). Those judging there to be a question constitute a sizable majority.

Sarah, like most of us, does not type out an interrogative sentence when she conducts her internet search. She does not, for instance, type 'where is the nearest butchers to my house.' The phrase Sarah searches with is an approximately arranged string of three words, related to the information she is looking for. It is not an interrogative sentence (in fact, it has no formal linguistic structure). Nonetheless, the majority judge there to be a question in this scenario. Notably, if Sarah had typed an appropriate interrogative sentence to conduct her search, she would probably have got the same results from Google. That is because, in both cases, Google assumes the same thing: that Sarah is trying to find the location of butchers near to her in Edinburgh. Google doesn't, in general, differentiate between searches like the one Sarah conducted and those constituting full interrogative sentences; both types of searches are conducted with the same basic aim and that is all Google needs to know.

In this respect, at least, it seems that Google imitates life. The fact that Sarah's search is not an interrogative sentence does not deter the majority of survey participants identifying a question in the GOOGLE scenario. The optional open comment section of the survey, where participants are invited to explain their response, provides an additional layer of insight. Among those who said yes, there is a question, participant comments reflect everyday experiences of internet searching and the language surrounding it. One participant, for example, writes, 'Searching on Google would be a question. It's used in speech as well 'let me ask Google''. Another comments, 'Searching for information on the internet is a form of question asking. The answering is done by algorithms rather than a person.' A third observes, 'We say, 'ask Google' and we have that shared understanding in English.'

Our common experiences of internet searching suggest that we do not rely on the interrogative form in order to either ask a question or to identify when one has been asked. The survey results reflect this. Notably, this is by no means the only context in which we identify questions without the use of interrogative sentences. We will see other examples of this throughout the paper. The case of internet searching is nonetheless helpfully illustrative, given the familiarity, indeed ubiquity, of this activity in the daily lives of many (of course, not all), in the twenty-first century. Our common experience shows that there are questions that do not take the form of interrogative sentences. Questions are not always interrogative sentences.

It is interesting, also, to look at a related, parallel conclusion: interrogative sentences are not always questions. Just as there are questions that do not take the form of interrogative sentences, so there are, arguably, interrogative sentences that do not amount to questions. This is suggested by a second key result from the survey, involving two further scenarios. I call these scenarios RAIN and DISINTERESTED. In RAIN, Sarah has just woken up and opened the curtains to discover that it is raining again, as it has been for the past two weeks. On seeing this she exclaims out loud 'will it ever stop raining'. Her partner, who is still in the bed behind her, shrugs. In response to this scenario, 35% of the survey participants judge there to be a question (2,115 participants), 58% judge there to be no question (3,432 participants), and 7% are unsure (406 participants).

In DISINTERESTED, Sarah has arrived at school and is walking to her classroom down a long corridor. She spots a particularly disliked colleague approaching from the other end. As they pass, despite having no interest whatsoever in his wellbeing, Sarah glances up and mutters 'morning, how are you'. In response to this scenario, 38% of the survey participants judge there to be a question (1,955 participants), 54% judge there to be no question (2,804 participants), and 8% are unsure (407 participants).

The results in response to both of these scenarios are remarkably similar. It is fair to say that they are also significantly less clear-cut than GOOGLE. That being said, it is interesting to note that these are the only two scenarios in the survey where the majority judge there to be no question. Again, the open comments provide an insight into the participants' responses. Among those who said no, there is no question in the RAIN scenario, one observes, 'It is a rhetorical response to the environment in the form of a statement that is not meant to be answered'. A second writes, 'Sarah's utterance seems like an expression of frustration to me. Don't think she is looking for a particular response from her partner.' A third notes, simply, 'it is a rhetorical question'. This last succinctly captures a plausible interpretation of the scenario in which the interrogative sentence, 'will it ever stop raining', is treated as a rhetorical question.

A similar set of comments accompanies the DISINTERESTED scenario, with many participants observing, in particular, that the interrogative sentence, 'how are you', in this context, serves as a convention of language reflecting a form of 'British politeness'. One participant who said no, there is no question in the DISINTERESTED scenario, writes, 'It's just a stock phrase, there isn't any inquiry here'. Another notes, 'Again, she wasn't really asking a question or seeking an answer. Her brief friendliness was more just the accepted way of conversing with a colleague'.

Significantly, in most (although not all) cases where the interrogative sentence in these scenarios is judged to be rhetorical or conventional, the majority also judge there to be no question. One participant, in response to DISINTERESTED, captures this neatly: 'Once again, a rhetorical question or formality, *not a question*' (emphasis mine). The participant here appears resolute. That said, intuitions certainly do diverge in this (and the previous) scenario. One participant who answered yes, writes: 'Still a question even if she couldn't care less about the answer or was doing it as just a formality'. However, for at least a notable proportion of the participants, these utterances are not judged to be 'real' or 'genuine' questions, even though they are expressed in the interrogative form. This suggests that, according to these participants at least, there are interrogative sentences that do not amount to questions.

The small margins in these last two scenarios render this conclusion tentative, as far as the survey is concerned. Intuitions diverge even to the extent that the same reading - that a question is rhetorical - can lead to directly opposing judgements. Nonetheless, these scenarios provide interesting grist for the mill when it comes to answering the Question Question. I will return, in particular, to discuss rhetorical questions in due course. For the time being, it is worth emphasising that, no matter how conclusive one takes the results of RAIN and DISINTERESTED to be, they are not necessary for establishing the conclusion we are after, given that GOOGLE was already sufficient for this. Questions are not always interrogative sentences.

In addition, there are, I think, many good reasons for holding that questions are not always interrogative sentences, beyond those discussed here. Consequently, despite mention of the interrogative form in several of the widely-used reference sources that I cited at the start of this section, I do not take this conclusion to be particularly contentious. One might happily concede that questions cannot be narrowly defined as interrogative sentences but nonetheless maintain that questions are a fundamental feature of language and are, therefore, always expressed in spoken or written word. Recall that all of the reference sources defined a question as some form of linguistic expression: a word, sentence, phrase or utterance. I will argue, however, that this is misguided. Just as questions are not always interrogative sentences, questions are not always expressed in language.

2.2 Questions are not always expressed in language.

Two further scenarios from the survey help to establish that questions are not always expressed in language. I call these scenarios DICTIONARY and ROAD. In DICTIONARY, our protagonist, Sarah, has arrived in her classroom and is checking through her teaching resources for the day. She notices a word that she is not familiar with and, in order to find out what it means, she looks it up in a dictionary. In response to this scenario, 81% of the survey participants judge there to be a question (4,119 participants), 14% judge there to be no question (725 participants), and 5% are unsure (260 participants). In ROAD, Sarah is trying out a new route to school. Along the route she comes to the side of a busy, unfamiliar road with no pedestrian crossing. She looks both up and down the road before crossing to check if there are any vehicles coming and then proceeds to cross safely. In response to this scenario, 66% of the survey participants judge there to be a question (3,670 participants), 28% judge there to be no question (1,589 participants), and 6% are unsure (352 participants).

In both scenarios, the majority judge there to be a question. This is despite the fact that Sarah uses no language, either written or spoken, in either case. This indicates that, for the majority, a question does not need to be expressed in spoken or written language in order to be a question. As before, the participants' comments add a layer of insight to their responses. Among those responding yes to the DICTIONARY scenario, for example, one participant comments, 'It is a clear attempt to find out something that was unknown to her'. A second writes, 'She needs to find the answer to something she does not know. That is questioning'. A third views the scenario as an almost paradigmatic instance of questioning: 'This seems to be quite a straightforward format of asking and answering a question: unknown information is indentified[sic] and a familiar, organised source is used to obtain it.' These comments reflect a common impression among participants who responded yes to this scenario. They, in turn, represent a sizable majority (81% - the largest we have seen so far). The fact that Sarah does not use any spoken or written language, does not deter the majority from identifying a question.

Interestingly, many of those responding yes to the ROAD scenario reflect on the absence of language explicitly. One participant, for example, writes:

> 'You could think about this scenario as Sarah asking herself: is there traffic coming from the right? no. The left? no. And even if she does not verbalize this in her head (or out loud for that matter), the underlying process is still the same.'

A second observes, 'Sarah checked to see if it was safe to cross the road, 'are there any cars coming?', could be an unspoken question in this scenario'. Another states simply, 'the non-verbal question: are there any vehicles on the road'. Again, the fact that a question is 'non-verbal' does not deter these participants from identifying a question in the scenarios. For the majority, at least, it seems that a question does not need to be expressed in language in order to be a question.

I think that this is the right result. However, it is fair to say that this conclusion is somewhat more contentious than the last. The participants' comments in response to ROAD and DICTIONARY reflect this. Some are less certain about the status of 'non-verbal questions'. For example, one participant, who answered unsure in response to ROAD, writes:

> 'Depends. Did she silently manifest a thought in a question form, 'Are there vehicles coming?' if she did then it was a question. if she just automatically, unreflectively scanned the street, then no, she did not ask a question.'

Similarly, in response to DICTIONARY, a different participant, who answered unsure, comments:

> 'Again, as with the crossing example, you could think of this process as Sarah verbalizing in her head 'hmmm, what does this word mean?'. And again, even if she doesn't, the process and the outcome are still the same. Does a question need to be verbalized in order to be a question? Does it need language to exist?'

These are certainly intriguing and relevant provocations in response to the scenario. One might argue that questions rely for their existence on some form of language, even if that language is expressed only internally or unconsciously. While this is fascinating in its own right, delving into this issue will take us well beyond the present investigation and into a further set of fundamental questions about the nature of language, consciousness and thought. Our focus on the Question Question will be lost. Bracketing these concerns for our purposes, then, the claim that questions are not always expressed in language is on relatively solid ground. Further support for this will emerge shortly when we turn to the positive thesis in Section 3.

Before doing so, one final observation is worth noting here. Readers will no doubt have noticed the lack of question marks in this paper. This is a practice that I adopted, again, about ten years ago, when I started thinking and writing about questions. The aim of the practice was, initially, to find out whether removing question marks from my writing, in all contexts from text messages to published work, affected anything in my life: my ability to ask questions, to communicate, to express sentiment, or to be understood by others. On the whole, I have found that it has not affected any of these things (with the one, intriguing exception that it is harder to express a sarcastic and typically rhetorical question in written form). One pleasing and unanticipated consequence of this practice has been its value as a provocation for talking with others about questions, especially those who find the lack of question marks itself intriguing or, in some cases, disquieting.

At any rate, in line with this practice, I included no question marks in the online survey. Notably, few survey participants, over the course of ten years, have referenced the fact that there are no question marks in the survey, including in any of the scenarios. As we have seen, the participants nonetheless judge there to be questions in many of the scenarios as described. This indicates, in line with my own experience of removing question marks from my writing, that questions do not require question marks in order to be identified as questions. Indeed, I have not yet come across anyone who considers the question mark a deal-breaker in this regard. I take this to be one minor, but further point in favour of a definition of questions that does not rely on their manifestation in language.

I have argued that a question is not always an interrogative sentence (and an interrogative sentence is not always a question), and that a question is not always expressed in language (nor does a question require a question mark to be a question). Consequently, in order to answer the Question Question, I believe we must look beyond language entirely. This is especially pertinent if the goal is to find an answer to the Question Question that responds to and reflects an everyday conception of questions, which has been my goal from the start. The survey results, in particular, indicate that many people see questions in everyday scenarios that do not involve interrogative sentences, linguistic expressions, or question-marks. What, then, are they seeing.

3. What a question is

In order to construct a satisfying answer to the Question Question, a shift in perspective is needed. I said earlier that defining questions as interrogative sentences represents a formal approach; one that prioritises question form as a means of identifying and analysing questions. This approach, broadly speaking, is also the one adopted by those working on questions in logic and linguistics; it is the source of the 'logician's answer', which we encountered at the start. While there is plenty to be said in favour of formal analysis, it is, I believe, not possible to derive a satisfying answer to the Question Question in this manner. The formal approach restricts analysis of questions to analysis of their form (be it their overt linguistic or underlying logical form). Yet, as we have seen from the preceding discussion, questions come in a multitude of forms. The questions I have in my question collection, and those identified in the survey scenarios, provide a broad illustration of this. What's more, we typically know questions when we see, hear and feel them, regardless of whether they come packaged up as neat interrogative sentences or as something else entirely. In everyday life, we do not identify questions by their form. Rather, I argue, we identify them by their *function*.

This shift in perspective can be articulated as a shift from formal to functional analysis. One makes the shift by changing the starting point. Instead of starting with questions as a feature of language (which, of course, they are), one starts with questions as a feature of everyday life (which, of course, they are). These two perspectives are not mutually exclusive – indeed, they overlap in interesting and important ways. But, as the starting point of analysis, they are distinct and lead to different lines of argument. By starting with questions as a feature of everyday life, it is more natural to focus on the role or function of questions (what do questions do), rather than on their logical or linguistic form (what form do questions take). In this respect, the Question Question is as much about what a question does, as what a question is. I construct my definition of questions with this in mind, beginning with an examination of questions as *acts* and proceeding to investigate what kind of act a question is. Ultimately, I argue that *a question is an information-seeking act*. This is my answer to the Question Question.

3.1 A question is an act.

What does it mean to say that a question is an act. In the first instance, it will help to elucidate this using speech act theory. Central to the idea of speech act theory is the thought that certain kinds of utterances are more than mere sentences but are, in themselves, acts. The philosopher of language, J. L. Austin (1962) writes of speech acts:

> 'to utter the sentence...is not to *describe* my doing of what I should be said in so uttering to be doing or to state that I am doing it: it is to do it' (Austin, 1962, p. 6, emphasis original).

Speech acts differ essentially from statements, or propositions, in the sense that the latter are used to describe or refer to states of affairs in the world, whilst the former are ways of acting in the world. Austin introduced the term 'performative' to describe a speech act in which, as he explains, 'the issuing of the utterance is the performance of an action' (1962, p. 6). A familiar instance of a performative utterance can be seen, for example, in the proclamation, 'I now pronounce you married'. Contrast this with the statement 'Lynn is my wife'. The statement describes a state of affairs whilst the performative, in virtue of its utterance, performs an act.

Spoken questions are performative speech acts. Another scenario from the survey will help to illustrate this. In this scenario, Sarah, is listening to a colleague describing a lesson he has just given on countries of the world. While he is talking, Sarah realises that she doesn't know how many countries there are and, as she is interested to know, she interjects saying 'how many countries are there'. Various colleagues respond with several different figures. I call this scenario COUNTRIES. COUNTRIES is by far the least contentious scenario in the survey. In response to this scenario, 95% of the survey participants judge there to be a question (4,711 participants), 3% judge there to be no question (147 participants), and 2% are unsure (94 participants). The vast majority judge there to be a question in this scenario.

Sarah's question is a performative speech act. By asking 'how many countries are there', Sarah is expressing a desire for information about how many countries there are, and requesting that her colleagues respond by providing the information if they have it. In other words, Sarah is not merely making a statement, she is performing an act. In contrast, imagine one of Sarah's colleagues recounting the staffroom conversation later in the day and saying, 'I think there are 192 countries but Julia thinks there are 196'. Sarah's colleague is making a statement; he is describing a state of affairs. A statement of this kind is not a performative speech act. Sarah's question is.

It is not, I think, surprising that a large majority responded yes to COUNTRIES (indeed, I find it surprising that 147 respondents judge there to be no question in this scenario, but I will leave that for another time). Most people see a question in this scenario. Interestingly, however, we can reasonably infer from GOOGLE, RAIN and DISINTERESTED, that the presence of an interrogative sentence in this scenario is not the determining factor for most people who judge there to be a question. If Sarah had expressed her desire for information without employing an interrogative sentence (as in GOOGLE), the majority would still see a question. On the other hand, if Sarah had, for some reason, employed this interrogative sentence as a matter of convention or rhetorical flourish (as in DISINTERESTED and RAIN), the majority would *not* see a question. Moreover, I have argued that questions are not always expressed in language. This was illustrated in DICTIONARY and ROAD. This suggests that, even if Sarah had avoided language altogether, for example, if she had consulted an encyclopaedia in order to find out how many countries there are, many (the majority) would still see a question in the scenario.

With each hypothesised scenario we move further and further from the interrogative sentence that Sarah uttered in COUNTRIES and yet, it seems reasonable to infer from the survey results that the majority would still see a question in each case. What explains this. What are the survey participants seeing. Speech act theory tells us that questions are performative speech acts. But, we have seen that questions can also occur without spoken or written language, as non-linguistic acts. So, questions can be both linguistic and non-linguistic acts. In other words, *questions are acts*. It is an act, I maintain, that the survey participants are seeing and this is what causes them to judge that there is a question in the scenarios discussed. Likewise, in the series of hypothesised scenarios just described, it is an act that would cause people to identify a question in each case. Sarah is, in essence, doing the same thing every time: she is trying to find out how many countries there are. It is, ultimately, this act that constitutes the question.

As noted earlier, the survey results are only intended as a prompt for reflection. They illustrate and support the underlying theoretical point, which is driven by the shift in perspective advocated earlier.

Questions are better defined in terms of their function, rather than their form. The survey results support this by indicating that we do indeed identify questions by function, rather than form. As per the functional approach, defining a question as an act forces us to move beyond the characterisation of questions as a linguistic expression. Now that this move is made, a further layer of analysis is required to complete the definition. It is clear, after all, that not all acts are questions; a question is a particular kind of act. But what kind of act is it. I argue that a question is an information-seeking act.

3.2 A question is an information-seeking act.

A question is an act and when we act we 'do'. So, what is it that we do when we ask questions. This question is brought about by the shift from formal to functional analysis. I argue that the answer to this question is information-seeking: when we ask questions, we seek information. It is this information-seeking act that is seen in the survey scenarios when a question is identified by participants. When Sarah asks 'how many countries are there', she is seeking information. Likewise, when she types 'local Edinburgh butchers' into Google, when she checks the dictionary for the meaning of a word, and when she looks both ways on an unfamiliar road. In all of these scenarios, Sarah is seeking information, and in all these scenarios the majority judge there to be a question.

Notably, this judgement is not affected by the success of Sarah's information-seeking attempts. In COUNTRIES, Sarah asks for information about how many countries there are and her colleagues respond with several different figures. As such, she does not receive a definitive answer to her question. Sarah may quite rightly feel that she has not actually acquired the information she was looking for. This isn't necessarily a failure of her information-seeking abilities or of her colleagues' general knowledge. Indeed, there is arguably no definitive answer to this question. Even among official sources, the number of countries ranges between 189 and 196, and most acknowledge the contentious nature of the topic. However, despite the fact that Sarah does not (and perhaps cannot) acquire the information she is looking for, the vast majority judge there to be a question in the scenario. This is because Sarah's utterance is an information-seeking act. A question is an information-seeking act. I call this the information-seeking account of questions.

Another scenario in the survey helps to add detail to the information-seeking account. In this scenario, Sarah is teaching her students basic arithmetic. One student shows her his answer to a question and she sees that it is wrong. In order to correct him, rather than telling him the answer, Sarah counts out ten pencils on the table in front of him, removes two and says 'how many pencils are left on the table'. I call this scenario PENCILS. In response to this scenario, 84% of the survey participants judge there to be a question (4,223 participants), 12% judge there to be no question (583 participants), and 4% are unsure (215 participants). A large majority judge there to be a question in this scenario.

This scenario is interesting because Sarah, of course, already knows the answer to the question that she asks. The majority, nonetheless, judge her to be asking a question and, indeed, I think that this result aligns with the information-seeking account. There is nothing in the account that requires a questioner to be seeking information for themselves. Questions often form part of an interaction between individuals and the information-seeking task is shared among those involved. The interaction between Sarah and her student in PENCILS illustrates this: the information-seeking task is distributed between the two parties. As such, by asking a question, Sarah is seeking information that she has but her student does not. She is asking in order to make this information manifest for the student; seeking on his behalf, as it were. Again, Sarah's utterance is an information-seeking act. A question is an information-seeking act.[4]

4. Objections considered

Having made the move from formal to functional analysis, I have arrived at the information-seeking account of questions with relative ease. One might be concerned that this is all too quick. In order to substantiate the account, I will address a series of relevant, interrelated objections. These all centre around the reasonable observation that we do not always have information-seeking in mind when we

[4] Note that I am relying on a commonplace understanding of key terms in the information-seeking account, namely, 'information', 'seeking' and 'act'. A more in-depth analysis would address and define each of these in turn and require a substantially longer (or supplementary) paper. I am, however, comfortable relying on a commonplace understanding of these terms given that my goal is to provide an answer to the Question Question that reflects an everyday conception of questions and I do not intend for any of these terms to be remotely technical. I will, therefore, leave detailed analysis of the component elements of the information-seeking account for another time.

ask questions. Indeed, we ask questions for a whole variety of different reasons: to demonstrate concern or care for another person, for example, or to provoke a response such as surprise or embarrassment. As such, one might argue that, while information-seeking is a common goal of question asking, it is not the only goal: questions are not always asked in order to seek information. Consequently, just as I have argued that a question is not always an interrogative sentence, a critic might contend that a question is not *always* an information-seeking act.

This objection is especially appropriate in light of COUNTRIES. In this scenario, Sarah is described as being 'interested to know' how many countries there are. As such, her information-seeking motive is written into the scenario and the dice are loaded, so to speak, in favour of the information-seeking account. Indeed, the account lines up perfectly with the survey results in this paradigmatic case. But the alignment is arguably too neat. There are a multitude of less paradigmatic, but no less familiar, scenarios in which most of us would identify questions without any overt information-seeking motive in sight. Further still, there are many scenarios in which most of us would identify questions where an entirely different, non-information-seeking motive is overtly in play.

A scenario of the latter kind is tested in the survey. In this scenario, Sarah is attending a staff meeting in which a colleague she doesn't particularly like (the one that provoked the disinterested 'how are you' from earlier) is being unhelpfully rude and obstructive regarding a particular issue. Sarah knows that he has not read the minutes from last week's meeting, which he did not attend, and in order to expose this she interjects at the end of his comments, saying, 'what did you think of the suggestion Julia made last week to address this issue'. I call this scenario EXPOSE. In response to this scenario, 62% of the survey participants judge there to be a question (3,038 participants), 29% judge there to be no question (1,391 participants), and 9% are unsure (430 participants). The majority judge there to be a question in this scenario.

Unlike in COUNTRIES, there is no information-seeking motive written into this scenario. In fact, the scenario attributes a different motive to Sarah; that of exposing the disliked colleague. One can imagine that she does this in order to embarrass him into dropping the subject about which he is being rude and obstructive, or force him to modify his behaviour in some way. At any rate, it seems that Sarah's motive for interjecting is explicitly not information-seeking. Despite this, the majority (albeit relatively small) judge there to be a question in the scenario. As such, EXPOSE appears to provide support for the objection that not all questions are information-seeking acts.

As with all the scenarios discussed, I think the majority are right in this case. There is a question in the scenario, despite the absence of an overt information-seeking motive. How can one make sense of this, given the information-seeking account of questions. The answer to this relies on a relatively subtle point. Put simply, to say that a question is an information-seeking act is not to attribute an overt or conscious information-seeking motive in every instance of question asking. In other words, I am not claiming that information-seeking is the only thing we do with questions or that we always have information-seeking on our minds, when asking questions. These would indeed run counter to an everyday conception of questions. Nonetheless, I maintain that a question is defined by its information-seeking function.

To elucidate, it is useful to think of a question as a tool. Tools are typically identified in terms of a defined function. A wrench, for example, is a tool for tightening and untightening screws. A hammer, on the other hand, is a tool for hammering in nails. These different functions are what makes one piece of metal a wrench and another, a hammer. This, however, does not mean that wrenches and hammers are only ever used to (un)tighten screws and hammer in nails. They can and are used for numerous other purposes: to prop open doors, to smash through glass panes, to display in sculptural art. These alternative uses do not change what it is to be a hammer or a wrench. To define a thing in terms of its function is not to determine every instance of its use. Rather, it is to identify the thing that makes it what it is, as opposed to something else. A question is a like a tool for seeking information; a cognitive tool, if you like. It is defined by its information-seeking function. This is what makes a question a question, as opposed to something else.

We can interpret EXPOSE with this in mind. Sarah is still engaged in an information-seeking act, even though her overt intention is not to seek information but to expose her colleague. In fact, she has chosen to expose him precisely by seeking information from him. The goal of exposing him is achieved by means of the information-seeking act; the question. Sarah could have chosen an alternative means, an assertion for example, in which case the colleague's absence would have been exposed in a different way. If, for example, Sarah had interjected with the statement 'you were not at the last staff meeting and haven't read the minutes' she would have achieved the desired effect with a statement, rather than a question. By asking a question, Sarah uses information-seeking to achieve this effect. Again, it is precisely the attempt to seek information from her colleague about what he thought of Julia's suggestion in last week's staff meeting that does the work of exposing the fact that he wasn't there and hasn't read the minutes.

Sarah uses a question to expose her colleague. The fact that she uses a question in this way does not change what it is to be a question. Again, to define a thing in terms of its function is not to determine every instance of its use. Rather, it is to identify the thing that makes it what it is, as opposed to something else. A question is defined by its information-seeking function, not by its role in exposing or embarrassing someone, or indeed, by anything else that we do with questions. This is the case, even when no overt or conscious information-seeking motive is present and some other motive is overtly in play, as illustrated by EXPOSE.

In fact, EXPOSE also illuminates a related issue mentioned earlier; that of rhetorical questions. Notice that the relatively small majority in EXPOSE (62%), is only slightly higher than the majorities seen in RAIN (58%) and DISINTERESTED (54%): the only two scenarios in the survey where the majority judged there to be no question. I think the relationship between these scenarios can be well accounted for by examining the place of rhetorical questions in relation to the Question Question. In turn, this will help to refine the contours of the information-seeking account, in light of the objection I have been addressing.

As noted, many of the survey participants interpreted RAIN and DISINTERESTED as containing rhetorical questions. For many (although not all), this had the effect of discounting the interrogative sentences in the scenarios as not 'real' or 'genuine' questions. Likewise, the interrogative sentence in EXPOSE can plausibly be interpreted as a rhetorical question. The survey participants' responses in the open comments section reflect this. One participant, for example, writes, 'the question seems like more of a rhetorical prop than a real inquiry for information.' Another comments, 'the question is mere rhetoric since Sarah knows that x has not read the minutes and did not attend the meeting.' A third participant makes an explicit connection between EXPOSE and RAIN: 'Like the rhetorical question about the rain, this question serves a purpose other than gaining an answer.'

As we saw with RAIN and DISINTERESTED, the survey participants are divided with respect to whether or not the interrogative sentence in EXPOSE is a rhetorical question. More tellingly, they are also divided on whether rhetorical questions should be counted as real questions. One participant, who responded 'yes', writes, 'I think probably it's a question, because it's not exactly rhetorical.' Another, who responded 'no', comments, 'There wasn't a question, or if there was, it was rhetorical.' This two-layered lack of consensus among the participants, regarding the nature and status of rhetorical questions, explains the relatively small majorities found in response to all three scenarios. The unclear place of rhetorical questions in relation to the Question Question leads to divergent responses in the survey. How, then, should rhetorical questions be interpreted when it comes to answering the Question Question.

There is not space to develop a full-bodied account of rhetorical questions in this paper. However, a preliminary analysis can be offered, using the functional approach, which distinguishes rhetorical from non-rhetorical questions along functional lines. The information-seeking account of questions provides grounds for this. Thus, I define a question as an information-seeking act and propose that a rhetorical question can be defined negatively by the absence of an information-seeking function. Whatever else is required in order to develop a positive account of rhetorical questions, the absence of an information-seeking function can be viewed as a necessary condition. There is plenty more to be said about rhetorical questions, in their own right. However, this distinction helps to further refine the contours of the information-seeking account of questions. We can see this in operation in the survey.

In EXPOSE, Sarah is using the information-seeking function of questions to expose her disruptive colleague. Again, it is precisely the fact that she is seeking information from him that does the work of exposing him in this way. In DISINTERESTED, Sarah is not perceived to be seeking information from the disliked colleague. As many of the survey participants observed, she is adopting a convention of British politeness that is, to some extent, defined by a shared understanding that the utterance 'how are you' in this context, is not made in order to seek information. As one participant observed, 'The intention isn't to gain information or understanding.' Likewise, in RAIN, Sarah's utterance is not made in order to seek information about whether it will ever stop raining. It is, as many participants commented, more like an expression of disappointment or frustration. In both DISINTERESTED and RAIN, there is no information-seeking taking place. In EXPOSE, Sarah is seeking information in order to achieve the goal of exposing her colleague. As such, the latter scenario contains a question, while the former do not. This is predicted by the information-seeking account of questions and reflected in the survey results.

The distinction between rhetorical and non-rhetorical questions (or just questions) adds further clarity to the claim that a question is an information-seeking act. It allows for certain predictions about what will and will not be identified as a question, according to an everyday conception. It can also be used as a method for including or excluding things from the question collection. If something is an information-seeking act, then it gets a place in the collection. If it is rhetorical or conventional or something else, then it does not.[5] Clarifying the nature and status of rhetorical questions helps to identify a clear, analytical boundary around the information-seeking account of questions. Intuitions may diverge on what counts as an information-seeking act, but whether or not something is a question is determined by the result.

That being said, everyday life is never as clean or ordered as conceptual analysis would like it to be. As such, there are inevitably many things that it is difficult to classify, even with the information-seeking account of questions in place. I think of these as grey area cases. Grey area cases reflect the need for a pragmatic attitude in any attempt to answer the Question Question (and, indeed, in the analysis of everyday concepts more generally).

One such grey area case is represented in the last scenario of the survey. In this scenario, Sarah is leaving work for the day and night has already fallen. She pauses at one point and looks up to the clear, dark sky above. Marvelling at the scale and beauty of the scene she says silently inside her head 'how big is the universe'. She considers this for several minutes and then continues home. I call this scenario SKY. In response to this scenario, 53% of the survey participants judge there to be a question (2,592 participants), 35% judge there to be no question (1,698 participants), and 12% are unsure (560 participants). The scenario elicits only a very small majority who judge there to be a question and the largest percentage of 'unsure' responses.

This is a grey area case. However, I think the lack of consensus reflected in the survey results for SKY can be explained by the information-seeking account of questions. It seems likely that Sarah knows that there is no possibility of her actually finding out how big the universe is by saying silently inside her head 'how big is the universe'. However, it is unclear whether this fact alone should or does prevent her from seeking information in this way. As one survey participant, who responded 'unsure', puts it:

[5] Actually, that's not quite true, there is a special section in the collection dedicated to 'non-questions'.

> 'this could go either way. Obviously she won't ever be able to answer the question of how big the universe really is, but she still asked the question to herself which led her to ponder the vastness of it all, which could be considered a question.'

The case is unclear precisely because it is unclear whether Sarah is really engaged in an information-seeking act. Does wondering, pondering or awe, inspired by genuine curiosity, amount to information-seeking. Perhaps in some primitive sense, it does. On the other hand, perhaps this is a different kind of act entirely. SKY represents a grey area case when it comes to answering the Question Question, even with the information-seeking account in place. This raises a suite of fascinating questions of its own (many of which are considered by the survey participants). The existence of grey area cases, however, does not undermine the information-seeking account of questions but rather serves to illustrate the complexity of the task one undertakes when attempting to provide a satisfying answer to the Question Question.

5. An answer to the Question Question

A question is an information-seeking act. This is my answer to the Question Question. If this answer seems intuitive to you (perhaps even bordering on the obvious or mundane) then I have done what I set out to do. As I said at the outset, my goal is to present an answer to the Question Question that responds to and reflects an everyday conception of questions. This aim goes far beyond that of constructing accessible prose. As a philosopher, it is my privilege to spend time engaging in abstract conceptual analysis. But the object of analysis, in this case, is not itself an abstract entity, detached from the practical concerns of daily life. Quite the opposite, in fact, questions are an integral part of the way that we communicate with each other, coordinate our social and epistemic interactions, and learn about the world in which we live. They are part of the stock of the world and a ubiquitous feature of human life. A satisfying answer to the Question Question should reflect this.

I observed, at the outset, that relatively few answers to the Question Question have been offered throughout the history of philosophy. There is, as far as I am aware, only one other English language paper with the title 'What is a question?'[6] This paper was written

[6] Of course, this is actually a different title, as it includes a question-mark.

by the logician and legal philosopher, Felix S. Cohen, in 1929. Cohen (1929) opens his paper with the following sentence: ''What is a question?' is a question which seems to have been almost totally ignored by logicians' (p.350). I submit that it is a question that has been almost totally ignored by philosophy at large (and, in fact, logicians and linguists have done by far the most work in this field). Philosophy has plenty more to offer on this topic.

The answer that Cohen (1929) provides is, as one might expect, a version of the logician's answer I quoted at the start: 'A question, it is submitted, is simply a propositional function (or propositional form)' (p.353). As before, this answer reflects a formal approach to the analysis of questions and understanding it requires one to know, at least, how the terms proposition, form and function, are used by logicians. It is, again, far from intuitive. Any answer to the Question Question that seeks to move beyond this kind of formal analysis and, most importantly, capture the value and significance of questions in our lives must, I think, respond to and reflect an intuitive, everyday conception of questions.

That said, I am not attempting to undermine the logician's answer to the Question Question. Nor, for that matter, to undercut the definitions provided in dictionaries and reference sources (although perhaps these could be tweaked). Both of these sources contribute something valuable to the interpretation and analysis of questions. Nonetheless, as I see it, there is a wide open space between dictionary definitions and logical constructs, where the everyday conception of questions resides. This paper is an attempt to fill some of that space with philosophical reflection on the nature of questions. More importantly, it is an invitation for others to do the same. In one sense, questions are abstract but in another they are familiar and tangible. We all know what it is like to ask a question. My hope is that this paper provides a stimulus for further thought and discussion about this familiar act, and the practice of questioning in which it is embedded.[7]

University of Oxford
Lani.Watson@philosophy.ox.ac.uk

[7] I am grateful to Joshua Habgood-Coote and Jared Millson for a very helpful exchange during the writing of this paper. I am also grateful to all those who have taken the 'What is a Question' survey and contributed to the Question Collection on my website. Particular thanks to the audience of my talk as part of the *Royal Institute of Philosophy*, London Lecture Series 2020, and to the organisers for inviting me to give it.

References

Maria Aloni, 'A formal treatment of the pragmatics of questions and attitudes', *Linguistics and Philosophy* 28 (2005), 505–539.

Lennart Åqvist, *A New Approach to the Logical Theory of Interrogatives,* (Uppsala: University of Uppsala, 1965).

John, L. Austin, *How To Do Things With Words: The William James Lectures delivered at Harvard Univ. in 1955,* (Oxford: Oxford University Press, 1962).

Nuel Belnap, 'Questions, Answers and Presuppositions', *The Journal of Philosophy* 63 (1966), 609–611.

Nuel Belnap and Thomas Steel, *The Logic of Questions and Answers,* (Connecticut: Yale University Press, 1977).

Sylvain Bromberger, 'Why-Questions'. In: *Mind and Cosmos: Essays in Contemporary Science and Philosophy* edited by Robert Colodny. (Pittsburgh: University of Pittsburgh Press, 1966) 68–111.

Ivano Ciardelli, 'A First-Order Inquisitive Semantics', In: *Logic, Language, and Meaning: Selected Papers from the Seventeenth Amsterdam Colloquium* edited by Maria Aloni, Harald Bastiaanse, Tikitu de Jager, and Katrin Schulz, (Berlin: Springer, 2010).

Felix. S. Cohen, 'What is a Question?' *The Monist* 39 (1929), 350–64.

Jonathan Ginzburg, 'Interrogatives: Questions, Facts and Dialogue', In: *Handbook of Contemporary Semantic Theory* edited by Shalom Lappin, (Oxford: Blackwell, 1997) 385–422.

Jereon Groenendijk, 'The Logic of Interrogation', In: *Semantics and Linguistic Theory* edited by T. Matthews and D. Strolovitch, (Cornell: Cornell University Press, 1999) 109–126.

Jeroen Groenendijk and Martin Stokhof, *Studies on the Semantics of Questions and the Pragmatics of Answers*, Joint Ph.D. thesis, University of Amsterdam, Department of Philosophy (1984).

Charles Hamblin, 'Questions in Montague English', *Foundations of Language* 10 (1973), 41–53.

David Harrah, 'A Logic of Questions and Answers', *Philosophy of Science* 28 (1961) 40–46.

Jaakko Hintikka, 'The Interrogative Model of Inquiry as a General Theory of Argumentation', *Communication and Cognition* 25 (1985) 221–42.

Jaakko Hintikka, 'The Role of Logic in Argumentation', *The Monist* 72 (1989) 3–24.

William Jaworski, 'The Logic of How Questions', *Synthese* 166 (2009 133–55.

Lauri Karttunen, 'The Syntax and Semantics of Questions', *Linguistics and Philosophy* 1 (1977), 3–44.

Ferenc Kiefer, 'On the Pragmatics of Answers', In: *Questions and Questioning* edited by Michel Meyer. (New York: De Gruyter 1988), 255–279.
Mary Prior and Arthur Prior, 'Erotetic Logic', *Philosophical Review,* 64 (1955) 43–59
Floris Roelofsen, 'Algebraic foundations for the semantic treatment of inquisitive content', *Synthese,* 190 (2013), 79–102.
Richard Whately, *Elements of Logic,* (London: J. Mawman, 1826).
Richard Whately, *Elements of Rhetoric,* (London: J. Mawman, 1828).
Andrzej Wisniewski, 'Erotetic Search Scenarios', *Synthese* 134 (2003), 389–427.

Index of Names